Latin American History
at the Movies

Latin American History at the Movies

Edited by Donald F. Stevens

ROWMAN & LITTLEFIELD
Lanham • Boulder • New York • London

Published by Rowman & Littlefield
An imprint of The Rowman & Littlefield Publishing Group, Inc.
4501 Forbes Boulevard, Suite 200, Lanham, Maryland 20706
www.rowman.com

86-90 Paul Street, London EC2A 4NE

British Library Cataloguing in Publication Information Available

Library of Congress Cataloging-in-Publication Data

Names: Stevens, Donald Fithian, 1953– editor.
Title: Latin American history at the movies / edited by Donald F. Stevens.
Description: Lanham : Rowman & Littlefield, [2023] | Series: Latin American silhouettes
    | Includes bibliographical references and index.
Identifiers: LCCN 2022019203 (print) | LCCN 2022019204 (ebook) | ISBN
    9781538152454 (cloth) | ISBN 9781538152461 (paperback) | ISBN
    9781538152478 (epub)
Subjects: LCSH: Latin America—In motion pictures. | Latin Americans in motion
    pictures. | Historical films—History and criticism.
Classification: LCC PN1995.9.L37 L38 2023 (print) | LCC PN1995.9.L37 (ebook) |
    DDC 791.43/628—dc23/eng/20220714
LC record available at https://lccn.loc.gov/2022019203
LC ebook record available at https://lccn.loc.gov/2022019204

For Madeleine,
who will write her own books

Contents

Illustrations

Acknowledgments

In the years since the publication of *Based on a True Story* in 1997, I have received countless suggestions for films to include in a future volume. I am grateful to everyone who shared their ideas and enthusiasm for the book, and I particularly want to recognize the persistence of William H. Beezley. I am certain that every time I saw Bill, he encouraged me to put together another collection of essays.

My original plan for this volume was to have it consist entirely of new essays since so many people had given me good ideas, and a few had even volunteered to write a chapter. Finding the right person to write was not always so easy though. Authors need to have expertise in the subject and time period, but they also need to have the disposition to write in a different genre. And they need to have time. We began this work before the COVID-19 pandemic began to make everyone's life more complicated and stressful. It was inevitable that several of the original authors would be unable to complete their chapters, which was a considerable loss for the book. In order to make the volume more comprehensive chronologically, it made sense to fill in some of the gaps with essays from the original book. I am especially indebted to Thomas H. Holloway and Susan Elizabeth Ramírez for revising their earlier chapters, to bring them up to date with the latest scholarship, on short notice. I am immensely grateful to every one of this distinguished group for their contributions and for producing their chapters on schedule, even in such trying times.

Without the dedicated staff of Drexel University Libraries, this project would never have been possible, especially during a pandemic. I thank you all.

Judy Silver watched the films with me, shared her thoughts and observations, and read every word. Her enthusiasm for this project never wavered, and I will always find it difficult to express my appreciation and gratitude sufficiently. Every day, I know how lucky I am.

D.F.S.

Philadelphia, PA
February 2022

Introduction

The nineteenth century was profoundly optimistic about the possibilities of recording objective reality in both words and images. The invention of photography in the 1820s, and its improvement by Louis Daguerre and George Eastman later in the century, coincided with the development of history as a profession. Both history and photography promised accurate descriptions of objective reality. As photographers recorded images of places, objects, and people unmediated (it was thought) by the artist's style, scholars believed that they could write history, in Leopold von Ranke's essential phrase, "as it really was."[1] Both history and photography became more methodologically and technically sophisticated. Further mechanical improvements made sequential photography possible, then kinetoscopes and peep shows. Finally, in 1895, the first true motion picture flashed on a theater screen.

As the movies and television reached ever-larger audiences in the twentieth century, the written products of the historical profession became increasingly specialized. Visual images became more attractive and pervasive; history became more disciplined, compartmentalized, and marginalized from the broader culture. During the nineteenth century, historical narratives by William H. Prescott, George Bancroft, and Thomas Carlyle had been widely read. Today, history is more likely to be interpreted by Werner Herzog, María Luisa Bemberg, or Oliver Stone. It may be that more people get their history in movie theaters and from cable television and streaming services than from reading print; Carl Sandburg is said to have remarked that Hollywood was a more effective educational institution than Harvard.[2] The products of Hollywood, Buenos Aires, São Paulo, and Churubusco are more economical and popular as well.

For much of the twentieth century, there were technological obstacles to using movies in classrooms. Films were expensive, even to rent. Finding suitable films took a great deal of time and effort. Showing them required a considerable investment in equipment that needed skill to operate and maintain. By the mid-1970s the commercial viability of videotape and VCRs made it

1

cheaper and less technically complex to use films in teaching, but the intellectual obstacles to films in the classroom may well have been greater than the technological ones.

Historians had some justification for intellectual suspicion and emotional resentment of films as a way of depicting the past. Movies are relatively short. Even a full-length feature film is seldom more than two hours long, so it can deal with only a relatively small amount of information. Since they may contain only about as much information as a chapter or an article, films can seem superficial to professionals who spend years immersed in the details of a particular subject and time. As Robert Rosenstone has written, "Let's face the facts and admit it: historical films trouble and disturb (most) professional historians. Why? We all know the obvious answers. Because, historians will say, films are inaccurate. They distort the past. They fictionalize, trivialize, and romanticize important people, events, and movements. They falsify history."[3]

Making films is nothing like book writing. Moviemaking is a gregarious activity; it appears glamorous, is always expensive, and is sometimes lucrative. Historians generally work on their own, in relative solitude, on restricted budgets for small audiences. But many of these ideas and attitudes will not stand up to scrutiny. As Rosenstone pointed out, a short work is not inherently less historical than a long one any more than an article is worse than a book or a two-hundred-page book less historical than five heavy volumes.[4] Brevity can be a virtue and an advantage, rather than a defect. As Mohamed Kamara writes on page 137 of this book in his analysis of Euzhan Palcy's *Rue Cases-Nègres*: "That it is possible to compress hundreds of pages and centuries of history into a few hours makes films more appealing and accessible to a much larger number of people."[5] And film has other merits of immediacy and emotional impact that make it more attractive to the wide audiences that somehow are not interested in professional historical writing. Most period movies nevertheless rely on historians' labor of one sort or another. Robert Brent Toplin has noted that filmmakers generally do not have a complete grasp of the appropriate scholarly literature but they do "frequently operate under the influence of specific works in print."[6] Historians have, for the most part, repaid this attention by neglecting films, leaving the analysis of visual media primarily to scholars trained in cinema studies, literature, and communications.[7]

Even the films that are most congruent with professional history require certain liberties that historians find troubling. They may complain that filmmakers concretize what is not known, that too much imagination is involved in making historical texts into visual representations and reenactments. Film demands specificity about many things for which we have insufficient evidence. As Rosenstone put it, the motion picture camera is "a greedy mechanism."[8]

Many of the same objections could be made to written history. Do we not do the same thing in our own minds (that is, visualize an imagined past based on the evidence) when we read traditional historical documents or narratives? Is there a clear distinction between trying to imagine what seventeenth-century peasant households looked like from reading inventories postmortem and assembling words or images to convey that knowledge?[9] Hayden White argues that the process is the same: "Every written history is a product of processes of condensation, displacement, symbolization, and qualification exactly like those used in the production of a filmed representation. It is only the medium that differs, not the way in which messages are produced."[10] E. Bradford Burns went even further, considering the clear communication of visual images a potential advantage of filmmaking over traditional historical writing. In his words, "the historian should note that in at least this respect the film could be less subjective than the written word since it transfers the image directly to the mind rather than requiring, as the written description does, the mind to create an image, one that naturally varies with each person. Thus, the film leaves less to the imagination, requiring perhaps less interpretation than other forms of communication."[11]

At the same time, even the most traditional approach to "facts" and "what really happened" cannot proceed without inspiration, assumptions, and questions. Imagination shapes the questions we ask about the past and helps us guess where appropriate sources might be found.[12] Films and filmmaking can encourage historical imagination. Natalie Zemon Davis found that the process of putting the story of Martin Guerre's disappearance and reappearance on film provoked questions that would not have occurred to her if she had only tried to tell the story in words. Making the movie led her to ask new questions not only about appearances but also about motivations: "I felt I had my own historical laboratory, generating not proofs, but historical possibilities."[13] Films can serve as an introduction to the past and an incentive to study history. Werner Herzog's *Aguirre, the Wrath of God* is a cinematic marvel with striking visuals of actors portraying sixteenth-century Spanish conquistadors descending from the mists of the Andes into the steamy jungles of the Amazon. Yet those who know something of the historical Lope de Aguirre will find the cinematic version disappointing. Aguirre's own story is stranger and more compelling than fiction, as Thomas H. Holloway demonstrates in chapter 2.

While the public hungers for something beyond a diet of dry facts, historians have a voracious appetite for scraps of paper hidden away in previously unexplored places. One of the wonders of historical research and writing is the way the sources both discipline and delight us. The past is a strange land, far more peculiar than we can imagine on our own. Historians will probably always be at odds with postmodern literary theory. "History is crucially distinguished from fiction by curiosity about what actually happened in the past. Beyond the self—outside the realm of the imagination—lies a landscape cluttered with the detritus of past living, a melange of clues and codes informative of a moment as real as this present one."[14]

Here is the crucial point: Where filmmakers and their mass audiences may be looking for the present and the familiar in the past, historians are attracted to its distinctiveness, its "otherness," and its peculiarities. As Davis puts it, "I wanted to shake people up, because I feel that is what history is about. It is not about confirming what you already know, but about stretching it and turning it upside down and then reaffirming some values, or putting some into question."[15] The best history allows the past to speak to us in its own strange way.

Since historians refuse to give imagination and invention free rein, they may perceive that what are called documentaries are closer to their stylistic preconceptions of how history should be portrayed on film. Even the term itself is reassuring and almost tranquilizing. "Documentary" sounds very much like the documents and manuscripts we usually study. The documentary style flatters historians while it relies on their authority as arbiters of the past; historians regularly appear as "talking heads" in this sort of movie. Often constructed out of "actuality footage" to distinguish them from re-creations, these films have the advantage of showing students actual people, places, and sounds from the past.[16]

Documentary films, though, are also mediated by our imaginations and can suffer from falsification through juxtaposition and problems of connecting images with texts.[17] Most of these difficulties are inherent even in the use of simple photographs. Were the photos spontaneous or posed? For most of the nineteenth century, subjects had to remain motionless for long periods. Even the minimum time under exceptional circumstances, about five seconds, was probably too long for spontaneous or candid photography. As late as the 1870s, studio portraiture required the subject to remain motionless from fifteen seconds to more than a minute.[18] Long exposure times made it nearly impossible not only to capture action but also even to record unaffected poses on film. Thus, Matthew Brady's Civil War battlefield views show the ideal photographic subjects of his time, corpses. Dead bodies did not move and blur the image. Even when faster film speeds made stop-action photography possible, anticipation, preparation, and even rehearsal were essential to successful images. The famous, dramatic photograph of Pancho Villa galloping on horseback during the Mexican Revolution of 1910 could only have been carefully staged after the filmmaker was sent out ahead to a suitable location and given ample time to prepare.[19] Robert M. Levine has also pointed out that as much as early photographers thought of themselves as scientists rather than artists, they "were first and foremost businessmen and could not afford to take [unflattering or bluntly realistic] pictures which could not be sold."[20]

Photographs do not speak for themselves; they must be spoken for.[21] Connecting text to image is not a self-evident process. Portraits of individuals used in traditional documentary films seldom show how they looked when the words, actions, or ideas attributed to them in the narration occurred. Even a photograph of someone seated at a desk, pen in hand, apparently in the act of writing, will likely bear no connection to the words read in the voice-over narration. We are inclined simply to accept the filmmaker's juxtaposition as accurate. Even when that narration contains the actual words, another fiction is created. The letters written by real Civil War soldiers to loved ones and family were some of the most emotionally evocative moments in Ken Burns's *The Civil War*. In listening to them, we imagine a voice from the past, but we are listening to the intonations and enunciations of professional actors hired to read the lines.

The boundary between dramatic re-creation and documentary can be clouded. In some of the best historical feature films, dialogue comes from the same sort of documentary sources. In María Luisa Bemberg's *Camila*, a cinematic melodrama set in mid-nineteenth-century Argentina, the actor playing the family patriarch reads chilling words actually written by Camila's father nearly two centuries ago.[22] The blurred boundary between documentary and feature or fictional film can also be a matter of interpretation as filmmakers attempt to tell the truth in spite of political interference. Héctor Babenco began to make a documentary about Brazil's juvenile detention system. When official obstruction made that project impossible, he told the story through fiction, writing and directing *Pixote*, a haunting and realistic vision of a child's life on the streets of São Paulo and Rio de Janeiro. The film was not only a powerful condemnation of Brazil's social crisis; it was also an international financial and critical success that foretold the tragic death of the film's own star, Fernando Ramos da Silva.[23]

Certainly, those who know Latin American and postmodern culture are familiar with the juxtaposition of what Julianne Burton has called "art and actuality, fabrication and found objects, the fictional and the factual."[24] Burton has pointed out that even earlier in the century, after the Mexican Revolution of 1910, "feature filmmakers, motivated by economy rather than by any will to authenticity, inserted actual documentary battle footage from the great unassembled 'archive' of the revolution into their fictional films."[25]

Privileging the empirical, however, is what historians have to do. One of the historian's fundamental propositions is that "the past does exist and that, contrary to some notion that the past is only in our minds, it has an existence independent of our knowledge of it."[26] If it seems that the boundaries are not as clear as they once were, perhaps they were never all that distinct to begin with.[27] E. Bradford Burns reminds us of the words of Louis Gottschalk, first published in 1950:

> It might be well to point out again that what is meant by calling a particular credible is not that it is actually what happened, but that it is as close to what actually happened as we can learn from a critical examination of the best available sources. This means verisimilar at a high level. It connotes something more than merely not being preposterous in itself or even than plausible and yet is short of meaning accurately descriptive of past actuality. In other words, the historian establishes verisimilitude rather than objective truth.[28]

Robert Rosenstone is the historian who has most clearly articulated the relationship between history on film and history in texts. He sees history on film as embodying a distinct type of complexity from history as written in books and academic journals.

> Film creates its own sort of truth, one that involves a multi-level past that has so little to do with language that it is difficult to describe adequately in words. . . . On the screen, several things occur simultaneously—image, sound, language, even text—elements that support and work against each other to create a realm of meaning as different from written history as written was from oral history.[29]

Rosenstone encourages historians to look beyond the question of whether or not the particular scenes or specific "facts" in a film can be aligned with written history and deemed "accurate." Instead, he encourages us to ask a broader question about films, "whether their overall portrait or vision has something meaningful and important to say about our past."[30] History on film is distinct from history in words; each genre has its own particular mixture of advantages and shortcomings. As Rosenstone wrote, "Even if film could deliver data as well as the written word (which it cannot, as a practical matter, do very well), what would be the point? We already have books."[31]

Just as fact and imagination are not always clearly separable, the advantages and disadvantages of using film to study history are not necessarily distinguishable either. Films have an emotional impact and a popular appeal that is usually missing from professional scholarship. Is this a disadvantage and reason to exclude them from classrooms and professional discussion, or an opportunity to reduce the marginalization that has accompanied the professionalization of historical research? The possibilities and the perils are not discrete items; they are valuations attributed to the same conditions. It is not a case of either/or but of both and more at once. Neither book-writing nor filmmaking provides a perfect window on the past. Neither is "true" and complete in itself, but historians need to take film seriously as a way of depicting the past.

The fifteen essays in this book are arranged in roughly chronological order beginning with the indigenous past before the Spanish arrived at the turn of the sixteenth century and continuing through the colonial period, the centuries after independence, to final reflections on the past (and the present) in the early years of the twenty-first century. Each essay is written by a scholar who is an expert on the time and the themes of each film.

1. Camilla Townsend recognizes the controversial character of Mel Gibson's *Apocalypto*, a fictional story set in indigenous communities in Mexico just before the arrival of the Spanish. She regards portions of it as sinister and stereotypical. At the same time, she also sees it as a remarkable film that breaks new ground in imagining preconquest history as well as exploring cultural difference and how much humanity really has in common.

2. Rather than focusing on the "great men" of the conquest, Werner Herzog has shown us an obscure conquistador in his *Aguirre, Wrath of God*. Thinking he can learn from history, Lope de Aguirre attempts to follow Hernán Cortées's path to victory, wealth, and power. Although Herzog presented Aguirre as deranged, the film has many redeeming aspects. Thomas H. Holloway concludes that Aguirre was not a madman but that he was angry (and articulate) about his legitimate grievances.

3. María Luisa Bemberg's *I, the Worst of All* is one of the best films about colonial Latin America. It visualizes the life of a Mexican nun, Sor Juana Inés de la Cruz, a remarkable intellectual who was also one of the greatest poets of Spain's Siglo de Oro. Susan Elizabeth Ramírez explores Sor Juana's life and her art, putting her in historical context to demonstrate her importance for understanding colonial Mexico.

4. One hundred years after Sor Juana's death, Miguel Hidalgo y Costilla was not yet a national hero. Instead, he was the parish priest in a small city called San Felipe. Rather than telling the well-known story of how Hidalgo set off Mexico's war for independence, director and scriptwriter Antonio Serrano focused on the less-familiar period of his life in *Hidalgo—La Historia Jamás Contada*. In the 1790s, Hidalgo made his home a cultural center, which became known as "Little France" because he treated everyone equally without regard to race or social status. Hidalgo loved music, dancing, and the theater, and he was alleged to have fathered several illegitimate children. Donald F. Stevens draws on the historical and biographical literature, as well as the Inquisition's records, to assess the veracity of the film.

5. The tension between romance, repression, and religion is also a theme in María Luisa Bemberg's *Camila*, the story of a young woman who eloped with a priest in mid-nineteenth-century Argentina. Stevens finds that there is historical evidence for Bemberg's feminist vision of Camila as an active instigator rather than a passive victim in her story. Camila's death was also a significant factor in undermining the tyranny of the federalist dictator Juan Manuel de Rosas.

6. Ciro Guerra's *Embrace of the Serpent* presents the story of an indigenous man named Karamakate and his interactions in the Amazon rain forest with two Western scientists over four decades in the early twentieth century. Daniel O. Mosquera sees the film not only as a reflection of the past but also as an opportunity to think about the future of the Amazon, and the planet.

7. The small Caribbean island of Martinique produced many outstanding intellectuals and authors in the twentieth century including Joseph Zobel, Frantz Fanon, and Aimé Césaire, as well as the filmmaker Euzhan Palcy. *Rue Cases-Nègres*, her adaptation of Zobel's autobiographical novel, follows José, a child born in poverty, as he and his grandmother struggle to escape from life on a sugar cane plantation. Mohamed Kamara sees Palcy's film as an opportunity to explore race, class, and gender as well as the contrast between José's formal French education, which attempted to erase the African past, and his informal education, which kept memories of his ancestors' history alive.

8. Education, this time mostly informal, was also an ingredient in the transformation of another student. A middle-class child born in Argentina, Ernesto Guevara took a detour on the way to his medical degree. On a lark, he set off on a motorcycle trip with a friend, but he ended up learning what life was like in other South American countries. Guevara began to see the necessity for political change. Thomas C. Field Jr. points out the ways in which the film *The Motorcycle Diaries* follows the itinerary of this remarkable individual, but he concludes that the film deliberately distorts Guevara's political transformation.

9. By the 1960s, thousands of people were inspired by the Cuban Revolution of 1959. They concluded that armed violence was the only way to overturn corrupt, authoritarian governments. When the Brazilian military deposed an elected government in 1964, even more people took up arms to end the repression there. James N. Green examines two films set in Brazil during the 1960s, *Four Days in September* and *Marighella*, explaining the historical context and analyzing their distinct answers to the important questions of those years: Was armed resistance justified? What should be their goal, restoration of democracy or socialist revolution?

10. In the middle of the twentieth century, Mexico was controlled by what some have called "the perfect dictatorship." *La Ley de Herodes* focuses on a fictional central character, a political flunky who becomes the interim mayor of a poor, indigenous village far from the benefits of electricity, education, health care, and "progress." Jürgen Buchenau and Madison Green contend that this character's story illustrates a great deal that was true about the ways politics really worked then and who benefited. Since Luis Estrada's film was the first to directly name the dominant party and to show the president as responsible for the corruption and authoritarian rule, the film also may have helped to undermine one-party rule when it was released later in the century.

11. Alfonso Cuarón's *Roma* is also set in Mexico, in the middle-class neighborhood where he grew up. The central character, Cleo, is a live-in domestic worker. Susie S. Porter explains how the film shows us lives shaped by consumer culture as well as how increasing economic and social inequality led to more dissatisfaction and organized protests. As Mexico's government began losing control, it resorted to increasing violence to suppress dissent, even against the middle class.

12. The Central American nation of El Salvador had a long history of using military violence to repress demands for social justice. John Duigan's *Romero* follows the life of Oscar Romero, who had been a relatively conservative Catholic priest before he was elevated to archbishop. As he faced the horrific violence being unleashed on peasants, students, and priests, Romero used his position to advocate for social justice and an end to the repression. Then he was killed by an assassin. Kevin Coleman finds that the film not only gets the facts right but that it played a crucial role in bringing the story of Archbishop Romero and the violence in El Salvador to audiences in the United States, Europe, and the rest of the world.

13. After the assassination of Archbishop Romero, El Salvador descended into civil war. Oliver Stone's *Salvador* focuses on the experiences of Richard Boyle, a troubled photojournalist from California who traveled to El Salvador to report on the increasing violence there. Stone co-wrote the script with the real Richard Boyle, who had reported from the country during those years. The film provides an outsider's point of view as Boyle tries to document what is happening there and to report on the role of the United States government in the conflict. Erik Ching describes the limitations of the film as well as what it gets right. He concludes that *Salvador* increased international awareness of El Salvador's civil war.

14. John Malkovich's *The Dancer Upstairs* is a fictionalized account of the search for the elusive leader of a revolutionary organization intending

to overthrow the government in an unnamed South American coun-try. Susan Elizabeth Ramírez explains how the film closely parallels the search for Abimael Guzmán, alias Presidente Gonzalo, the leader of a Maoist guerilla organization in Peru called Sendero Luminoso (Shining Path).

15. In *Even the Rain*, a fictional filmmaker travels to Cochabamba, Bolivia, to make a historical film about the exploitation of the indigenous people of Hispaniola after 1492. Leo J. Garofalo points out that this temporal and geographic incongruity enables the film to address debates about two historical time periods: the first years of European exploitation in the Caribbean and neoliberal domination by foreign corporations in the twenty-first century.

Each film, and each essay, is an invitation to further investigation. Movies are a vivid way to present the past, but film is an expensive medium and one that necessarily presents only a brief time span and a limited point of view. So every author has provided a list of additional resources at the end of each chapter, to enable those who would like to learn more about the evidence, the broader contexts, and the debates. There is a lot of history to explore.

ADDITIONAL RESOURCES

Burns, E. Bradford. *Latin American Cinema: Film and History*. Los Angeles: UCLA Latin American Center, University of California, 1975. A classic work by one of the first Latin American historians to use films in teaching history.

Davis, Natalie Zemon. *Slaves on Screen: Film and Historical Vision*. Cambridge: Harvard University Press, 2000. Includes a chapter on Gillo Pontecorvo's *Burn!* (1969) and Tomás Gutiérrez Alea's *The Last Supper* (1976), as well as Davis's conclusions about the relationship between written and cinematic history.

King, John. *Magical Reels: A History of Cinema in Latin America.* New ed. London: Verso, 2000. A comprehensive history of filmmaking in Latin America from the silent era to the late twentieth century.

Levine, Robert M. *Images of History: Nineteenth-and Early Twentieth-Century Latin American Photographs as Documents*. Durham, NC: Duke University Press, 1989. Not only a guide to the literature on photography in Latin America but also an essential discussion of images as documents.

Novick, Peter. *That Noble Dream: The "Objectivity" Question and the American Historical Profession*. Cambridge, England: Cambridge University Press, 1988. A fascinating look at the professionalization of history and the debate on the ideal of "what really happened."

O'Connor, John E., ed. *Image as Artifact: The Historical Analysis of Film and Television*. Malabar, FL: R. E. Krieger, 1990. Essays analyzing film and television as a series of "frameworks" including representations of history; evidence of facts, events, and culture; and the development of the motion picture industry.

Rosenstone, Robert A. *History on Film/Film on History*. Third ed. London: Routledge, 2018. Based on his five decades of thinking, writing, and filmmaking, this is the most important book on the relationship between written history and film.

Rosenstone, Robert A., ed. *Revisioning History: Film and the Construction of a New Past*. Princeton: Princeton University Press, 1995. An important collection of essays that includes John Mraz on Tomás Gutiérrez's *Memories of Underdevelopment* (1968) and Rosenstone on Alex Cox's *Walker* (1987).

NOTES

1. For the professionalization of history and its idea of "objectivity," see Peter Novick, *That Noble Dream: The "Objectivity" Question and the American Historical Profession* (New York: Cambridge University Press, 1988). Ranke's words, in the original German, were "*wie es eigentlich gewesen.*" See page 28 for discussion of whether the phrase should be translated "as it really was" or "as it essentially was." The difference is significant. On the development of photography, see Robert Taft, *Photography and the American Scene: A Social History, 1839–1889* (New York: Macmillan, 1942).

2. See John E. O'Connor, "History in Images/Images in History: Reflections on the Importance of Film and Television Study for an Understanding of the Past," *American Historical Review* 93, no. 5 (December 1988): 1201; Sandburg as paraphrased by E. Bradford Burns, *Latin American Cinema: Film and History* (Los Angeles: UCLA Latin American Center, University of California, 1975), 14.

3. Robert A. Rosenstone, "The Historical Film as Real History," *Film-Historia* 5, no. 1 (1995), 5.

4. Robert A. Rosenstone, "History in Images/History in Words: Reflections on the Possibility of Really Putting History onto Film," *American Historical Review* 93, no. 5 (December 1988): 1178–79.

5. Mohamed Kamara, "History, Autobiography, and Truth in Euzham Palcy's *Rue Cases-Nègres*," in this volume, 146.

6. Robert Brent Toplin, "The Filmmaker as Historian," *American Historical Review* 93, no. 5 (December 1988): 1227.

7. Robert A. Rosenstone, *History on Film/Film on History*, third ed. (London: Routledge, 2018), xvi.

8. Rosenstone, *History on Film*, 139.

9. See Davis's remarks as quoted in Ed Benson, "Martin Guerre, the Historian and the Filmmakers: An Interview with Natalie Zemon Davis," *Film & History* 13, no. 3 (September 1983): 49–65, especially 62.

10. Hayden White, "Historiography and Historiophoty," *American Historical Review* 93, no. 5 (December 1988): 1194.

11. Burns, *Latin American Cinema*, 6.

12. Robin W. Winks portrays the historian as "like Sergeant Friday, he only wants to get the facts." Nevertheless, the stories he excerpts of searches for manuscripts also show that success requires imagination and even luck. See Robin W. Winks, ed., *The Historian as Detective: Essays on Evidence* (New York: Harper and Row, 1968).

13. Natalie Zemon Davis, *The Return of Martin Guerre* (Cambridge, MA: Harvard University Press, 1983), viii.

14. Joyce Appleby, Lynn Hunt, and Margaret Jacob, *Telling the Truth about History* (New York: W.W. Norton, 1994), 259.

15. Quoted in Barbara Abrash and Janet Sternburg, eds., *Historians & Filmmakers: Toward Collaboration; A Roundtable Held at the New York Institute for the Humanities, New York University, October 30, 1982* (New York: Institute for Research in History, 1983), 12.

16. Burns, *Latin American Cinema*, 7–13; Pierre Sorlin, "Historical Films as Tools for Historians," in *Image as Artifact: The Historical Analysis of Film and Television*, ed. John E. O'Connor (Malabar, FL: R. E. Krieger, 1990), 42–68.

17. Bill Nichols argues that "the categories and boundaries surrounding documentary and reality, fact and fiction, defy hard and fast definition." See Nichols, *Blurred Boundaries: Questions of Meaning in Contemporary Culture* (Bloomington: Indiana University Press, 1994), xiii.

18. Taft, *Photography*, 310, 347.

19. The photograph that I have in mind is number 86 in Anita Brenner's *The Wind That Swept Mexico: The History of the Mexican Revolution, 1910–1942* (Austin: University of Texas Press, 1943, 1971); and number 31 in Aurelio de los Reyes, *Con Villa en Mexico: Testimonios sobre camarógrafos norteamericanos en la Revolución, 1911–1916* (Mexico: Universidad Nacional Autónoma de Mexico, 1985). Kevin Brownlow, *The War, the West, and the Wilderness* (New York: Alfred A. Knopf, 1979), 88–89, showed the full, original frame enlargement, whereas the previous citations published a version that was cropped to make Villa appear more prominent. See also Brownlow's discussion of the circumstances of this filmmaking on his page 92. I am grateful for the observations of Dr. Friedrich Katz on Villa's relationship to the film industry.

20. Robert M. Levine, *Images of History: Nineteenth-and Early Twentieth-Century Latin American Photographs as Documents* (Durham, NC: Duke University Press, 1989), 9, 184–85. See also Robert M. Levine, ed., *Windows on Latin America: Understanding Society through Photographs* (Miami: North-South Center, 1987).

21. See Alan Trachtenberg, "Albums of War: On Reading Civil War Photographs," *Representations* 9 (Winter 1985): 1–32. Nancy Leys Stepan, "Portraits of a Possible Nation: Photographing Medicine in Brazil," *Bulletin of the History of Medicine* 68, no. 1 (Spring 1994): 136–49, finds certain uncaptioned Brazilian photographs mute. As Stepan is an expert on race, she comes to the altogether unsurprising conclusion that the photographs speak to that issue.

22. See Chapter 5.

23. See Robert M. Levine, "*Pixote*: Fiction and Reality in Brazilian Life," in *Based on a True Story: Latin American History at the Movies*, ed. Donald F. Stevens

(Wilmington, DE: SR Books, 1997; later printings, Lanham, MD: Rowman & Little-field, 1998).

24. Julianne Burton, "Toward a History of Social Documentary in Latin America," in *The Social Documentary in Latin America*, ed. Julianne Burton (Pittsburgh: University of Pittsburgh Press, 1990), 21.

25. See Burton, "Toward a History of Social Documentary," 13.

26. Robert Sklar, quoted in *Historians & Filmmakers*, 10.

27. The ideal of "objectivity" has been contested within the historical profession since the First World War. Novick, *That Noble Dream*, chap. 5.

28. Quoted in Burns, *Latin American Cinema*, 16–17. Burns cites the 1964 publication, but the first edition of Gottschalk's *Understanding History* appeared in 1950.

29. Rosenstone, *History on Film*, 139.

30. Rosenstone, *History on Film*, 43.

31. Rosenstone, *History on Film*, 141.

Chapter 1

Jaguar Paw's World

Thoughts on Apocalypto *and Mesoamerican History*

Camilla Townsend

Apocalypto *(2006); produced by Bruce Davey and Mel Gibson; directed by Mel Gibson; written by Mel Gibson and Farhad Safinia; color; 239 minutes; Icon Productions. A peaceful Mesoamerican villager is taken captive by Mayan (or possibly Aztec) warriors and brought to their capital for sacrifice before making a daring escape.*

When Mel Gibson's *Apocalypto* appeared in 2006, it had an effect that was, to put it mildly, polarizing. Many condemned the work for its over-the-top violence, others for its inaccuracy on a basic level: though the script was in Yucatec Mayan, the plot was utterly divorced from Mayan history as it really was in the early 1500s.[1] Many others truly loved the film, however—among them Robert Duvall, Quentin Tarantino, Martin Scorsese, Eduardo James Olmos, and Spike Lee.[2] A survey revealed that 80% of Mexicans responded very positively.[3] People who liked it said they learned something important about preconquest Mesoamericans. Clearly, there is a phenomenon at work that deserves to be better understood. Why would serious and well-intentioned people disagree about the film on such a visceral level?

Part of the answer lies in the fact that people love to hate (or sometimes love to love) Mel Gibson himself, who wrote and directed the film—though he worked with the Iranian American scriptwriter Farhad Safinia. Gibson is known for drinking too much, spouting anti-Semitic statements that he then recants, and occasionally embracing far-right views. None of these qualities endeared him to the type of person who would be most likely to take an interest in a film on preconquest Mexico. But we don't have to like a person to acknowledge that he or she occasionally exhibits streaks of genius in their work. A truly great film—like any truly great art—opens up the possibilities, complexities, and contradictions of a moment; it does not offer just one point of view and hammer it home. *Apocalypto* certainly does not.

A greater share of the explanation for the polarized reactions to the film is probably due to the fact that human beings still disagree profoundly about how much we have in common and how much we do not—about what cultural difference really is. For many centuries, Western commentators took for granted their own cultural superiority. It was a great step forward when, in the early twentieth century, Franz Boas of Columbia University in effect invented the field of anthropology and began to assert the need to study each human culture in depth and on its own, as a world unto itself, with its own complexities, equal in moral worth to any other culture.[4]

By the late twentieth century, however, even that notion had grown dangerous, as it necessarily implied discrete and unchanging cultures. Isolated or relatively isolated peoples were apparently trapped in their traditional worldviews. A world struggling against racism could not accept this vision of black and brown people who lived far from the main currents of "Western civilization" in purportedly static mental frameworks. So it was that in the 1980s and 1990s, the notion that each human was simply a product of their culture almost visibly imploded. In 1982, Eric Wolf demanded, "What if we take cognizance of *processes* that transcend separable cases [of cultural groups], moving through and beyond them and transforming them as they proceed? . . . for example, the North American fur trade, and the trade in native American and African slaves."[5] Academic conversation swirled and eddied along these themes. By 1988, James Clifford would say, "I argue that identity, considered ethnographically, must *always* be mixed, relational and inventive."[6] Every person, scholars began to recognize, is always in the process of inventing his or her cultural identity; all socially constructed ideas (not just European-descended ones) are inherently unstable. Such, indeed, had to be the very definition of culture. "Culture," John and Jean Comaroff concluded, "always contains within it polyvalent, potentially contestable messages, images and actions. It is, in short, a historically-situated, historically unfolding ensemble of signifiers-in-action."[7]

Yet in the early decades of the twenty-first century, this notion has been applied unevenly in the aggregate, and certainly differently by different individuals. Historians have tended to encourage our students not to overidentify with the past but to acknowledge that circumstances and context and thus culture have changed so much over time that we cannot be immediately certain that we know what an eighteenth-century white man, for instance, was talking about when he referred to "liberty" or "Christian beliefs." But when, on the other hand, students assume that global people we are studying *do* come from profoundly different and entirely separate, even unfathomable, cultures, we have not been as quick to remind them of the inverse—that in such a case we should assume *more* commonality than we have been in the habit of doing. These people, too, had certain human problems to solve and were caught up in comparable wars and likewise faced political power imbalances. Individuals in those worlds also had access to different worldviews and likewise, were adept at mentally integrating whatever they needed in order to cope with their shifting world.

In the course of *Apocalypto*'s first half hour, viewers meet with hunter-gatherers who are different from all those who have ever before appeared on film. After a brief period of feeling culturally alien, the forest dwellers resolve into a world of people who seem on some level recognizable. In 2006, the reviewer for *The New York Times* did not like this one bit. He said that their cinematic village "might double as a nostalgic vision of small-town America were it not for the loin cloths, the tattooed buttocks and the facial piercings."[8] Looked at from another angle, however, that is precisely the point. Despite innumerable cultural differences, we moderns sitting in the audience do not feel like we are a different species. Yes, the actors are speaking fluent Mayan and are of indigenous descent themselves. They wear loincloths and tattoos. They live in a rain forest (the movie was filmed in a real one in Mexico) and use brilliantly clever contraptions made of wood that none of us in the audience would have any idea how to construct. They think like many ancient indigenous people of Mesoamerica—telling stories about jaguars who speak, for instance, and teasing mercilessly a young couple who do not have children. Yet despite all this, we do not feel a chasm of distance but rather, a wish to know these people better. The film does not exoticize them but rather, renders them real to us.

How does this segment of the film manage to convey forcefully that these are indigenous Mesoamericans from an earlier era without imposing excessive distance? First, the filmmakers cast indigenous-descended people, so we are not left consciously or unconsciously thinking about modern Mexico. The main character, Jaguar Paw, is played by Rudy Youngblood, an Oklahoman of Comanche descent. And Jaguar Paw's father is played by Morris Birdyellowhead, of Canada's Paul First Nation. Many of the other actors are Mexican but not Mexicans who look more Spanish than anything else but rather, Mexicans who manifest their indigenous genes in their faces. This fact, along with the genuine forest setting, allows us to be transported to another era. The people speak a real indigenous language, not a fake one,[9] and definitely not English or Spanish. Yet the scriptwriter adeptly moves the plot along without lengthy or complex dialogue, so we are not scrambling to read long subtitles and connect them to the action. In this way, we are brought into the world of another language without the psychological alienation that generally occurs when we hear people speaking a tongue we do not understand. Finally, this part of the film revolves around humor, a rather dreadful practical joke. Most modern people would not find it funny in their own lives, but that does not matter. What does matter is that we see people arguing and laughing, as all humans do, in all cultures, albeit for different reasons.

The people do not live in a simple, unchanging idyll. We know this because during the course of a hunt, Jaguar Paw and his father run across a group of fugitives who have been uprooted by some sort of an attack on their homeland. We know nothing of whatever war they have been involved with, only that war exists in this world; as in all places, there are political complexities that outsiders are ignorant of. And the people in Jaguar Paw's milieu disagree about how best to handle the situation: Jaguar Paw wants to talk to the people to learn what he needs to know about the events they have experienced, but his father argues that their fear may be contagious and shuts down the conversation. We see the dissatisfaction on Jaguar Paw's face. He is a product of his father's worldview, but he is not trapped by it.

OLD IDEAS: BRUTAL SAVAGES VS. NOBLE SAVAGES

This initial segment of the film—a cinematic triumph, in my view—is not the end of the story. Perhaps it was too much to hope that someone like Mel Gibson could keep up this level of sophistication. As the main action begins, the film devolves into yet another work portraying indigenous people as vicious savages: Jaguar Paw's remote village is attacked by mind-bogglingly sadistic warriors (who look like "slavering, brain-dead orcs," in the words of one scholarly reviewer[10]) from an unidentified powerful civilization. Their leader wears human jawbones as part of his outfit. He and others laugh with pleasure as they kill without rhyme or reason, except when it is for spite. They rape and murder young women—which literally almost never happened in indigenous warfare (for young women, as future mothers, were valuable adoptees). Jaguar Paw and numerous others are taken prisoner. His wife and child hide down a cenote, or natural well, and he is marched away, desperate to try to save them but doubtful that he will ever see them again.

The first problem is that the film purports to be about Mayans of Yucatán—the people are certainly speaking a Mayan language—and yet it is really about the Nahuas, that is, the Aztecs and their neighbors in the central valley of Mexico.[11] Scriptwriter Farhad Safinia has confessed that at first, he and Gibson did not really care whether the film was about the Mayas or the Aztecs. They looked into matters, reading older works, and unbeknownst to them, met with a barrage of stereotypes. "The Mayas were far more interesting to us," Safinia remembered. "You can choose a civilization that is bloodthirsty [referring to the Aztecs], or you can show the Maya civilization that was so sophisticated."[12] Though it was inaccurate, the traditional literature did used to show the Aztecs as dedicated to death and the Mayas as talented astronomical observers, complex thinkers who had fallen from power for mysterious reasons. The latter idea delighted the two filmmakers, who became determined to make a movie about corruption and evil ways bringing a civilization down from within. The two happily toured Mayan sites and consulted with a professor of Mayan history.[13] Problematically, however, the Mayan power centers had declined many centuries before the arrival of the Spaniards, which is where Gibson wanted to end up. In the early 1500s, there were no longer any great urban centers in the Mayan world towering over all other people for hundreds of miles around.

In the central valley of Mexico, however, the Aztec capital of Tenochtitlan did just that. And so, with a sleight of hand that was invisible to many viewers, the filmmakers made a movie that was really about captives being taken to Tenochtitlan, even though it purported to be about the Mayan world. In a physical sense, the great city that appears in the movie with its towering pyramids, bright colors, and huge marketplace closely matches the descriptions left by the Spanish conquerors of the Aztecs in the sixteenth century.[14] Thus, Gibson was able to advertise to the world a movie about the famously sophisticated Mayas but then sneak in the "bloodthirsty" Aztecs after all, as more closely corresponding to the powerful and "corrupt" people he envisioned.

This bait-and-switch would not, on its own, be a serious problem for a pop culture movie. But sadly, although the filmmakers believed in Jaguar Paw's village, they did not truly believe in the Aztec empire. And since it was not real to them, they were not invested in making it real to the audience. Viewers are thus asked to believe that though Jaguar Paw's village was only a couple days' march away from a great and powerful city, they had never even heard of it. The audience is likewise expected to accept that the awe-inspiring city (where tens of thousands of people, possibly more, apparently live) is surrounded not by miles and miles of agricultural villages (as Tenochtitlan was, and the great Mayan complexes had been) but by forestland populated by small, self-sufficient groups of hunter-gatherers. One doesn't have to be a specialist in ancient Mesoamerica to find this scenario confusing. Large and populous cities are, always have been, and must be dependent on areas producing excess, storable food through extensive farming.

Within days, as the prisoners approach the outskirts of the great city, the inaccuracy (and thus, the audience's confusion) only multiplies. The prisoners come across a young girl stricken with a strange disease that seems a great deal like smallpox. She predicts disaster for the captors, for "the vile" people, as she calls them, claiming that a jaguar man will lead them to someone who will eventually destroy them. Her mother lies dead behind her, and her own face is marred by the pox. But there were no such horrific sicknesses in the New World before the Europeans arrived; across the sea, the great variety of deadly ailments existed as a result of the Old World's many millennia of agricultural lifestyle, which involved living with their farm animals.[15] Since most audience members are well aware that the Europeans brought the epidemics with them, and we have been given absolutely no reason to think that the Spaniards have already arrived, this moment, too, is perplexing. The director seems to have been so eager to prove his beloved theory that the "corrupt" society was on the edge of collapse that he allowed himself to make mistakes harmful to the integrity of the film.

The prisoners pass through an area where laboring slaves are covered in some sort of white powder. Are they working in a salt mine? Preparing chalk mixtures to make lime-based whitewash? (The filmmakers later said it was the latter, having read that painting the pyramids required exorbitant amounts of lime, and in a brief flash we see a building being coated.[16]) Either would be possible, but what seems strange is that there appear to be hundreds, potentially thousands, of enslaved people working on behalf of the city in a sort of proto-industrial neighborhood. Nothing could have been further from Tenochtitlan's truth, which is known to have been a breathtakingly beautiful city of gardens, where the percentage of the enslaved was always small. (It would not even have been possible for a people without a standing army to maintain a large segment of its people in brutal conditions for the long term.) How easy it would have been for the filmmakers to show something of the city's grandeur and sophistication—the embroidered clothing, the golden dragonflies in the girls' hair, the poetic songs, the screen-fold books, the zoological garden.[17] Such a place could have been just as frightening to the newly arrived Jaguar Paw. (Indeed, newcomers to the city always described it as awe-inspiring.) But none of this is anywhere to be seen, as Gibson was interested only in the idea that the place had rotted through, corrupt to the core.

As the newcomers enter the city proper, the women are sold into servitude—auctioned off from a raised platform, like enslaved people in the U.S. South—and the men are taken to be sacrificed atop a great pyramid. And here, we move beyond the point of error or omission to something more sinister. The movie departs radically from what we know about the ceremonies of sacrifice, based on indigenous-language sources, and instead conveys a horrific message about Native Americans. The killings in the film happen en masse, in numbers no preindustrial society could ever have managed: at one point we see hundreds of corpses in an open pit. We see dozens of heads on skewers and even a woman sitting next to a huge pot full of heads. Thousands of watchers are packed into the town square, swaying and screaming for blood. They literally jump for joy at every death. Some participants seem almost to be in a state of ecstasy. The scene takes on the look of a cult's violent, frenzied orgy.

No society in human history has ever lived regularly like this, and the Aztecs certainly did not. The sources that say they did were written by Spaniards, eager to assert that their own conquest of Mexico had the blessing of God. We get a different sense of things when we read what they wrote in their own language of Nahuatl.[18] The Aztecs themselves had been relative newcomers, migrants to the area, only a century before, and they themselves knew what it was to have often been clobbered by their better-established enemies. Over the course of generations, they cleverly allied with certain other groups and turned the tables on the royal line of the region's most powerful city-state, rising to become top dogs themselves. It was a nearly ubiquitous practice in the New World to sacrifice an occasional prisoner of war—indeed, archaeologists suspect that the practice occurred everywhere on earth at one time.[19] But now, as the Aztecs rose to power and feared that they might one day lapse back into their former state of vulnerability, they transformed the practice into something more frightening, a fate that was meted out to large numbers of prisoners of war, occasionally even to dozens at once. At the same time, they continued to hew to the old way of thinking, that the sacrifice of a human life was a great and worthy gift to the gods, in exchange for which the gods would keep the universe going. Though they had offloaded the role of sacrificial victim onto the shoulders of their enemies, they nevertheless took the ceremonies very seriously and did not seem to get joy or a wild satisfaction out of them. Instead, they stood quietly and reverently, holding sacred flowers, or garlands, or figures of the gods, depending on which holy day it was.[20]

GLIMPSES OF TRUTH

Nevertheless, despite his hideous distortion of what used to happen, Gibson does in the midst of this wild exaggeration stumble upon a germ of truth. The start of the film flashes a quotation from Will Durant: "A great civilization is not conquered from without until it has destroyed itself from within."[21] On one level, this is a cruel condemnation of the Aztecs (or of the Mayas), an insistence that they were destined to fall from power because of their own evil. The idea seems to echo older, colonialist views that the people of the New World deserved everything they got. But Will Durant was not talking about the Mesoamericans. He was simply observing that when nations grow very powerful, they sometimes destroy themselves. It is an old and oft-seen pattern in the history of the world.

There is in fact evidence, which historians have frequently noted, that the Aztec state had overreached itself and thus, made too many enemies to withstand the fracturing that occurred when the Europeans arrived. Most scholars today believe that the conquest would never have happened if so many indigenous people hadn't chosen to ally themselves with the Spaniards.[22] Why were they so embittered? After all, the practice of human sacrifice on a small scale as an element of warfare was nearly universal in the region, and the Aztec royal family had worked hard to intermarry with other noble lines far and wide. But in their efforts to cement their power, the Aztecs had grown the practice of human sacrifice too much and too quickly for the shift to be accepted easily. It may have been nonsensical for the makers of *Apocalpyto* to have imagined that a village like Jaguar Paw's would never have heard of the Aztecs, but it wasn't nonsensical to point out that small, rural villages were vulnerable to Aztec power. The Aztecs and their allies regularly made war on the frontiers of the known world, to gain more tribute payers and a wider array of resources, and in those wars, they took prisoners. As the years went by, more and more of those prisoners faced the cutting stone. All of Mesoamerica knew what was going on. Even Aztec poets, singing around bonfires of an evening in their beautiful city, lamented the reality of the ceaseless warfare. "Let there be more living on the earth," or "Let life continue on the earth," (*ma çan oc huel nemohua on in tlalticpac*), they would sing.[23] In short, the violent enslavement espoused by the Aztec political class was indeed the key to the fault lines that existed in their world. And those thin lines would crack wide open when the Europeans arrived and asked for help in bringing the Aztecs down.

It wasn't just the level of violence but also the associated tribute payments that people resented. After the destruction brought about by war and the taking of prisoners, conquered polities were left with the duty of collecting and submitting annual payments of goods. Sometimes, the assigned amounts were onerous and caused hardship. Sometimes, the tasks themselves were designed to remind people that they lived at the whim of Tenochtitlan. The historian Inga Clendinnen once described what happened to the town of Cuetlaxta after the people dared to rebel against Aztec requirements:

> After their military punishment the town's tribute was doubled, which was burdensome enough. But the townsfolk were also obliged to provide a number of live snakes and other animals, including (obviously outrageously rare) white-furred ocelots. "Symbolic" is possibly the wrong word to use of this brand of punitive strategy: wriggling miserably around in a snake-infested cave clutching one's snake-catching stick must have brought the might of Moctezuma very near.[24]

Apocalypto's audience sees a bit of this dangerous spirit of rebellion. The heart of the film is the next segment of the movie, in which Jaguar Paw escapes sacrifice, eludes his captors, and breaks for home. The savage city dwellers are at his heels, however, and one of the greatest chases of cinematic history ensues, prompting one reviewer to say that despite the Mayan dialogue, "the film's real language is Hollywood's, and Mr. Gibson's, native tongue."[25] In short, even the most hostile of reviewers must acknowledge that as the events unfold, we root for Jaguar Paw with every fiber of our being. This in itself seems to me to be a great development: how often in our lives do we root for a loincloth-wearing tribesman armed with blow darts?

Moreover, although Gibson almost certainly did not know this, the whole set of events is at root evocative of real occurrences in the Aztec world, c. 1500. Toward the peak of their power, when the sacrifice ceremonies were being used to terrorize neighboring states into obedience, they developed the practice of kidnapping young men from the region they were interested in incorporating into their empire and bringing them to Tenochtitlan. They forced them to watch the worst of the sacrificial ceremonies and then let them run home—undoubtedly, with the sensation that they were being followed, though they were not. What really followed them was the horror of what they had seen, the knowledge that the Aztecs would arrive in their village sometime soon, and the conviction that they must agree to the Aztecs' terms for tribute payments, whatever they were, rather than fight them and risk having prisoners taken. They should not even try to ally with others; the risk of disaster was too great. An Aztec elder later described the tactic: "Things were shown to them and they were stunned. Thus, they were undone, disunited." (*Tlattitiloia, tlamauizoltiloia; niman ic xitinoa, necacaoal.*)[26]

Like so many aspects of the film, the question of the women's roles can be read in either of two dramatically different ways. On the one hand, the movie is a classic "male fantasy": a young hero has the nearly superhuman strength and courage needed to survive untold horror, which he does successfully specifically because he holds the hope of being able to rescue his beautiful wife and his trusting son. Nowhere in evidence is anyone like Chimalxochitl, or Shield Flower, an old cultural heroine of the Aztecs who in their legendary histories showed extraordinary strength in the face of sacrifice and enormous dedication to her people and to posterity.[27] Never do we glimpse women fighting back with weapons, as Mesoamerican women were sometimes known to do.[28] And yet despite this, Gibson does allow indigenous women their due, often conveying what needs to be conveyed without falling into any of the usual traps. He wants to show that the women prisoners were sold into slavery rather than being sacrificed on the stone, as indeed they generally were, so the camera lingers on their fate for a while (albeit with inaccuracies).

He wishes to show that in this climate, people did not wear much, yet he wants to avoid ubiquitous, naked female breasts, which become a distraction and say something quite different in the modern world than they did at the time. So Jaguar Paw's wife wears hemp-woven cords full of beads, just as she really might have done. (Some of the people also wear woven cloth, which hunter-gatherers would not have had unless they bought it in Tenochtitlan. But let's let the small things go.)

Perhaps most importantly, Seven, the wife (played by Dalia Hernández), demonstrates exactly the kind of courage that was most often asked of indigenous women in ancient America: that she find the strength to stay alive and bear her child, come what may, thus bringing her people into the future. They were rarely wanted on the battlefield; girls were raised to do exactly what she did when she was trapped in the cenote—find the courage and wit to postpone death as long as possible in case the gods chose to be kind before it was too late. When she gives birth in the water to her infant, we are treated to a scene richly evocative of Mesoamerican belief: that birthing mothers were heroes, capturing a soul from the universe and bringing it home to their people. There isn't a trace of the European idea that a woman must suffer in birth as a descendant of Eve. The character Seven may not have much screen time, but she does not end up appearing as Hollywood's usual screaming, panicked woman.[29]

Jaguar Paw does return in time to save his wife, young son, and brand-new infant. He has previously seen some European ships arrive and two of his pursuers from the city move toward them, fascinated. (They clearly do not realize that this is the fulfillment of the sick girl's prophecy from earlier in the film.) Some scholars have argued this moment is meant to symbolize the advent of the Europeans as saviors of the people.[30] But after being rescued, Seven asks if they should also seek an alliance with the newcomers, and Jaguar Paw decides that they should not, that they should try to avoid them at all costs. He and his family move deeper into the forest. James Lockhart, a leading historian of the Nahuas, once argued that this is exactly what most indigenous people did in the wake of the arrival of the strangers, that is, attempt to carry on as usual as much as possible for as long as they were able.[31] In the end, then, the film remains a stubbornly indigenous tale from first to last, even after the arrival of the strangers from the sea. That in itself is remarkable for a Hollywood movie.

Apocalypto could have been an even better movie. It did not have to reduce the powerful Aztecs (or the Mayas) to the worst stereotypes imaginable. But that was hardly the only vision of indigenous people that the film offered. It was, I would argue, an essential step in the first decade of the twenty-first century, a necessary break from what had been done in past movies regarding the wearers of loincloths. The greater movies of the future that will tell stories of preconquest America will be able to be made because this one exists.

APPENDIX:

A DESCRIPTION OF TENOCHTITLAN ON
THE EVE OF THE SPANISH CONQUEST[32]

Bernal Díaz, one of the Spaniards who first approached Tenochtitlan in the expedition of Hernando Cortés, later wrote about what he saw at the moment of arrival. He did not describe the "bloodthirsty savages" that other Europeans would soon delight in evoking. Rather, he recalled a lovely, cosmopolitan city.

When we saw all those cities and villages built in the water,[33] and other great towns on dry land, and that straight and level causeway leading to the [city of] Mexico, we were astounded. These great towns and pyramids and buildings rising from the water, all made of stone, seemed like an enchanted vision from the tale of Amadis.[34] Indeed, some of our soldiers asked whether it was not all a dream. It is not surprising therefore that I should write in this vein. It was all so wonderful that I do not know how to describe this first glimpse of things never heard of, seen, or dreamed of before.

When we arrived near Iztapalapa[35] we beheld the splendor of the other caciques[36] who came out to meet us, the lord of that city, whose name was Cuitlahuac, and the lord of Culhuacan, both of them close relations of Montezuma. And when we entered the town of Iztapalapa, the sight of the palaces in which they lodged us! They were very spacious and well built, of magnificent stone, cedar wood, and the wood of other sweet smelling trees, with great rooms and courts, which were a wonderful sight, and all covered with awnings of woven cotton.

When we had taken a good look at all this, we went to the orchard and garden, which was a marvelous place both to see and walk in. I was never tired of noticing the diversity of trees and the various scents given off by each, and the paths choked with roses and other flowers, and the many local fruit-trees and rose bushes,[37] and the pond of fresh water. Another remarkable thing was that large canoes could come into the garden from the lake, through a channel they had cut, and their crews did not have to disembark. Everything was shining with lime[38] and decorated with different kinds of stonework and paintings which were a marvel to gaze on. Then there were rare birds of many breeds and varieties which came to the pond. I say again that I stood looking at it, and thought that no land like it would ever be discovered in the whole world. . . . But today all that I then saw is overthrown and destroyed; nothing is left standing.

ADDITIONAL RESOURCES

Ardren, Traci. *Social Identities in the Classic Mayan Northern Lowlands: Gender, Age, Memory, Place*. Austin: University of Texas Press, 2015.

Carrasco, Davíd, and Scott Sessions. *Daily Life of the Aztecs*. Indianapolis: Hackett Publishing, 1998.

Clendinnen, Inga. *Aztecs: An Interpretation.* New York: Cambridge University Press, 1995.

Hansen, Richard D. "Relativism, Revisionism, Aboriginalism and Emic/Etic Truth: The Case Study of *Apocalypto*," in Richard Chacon and Rubéen Mendoza, eds., *The Ethics of Anthropology and Amerindian Research* (New York: Springer Press, 2012), 147–90.

Matthew, Laura, and Michel Oudijk, eds. *Indian Conquistadors: Indigenous Allies in the Conquest of Mexico*. Norman: University of Oklahoma Press, 2007.

Sousa, Lisa. *The Woman Who Turned into a Jaguar and Other Narratives of Native Women in Archives of Colonial Mexico.* Stanford, CA: Stanford University Press, 2017.

Taylor, Tim. "Ambushed by a Grotesque: Archaeology, Slavery and the Third Paradigm," in *Warfare, Violence and Slavery in Prehistory*, ed. Michael Parker Pearson and I. J. N. Thorpe (Oxford, UK: Archaeopress, 2005), 225–32.

Townsend, Camilla. *Annals of Native America: How the Nahuas of Colonial Mexico Kept Their History Alive.* New York: Oxford University Press, 2016.

Townsend, Camilla. *Fifth Sun: A New History of the Aztecs*. New York: Oxford University Press, 2019.

Wolf, Eric. *Europe and the People Without History.* Berkeley: University of California Press, 1982.

NOTES

1. For the most thorough of these responses, see the piece by leading Mayanist David Stuart, "An Old Unpublished Review of *Apocalypto*," November 18, 2007, mayadecipherment.com. The review was written for the *Washington Post* but arrived too late to appear there. It has been widely read and cited by other commentators.

2. David Carr, "Apocalypto's Biggest Fan," *New York Times*, February 12, 2007; "Robert Duvall Interview," *Premiere*, March 2007; "Interview with Quentin Tarantino," *FilmInk*, August 2007; "Spike Lee's Essential List of Films for Filmmakers,"

Vulture.com, July 26, 2013; Robert Welkos, "Gibson Dives In," *Los Angeles Times*, November 13, 2006.

3. *La Reforma*, January 30, 2007.

4. There is an extensive literature about Boas and the field of anthropology, as well as one on the concept of culture. Students might want to begin with a volume that was prepared before the later extensive critique was underway: George Stocking, ed., *A Franz Boas Reader: The Shaping of American Anthropology* (Chicago: University of Chicago Press, 1974).

5. Eric Wolf, *Europe and the People Without History* (Berkeley: University of California Press, 1982), 17.

6. James Clifford, *The Predicament of Culture* (Cambridge: Harvard University Press, 1988), 10.

7. John Comaroff and Jean Comaroff, *Ethnography and the Historical Imagination* (Boulder, CO: Westview Press, 1992), 27.

8. A. O. Scott, "The Passion of the Maya," *New York Times*, December 8, 2006. Scott bemoaned the fact that Gibson had not turned out to be another Werner Herzog, director of *Aguirre: Wrath of God* (1972), in which a trip down the Amazon brought people in touch with their inner animal natures, an example of the perennial *Heart of Darkness* narrative associated with forests and the people who live in them. For more on that film, see Chapter 2 in this volume.

9. Comparable films have resorted to creating an indigenous language. See, for instance, Terrence Malick's *The New World* (2005).

10. Andrea Stone, "Orcs in Loincloths," Archaeology.org Online Reviews, January 3, 2007.

11. No people ever actually called themselves "the Aztecs." That was an invention of scholars of the eighteenth and nineteenth centuries. The Mexica (Me-SHEE-ka) were the ethnic group who rose to power in the central valley of Mexico. They spoke the Nahuatl (NA-wat) language, as did almost all of their neighboring city-states; all the residents of the valley were thus Nahuas. For ease of communication, this essay will rely on the term "Aztec."

12. Safinia's comments were quoted in Nicole Sperling, "With help from a friend, Mel cut to the chase," *Washington Post*, December 15, 2006.

13. Needless to say, the scholar whom they worked with, anthropologist Richard D. Hansen, does not approve of all the decisions made by Gibson. He has written a fascinating piece about the need to take risks in fiction and how much damage can equally well be done by ham-fisted documentaries. See his "Relativism, Revisionism, Aboriginalism and Emic/Etic Truth: The Case Study of *Apocalypto*," in *The Ethics of Anthropology and Amerindian Research*, ed. Richard Chacon and Rubéen Mendoza (New York: Springer, 2012), 147–90. He includes an extremely thorough bibliography, including all the responses to the film he has found.

14. The most compelling contemporary account is that of Bernal Díaz del Castillo. Many excellent editions exist, including that edited by J. M. Cohen and titled *The Conquest of New Spain* (London: Penguin Books, 1963). See the excerpt in the appendix above, p. 25.

15. There is an extensive literature on the transfer of European disease to the New World. Students are advised to start with a classic: Alfred Crosby, *The Columbian Exchange* (Westport, CT: Greenwood Publishing, 1972).

16. IMDB.com/Apocalypto. See "Trivia."

17. See Davíd Carrasco and Scott Sessions, *Daily Life of the Aztecs* (Indianapolis: Hackett Publishing, 1998).

18. Spanish friars taught indigenous students the Roman alphabet so that they could learn to read the Bible. They took the new tool home with them and used it to transcribe traditional, oral recitations of history. See Camilla Townsend, *Annals of Native America: How the Nahuas of Colonial Mexico Kept Their History Alive* (New York: Oxford University Press, 2016).

19. Tim Taylor, "Ambushed by a Grotesque Archaeology, Slavery and the Third Paradigm," in *Warfare, Violence and Slavery in Prehistory*, ed. Michael Parker Pearson and I. J. N. Thorpe (Oxford, UK: Archaeopress, 2005), 225–32.

20. For more on the real Tenochtitlan, see Camilla Townsend, *Fifth Sun: A New History of the Aztecs* (New York: Oxford University Press, 2019). This work was based almost entirely on sources written by the Aztecs in their own language; thus, it brings us closer to knowledge of who they were.

21. Will Durant (1885–1981) was a famous American historian who wrote prolifically in the era of Gibson's parents: they are likely to have been the ones who passed on knowledge of him, as he is no longer widely cited by today's historians. Durant's eleven-volume work *The Story of Civilization* was published between 1935 and 1975 and was widely read. It treated only the Old World and did not cover the Mayas or the Aztecs.

22. See, for instance, Laura Matthew and Michel Oudijk, eds., *Indian Conquistadors: Indigenous Allies in the Conquest of Mesoamerica* (Norman: University of Oklahoma Press, 2007).

23. This line appears several times in the *Cantares Mexicanos*, traditional Aztec song lyrics that the Franciscans urged their aides to write down in the mid-sixteenth century. There is as yet no good English edition of this text.

24. Inga Clendinnen, *Aztecs: An Interpretation* (New York: Cambridge University Press, 1995), 35.

25. Scott, "Passion of the Maya."

26. Arthur J. O. Anderson and Charles Dibble, eds., *Florentine Codex: General History of the Things of New Spain. Book 2: The Ceremonies* (Santa Fe, NM: The School of American Research, 1951), 53. After the conquest, indigenous elders spoke of the past, and aides to the Franciscan friar Bernardino de Sahagún recorded what they said.

27. Townsend, *Fifth Sun*, 13–16.

28. See Lisa Sousa, *The Woman Who Turned into a Jaguar and Other Narratives of Native Women in Archives of Colonial Mexico* (Stanford, CA: Stanford University Press, 2017), 263–65.

29. For more on the notion of gender complementarity and women's version of courage, see Clendinnen, *Aztecs*, especially the chapters on "Wives" and "Mothers," as well as Sousa, *Woman Who Turned into a Jaguar*, throughout.

30. Traci Ardren, "Is *Apocalypto* Pornography?" Archaeology.org Online Reviews, December 5, 2006.

31. James Lockhart, *The Nahuas after the Conquest* (Stanford, CA: Stanford University Press, 1992). Lockhart also collected all Nahuatl-language testimonies about the conquest itself in *We People Here* (Los Angeles: University of California Press, 1993).

32. Source of translation: Bernal Díaz, *The Conquest of New Spain*, ed. by J. M. Cohen (London: Penguin Editions, 1963), 214–15. (Notes are my own.)

33. They were not really built in the water but rather on a cluster of islands in the middle of a lake.

34. A popular romance in Spain.

35. A town on the lakeshore, near the causeway leading to the city proper.

36. Chiefs or kings. This was an Arawak word quickly adopted by the Spaniards to describe all chiefs in the Americas.

37. European roses were not native to the area. Díaz would have seen other beautiful flowers whose names he did not know, and he called them "roses." The indigenous people soon began to grow roses, and they called them *castillan xochitl*, or "Spanish flower."

38. Painting with lime produces a glistening white surface.

Chapter 2

Whose Conquest Is This, Anyway?
Aguirre, the Wrath of God

Thomas H. Holloway

Aguirre, der Zorn Gottes *(1972), or* Aguirre, the Wrath of God; *produced by Werner Herzog; directed by Werner Herzog; written by Werner Herzog; color; 90 minutes; Werner Herzog Filmproduktion/New Yorker. Sixteenth-century explorer Lope de Aguirre (Klaus Kinski) rebels against Spanish authority and takes charge of an expedition into the Amazon basin looking for gold and leads it down the Amazon River.*

The Werner Herzog film *Aguirre, the Wrath of God* is based minimally and loosely on a true story, a history that must forever remain elusive, despite the existence of several independent accounts left by participants and the preservation of extended statements by Aguirre himself. All versions left by eyewitnesses and participants, as well as the interpretive positions developed in the more recent renewal of interest in the Aguirre story, many of them heavily researched, have a vested interest in one or another interpretation among the several possible. Furthermore, the Aguirre story has become the subject of numerous fictionalized or literary accounts, some of which themselves are based to a considerable extent on histories and chronicles but which add yet another voice, one deliberately creative even as it seeks to develop a view of the "true" Aguirre through such imaginative embellishment.

THE FILM

Herzog's film, on the other hand, is no docudrama attempt to expand on the historical record in a way that remains true to what is known, while filling in the blanks for dramatic interest and narrative continuity. The film is inspired more by the legends that have built up around the story of the Ursúa expedition and Aguirre's mutiny, as well as the filmmaker's imaginative extension of general myths and stereotypes regarding the Spanish conquistadors, native peoples, and the luxuriant tropical environment of the Amazon region. Its basis in history aside, it is a tale of obsessive fixation on fortune and fame, jealousy and lust, honor betrayed and defended, and ultimately, paranoid delusions. The film suggests that such an intense mix, stripped of the inhibitions and restrictions of civilized society, immersed in the power of nature, can lead to brutal and deadly strife, delirium, and destruction. As Herzog himself has said, "This film, I think, is not really a narrative of actual happenings or a portrait of actual people. At any level it is a film about what lies behind landscapes, faces, situations, and works."[1]

Such an approach, of course, is well within the prerogatives of the filmmaker. But just as Herzog is free to do with the story whatever his creative urges dictate, it is also legitimate, even worthwhile, for historians and students of history to examine the film from their own point of view. Those who seek a historical version of these events can approvingly comment on many of the visual images Herzog evokes: the grimy coarseness of the ragtag band of would-be conquerors of yet another rich indigenous kingdom; bits and pieces of dented and rusty armor over the tattered remains of once-fine costumes rotting in the tropical humidity; stubble beards and stringy hair and wild looks; the dense, dripping foliage and precipitous paths of the eastern Andes; the mighty river, alternately roiling through rapids that toss huge rafts like toy boats or so calm and vast as to induce lethargy and despair. This is no Technicolor swashbuckler reconstructed on a sanitized Hollywood backlot, and the film is well worth seeing for these cinematographic aspects alone.

At the same time, however, any historical commentary must also point to several egregious examples of creative license that go far beyond allegorical symbolism and surreal images of caravels in treetops. First, the priest Carvajal, voice-over narrator and recurring foil for Aguirre's excesses in the Herzog film, was not a member of the expedition, did not write about it, and had nothing to do with it. He was, instead, the chronicler of the first Spanish expedition down the Amazon from Peru, that of Francisco de Orellana in 1542, nineteen years before the Ursúa–Aguirre trip. There are six eyewitness chronicles extant by participants in the latter expedition,[2] which together provide a rich if unavoidably biased narrative, but none of those authors figures as an important character in the film. Second, all the chroniclers agree that the murder of Ursúa by a gang of mutineers was a swift and definitive surprise attack. In the film version, he is first, only wounded; then lingers in convalescence and is given a pardon by his successor Guzmán; and later, is surreptitiously taken into the forest and hanged by the plotters. Finally, the film suggests that the orgy of internecine strife and suicidal obstinacy, culminating in the fiendish delirium of Aguirre himself, leads to the complete destruction of the entire company, lost in the midst of the Amazon river-sea.

In the historical accounts, the mutiny and murder of Ursúa during the trip down the river and the subsequent assumption of command by Aguirre set the stage for considerable give-and-take between the rebels and forces loyal to the crown, over several months, once the survivors made it back to the island of Margarita and the adjacent mainland of what is today Venezuela. While they were in that region, the mutineers terrorized several towns and supposedly schemed to move overland and reconquer Peru for themselves, but many defected to the royalist side in return for clemency, further isolating the ringleaders. While in Venezuela, Aguirre wrote and dispatched several letters, the texts of which have been preserved, and killed his own daughter before being shot dead by one of his former comrades. None of this appears in Herzog's film, and consequently, anyone aware that there was a historical Aguirre might wonder how any account of the trip survived if all those involved perished in the jungle.[3]

This essay provides a descriptive outline of the career of Lope de Aguirre, focusing on his role in the ill-fated Ursúa expedition into the Amazon (called the Marañon at the time, from which the veterans of the trip called themselves Marañones). It then takes up briefly the various explanations of those events that have been developed in recent times and concludes with a historical interpretation, that is, one that attempts to understand the events in their own context and to take Lope de Aguirre on his own terms.

CHRONOLOGY

Lope de Aguirre was born in the town of Oñate, in the Basque province of Guipúzcoa, probably in 1514 or a little earlier.[4] As a youth and later in Peru, he worked at taming horses—the only vocation other than soldier associated with him. He shipped out of Seville probably in 1534; appeared in Cartagena de Indias in 1536; and spent a career in the service of arms, always on the royalist side as far as has been determined, through the most turbulent period of the postconquest civil wars in Peru between Pizarristas and Almagristas and subsequent efforts of royal agents Blasco Núñez Vela and Pedro de la Gasca to impose royal authority on the new colony. He fought in the 1555 battle of

Figure 2.1: Lope de Aguirre (Klaus Kinski) seeks fortune and fame but finds envy and despair as he and his dwindling expedition drift down the Amazon River. (Photofest)

Chuquinga against the last of the great rebels, Francisco Hernández Girón, receiving a leg wound from which he limped ever after. In 1560, nearing age fifty, long in the royal service but enjoying few lasting personal rewards for his efforts, he responded to the call to join a new expedition in search of the land of El Dorado, the Gilded One, an Indian kingdom to the east of Peru where gold was said to be so plentiful that it was thrown into a sacred lake in an annual ritual.[5]

The appointed leader of the expedition was Pedro de Ursúa (or Orsúa), a Navarrese of the lesser nobility from near Pamplona, born about 1525, who had arrived in Cartagena in 1546 in the entourage of his uncle, the Visitador Armendariz, and subsequently commanded several other expeditions of exploration and campaigns against Indian uprisings. His reputation for decisive and ruthless action grew when, after putting down a slave rebellion in Panama, he turned over several of the captured Africans to his mastiffs to kill and eat, as an example to others. This successful military and administrative career put Ursúa, at age thirty-five, in a position to take the governorship of the province of Omagua, yet to be consolidated in eastern Peru, and command of the expedition to search there for the land of gold. Although it is often suggested that one purpose of such expeditions, or entradas, into unexplored territory was to rid the consolidating core areas of the Spanish colonies of surplus adventurers and fortune seekers as the era of conquest wound down, the successes of the previous few decades had shown the potential that came along with the risk. Joining such an expedition was well within the rational choices available to those men of arms who had yet to achieve the secure rewards that had accrued to a minority of their comrades through division of the spoils of conquest, encomienda grants, and administrative sinecures.

The company was assembled in the eastern foothills of the Andes, where a makeshift boatyard was set up along the Huallaga River to build the necessary vessels for the river trip east. The expedition took to the water in late September 1560 on numerous rafts and keelboat-like brigantines, with some three hundred soldiers (nearly twice the number that had accompanied Francisco Pizarro on his original entrada into the Peruvian interior in 1532) along with a large entourage of African slaves, Indian bearers, horses, munitions, equipment, and supplies. Among the party were several women, including Ursúa's creole mistress, Inés de Atienza, and Aguirre's mestiza daughter, Elvira, a girl in her early teens from a now-forgotten liaison with an Indian woman. River rapids and faulty construction with unseasoned timber soon took their toll on the heavily laden vessels, costing supplies and horses. As word passed along the shore that the immense expedition was approaching, the Indians faded into the jungle, leaving abandoned communities where the Spaniards had hoped to obtain information about what lay ahead and empty storage bins where they might have resupplied. Delays on shore for rest, repairs, and the building of new boats were interspersed by periods of the river sweeping them inexorably eastward, farther from familiar bases and into the unknown heart of the continent. In the sweltering heat, as endless miles of jungle passed by, morale began to sag.

Any assessment of the subsequent internecine strife must accept the versions of one or another of the chroniclers, all of whom had very personal reasons for laying blame in certain quarters and exonerating others, but through the maze of charges and innuendo, the basic outline of events emerges fairly clearly. None of the surviving accounts clarifies the specific cause of the original mutiny, but Ursúa's leadership seemed wanting, lax, or ruthless by turns, whether because he was ill, depressed, or spending too much time in the arms of his mistress. He delayed in appointing officers from among the ranks, but slowly the table of organization was filled. Among those placed in positions of authority were Fernando de Guzmán, a nobleman from Seville in his mid-twenties, and the veteran Lope de Aguirre. But from the continued drift, real or imagined offenses, or jealousy over the fair Ines, grumbling discontent coalesced into a plot to eliminate Ursúa and replace him with Guzmán. Ursúa was killed on New Year's Day 1561, surprised in his tent by a gang of thirteen heavily armed conspirators, one of whom was Aguirre, who subsequently made a speech bluntly laying out the alternatives: either they return to the realm of royal authority and assume responsibility for their actions or they "denaturalize" themselves from Spain and assume responsibility for themselves.

The group took the latter course by subsequently swearing allegiance to Guzmán as their "prince, lord, and rightful king" and cowing or killing the few men who dared to stand in their way. Jockeying for control and defensive intrigues persisted, with Aguirre emerging as the most outspoken and decisive of the several faction leaders. In May 1561, during another extended shore encampment, Aguirre ordered his men to kill Ines de Atienza, "King" Fernando de Guzmán, and several of their allies and followers. In the wake of this new round of murderous strife, Aguirre made an impassioned speech in which he gave himself the titles "Wrath of God, Prince of Liberty, and of the kingdom of Tierra Firme and the Provinces of Chile," or in other words, ruler of most of Spanish South America. In a high-risk game of kill or be killed in which more than sixty people met a violent end at the hands of erstwhile comrades in arms or protectors, Aguirre and those loyal or submissive to him were the eventual survivors. Others not murdered outright were lost to disease and to the river or never returned from reconnaissance forays.

In two new brigantines constructed en route, the remnants of the expedition sailed on down the Amazon, proceeded up the coast—abandoning their now superfluous Indian servants on shore along the way—and reached Margarita Island on July 20, 1561. There, the small Spanish outpost was overwhelmed by the sudden appearance of some two hundred desperate and heavily armed outlaws ravaged by their experiences of the previous ten months. There followed an inconclusive near encounter with Friar Francisco de Montesinos, provincial of the Church in Santo Domingo and captain general of the subordinate zone on the Spanish Main, whose ship coincidentally arrived offshore. The party that Aguirre sent to confer with Montesinos defected to the royalist side, but the military force thus under the Dominican friar's command, though formidable, was still no match for Aguirre's remaining legion. Aguirre sent a letter to Montesinos, laden with ironic references to the standoff, to remind the turncoats, now siding with the friar, that their signatures were on various documents and thus, implicating them in their actions while on the Amazon and with subtle menace, suggesting that "we now live in a state of grace, after being threatened with death by the river, the sea, and hunger, and thus any who challenge us are coming to fight the ghosts of dead men. By fate we only know how to make arquebus balls and sharpen lances, which is the coin that circulates among us. If where you are there is need of such small things, we will provide you with some of what we have."[6] Montesinos thought it better to return to Santo Domingo and spread the word of the threat of the Marañones than to directly challenge the rebels.

Aguirre's party, now numbering about 160 men, left Margarita at the end of August, coasted westward, and arrived on the mainland on September 12.

They struggled inland as far as Valencia by early October, where Aguirre paused to dictate his famous letter to King Philip II of Spain, of which more will be said. He gave the letter to a priest being held by the party, Father Pedro de Contreras, forcing him on bended knee to swear to deliver the missive to the Audiencia in Santo Domingo, from where it was to be delivered to the king. Although no manuscript that can be called original is now extant, several versions have come down to the present. They differ only in minor grammatical points, which suggest that the letter was copied several times at the time of its drafting.[7]

During this period, increasing numbers of the Marañones defected, either fading into the hills to fend for themselves or going over to the loyalist forces who waited for an opportune moment to challenge the dwindling band of intruders. Recognizing their position as hopeless, Aguirre and his close supporters forged on. They burned Valencia behind them and pushed on to the town of Barquisimeto, which the inhabitants had abandoned in advance. In a letter to local governor Pablo Collado, Aguirre laid out his interpretation of the rights of offended vassals to break the bonds of subservience: "You cannot say that we do not serve the King, because I and my companions intend to do by arms what our ancestors did. He who fulfills his obligation to us will be our lord, and he who does not, we do not recognize. Many days ago we denaturalized ourselves from Spain and denied her King, so we have no further obligation to serve him. We made our own King, whom we obey, and as vassals of another lord we may well wage war against whom ever we have sworn to do so, innocent of the accusations made against us."[8] Collado's more pragmatic response was to offer clemency to any of the rebels who would surrender peacefully, and more responded to his call.

The end came on October 27, 1561, when Aguirre and his immediate party were surrounded by loyalist troops, including several former Marañones. Among his last acts was to call his daughter Elvira to his side and stab her to death, telling her that such a fate was preferable to living a life of infamy as the child of a traitor and becoming the sexual victim of whichever soldier claimed her after her father and protector was gone. He then faced the arquebus balls of the encircling soldiers, two of which brought him down. His corpse was beheaded and quartered, and parts were put on public display or given to towns that his party had passed through as trophies of their involvement in the affair.

SEVERAL AGUIRRES

One Aguirre is the insolent and murderous traitor who had dared to "denaturalize" himself and his followers from allegiance to Spain and its king during a period when centralized royal authority was determined to overtake the contractual forms of reciprocal obligation and responsibility on which medieval allegiance had been based, particularly in the tradition of armed bands of the military reconquest of Iberia that had extended over the preceding half-millennium. That tradition, as expressed in the letter to Governor Collado, still formed the political culture of the independent Spanish soldier–hidalgo that Aguirre and hundreds of his fellow conquistadors shared and were motivated by. It conflicted sharply with the bureaucratic imperatives of the centralizing state, the new mode of governance that heavily depended on the earlier one to accomplish its ends in acquiring new territory and consolidating the far-flung Spanish empire.[9] Compounding the specific offense was the general threat that any successful challenge to royal control might have posed in situations similar to the Ursúa–Aguirre expedition in remote and isolated corners of the expanding empire, where the principles of monarchical authority necessarily had to be mitigated by a considerable measure of independent initiative in response to specific and changing local circumstances. Such a brazen challenge to constituted authority, once eliminated, was better ignored as completely and for as long as possible among defenders of Spanish legal tradition, creating what might well be called the "suppressed" version of Aguirre's story.

This suppressed Aguirre is in many ways consistent with the "cruel tyrant" version of the self-interested chroniclers themselves, the "insane" version of Spanish nationalists, the "brave resister of Castillian authority" of the Basque nationalists, and the "first freedom fighter" of the Venezuelans and other modern Latin American writers. Such interpretations either deny the validity of Aguirre's actions and the principles on which they were based, calling them illegal at best and the evil actions of a deranged mind at worst, or anachronistically appropriate the memory of Aguirre and his band for political causes relevant in times and places different from the world in which he lived and died.

A view shared in some measure, among these interpretations of the Aguirre story and the film version by Herzog is that Aguirre went insane or was at least irrational and mentally unbalanced. Such a view is perpetuated by modern writers who take Aguirre to task for not making his various letters to authorities more coherent and transparent to those who, four and a half centuries after the events, presume to know how Aguirre should have acted to survive in the conditions of the expedition in which he took part and who take the self-serving tirades of the several chroniclers uncritically as simple descriptions of events. But accusations of insanity or irrationality are too often the refuge of those who have no basis for or who refuse to consider an interpretation that is more sensitive to the moment and circumstances in question and is truer to the memory of historical actors who cannot defend themselves from such ahistorical vilification.

Lope de Aguirre should not be made into a tragic but misunderstood hero, nor should one excuse, defend, or glorify his remarkable life, much less the Spanish conquest of America generally. Nor should it be denied that he killed people. If the latter were a criterion for insanity, then much historical interpretation would be the study of psychopathology. But in an attempt at historical understanding, it is only fair to the memory of Aguirre and those whom his actions affected to put the story in its own context and take him at his own word. Such an approach listens to one of the few voices of the rank and file of the hundreds who shared a vision of brave action and loyal service, for which they expected rewards that accrued to only a small minority. Their initial shares of booty, tribute, and conquered land were already in his lifetime being eroded by the encroachment of grasping royal agents, corrupt bureaucrats, and venial priests. Aguirre was representative of the resentful late arrivals among the rank and file of the conquistador generation[10]; he toiled for years and risked his life with little compensation and found himself forsaken in an ill-fated expedition during which the situation deteriorated from bad to worse to desperate. Survival required that someone take charge, despite the eventual reckoning of jurists and bureaucrats and more important, the judgment of God. Aguirre took charge and paid the price.

A POLITICAL TESTAMENT

Knowing that his cause was lost, he took a last opportunity to make a statement. While taking responsibility for his actions of the previous few months, he tried to put them in the context of an expedition falling apart. He decided to go beyond the particulars of the situation to vent the frustrations of his career, which he felt that many of his comrades in arms shared. He took the trouble to recall the names of several former conquistadors whom he thought had been unjustly treated and concluded with a list of those in solidarity with him. By example and by citing principle, he indicted the entire administrative apparatus of the colonies and the responsibility of the monarch for it. By his own word, he was a soldier of fortune, not one of the *letrados* (men of letters) he took to task, and he may be forgiven if in the press of the circumstances, his letter to the king lacks some of the polish and orderly structure that a final editing might have provided. We do not have to agree with what Aguirre did nor approve of his worldview to conclude that this letter is not the raving of a madman. Some of the sardonic tone and not-so-subtle turn of phrase of this letter appear in earlier missives to Friar Montesinos and Governor Collado, but they were intermediaries. Some interpreters have taken too literally the ironic and sarcastic references scattered throughout the document, and they have failed to see the bemused resignation behind the officious bluster in some passages. The general tone is one of outrage and despair that comes from an aging soldier of the conquest who felt betrayed by what today is called "the system" and who, denying nothing of the accusations directed against him, persisted in the hope that his position would receive a hearing. I urge modern readers to ponder the voice of Lope de Aguirre as, facing certain death, he directed his message to the highest authority he could hope to reach in this world.

DOCUMENT

Lope de Aguirre's Letter to King Philip II of Spain, September 1561[11]

To King Philip, native of Spain, son of Charles the Invincible:

From Lope de Aguirre, your lesser vassal, old Christian, of middling parents but fortunately of noble blood, native of the Basque country of the kingdom of Spain, citizen of the town of Oñate.

In my youth I crossed the sea to the land of Peru to gain fame, lance in hand, and to fulfill the obligation of all good men. In twenty-four years I have done you great service in Peru, in conquests of the Indians, in founding towns, and especially in battles and encounters fought in your name, always to the best of my power and ability, without requesting of your officials pay or assistance, as can be seen in your royal records.

I firmly believe, most excellent King and lord, that to me and my companions you have been nothing but cruel and ungrateful. I also believe that those who write to you from this land deceive you, because of the great distance.

I demand of you, King, that you do justice and right by the good vassals you have in this land, even though I and my companions (whose names I will give later), unable to suffer further the cruelties of your judges, viceroy, and governors, have resolved to obey you no longer. Denaturalizing ourselves from our land, Spain, we make the most cruel war against you that our power can sustain and endure. Believe, King and lord, we have done this because we can no longer tolerate the great exactions and unjust punishments of your ministers who, to make places for their sons and dependents, have usurped and robbed us of our fame, life, and honor. It is a pity, King, the bad treatment done to us.

I am lame in the right leg from the arquebus wounds I received in the battle of Chuquinga, fighting with Marshal Alonzo de Alvarado, answering your call against Francisco Hernández Girón, rebel from your service as I and my companions presently are and will be until death, because we in this land now know how cruel you are, how you break your faith and your word, and thus we in this land give to your promises less credence than to the books of Martin Luther.

Your viceroy the marquis of Cañete hanged Martín de Robles, a man distinguished in your service; and the brave Tomás Vásquez, conquistador of Peru; and the ill-fated Alonso Días, who worked more in the discoveries of this kingdom than did the scouts of Moses in the desert; and Piedrahita, a good captain who fought many battles in your service. In Pucara they gave you victory; and if they had not, Francisco Hernández would now be the king of Peru. Don't give much credence to the claims your judges make of services performed, because it is a great myth, unless they call a service having spent 800,000 pesos of your royal treasury for their vices and evil deeds. Punish them as evil-doers, as such they certainly are.

Look here, King of Spain! Do not be cruel and ungrateful to your vassals, because while your father and you stayed in Spain without the slightest bother, your vassals, at the price of their blood and fortune, have given you all the kingdoms and holdings you have in these parts. Beware, King and lord, that under the title of legitimate king, you cannot take any benefit from this land where you risked nothing, without first giving due gratification to those who have labored and sweated in it.

I am certain that very few kings go to Hell because there are few kings, but if there were many of you, none could go to Heaven. Even in Hell you would be worse than Lucifer because you all thirst after human blood. But I don't marvel nor make much of you, who are like children, and any man naively innocent of this is crazy. For certain, I and my two hundred arquebus-bearing Marañones, conquistadors and hidalgos, swear solemnly to God that we will not leave a minister of yours alive, because I already know how far your clemency reaches. Today we consider ourselves the luckiest men alive, because in these parts of the Indies we are maintaining all that is preached by the Holy Mother Church of Rome, with faith in God's commandments full and uncorrupted as Christians; and we intend, though sinners in life, to achieve martyrdom through God's commandments.

Upon leaving the Amazon river, called the Marañon, on an island inhabited by Christians called Margarita, I saw some reports from Spain regarding the great schism of Lutherans there, which caused us to be frightened and surprised. In our company there was a German named Monteverde, and I ordered him cut to pieces. Destiny rewards the prudent. Believe this, excellent Prince: Wherever we are, we ensure that all live perfectly in the Christian faith. The dissolution of the priests is so great in these parts that I think it would be well that they feel your wrath and punishment, because there is now none among them who sees himself as less than governor. Look here, King, do not believe what they might tell you, because the tears they shed before your royal person is so that they can come here to take command. If you want to know the life they lead here, it is to deal in merchandise, seek and acquire temporal goods, and sell the Sacraments of the Church for a price. They are enemies of the poor, uncharitable, ambitious, gluttonous, and arrogant, so that even the lowest of the priests tries to command and govern all these lands. Correct this, King and lord, because from these things and bad examples faith is not impressed upon nor instilled in the natives. Furthermore, if this dissolution of the priests is not stopped, there will be no shortage of scandal.

If I and my companions, by the correct position we have taken, are determined to die, for this and for other things that have happened, singular King, you are to blame, for not duly considering the labor of your vassals and for not thinking of what you owe them. If you do not look out for your vassals, and your judges do not take care of this, you will never succeed in government. Certainly there is no need to present witnesses, but simply to point out that each of your judges has 4,000 pesos in annual salary, plus 8,000 pesos for expenses, and after three years in office each has 60,000 pesos saved, along with properties and possessions. Despite all this, we would be willing to serve them as we do, except that for our sins they want us to drop to our knees wherever we meet and worship them like Nebuchadnezzar. This is intolerable. Just because I am an unfortunate man made lame in your service (and my companions long and weary in the same), I should not fail to advise you never to trust your conscience to these learned persons. It is in your royal interest to watch out for them, as they spend all their time planning the marriages of their children, and care for nothing else. The common refrain among them is: "To the left and to the right, I possess all in my sight."

The friars do not want to bury poor Indians, and they are lodged in the best estates in Peru. The life they lead is bitter and burdensome, as each one has as a penance a dozen young women in his kitchen, and as many boys engaged in fishing, hunting partridges, and bringing fruit! They get a share of everything. In Christian faith I swear, King and lord, that if you do not remedy the evils of this land, divine punishment will come upon you. I tell you this to let you know the truth, even though I and my comrades neither expect nor want mercy from you.

Oh, how sad that a great Caesar and Emperor, your father, should conquer great Germany with the power of Spain, and should spend so much money from these Indies discovered by us, and that you should not concern yourself with our old age and weariness enough to assuage our hunger for a day.

You know that we know in these parts, excellent King and lord, that you conquered Germany with arms, and Germany has conquered Spain with vices. We over here are more content with just corn and water, to be far removed from such a bad irony. Let those who have fallen into such a situation keep their reward. Let wars spread where they may, and where men make them, but we will never cease to be subject to the teachings of the Holy Mother Church of Rome, no matter what adversity might come upon us.

Excellent King and lord, we cannot believe that you would be so cruel to such good vassals as you have in these parts. Your judges must be acting this way without your consent. I say this, excellent King, because two leagues from the City of Kings [Lima], there was discovered near the sea a lake where there were some fish God permitted to exist there. To profit from the fish for their pleasures and vices, your evil judges and officials leased them in your name, giving us to understand, as though we were fools, that this was done by your will. If this is so, lord, let us catch some of the fish, because we worked to discover it, and because the King of Castile has no need for the 400 pesos they leased it for. Illustrious King, we are not asking for grants in Cordoba or Valladolid, nor in any part of Spain, which is your patrimony. Deign to feed the weary and poor with the fruits and proceeds from this land. Remember, King and lord, that God is the same for all, and the same reward and judgment, Heaven and Hell.

In the year 1559 the marquis of Cañete entrusted the expedition of the river of the Amazons to Pedro de Ursúa, Navarrese, or rather, a Frenchman. He delayed the building of the boats until the year 1560 in the province of the Motilones, in Peru. The Indians are called Motilones because they wear their heads shaved. These boats were made in the wet country, and upon launching, most of them came to pieces. We made rafts, left the horses and supplies, and took off down the river at great risk to our persons. We then encountered the most powerful rivers of Peru, and it seemed to us to be a fresh-water sea. We traveled in the first phase 300 leagues from the point of launching.

This bad governor was so perverse and vicious and miserable that we could not tolerate it, and it was impossible to put up with his evil ways. Since I have a stake in the matter, excellent King and lord, I will say only that we killed him; a very swift death, for sure. We then raised a young gentleman of Seville named Don Fernando de Guzmán to be our king, and we made an oath to him as such, as your royal person will see from the signatures of all those who were in this, who remain on the island of Margarita, in these Indies. They appointed me their field commander, and because I did not consent to their insults and evil deeds, they tried to kill me; and I killed the new king, the captain of his guard, the lieutenant general, his majordomo, his chaplain, a woman in league against me, a knight of Rhodes, an admiral, two ensigns, and another six of his allies. It was my intention to carry this war through and die in it, for the cruelties your ministers practice on us, and I again appointed captains and a sergeant major. They tried to kill me, and I hanged them all.

We went along our route down the Marañon river while all these killings and bad events were taking place. It took us more than ten and a half months to reach the mouth of the river, where it enters the sea. We traveled a good hundred days, covering 1,500 leagues. It is a great and fearsome river, with 80 leagues of fresh water at the mouth. It covers vast lowlands, and for 800 leagues along its banks it is deserted, with no towns, as Your Majesty will see from the true report we have made. Along the route we took, there are more than six thousand islands. God only knows how we escaped from such a fearsome lake! I advise you, King and lord, not to attempt nor allow a fleet to be sent to this ill-fated river, because in Christian faith I swear, King and lord, that if a hundred thousand men come, none will escape, because the stories are false and in this river there is nothing but despair, especially for those newly arrived from Spain.

The captains and officers with me at present, and who promise to die in this demand like pitiful men are: Juan Jerónimo de Espínola Ginovés, admiral; Juan Gomez, Cristóbal Garcia, captain of infantry, both Andaluz; mounted captain Diego Tirado, Andaluz, from whom your judges, King and lord, with great injury, took Indians he had earned with his lance; captain of my guard Roberto de Sosaya and his ensign Nuflo Hernández, Valencian; Juan López de Ayala, from Cuenca, our paymaster; general ensign Blas Gutiérrez, conquistador for twenty-seven years; Juan Ponce, ensign, native of Seville; Custodio Hernández, ensign, Portuguese; Diego de Torres, ensign, Navarrese; sergeant Pedro Gutiérrez Visa and Diego de Figueroa; Cristóbal de Rivas, conquistador; Pedro de Rojas, Andaluz; Juan de Saucedo, mounted ensign; Bartolomé Sánchez Paniagua, our lawyer; Diego Sánchez Bilbao, supply; García Navarro, inspector general; and many other hidalgos of this league. We pray to God our Lord that your fortune ever be increased against the Turk and the Frenchman, and all others who wish to make war on you in those parts. In these, God grant that we might obtain with our arms the reward by right due us, but which you have denied.

Son of your loyal Basque vassals, I rebel against you until death for your ingratitude.

Lope de Aguirre, the Wanderer

ADDITIONAL RESOURCES

Historical Treatments and Document Collections

Aguilar y de Córdova, Diego de. *Libro primero del Marañon, año de 1578.* Manuscript in the British Museum, MSS Add. 17,616. One of the earliest known copies of Aguirre's letter to Philip II is in chapter 2 of book 3 of this document, produced seventeen years after the events.

Balkan, Evan. *The Wrath of God: Lope de Aguirre, Revolutionary of the Americas.* Albuquerque: University of New Mexico Press, 2011. Compiled from secondary sources, uncritically perpetuating the consensus that Aguirre was mentally deranged.

Bayo, Ciro. *Los Marañones: Leyenda aurea del nuevo mundo.* Madrid: Bailly-Baillière, 1913. Narrative based primarily on the Vásquez and Almesto eyewitness chronicle.

Caro Baroja, Julio. *El Señor Inquisidor y otras vidas por oficio.* Madrid: Alianza, 1968. Includes (chaps. 2 and 3) insightful interpretive essays on the careers of both Aguirre and his nemesis, Pedro de Ursúa.

Jos, Emiliano. *La expedición de Ursúa al Dorado y la rebelión de Lope de Aguirre y el itinerario de los "Marañones," según los documentos del Archivo de Indias y varios manuscritos inéditos.* Huesca, Spain: V. Campo, 1927. One of the first major modern treatments, based on exhaustive research, during which the author concluded that there is probably no original manuscript of Aguirre's letter to Philip II in the Archive of the Indies: "We are inclined to believe that if the letter arrived in Philip II's hands he would have taken measures so that no one could read its contents, but because Lope permitted and even sought that his writings be made known among his soldiers, some of the latter made copies, by which the famous document has survived to our day" (111). The version of the letter Jos used, which has subsequently been reprinted in various forms, is based on the one included in the Vásquez and Almesto chronicle. It differs only slightly from the version in the 1578 Aguilar manuscript in the British Museum, listed above.

————. *Ciencia y osadia sobre Lope de Aguirre el Peregrino, con documentos inéditos.* Seville: Escuela de Estudios Hispano-Americanos, 1950. Largely a critique of other authors, whom Jos maintains distorted or plagiarized his fundamental 1927 study, that reiterates the basic conclusion of the earlier work—that Aguirre was insane—with "confirmation" from psychohistorical analyses of his career.

Lope de Aguirre descuartizado. San Sebastian: Auñamendi, 1963. A collection of papers given at a meeting of the Basque "Academia Errante" in October 1961, marking the four-hundredth anniversary of the death of Aguirre—who had become a figure of admiration among Basque nationalists—beginning with the revisionist writings of Segundo de Ispizua in his multivolume *Los Vascos en América, 1914–1918.* The title evokes the usual execution method for rebels in an earlier age, drawing and quartering, here referring ironically to an analytical dissection of the case.

Lowry, Walker. *Lope de Aguirre, the Wanderer.* New York: Bookman Associates, 1952. A brief (seventy-four-page) narrative of the excursion, competent in description but short on interpretation.

Mampel González, Elena, and Neus Escandell Tur. *Lope de Aguirre: Crónicas, 1559–1561.* Barcelona: 7 1/2, 1981. An indispensable compilation of the accounts of Gonzalo de Zúñiga, Toribio de Hortiguera, Pedro de Monguia, Custodio Hernández, Vásquez and Almesto, and an unidentified chronicler, with a historical/historiographical prologue; additional documents; an extensive bibliography; and selected maps, photographs of manuscript pages, and signatures.

Oviedo y Baños, José de. *Historia de la conquista y población de la Provincia de Venezuela.* Madrid: Imprenta de Gregorio Hermosilla, 1723. A detailed account (on pp. 173–224) of Aguirre's activities on Margarita Island and the Venezuelan mainland, including the circumstances of his death. Includes transcriptions of Aguirre's letters to Fray Francisco de Montesinos, Governor Pablo Collado, and King Philip II (the latter differing in minor details from the translation given above). Available for download from Google Books.

Piedrahita, Lucas Fernández. *Historia general de las conquistas de Nuevo Reino de Granada.* Madrid, 1688. Probably the earliest published account (pp. 566–86) of Aguirre's career, focusing on the events on Margarita island and mainland Venezuela. Briefly alludes to the letter to Philip II, claiming that "its contents are not known" (p. 576) but then suggesting it was the work of someone gone mad and filled with "the sort of foolishness one would expect from a belligerent mule tamer." Available for download from Google Books.

Poggi, Alfredo Ignacio. *Lope de Aguirre, Hugo Chávez, and the Latin American Left: The Wrath of Liberation.* Lanham, MD: Rowman & Littlefield, 2020. Updates the ahistorical tradition of treating Aguirre as the precursor of modern anticolonial struggles, to include the rhetoric of *chavismo* in recent times.

"Relación del descubrimiento del río Marañon" (c. 1570), Archivo General de Indias ES.41091.AGI/PATRONATO,29,R.13. This manuscript document, digitized for viewing online, provides an account of the Ursúa–Aguirre expedition and a copy of Aguirre's letter to Philip II (folios 19d–23).

Southey, Robert. *The Expedition of Orsúa; and the Crimes of Aguirre.* London: Longman, Hurst, Rees, Orme, and Brown, 1821. An early version of the story in English, by a major English historian of the Romantic era. Available for download from Google Books.

Fictionalized and Literary Versions

Acosta Montoro, José. *Peregrino de la ira: Narracicón dramático sobre la aventura de Lope de Aguirre.* San Sebastián: Auñamendi, 1967. A drama presented in bilingual form, with Spanish and Basque on facing pages.

Arciniega, Rosa. *Dos rebeldes españoles en el Perú.* Buenos Aires: Sudamericana, 1946. Separate narrative accounts of the careers of Gonzalo Pizarro, "el gran rebelde," and Lope de Aguirre, "el cruel tirano." Frontispiece is a photographic reproduction of Aguirre's signature from his letter to Friar Montesinos.

Funes, Jorge Ernesto. *Una lanza por Lope de Aguirre.* Buenos Aires: Platero, 1984. An imagined interview of Aguirre by a time-traveling "chronicler."

Lewis, Bart L. *The Miraculous Lie: Lope de Aguirre and the Search for El Dorado in the Latin American Historical Novel.* Lanham, MD: Lexington Books, 2003. Analysis of five literary works dealing with the topic.

López, Casto Fulgencio. *Lope de Aguirre, el Peregrino: Primer caudillo de América.* Madrid: Plon, 1977. First published in Venezuela in 1947, this novelistic re-creation of the Ursúa–Aguirre story is based on considerable archival and bibliographical research. It presents a heavily embellished account favorable to Aguirre as the issuer of the first "cry of freedom" of Spanish America.

Minta, Stephen. *Aguirre: The Re-creation of a Sixteenth-Century Journey across South America.* New York: Henry Holt, 1994. A modern travelogue retracing the route of the Ursúa–Aguirre expedition interspersed with historical rumination and commentary on the events of the earlier trip, perpetuating the consensus that Aguirre was deranged and that his letter to Philip II "is not the work of a rational mind" (210).

Otero Silva, Miguel. *Lope de Aguirre, Principe de la Libertad.* Barcelona: Seix Barral, 1979. Novelized version of the story by a distinguished Venezuelan writer.

NOTES

1. Quoted in S. S. Prawer, *Caligari's Children: The Film as Tale of Terror* (New York: Oxford University Press, 1980), 19.

2. Elena Mampel González and Neus Escandell Tur, *Lope de Aguirre: Crónicas, 1559–1561* (Barcelona: 7 1/2, 1981), is an indispensable compilation of the accounts of Gonzalo de Zúñiga, Toribio de Hortiguera, Pedro de Monguia, Custodio Hernández, Vásquez and Almesto, and an unidentified chronicler.

3. This question is raised by Luisela Alvaray in "Filming the 'Discovery' of America: How and Whose History Is Being Told," *Film-Historia* 5, no. 1 (1995): 37.

4. This summary is drawn from the secondary literature and the chronicles and documents related to the case listed in Additional Resources. The most complete modern compilation of contemporary documents is Mampel González and Escandell Tur, *Crónicas.*

5. An extensive review of the El Dorado legends and efforts to confirm them, including the involvement of Sir Walter Raleigh in South America, is Demetria Ramos Pérez, *El mito del Dorado: Su genesis y proceso* (Caracas: Academia Nacional de la Historia, 1973; second ed. enlarged, Madrid: Ediciones Istmo, 1988). See also John Hemming, *The Search for El Dorado* (New York: Dutton, 1979). Playing on the Spanish explorers' manifest desire for precious metals, indigenous informants apparently concluded that they could be rid of passing bands of Europeans by spinning tales of gold for the taking in some far-off location. An ethnographic basis for the legends involved rituals among indigenous peoples of the northern Andes in which a priest or prince periodically applied gold dust to his body and swam in a sacred lake, into which other gold offerings were tossed. Lake Guatavita, not far from Bogotá, Colombia, has been identified as one site of such rituals. These legends emerged during the first Spanish forays into South America in the 1520s and persisted well into the seventeenth century.

6. The letter to Montesinos is reproduced in several studies, including Mampel González and Escandell Tur, *Crónicas*, 285–86.

7. Emiliano Jos, *La expedición de Ursúa al Dorado y la rebelión de Lope de Aguirre y el itinerario de los "Marañones," segun Los documentos de Archivo de Indias y varios manuscritos inéditos* (Huesca, Spain: V. Campo, 1927), 111. A manuscript copy of the letter, from c. 1570, is included in the "Relación del descubrimiento del río Marañon," Archivo General de Indias (Seville), ES.41091.AGI/PATRONATO,29,R.13, folios 19d–23, digitized for viewing online.

8. Jose de Oviedo y Baños, *Historia de la conquista y población de la Provincia de Venezuela* (Madrid: Imprenta de Gregorio Hermosilla, 1723), 215.

9. On the tradition of the semiautonomous armed bands in the reconquest of Iberia and the conquest of America, see Matthew Restall, "The Myth of the King's Army," in *Seven Myths of the Spanish Conquest* (Oxford, UK: Oxford University Press, 2003).

10. For a detailed reconstruction of the world of the conquistadors, see two works by James Lockhart, *Spanish Peru, 1532–1560* (Madison: University of Wisconsin Press, 1968), and *The Men of Cajamarca* (Austin: University of Texas Press, 1972), the latter a collective biography of the 167 men who shared in the ransom of the Inca emperor Atahualpa. A good overview of the era is John Hemming, *The Conquest of the Incas* (New York: Harcourt, Brace, Jovanovich, 1970).

11. This translation is by Thomas Holloway of the text published in A. Arellano Moreno, comp., *Documentos para la historia económica de Venezuela* (Caracas: Instituto de Antropología e Historia, Facultad de Humanidades y Educación, Universidad Central de Venezuela, 1961), 291–97, which in turn is from that published in Casto Fulgencio López, *Lope de Aguirre, el Peregrino: Primer caudillo de América* (Madrid: Plon, 1977), 234–40, after Jos, *La expedición de Ursúa al Dorado*, 196–200, and checked against the versions in the Vázquez and Almesto chronicle (Mampel González and Escandell Tur, *Crónicas*, 255–59), the version in José de Oviedo y Baños, *Historia de la conquista y población de la Provincia de Venezuela* (Madrid: Imprenta de Gregorio Hermosilla, 1723), 206–209, and the Aguilar y de Córdova version in the British Museum, dated 1578. All these iterations differ slightly from one another but not in ways that add or subtract sections or change the thrust of the document.

Chapter 3

I, the Worst of All
The Literary Life of Sor Juana Inés de la Cruz

Susan Elizabeth Ramírez

Yo, la Peor de Todas *(1990), or* I, the Worst of All*; produced by Gilbert Marouani and Lita Stantic; directed by María Luisa Bemberg; written by María Luisa Bemberg and Antonio Larreta based on* Sor Juana, or, The Traps of Faith *by Octavio Paz; color; 105 minutes; GEA Cinematográfica. Sor Juana Inés de la Cruz (Assumpta Serna), the famous seventeenth-century Mexican nun, writes poetry and plays under the patronage of the viceroy (Héctor Alterio) and his wife (Dominique Sanda) until they are recalled to Spain. Then a misogynistic archbishop tries to restrict Sor Juana activities to more humble and traditionally religious pursuits.*

Despite a growing number of books and articles on her life and times, Sor Juana Inés de la Cruz remains an enigma in many respects. Assiduous searches by scholars in archives and libraries all over the world have been unable to find many sources on her life other than those that she herself wrote. And many of these are poems and plays and other literary works, which although they reflect her life and concerns, do not and were not meant to provide facts on or explain her existence. Nevertheless, what remains of her work (because much of it has been lost) allows her to retain much of the power of description, even centuries after her premature death from the plague in 1695. Her writings provide the bare outlines of a self-portrait and representation. Hence, it is largely her own creation that historians, poets, filmmakers, and the many others interested in this seventeenth-century woman and nun have attempted to synthesize and analyze.[1]

The interpretation of Argentine director María Luisa Bemberg follows closely the Mexican Octavio Paz's masterful biography, *Sor Juana, or, The Traps of Faith*.[2] Each leaves some of the questions about Sor Juana's life unresolved. Both show her to have been a woman of strength who chose the cloistered life of a convent to gain the freedom to pursue her art. She is shown as a forceful, willful, intelligent, creative, and even gifted individual who could not escape the political, economic, and social conjuncture that surrounded her. Bemberg carefully reconstructs these larger circumstances, especially the conflicts between the church and the state, to explain the trajectory of her singular and exemplary life.

JUANA INÉS

Bemberg's story focuses on Sor Juana's life during the viceregal reign of the marquis de la Laguna (1680–1686), during which she wrote some of her most memorable work, and the increasingly sad and crisis-ridden years that followed his return to Spain. The film opens with a brief, darkly shadowed scene in which a new viceroy toasts the archbishop. The two promise to save New Spain from license and irreligiosity by governing together. We then see the sunny courtyard of the Convent of San Jerónimo in Mexico City, where nuns and novices are playing and singing. Inside her contrastingly quiet cell, Sor Juana, surrounded by books, scientific instruments, and oddities, is busy at her desk. Thus, we encounter an adult Sor Juana, already a professed nun, writing for an elite and educated audience. About her early childhood we know very little. Throughout the film and not necessarily in chronological order, using flashbacks and other devices, Bemberg provides the viewer with the salient points in young Juana Inés's life. Late in the film, Bemberg reminds viewers of her illegitimate birth as Juana Ramírez or Juana Ramírez de Asbaje in Chimalhuacán, in the scene set in 1688 in which she tries to find out who her father was as her mother (Isabel Ramírez de Santilla) lays dying. This interpretation is consistent with Paz's belief that this girl never knew her father, who was from Vizcaya (Spain) and may have been the local priest. Based on a baptismal record and Isabel Ramírez's will, Paz believes that Juana Inés was one of six illegitimate children whom her mother bore: the first three by Pedro Manuel de Asbaje y Vargas Machuca and the last three by Captain Diego Ruiz Lozano. Juana Inés was the youngest of the first set of children. Given these origins, she always relied on and lived with her maternal relations.

It was there in Chimalhuacán that as Juana says in her *Respuesta a Sor Filotea de la Cruz*, she learned to read when she was three years old with the help of a teacher of an older sister.[3] By age six or seven, by her own account, she could read and write. Then it occurred to her to ask her mother to send her to the university. Because the seventeenth-century university was open only to males, she promised to dress as a man. When the response was negative, Juana consoled herself by reading and studying in the library of her maternal grandfather on the Hacienda Panoayán. When her grandfather died in 1656, eight-year-old Juana was sent to Mexico City to live with a maternal aunt, Doña María Ramirez, and her wealthy husband, Juan de Mata.

In her aunt's home, she learned Latin from Martín de Olivas and developed into a lovely young lady. Perhaps because her relatives decided that they did not want the responsibility for the ultimate fate of a pretty, virginal, and wayward relative or because the court might give her a better context for developing herself, her relatives presented her to the just-arrived Doña Leonor Carreto, the marquise de Mancera, who accepted Juana Inés as a favored lady-in-waiting.

The court of Viceroy Antonio Sebastián de Toledo, the marquis de Mancera, must have been stimulating to a precocious adolescent such as Juana Inés. Her four years there left a lasting impression on her. The marquise was ingenious, vivacious, and like her husband, a lover of pomp and pageantry. The Manceras were known for their prodigality: they spent lavishly, arrived late to Mass, and loved literature. Undoubtedly, the opportunities to attend receptions, parties, and dances and to see processions and ceremonies contributed to Juana Inés's reputed liveliness, joviality, narcissism, and flirtatious nature.

However, while at court, she also became known for her learning. At one point, the marquis assembled forty professors, professionals, and other learned men, among them theologians, writers, philosophers, mathematicians, historians, and poets, to test her knowledge. As Bemberg's film shows, Juana Inés answered the questions of this scholarly assemblage with aplomb and to the satisfaction and even astonishment of those present.

It is after this point in her life, in 1667, that she first tried the religious life. At age nineteen she became a novice at the Convent of San José de las Carmelitas Descalzas.[4] The order proved too severe for Juana Inés, and she abandoned this attempt soon after she entered. A year and a half later she professed at the Convent of San Jerónimo, known for the laxity of its discipline. At age twenty-one, in 1669, she took her final vows.

The Convent of San Jerónimo, in contrast to that of San José, was a very good choice for Juana Inés. Unlike many other convents in Mexico at the time, the rule at San Jerónimo was often observed more in the breach. In San Jerónimo, the sisters followed a "private life." Instead of living and eating together communally, each nun lived separately in her own cell, where she took meals, worked, prayed, and received other nuns. Sor Juana's cell, or apartment, was a duplex with one large room divided into bedroom and study, another that served as salon and library, a bath, and a kitchen. Where poverty was the rule at other convents, in San Jerónimo nuns had their own possessions. Sor Juana was able to maintain an extensive library of some four thousand volumes,[5] reputed to be the largest in New Spain at the time. Nearby, she kept a disparate array of prized objects, such as her telescope, astrolabe, obsidian mirror, and feather headdress. Although the sisters were forbidden to accept gifts, Sor Juana received many presents, especially from the viceroy's wife. The convent, furthermore, was known as a center of culture and learning. It was celebrated for its classes in music, dance, and theater. Sor Juana was a natural to assume the task of music mistress. Over the years, she wrote songs and lyrics for dances and participated in musicals and plays. We see one of these theatrical events in the opening scenes of the motion picture.

The only rule that was observed was that of cloister, which restricted the visits of friends and acquaintances and prohibited nuns from leaving the convent except under extraordinary conditions, such as the death of a mother.[6] When visitors were permitted, they were usually separated from the sisters by wooden bars. Viceroys and their followers visited often. The Manceras often heard Vesper prayers in the chapel and then went to the parlor to talk with Sor Juana. They were joined by other clerics and literary people for a lively exchange and debate. The nuns also received guests in the sacristy, usually with their faces uncovered. In San Jerónimo, says Paz, there was conversation, debate, poetry recitals, and musical performances—both secular and sacred.

SOR JUANA

The main focus of the film is a conflict between church and state and the political intrigues and personal animosities that eventually catch Sor Juana in their webs, defeat her passion for literature, and speed the end of her life. The script of the movie starts sometime after November 1680, emphasizing the years that New Spain was governed by Viceroy don Tomás Antonio de la Cerda, the third marquis de la Laguna[7] and the younger brother of the eighth duke of Medinaceli—that is, a member of the highest nobility of Spain.[8] He is accompanied by his wife, the *virreina*, also a well-born lady, María Luisa Manrique de Lara y Gonzaga, the condesa de Paredes. Both loved the arts, poetry, theater, and music. Even before the new viceroy arrived, he had heard of Sor Juana, whom he called the *decima musa* (the tenth Muse), an allusion to the nine sister goddesses in Greek mythology who presided over song, poetry, and the arts and sciences.

According to the movie, after don Tomás's arrival and at the performance of one of Sor Juana's plays at the convent, the delighted viceroy and his wife, although acknowledging that it was "crazy" for a woman to want to think and write, decide to adopt her. In reality, Sor Juana met the new viceroy as the result of a commission from the town council to write a poem for one of the arches erected to honor him upon his arrival in late 1680. Nevertheless, the outcome was the same; she would work thereafter under his patronage and favor. This episode initiates one of the most fecund times in her literary life, during which she composed the poems *El divino narciso* and *Primero sueño*. A foreshadowing that the proverbial storm clouds were already gathering around her is the attitude of the archbishop of Mexico, Francisco de Aguiar y Seixas, a misogynist who clearly does not share the viceroy's delight, as he mumbles something about the convent as bordello. The archbishop leaves, already thinking of revenge.

In the scenes that follow, we see the life of Sor Juana up close. Unlike a woman living the stereotypical life of a nun, Sor Juana spends her days thinking, reading (sometimes books prohibited by the Inquisition), and writing. (At this time, she was working on her famous *Primero sueño*.) She watches the heavens through her telescope, plucks her lyre, and splashes on perfume and gazes into a mirror to adjust her veil and jewelry before receiving visitors, an allusion to her vanity and narcissism.

One of her most frequent visitors (according to Bemberg) is the *virreina*. In a long conversation in an early scene, the two discuss their lives. Sor Juana lists the advantages of her chosen path. The convent allows her to write and think. In response to a question about loneliness, she says that she has been alone since she was a child—a reference undoubtedly to her early life: to an absent father, to her dead grandfather, and to a mother and aunt who sent her away. The *virreina* sees the parallels with her own life; both are locked in by either a rule (of the convent) or a protocol (of the diplomat's wife). Both have a circumscribed world. They become the best of friends. The *virreina* thereafter comes frequently to Sor Juana's cell. They talk of books. They acknowledge the potential for problems with the Holy Inquisition because of the "dangerous" volumes that Sor Juana reads by Gassendi, Kircher, Kepler, Copernicus, and Descartes. The *virreina* brings her gifts in return for her laudatory poems and admires Sor Juana's "children": her telescope, sundial, astrolabe, and magnets.

Another frequent visitor is her confessor, the Jesuit father Antonio Núñez de Miranda, sometimes described as an "intellectual luminary" and known to believe that women were inferior to men and unsuitable for scholarly pursuits because of their lack of intelligence and physical strength. He was a theologian, philosopher, professor, preacher, and instrument of the Inquisition. He served as confessor to viceroys and as spiritual director to nuns. Bemberg accepts his reputation for having convinced or influenced Juana Inés to profess thirteen years earlier, going so far as to arrange for don Pedro Velásquez

de la Cadena to pay her three-thousand-peso dowry.[9] We see him rebuking
Sor Juana for her vanities. She writes praises for viceregal authorities. He
asks, "What about God?"[10]

In contrast to these light and happier scenes are those that allude to the
growing adversity that Bemberg inserts, ever more often, as the film pro-
gresses in dark and muted colors. Already, in one of the first scenes, we know
that Mother Nature is not cooperating. In the same scene in which the abbess
announces the first visit of the viceroy de la Laguna to the convent, we are told
that there is a drought in Mexico that makes the convent's rent collections slow
and difficult. The nuns are admonished to work harder. The archbishop reap-
pears complaining about the lax rule in the convent. He is a fanatically religious man who hates women. So fearful of temptation is he that he will not sit
at a table with one. The archbishop begins meddling with the upcoming secret
elections for the new abbess. He wants a stricter nun to govern the sisters, even
if it means using influence and promises to win the needed additional votes.
Subsequently, a scene shows nuns clandestinely copying the *Primero sueño* in
the depths of the night and the members of a divided Inquisition tribunal dis-
cussing its merits and demerits. But as long as the marquis de la Laguna rules
Mexico, Sor Juana and her creations are safe. Orders to give up some books
go nowhere as long as the *virreina* is at Sor Juana's side.

Once the viceroy de la Cerda is recalled and leaves Mexico at the end of
1688, the conjuncture of forces and the vicissitudes of nature combine to
doom Sor Juana and the products of her quill pen.[11] Paz reminds us, "After
María Luisa and her husband left, Sor Juana must have felt abandoned. To
live without protectors in a world that was a web of alliances, friendships
and reciprocal favors was like being in deep water without a lifebuoy to
cling to."[12]

Perhaps in seeking to please another protector, the bishop of Puebla, Sor
Juana makes a fatal mistake. Manuel Fernández de Santa Cruz, the bishop
of Puebla, had a personal grudge against the archbishop of Mexico and had
asked Sor Juana to write a critique of a sermon by one of the archbishop's
favorite Portuguese theologians. This writer, Father Antonio Vieyra, had
refuted the opinions of three saints (Augustine, Thomas Aquinas, and John
Chrysostom) about Christ in his last days. Bemberg's film suggests that Sor
Juana accepted the assignment to show her erudition in a field that was the
exclusive preserve of men and that she ignored repeated warnings about
the power of the Inquisition in New Spain.[13] In Bemberg's film, Sor Juana
accepts the challenge despite stories of Spanish autos-da-fée in which scores
were burned at the stake to amuse the populace and take people's minds off
larger socioeconomic problems. Furthermore, Bemberg suggests that Sor
Juana could not resist the opportunity to attack a man who hated women, who
had initiated an era of austerity and prohibited friends' visits to the convent

Figure 3.1: As religious pressure to obey increases, Sor Juana (Assumpta Serna) learns that her patrons must return to Spain. (Photofest)

parlor and who damned public spectacles such as plays, bullfights, and cock-fights. Paz suggests that Sor Juana regarded the archbishop with a mixture of fear and repugnance. She may have thought that his rejection of the theater and poetry was a condemnation of her life and work. In this one instance, Sor Juana's pride in her accomplishments and her abilities led her to abandon her heretofore extreme prudence and reserve when it came to the Inquisition and the power of the church—as epitomized by the archbishop of Mexico.

Although declared not heretical, Sor Juana's critique was condemned in Mexico. Dorothy Schons explains why: the Jesuits were all powerful. They were practically in control of the Inquisition. Father Vieyra was a Jesuit, and it was thought that the critique was an attack on that order. To attack Vieyra or the order was to attack Aguiar y Seixas himself. Worse, when confronted by the archbishop and asked for the name of the person behind the critique, she responded with the pseudonym Sor Filotea (really the bishop of Puebla, Fernández de Santa Cruz) under which it was published. Paz sums up the situation, saying that "Sor Juana intervened in the quarrel between two powerful Princes of the Roman Church and was destroyed in the process."[14] Only a few months later, she dictated another treatise (*Respuesta a Sor Filotea de la Cruz*, March 1, 1691) to defend the right to study and write.[15]

In the end, her confessor not only did not defend her but also abandoned her. So did the cautious Fernández de Santa Cruz, an origin of her troubles. Envy, fear, hatred of women, and suspicion prevailed under the guise of orthodoxy.

Meanwhile, Mexico was afflicted by unceasing rains, from the summer of 1691 into 1692, and disease, both of which were seen as a sign of God's condemnation of the immorality of society. Social upheaval broke out in June 1692 in Mexico City, where natives rioted and attacked the viceregal palace. Trouble erupted too in Tlaxcala, Guadalajara, and elsewhere. Processions and prayers did little to assuage the scarcity of provisions that continued into 1693. At this point, Bemberg makes Sor Juana look worn and aged (notice that she wears spectacles for the first time). Paz says that she felt culpable. Subsequently, we see her washing floors in the medical ward. Such self-sacrifice in the service of God brought the peripatetic confessor back to her side. Her renunciation of the material world and herself and her art began. Paz believes that she had lost her faith in herself. With no protectors, she needed to find refuge. The only option in such a situation was one of submission. Núñez de Miranda told her that God wanted a different Juana, so Sor Juana renounced her books, her fame, her vanity, and her "satanic" ideas and as penance, gave up all her worldly effects. She presented a petition to the Holy Tribunal in which she pleaded for pardon from her sins. Father Juan Oviedo, S.J., states that "she rediscovered how to be 'alone with her Husband [Jesus Christ], and considering Him nailed to the cross for the sins of men,

her love gave her inspiration to imitate Him, trying with all her might to cru-
cify her passions and her appetites with such rigorous fervor in the penitence,
that she needed the prudent advice and attention of Father Antonio to hold
her back, lest her fervor would end her life. And Father Núñez used to say,
praising God, that Juana Inés was not running, but flying to perfection.'"[16]

Her first biographer, the Jesuit Diego Calleja, reports much the same
story.[17] In February 1694, Sor Juana signed in her own blood another text,
entitled *Docta explicación del misterio, y voto que hizo de defender la
Purísima Concepción de Nuestra Senora*, in which she pledged to defend
that mystery, and announced a special devotion to the Virgin Mary and the
Immaculate Conception.[18] The previously defiant, audacious, nonconforming
and unconventional nun gave up her books and possessions; the proceeds of
their sale provided for the poor. This act marks a move toward the spiritual
and penitential. She became humble, obedient, and pious, and she began to
scourge her own flesh. In short, the renunciation was so complete that she lost
her spirit and came to believe that she was "the worst of all."[19]

FILM AS INTERPRETATION

Bemberg succeeds admirably in portraying many of the known details of
Sor Juana's life. In so doing, her presentation touches on several themes
that have attracted scholarly attention in the last few years. One of these
debates concerns the reasons why Juana Inés originally professed. Bemberg
emphasizes the relative freedom that cloistered life promised to continue her
studies. Sor Juana complained, after twenty-two years of religious life, that
the spiritual duties and expectations and interruptions of the community of
sisters robbed her of some of her time (she served as archivist and secretary
of San Jerónimo),[20] yet it was still her best option. Thus, love of learning is
one answer to the question of why she professed. The film also alludes to
her aversion to marriage and children. Sor Juana admits the "total antipathy I
felt for marriage" and her lack of domestic aptitude.[21] In the scene where Sor
Juana holds the *virreina*'s newborn son, the baby elicits a reflection from her
instead of a caress. Once again, the role of Núñez de Miranda as confessor is
highlighted. Indirectly, too, there are quick allusions to Juana's illegitimacy,
the absence of a father, her probable relative poverty, and the consequent
lack of the dowry necessary for a suitable marriage. But Bemberg makes
no reference to the popular belief that she professed as a reaction to a failed
love affair, a point that Paz energetically rejects in part based on Sor Juana's
own words:

and so, beloved of so many,
I took not one into my heart.[22]

Bemberg fails to put Juana's profession into historical context. A woman
need not have a true vocation to enter a convent; one only had to be a sin-
cere, orthodox Catholic. Women might choose the convent for other reasons.
Families frequently disposed of unmarried daughters by putting them in
a convent. Asunción Lavrin states, "She professed knowing that life in a
convent entailed certain conditions 'most repugnant to my nature; but . . .
conventual life was the least unsuitable and most desirable I could elect.'"
Becoming a nun was seen as a career or occupation, a means to earn a living
and maintain social respectability. To remain a spinster was not an option.
Paz concludes a long analysis of this question: "It was a prudent decision
consistent with the morality of the age and the habits and convictions of her
class. The convent was not a ladder toward God but a refuge for a woman
who found herself alone in the world."[23]
    Another issue left somewhat underdeveloped and unresolved by Bemberg
is whether or not Sor Juana exhibited homosexual tendencies, especially
toward the wives of the two viceroys whom she encountered during her
adult life. Sor Juana did not have a high opinion of men: recall the *"Hombres
necios"* (Foolish men) poem recited in the film.[24] In contrast, many point to
her poetry as clear evidence of the love she felt for the condesa de Paredes.
For example:

There is no obstacle to love
in gender or in absence,
for souls, as you are well aware,
transcend both sex and distance.[25]

Bemberg features their relationship in several scenes from quiet con-
tentment and formal familiarity in the adoption scene, to declarations of
protection in the court scene in which the pregnant condesa faints, to the
close intimacy in the scene in which the condesa asks Sor Juana to loosen
her bodice.
    Paz explains away the lesbian suggestions, reminding us that of 216
known poems penned by Sor Juana, 52 (or one-quarter) were dedicated to
the Manceras and that more than half of her works were *piezas de ocasión*
(occasion pieces)—homages, epistles, felicitations, verses to commemorate
the death of an archbishop or the birthday of a magnate. Most are written
between 1680 and 1688, coincident with the stay in Mexico of Viceroy de la
Laguna, and almost all are dedicated to him; his wife; or his son, José María
(born in 1683). Paz argues that it makes no difference that these expressions

and adulations grew ever more familiar and friendly, ever more exaggerated and exalted. He reminds us that New Spain, in the late seventeenth century, was regimented by a very strict social order, a chain of powers, loyalties, and subordinations. Sor Juana's work reflected the position she held in society. One had to seek support of another power, which she learned to do well at a young age given the circumstances of her birth and upbringing. She became a friend and confidant of the condesa de Paredes, a woman only one year her junior. Her ever more fervent works of praise to her protectors were natural in that era, an expression of her subordinate and (in some ways) dependent status. Paz concludes that "the sensual expressions and amatory images could be accepted and read as metaphors and rhetorical figures of two true sentiments: appreciation and an inferior's devotion to her superior. In Sor Juana's poems to the Countess of Paredes we find all the motifs of traditional amatory poetry transformed into metaphors of the relationship of gratitude and dependence that united the nun with her Vicereine."[26]

Sor Juana's first book of poetry, a volume published at the behest of the condesa in Spain, was "an homage to her and to the house of Laguna."[27] Most of the poems were written to accompany presents or to thank the giver for one. Paz concludes that modern readers confuse eroticism with feudal submission, reminding us that "an unmarried girl, especially one in Juana Inés's peculiar circumstances, who displayed her love for a man in public would have lost her reputation immediately; on the other hand, a loving friendship between women was permissible if they were of elevated rank and their sentiments idealized."[28]

Bemberg differs from Paz in leaving the issue ambiguous. On the one hand, she acknowledges that many of Sor Juana's poems are an homage to the viceroy and his wife—an argument against claims of homosexuality. Yet later, Bemberg directs the condesa to say that she does not want to hear of another viceroy's wife from the lips of her favorite nun (an indication of jealousy?). Meanwhile, Sor Juana's confessor warns her of "excessive loves" (amores excesivos). And finally, the viceroy's wife wants to know the details of Sor Juana's solitary life and requests that she take off her veil. The script continues with phrases such as "Juana is mine, only mine" coming from the condesa's lips, followed by a deep kiss so that she will remember. Bemberg is not convinced by Paz's reasoned arguments to the contrary and by his reconstruction of the past.[29]

Another issue that recent studies have raised is whether or not Sor Juana was a feminist. If among feminists one includes those persons who use their abilities to defend and advance the position and power of women, then there can be no doubt about Bemberg's interpretation of Sor Juana. In one scene, music teacher Sor Juana tells her students that women are intelligent and that intelligence has no gender. Her students must keep their eyes and ears open to perceive everything. This viewpoint is coincident with Sor Juana's own words. In her *Respuesta a Sor Filotea*, she reiterates these beliefs. Paz states, "She scoffs at the idea, current in her day, that women are intellectually inferior. As stupidity is not confined to women, neither is intelligence an attribute only of men."[30]

Already mentioned are her thoughts about men. Who is to blame, Sor Juana asks, "she who sins and takes the pay,/or he who pays her for the sin?"[31] She lashes out at the double standard and the hypocrisy of the male-dominated culture and society. Hers, says her biographer, was a "resolute feminism."[32] Although the concept of feminism (as such) did not exist in her day, there can be no doubt that this freethinker and prolific author was one of the movement's precursors.

Finally, we might ask whether or not Sor Juana was a typical nun, a topic mentioned in passing above. Lavrin states that she was both atypical and typical at different times of her life. She was unlike Isabel de la Encarnación, a discalced Carmelite in the Convent of Puebla, who had felt a religious vocation since the age of nine. She did not live the life of a nun from the time she was a little girl, like Sor María Josefa Lino de la Canal, who founded the Convent of La Concepción in San Miguel Allende.[33] As seen in the film, she does not spend long hours on her knees either praying or scrubbing floors; she does not seem overly inclined to charity, sewing, or other "sisterly" pursuits. In short, she did not have a strong vocation for the religious life. Her motives for moving into the convent were opportunistic.

Her writing was also atypical. Many other nuns wrote autobiographies, usually at the instigation of a confessor.[34] Lavrin says that the "confessional character" of the latter condemned these works to oblivion.[35] They were regarded as a means of achieving self-perfection and were not meant to be literary works of art, as were Sor Juana's. Nuns also wrote biographies, histories of convents, plays, poetry, and personal letters, but few of these are known. It is only during the last years of her life that we know she practiced asceticism and repented for her worldliness.[36] Sor Juana was not humble, meek, and self-effacing like other nuns. Lavrin remarks that not until her "final spiritual transformation" in 1693 do expressions of humility find their way into her writings. She quotes from the *Petición causidica*: "I, Juana Inés de la Cruz, the most insignificant of the slaves of the Blessed Mary," and "Juana Inés de la Cruz, the most unworthy and ungrateful creature of all created by your Omnipotence."[37] Sor Juana admitted having lived a religious life without religion.[38] Bemberg, fittingly, portrays her death after self-sacrificing scenes of her aiding the ailing. One suspects, though, that she died "although virgin, pregnant with divine concepts."[39]

ADDITIONAL RESOURCES

Juana Inés de la Cruz, Sister. *A Sor Juana Anthology*. Translated by Alan S. Trueblood. Cambridge, MA: Harvard University Press, 1988. This collection of Sor Juana's writings is helpful for an English-reading audience.

Juana Inés de la Cruz, Sor. *Obras completas*. 4 vols. Mexico: Fondo de Cultura Economica, 1951. A popular edition of Sor Juana's known writings.

————. *Sor Juana Inés de la Cruz: Sus mejores poesías*. Mexico: Gómez Hermanos Editores, 1980. A collection of some of Sor Juana's best poems in a single volume.

Franco, Jean. *Plotting Women: Gender and Representation in Mexico*. New York: Columbia University Press, 1989. This interesting book focuses attention on women in Mexico. Chapters mention individuals such as Sor Juana and Frida Kahlo as well as whole classes of women, such as the deluded women of colonial times.

Kirk, Stephanie. *Sor Juana Inés de la Cruz and the Gender Politics of Knowledge in Colonial Mexico*. New York: Routledge, 2016.

Lavrin, Asunción. "Unlike Sor Juana? The Model Nun in the Religious Literature of Colonial Mexico," *University of Dayton Review* 16, no. 2 (Spring 1983): 75–92. Lavrin has written a good article that stresses the fact that Sor Juana was both typical and atypical of other women who entered convents in colonial Mexico at different times in her life.

Ludmer, Josefina. "Tricks of the Weak." In *Feminist Perspectives on Sor Juana Inés de la Cruz*, edited by Stephanie Merrim, 86–93. Detroit: Wayne State University Press, 1991. An in-depth analysis of Sor Juana's Respuesta a Sor Filotea de la Cruz.

Merrim, Stephanie. "Toward a Feminist Reading of Sor Juana Inés de la Cruz: Past, Present, and Future Directions in Sor Juana Criticism." In *Feminist Perspectives on Sor Juana Inés de la Cruz*, edited by Stephanie Merrim, 11–37. Detroit: Wayne State University Press, 1991. Merrim asks the question: Is Sor Juana a feminist?

Myers, Kathleen A. "The Addressee Determines the Discourse: The Role of the Confessor in the Spiritual Autobiography of Madre María de San Joseph (1656–1719)." *Bulletin of Hispanic Studies* 69 (1992): 39–47. Myers analyzes New World nuns' writings, especially those that were composed at the behest of a confessor. She mentions the work of Sor Juana as well as that of a contemporary, the Augustinian Recollect nun from Puebla, Madre María de San Joseph.

Paz, Octavio. *Sor Juana, or, The Traps of Faith*. Cambridge, MA: Belknap Press, Harvard University, 1988. This fat tome is the definitive biography of Sor Juana, written by an admiring modern Mexican poet. The depth of his knowledge and the acuity of his interpretation of his subject are unrivaled.

Prendergast, Ryan. "Constructing an Icon: The Self-Referentiality and Framing of Sor Juana Inés de la Cruz," *Journal for Early Modern Cultural Studies* 7, no. 2 (2007): 20–56. This analysis compares known portraits of Sor Juana and her self-references in her published work.

Schons, Dorothy. "Some Obscure Points in the Life of Sor Juana Inés de la Cruz." In *Feminist Perspectives on Sor Juana Inés de la Cruz*, edited by Stephanie Merrim, 38–60. Detroit: Wayne State University Press, 1991. Schons provides a short analysis of various points of Sor Juana's life, based on the nun's writings and other documents.

NOTES

1. On Sor Juana's self-descriptions, see the analysis by Ryan Prendergast, "Constructing an Icon: The Self-Referentiality and Framing of Sor Juana Inés de la Cruz," *Journal for Early Modern Cultural Studies* 7, no. 2 (2007): 20–56.

2. Octavio Paz, *Sor Juana, or, The Traps of Faith* (Cambridge, MA: Belknap Press, Harvard University, 1988). Paz is a celebrated author, philosopher, poet, and winner of the Nobel Prize for literature in 1990. One of his most famous works is *Labyrinth of Solitude*. Bemberg was a scriptwriter and director, who also brought to the screen *Momentos* (1981), *Senora de Nadie* (1981), and such perennial favorites as *Camila* (1984) and *Miss Mary* (1987). She made *Yo, la Peor de Todas* in 1990. Bemberg was born in Buenos Aires in 1925. Her first screenplay, *Cronica de una senora*, dates from 1971.

3. Paz, *Sor Juana*, 109; but Paz says later (123) that she was self-taught.

4. Dorothy Schons, "Some Obscure Points in the Life of Sor Juana Inés de la Cruz," in *Feminist Perspectives on Sor Juana Inés de la Cruz*, ed. Stephanie Merrim (Detroit: Wayne State University Press, 1991), 39; Schons says that she was not quite sixteen when she professed.

5. Paz, *Sor Juana*, 248, reports that the number may be exaggerated. He concludes that it is impossible to know the true number of the volumes in her personal library.

6. Cloister also refers to the enclosed part of a religious house where none but the religious themselves may enter. The rules of cloister, or enclosure, restrict the entry of outsiders to maintain religious retirements and to prevent unnecessary worldly distractions. Violation of strict cloister results in automatic excommunication.

7. Also known as the Count of Paredes, though he held this title only as consort.

8. The marquis de la Laguna was named viceroy in a decree on August 8, 1680; he arrived in Mexico in November. He took possession on November 7, 1680, and passed on the staff of authority on November 30, 1686. Paz, *Sor Juana*, 147, 191, 265.

9. Her confessor helped pay other expenses for clothes and the purchase of a cell as well as provision for slaves or servants. Asuncion Lavrin, "Unlike Sor Juana? The Model Nun in the Religious Literature of Colonial Mexico," *University of Dayton Review* 16, no. 2 (Spring 1983): 75.

10. On Father Núñez, see María Águeda Méndez, "Antonio Núñez de Miranda, confessor de Sor Juana, y las mujeres," *Caravelle* (2001): 76–77, 411–20; and Virginia M. Bouvier, "Sor Juana y la Inquisición: Las paradojas del poder," *Revista de Crítica Literaria Latinoamericana* 25, no. 49 (1999): 63–78, on Núñez's role in the Inquisition, especially p. 65. The article also includes statistics on the persons condemned by the Inquisition for crimes against Catholic orthodoxy. Stephanie Kirk also adds his beliefs regarding women. See her book, *Sor Juana Inés de la Cruz and the Gender Politics of Knowledge in Colonial Mexico* (New York: Routledge, 2016), especially 8, 81.

11. Her poems are silent, with one exception, about the next viceroy, don Melchor Portocarrero y Lasso de la Vega, conde de Monclova, who remained in office from 1686 to 1688, when he was transferred to Peru. His replacement, don Gaspar de Sandoval Cerda Silva y Mendoza, conde de Galve (September 1688 to February 1696 [Paz, *Sor Juana*, 269]), was part of a faction opposed to de la Cerda. Although on friendly terms with the conde, Sor Juana dedicated only a few poems to him and his wife (Schons, "Some Obscure Points," 47). None of these men seems to have played as prominent a role of protector as the marques de la Laguna.

12. Paz, *Sor Juana*, 266.

13. Irving A. Leonard believes that legislation limiting the circulation of certain books in New Spain was only enforced at the end of the seventeenth century (Paz, *Sor Juana*, 248). Schons, "Some Obscure Points," in contrast, talks of "strict censorship on books that existed in New Spain" (49; see also her footnote 28, 59).

14. Paz, *Sor Juana*, 403.

15. Schons, "Some Obscure Points," 52, characterized it as "a defense of the rights of women, a memorable document in the history of feminism."

16. As quoted in Lavrin, "Unlike Sor Juana?" 86.

17. See Paz, *Sor Juana*, 450–70.

18. Paz, *Sor Juana*, 461–62.

19. Little reliable information about Sor Juana's library, said to be one of the greatest of her era in New Spain, is available. Estimates of its size, as mentioned above, range from four hundred to four thousand volumes. Furthermore, scholars differ on whether Sor Juana voluntarily gave up her possessions or was ordered to do so by ecclesiastical authorities. Bolstering the former interpretation is a clause in a cleric's testament stating that he sold her books at her request. Kirk cites recent scholarship that indicates that Sor Juana, almost immediately after she authorized the sale of her books, began to acquire others, accumulating 180 volumes in the two years before her death (Kirk, *Sor Juana*, 13, 16, 21, 25, 31–33, 35).

The phrase "the worst of all" was used commonly by the religious—both male and female—of her time. Its source is biblical, from Paul's first epistle to Timothy: "Christ Jesus came into the world to save sinners, of whom I am the worst of all" (1 Timothy 1:15). Sor Juana wrote the phrase in the margins of her books (Paz, *Sor Juana*, 448). She also actually signed her name below a statement in the Book of Professions (*Libro de profesiones*) that read: "Here above the day, month and year of my death shall be recorded. I beg, for the love of God and of his Purest Mother, my beloved religious sisters, . . . to entrust me to God, I have been and am the worst of all. To all I ask pardon for the love of God and of his Mother. I, the worst one of the world."

Paz believes that she wrote these words months before her death. Ezequiel Chavez believes that this statement was not written by Sor Juana but only signed by her (Lavrin, "Unlike Sor Juana?" 81; Paz, *Sor Juana*, 464–65). The *Libro de profesiones* was purchased by Schons and is today in the library of the University of Texas at Austin.

20. Paz, *Sor Juana*, 102; Lavrin, "Unlike Sor Juana?" 78.

21. Josefina Ludmer, "Tricks of the Weak," in *Feminist Perspectives*, 88; Jean Franco, *Plotting Women: Gender and Representation in Mexico* (New York: Columbia University Press, 1989), 24, 27.

22. Paz, *Sor Juana*, 101. See also Schons, "Some Obscure Points," 39.

23. Paz, *Sor Juana*, 110. See his wider discussion of the question from 100–111.

24. For the complete text of "*Hombres necios*," see Sor Juana's *Sor Juana Inés de la Cruz: Sus mejores poesías* (Mexico: Gomez Hermanos Editores, 1980), 57–59.

25. Paz, *Sor Juana*, 219. See the rest of Paz's chap. 15, "Religious Fires," for his interpretation of Sor Juana's love.

26. Paz, *Sor Juana*, 201, 202.

27. Paz, *Sor Juana*, 199.

28. Paz, *Sor Juana*, 101–102. For more on this topic, see Paz, pt. 4, chap. 14.

29. See also Stephanie Merrim, "Toward a Feminist Reading of Sor Juana Inés de la Cruz: Past, Present, and Future Directions in Sor Juana Criticism," in *Feminist Perspectives on Sor Juana Inés de la Cruz*, ed. Stephanie Merrim (Detroit: Wayne State University Press, 1991), 18, on this issue.

30. Paz, *Sor Juana*, 423.

31. Paz, *Sor Juana*, 304.

32. Paz, *Sor Juana*, 300.

33. Lavrin, "Unlike Sor Juana?" 77.

34. Kathleen A. Myers, "The Addressee Determines the Discourse: The Role of the Confessor in the Spiritual Autobiography of Madre María de San Joseph (1656–1719)," *Bulletin of Hispanic Studies* 69, no. 1 (January–March 1992): 39–47.

35. Lavrin, "Unlike Sor Juana?" 84.

36. Lavrin, "Unlike Sor Juana?" 85.

37. Lavrin, "Unlike Sor Juana?" 81.

38. Schons, "Some Obscure Points," 56.

39. Paz, *Sor Juana*, 77. These were words used by Sor Juana to describe the pythoness of Delphi in "El epinicio al conde de Galve."

Chapter 4

A French Comedy, the Inquisition, Dirty Dancing, and a Sociopath

Hidalgo—La Historia Jamás Contada

Donald F. Stevens

Hidalgo—La Historia Jamás Contada *(2010): produced by Lourdes Garcia and Luis Urquiza; directed by Antonio Serrano; written by Leo Eduardo Mendoza and Antonio Serrano; color; 115 minutes; Astillero Films. As he awaits his execution, Miguel Hidalgo (Demián Bicher) reflects on his life before Mexico's War for Independence.*

So much has been written about the life of Miguel Hidalgo y Costilla that it may be difficult to imagine what stories might be left untold to fulfill the promise of this film's title. Hidalgo is famous as the man who began Mexico's war for independence from Spain. After midnight on September 16, 1810, Hidalgo called on the Mexican people to rise up against Spanish tyranny. His exact words are unknown, but Hidalgo's exhortation became known as the "Grito de Dolores" for the town where Hidalgo initiated the movement, and the date is celebrated every year as Mexico's Independence Day. Hidalgo's call was answered by tens of thousands of ordinary people. His massive army of poorly armed volunteers was allied with a few militia units. Hidalgo's goal was not just independence but social justice, so he decreed the abolition of slavery and the discriminatory head tax on Indigenous men. His army won a few victories but suffered massive casualties. They were decisively defeated by royalist troops near Guadalajara in January 1811. Hidalgo was captured two months later. He was tried by a military tribunal and executed in July

1811, but the movement he inspired continued the war. After more than ten years, Mexico finally achieved independence from Spain in 1821.

The private lives of many great men are overshadowed by their public roles in history. As one prominent historian wrote, "The biography of Hidalgo tends to be lost in the history of the war."[1] In fact, "the untold story" in this film's title is a phrase that someone in the marketing department wrote well after the project was finished. The subtitle tells potential filmgoers that this will not be the usual hagiographic treatment, repeating what they already know about the historic actions of Mexico's foremost independence hero.[2] Fair enough. After all, I wrote the title for this chapter with the same motivation: to get your attention and to suggest that this will not be dull. This biopic does tell some stories that are not *often* told but were based on facts, other stories that were only rumors or allegations during Hidalgo's lifetime, a few stories that seem to have been conceived generations after his death, and some others that were only recently invented for the film's script.

A FRENCH COMEDY

The original working title for the film was *Hidalgo Molière*. That would have been a more enigmatic designation and perhaps one that would have been harder to sell. Yet Leo Mendoza (the scriptwriter), Damián Bicher (the star and co-producer), and Antonio Serrano (the director) regarded the name "Molière" as essential to the soul of their project.[3] Molière was the stage name and nom de plume adopted by Jean-Baptiste Poquelin, a seventeenth-century French actor and playwright who is best known today for his comedies, one of which, *Tartuffe* (1664/1669), is the focus of several scenes in this film. Miguel Hidalgo was a big fan of French culture in general and French theater in particular. Molière's *Tartuffe* was one of his favorite comedies. In fact, Miguel Hidalgo might well have been the first to translate *Tartuffe* into Spanish. He organized and directed several productions of the play in his home while he was the curate in San Felipe.[4] The question is, why was Hidalgo so fond of this play?

Molière was a great innovator in French comedy. Rather than employing the usual stock characters and customary costumes that were routine up to his time, he created original, more natural roles for himself and his acting troupe. He wrote, produced, and acted in comedies that reflected the times in which they were living. Molière used the theater to poke fun at people in situations that were familiar to his audiences. So it follows that Molière's plays were often controversial. In *Tartuffe*, the title character is a trickster. Moralists have traditionally objected to this age-old comedic motif because the audience is invited to find amusement in dishonesty and to see deceptions as entertaining.

Spectators generally find themselves applauding the tricksters and laughing at how clever they are, even though they would (and should) despise such characters in real life. This "suspension of moral disapproval" is part of the reason that prudes and saints have seen the theater as a disreputable pastime.[5] In this particular comedy, Molière amplified this existing fault by introducing religion into the mix; he made his title character a hypocrite who feigns sanctity to manipulate a respectable bourgeois patriarch named Orgon. Although the rest of his family sees who Tartuffe really is, Orgon is beguiled until it is too late: Orgon insists that his daughter must marry Tartuffe; he will not believe his wife when she tells him that Tartuffe has tried to seduce her; and eventually, Orgon turns all of his property over to Tartuffe. Then suddenly, a surprise ending restores good order so that the play can be a comedy rather than a tragedy.

Tartuffe eventually became a great success with Molière playing the role of Orgon, but it got off to a rocky start. When it was first performed in 1664 for the royal court at Versailles, King Louis XIV thought the play was funny enough and essentially harmless, but some prominent courtiers were so aghast, shocked, and agitated that the king banned the play a few days later, "until it could be revised." The prohibition lasted for five years.[6]

More than a century later and a quarter of the way around the world, what did this comedy mean to Hidalgo? In the film, Hidalgo's motivation for choosing to produce this play is focused on an individual character, a priest named Ramírez, who is Hidalgo's subordinate in the parish. Ramírez is an invented character who stands in for all that is conventional and conservative and dull and repressive. In fact, the role and the circumstances are not true to history since Hidalgo, as the parish priest, had control over the other priests employed in his parish. When Hidalgo began his tenure in San Felipe, there were at least seven vicars, chaplains, and lieutenant priests in the parish.[7] Hidalgo paid their salaries. If any of these subordinates had annoyed him, Hidalgo could reprimand them. And if that did not work, he could replace them.

In any case, this fictional character, Ramírez, is used to introduce the problem of a debt that Hidalgo was accused of owing to the Colegio de San Nicolás. Ramírez travels to the provincial capital, Valladolid, to complain to the bishop about Hidalgo's staging of "that troublemaker" Molière's play. The bishop calmly grooms his beard and brushes lint off his robe while remarking that Hidalgo may be rebellious, arrogant, and vain but that his "little play" is of no concern. (Moliere's play was never banned in New Spain.) What does matter to the bishop is the debt that Hidalgo owes: eight thousand pesos from when he was in charge of the Colegio de San Nicolás. The bishop's assistant explains that Hidalgo was "too generous" with the school's money and that he had given each of the resident students *two blankets* in the winter.[8]

Although the film names this bishop as Manuel Abad y Queipo, that cleric did not become the acting bishop of Valladolid for almost another twenty years. While Hidalgo was in San Felipe, Abad y Queipo was serving as a subordinate official in the diocese, while the bishop of Valladolid at the time was a Hieronymite friar named Antonio de San Miguel. Both Bishop San Miguel and his subordinate, Abad y Queipo, were favorably disposed toward Hidalgo. Much later, after Hidalgo had started the war in 1810, Abad y Queipo was criticized for his earlier friendship with Hidalgo. As acting bishop by that time, Abad y Queipo furiously denounced his former friend and excommunicated Hidalgo.[9]

Even if the character "Ramírez" was invented for the film, the historical Miguel Hidalgo did have real debts. Hidalgo had borrowed eight thousand pesos from the *Juzgado de Testamentos y Capellanías* (a sort of ecclesiastical bank) to improve haciendas he owned near Taximaroa. Hidalgo reached an agreement to pay it back that was approved by Abad y Queipo.[10] It was not unusual for secular priests to have business interests since only a few of them were able to make a living as parish priests. Once they had completed their educations, graduates had to prove that they had sufficient income before they could be ordained as priests. Most priests found it difficult to find a suitable parish. While they waited for an opportunity, they accepted less remunerative jobs, such as teaching or as an assistant priest (*teniente de cura*) in the same way that Hidalgo had employed other priests in his parish in San Felipe.[11] Although the film presents Hidalgo's transfer from his position at the Colegio de San Nicolás to the post as parish priest at San Felipe as a punishment and a demotion, Hidalgo would not have viewed the change of circumstances that way. Being a parish priest was not only a more prestigious job than teaching or academic administration; it paid better as well. Hidalgo's income as the parish priest of San Felipe was four times greater than his income as rector and treasurer of the Colegio in Valladolid. Hidalgo needed the money because as is correctly depicted in the film, he had a large family who depended on him financially. San Felipe was also much closer to Hidalgo's beloved older brother, Joaquín, who was the parish priest of the nearby city of Dolores.[12]

So Hidalgo did owe the bishopric eight thousand pesos, but he had arranged to pay it back. The film features a different "debt," one that was related to Hidalgo's administration of the Colegio de San Nicolás when he was treasurer and rector there between 1787 and 1792. Subsequent audits of the books of the Colegio came to quite different conclusions. At first, in 1797, it appeared that the Colegio owed money to Hidalgo. The amount was reckoned to be 1,282 pesos, although the surplus was later reduced to 400 pesos. Two years after that, another accounting concluded that Hidalgo owed the Colegio 7,069.30 pesos, most of which was attributed to what the auditor regarded as excessive spending on food: Hidalgo's policy had been to serve meat to the students every day, while his successor believed that they should have been restricted to a more austere diet. It was not until 1805, a year after the death of his friend Bishop San Miguel, that Hidalgo finally agreed to pay one thousand pesos of this "debt."[13] You can see why Hidalgo (in the film) refers to the "invented" character of this debt to the Colegio.

In the film, Hidalgo decides to produce Molière's comedy in order to humiliate "Ramírez," the fictional character who has been spying on him and agitating for his payment of the "debt" to the Colegio. Ramírez, then, was not a historical person, and the real story behind Hidalgo's interest in this French comedy is more interesting. Carlos Herrejón Peredo, the most meticulous and insightful of Hidalgo's many biographers, suggests that Hidalgo saw Molière's *Tartuffe* as an allegory of the eighteenth-century royal court in Spain, with the deluded Orgon standing in for King Charles IV and Tartuffe for the king's favorite, Manuel de Godoy. Tartuffe's attempted seduction of Orgon's wife, Elmire (in the play), was a symbolic representation of Godoy's relationship with the king's wife, María Luisa, who was rumored to be having an affair with Godoy.[14] In Act IV, Scene 5 of Molière's play, Tartuffe tries to convince Orgon's wife to have sex with him. As Tartuffe says to her, "Something is scandalous only when it is known; sin that no one knows is no sin."[15]

Sins that were unknown to anyone living in Hidalgo's time are presented as historical facts in Serrano's film. Hidalgo is shown violating his clerical vow of chastity with two different women. When the cinematic Hidalgo first moves from the provincial capital to his new parish in San Felipe, he leaves behind his two children, Agustina and Lino Mariano, and their mother, Manuela Ramos Pichardo. Later in the film, Hidalgo has a passionate sexual relationship with a beautiful young woman named Josefa Quintana, whose father has bought her an impressive wardrobe of sumptuous, lowcut gowns in hopes of attracting a husband for her.

These characters provide an opportunity for some of the film's brief allusions to the historical problems that motivated the independence movement. Even before he hears the news Manuela has been persuaded to enter a convent, when he first learns that "the new bishop" is Abad y Queipo, Hidalgo interrupts with: "Damned Spaniards! Always passing the job between themselves." In contrast, Josefa's father, José Quintana, is portrayed as an amiable wealthy man who pays his tithes punctually and cheerfully, but he complains to Hidalgo about the taxes and the forced loans that he must pay for the Spanish government's wars against the English. "They are ruining us," he says. Hidalgo mentions the rebellion of the English colonies in North America, and both men agree that independence from Spain would be a solution to Mexico's problems. They quickly drop such a dangerous subject.

After a pause, José Quintana says that he would really like to be on the stage again and offers to pay the expenses if Hidalgo would put on a play. Once in the film Hidalgo has decided that their play will be Molière's *Tartuffe*, he asks José Quintana to play the role of the deluded patriarch, Orgon. Soon after Hidalgo meets Quintana's beautiful daughter, Josefa, he recruits her as well. Miguel and Josefa find each other attractive and end up in bed together. On the morning of their first performance of *Tartuffe*, when Josefa's father discovers their affair, he punches Hidalgo in the eye. After cooling off, he forgives Hidalgo just in time for the curtain to rise on their first (and only) truncated public performance of Molière's comedy, as the Inquisition's soldiers sweep in to stop the show and chase the audience away.

There is no contemporary evidence from Hidalgo's lifetime for either of these affairs with Manuela Ramos Pichardo or Josefa Quintana. There were only rumors that Hidalgo had an illegitimate child. We know about those stories because they appear in one of the most important sources for this period, the work of Miguel Alamán, a prominent conservative politician and historian who had grown up in Guanajuato and had met Hidalgo before the revolution. In writing his massive history of the wars of independence, first published in 1849, Alamán was always eager to include anything, however speculative, that would cast an unfavorable light on Hidalgo. Alamán repeated several variations of the gossip that circulated at the time about "la Fernandita," an attractive young woman who rode with Hidalgo in his coach as he traveled from Valladolid to Guadalajara in 1811. Alamán's preference among these rumors was that "it seems" that the mysterious young woman was Hidalgo's illegitimate daughter whose mother was the wife of a Spaniard. This would make the "daughter" a particularly reprehensible type of illegitimate child whose father was violating his vow of celibacy and whose mother was breaking her marriage vow.[16]

The stories about Manuela Ramos Pichardo and Josefa Quintana were not published until a hundred years or more after these sexual relationships were supposed to have taken place.[17] In 1891, Pedro González wrote that Hidalgo had had "intimate relations" with a señorita named Josefa Quintana, who gave birth to two daughters, but González did not cite any sources.[18] As time passed, others built on this flimsy foundation and embellished it with further unsubstantiated details. In 1910, José María de la Fuente added more descendants to the story.[19] It was not until 1948 that José Castillo Ledón became the first to claim that Josefa had performed in Hidalgo's theatrical productions in San Felipe, although in his words, Josefa Quintana was the "beautiful interpreter of the [tragic] heroines of [Jean] Racine" rather than an actress in the comedies of Molière.[20] Nothing in the earlier historiography before the middle of the twentieth century suggested that Josefa Quintana was unusually attractive or that she had appeared in any of Hidalgo's plays, whether comedic or tragic.[21]

The historiography of Hidalgo's supposed relationship with Manuela Ramos Pichardo follows a similar trajectory. There is no documentation from Hidalgo's lifetime and nothing at all in the secondary literature for many years. Then, after more than a century had passed, there is the same gradual accumulation of specific details without foundation in reliable primary sources. In 1897, a relatively new Mexico City newspaper, *El Imparcial*, published an anonymous article claiming that Miguel Hidalgo had a son named Mariano with Manuela Ramos y Pichardo.[22] Just in time for the centennial of Mexican Independence in 1910, José M. de la Fuente accepted as fact what even Alamán had described as only a rumor, that is, that Hidalgo's daughter was "la Fernandita" who dressed as a man to travel with Hidalgo in 1811. De la Fuente concluded that two children had been born from Hidalgo's relationship with Manuela Ramos Pichardo.[23] At mid-century, Luis Castillo Ledón repeated the story of the supposed affair with Manuela Ramos Pichardo and the two children, but he appeared to be confused about what happened to them. First, he said that Manuela had entered a convent (as in the film), and a few pages later, he wrote that the mother and children were living in Mexico City, where she was raising the children herself.[24]

None of these authors cite any contemporary documentary evidence for these children or the supposed affairs or even any verification that these stories circulated during Hidalgo's lifetime. All the same, these biographers were articulate in explaining the importance of these supposed affairs and imaginary children in shaping their views of Miguel Hidalgo as a vigorous, virile man. For Amaya, "Miguel Hidalgo Costilla y Gallaga was a normal man, complete in every sense. He loved life in all its aspects."[25] Castillo Ledón described Hidalgo this way: "With a strong and robust constitution, full of curiosities, driven and warmed by the fire of young blood, it was most natural that Miguel, like all men who stand out from the rest, had vivid passions."[26] In contrast, Herrejón Peredo concluded that these stories about Hidalgo's relationships with Manuela Ramos Pichardo and Josefa Quintana contain "absurdities that are out of touch with reality."[27] He also pointed to the absence of evidence: not only was Alamán silent about these women and their children, but if Hidalgo was having sexual relationships and fathering children with various women, why was there no testimony about any of them in the records of the Holy Office of the Inquisition?[28]

THE INQUISITION AND DIRTY DANCING

In Serrano's film, the Inquisition is represented by men in yellow uniforms. In San Felipe, these soldiers abruptly disrupt Hidalgo's presentation of Molière's play and violently disperse the audience. In an earlier scene, soldiers wearing the same yellow uniforms burst into a pulquería to arrest Hidalgo's friend Ascanio, probably on charges of sorcery. Some of the Inquisition's violence is implicit in the film. We see the preparations for burning Ascanio at the stake as well as the smoldering ashes that remained the next morning as Hidalgo rides away from Valladolid. None of this appears in the historical record. Ascanio is another fictional character. His role is to augment our appreciation of Hidalgo's rural background and his real connections with the indigenous communities, but the Mexican Inquisition did not have jurisdiction over Indigenous people and rarely executed anyone in the late eighteenth century.[29]

The film's cinematic scenes of Inquisitorial violence stand in dramatic contrast to the slow, methodical research that the Holy Office is known to have carried out before an arrest would be made. Such investigations typically began with a denunciation, something like the one that the two women from the church in San Felipe make in the film when they complain to "Ramírez" about Hidalgo's shocking behavior as a priest. Most of their charges are merely characterizations; they describe Hidalgo as a "lascivious beast," a "lustful monster," and a "horseman of the Apocalypse." The one specific charge they make is that Hidalgo had hidden the consecrated Host (*el Santísimo*) in the church and had his friends look for it blindfolded.[30]

In fact, the Inquisition carried out an extensive examination of Hidalgo's life during his years in San Felipe. That investigation began after two Mercedarian friars, Joaquín Huesca and Manuel Estrada, denounced Hidalgo to the Holy Office. Estrada and Huesca had met Hidalgo in the home of the parish priest of Taximaroa (known today as Ciudad Hidalgo), a city not far from Valladolid and near the haciendas Hidalgo owned. They all were attending a party during the celebrations of Easter in April 1800. After mulling the matter over for three months, Huesca finally reported to the Inquisition's commissioner in Valladolid that Hidalgo had said a number of things that he thought were heretical. According to Huesca, one of those heresies concerned an error in the Bible. In a conversation with Hidalgo, Huesca had quoted the Old Testament prophecy of Isaiah that "a virgin will conceive and give birth." Hidalgo replied that this was a mistranslation from the ancient text into Greek and that the original author had used the Hebrew word for "woman" rather than "virgin."[31] In addition to disputing Isaiah's prophecy of the virgin birth, Huesca said that Hidalgo had spoken disrespectfully about several popes and that he had questioned the interpretation of Saint Paul's letter to the Corinthians. Huesca also reported that he had heard from Estrada that Hidalgo had said that Santa Teresa had had visions because she did not eat and did not sleep. A few weeks later, Estrada made his own statement to the Inquisition about the shocking things he had heard Hidalgo say in Taximaroa.[32]

Once an investigation began, the Inquisitors proceeded by calling people in for interviews or visiting them and asking a series of open-ended questions. For example, two of their witnesses reported that when Hidalgo was living in Valladolid, he had often visited the home of a vivacious young woman, Guadalupe Santos Villa, who was known to be fond of comedies. Before long, she entered a convent in Puebla because she wanted to get away from "someone who was so free in his conversations."[33] The inquisitors duly followed up by interviewing the other members of the household. Eventually, they even sent their commissioner in Puebla to the convent to interview the woman, who by then was a thirty-eight-year-old nun known as María Teresa Josefa del Salvador. The inquisitor first asked her if she knew why he was questioning her. Next, he asked if she knew of "anyone who had said or done anything that was or might appear to be against our Holy Catholic Faith, the Evangelical Law that the Holy Mother Roman Catholic Church preaches and teaches, or against the correct practice of the Holy Office?" The commissioner followed up with a more direct, yet still carefully vague, question: "did she know, or had she heard, that 'someone had said to another person that she had been eager to become a nun to avoid someone who was too free in his conversations?'" Then, the inquisitor tried one more time to elicit a response that was something more than a simple denial: "that for reverence of God she was asked to search her memory and say the whole truth." Sister María Teresa Josefa del Salvador had responded to every previous question with short statements that she did not know or could not presume to say, but her last reply was longer and more emphatic: "She said that she knows nothing about what she was asked nor of any other person and that she would have said so if she had remembered anything, and that she was withholding nothing, and that is the truth as she had sworn to tell it."[34]

That line of inquiry reached a dead end, but the Inquisitors had asked many more people many more questions about Hidalgo. The Inquisition's initial investigation lasted for fifteen months, and their file on Hidalgo in these years consists of seventy-five documents. They were slow and methodical. About six months after the investigation began, they interviewed Juan Antonio Romero, the vicar of Irimbo, a town near Taximaroa, who had also attended the Easter fiestas. He testified that "Hidalgo is one of the finest theologians of this diocese." The summary of Romero's testimony continued, "that he has known Hidalgo for about fifteen years and has never noticed bad habits, nor anything that would contradict the Christian Religion."[35] After nearly a year had passed since Huesca's and Estrada's original denunciations, the Inquisitors asked their own notary and censor (the same man who had witnessed Huesca's original denunciation) what he knew about whether Hidalgo had been reading prohibited books. José María Pisa had no evidence about forbidden texts, though he had heard the story about Guadalupe Santos Villa. He also testified that "in the times that we were together, or I heard him speak, I took him for a man with solid reasoning, capable of making himself an honorable, distinguished man of letters."[36]

Hidalgo had already distinguished himself as a theologian. Like many academics, Hidalgo's career moved slowly in the beginning as he waited for opportunities to open up. Just before his twenty-fourth birthday, the Colegio de San Nicolás had invited him to give a lecture to welcome the new bishop, Juan Ignacio de la Rocha, in 1777. The new bishop was impressed by the young theologian, and the Colegio was pleased. But Hidalgo's academic career still moved slowly. Since he was underemployed, at first, Hidalgo had time to read whatever theology and ecclesiastical history he wanted and to practice the violin. Although Hidalgo had completed his education and gathered sufficient funds to receive his doctorate in theology, his father was dying in 1783, so Hidalgo never went to Mexico City to receive his degree formally. He taught Latin and philosophy and substituted for the ailing professor of theology. It was not until 1784 that he won the competition for the permanent post of professor of theology. He continued to receive additional recognition for his proficiency and expertise in theology. Hidalgo won a prize for a thesis he wrote on the proper way to study scholastic theology. In 1785, Hidalgo organized and presided over an academic conference that was impressive enough to be praised in the viceregal capital's *Gaceta de México*.[37]

After fifteen months of investigation, in July 1801, the inquisitors filed their paperwork and stopped asking questions. They brought no charges, noting that in any case, Hidalgo had changed his behavior. He gave fewer parties and devoted more of his energy to economic development projects. (As his accusers in the film said, Hidalgo was "teaching the Indians to do things.") Even though the inquisitors decided not to proceed with their investigation and closed the files, they continued to be a threat. Hidalgo's friends Martín García de Carrasquedo and José Antonio Rojas were charged and received more serious sanctions. Even Abad y Queipo and Manuel Estrada (one of Hidalgo's original accusers) were investigated by the Inquisition. After 1808, Hidalgo spent more of his time secretly conspiring for independence. Once his activity became known, the Inquisition reopened its investigation.[38]

Since the Inquisition had conducted such a thorough investigation during the years when he was the parish priest in San Felipe, we know quite a lot about Hidalgo's life there. In addition to his love of theater, Hidalgo was also an accomplished violinist who loved music, both sacred and secular. In

San Felipe, he kept a small orchestra employed to provide music for church services and to perform for the frequent parties in his home. Hidalgo treated everyone equally without regard to gender, race, or class, so his home became known as "*la Francia chiquita*" ("little France"). A scene in the film depicts one of these parties. Late one evening, after the guests have gone home, Hidalgo's musicians suggest a new song that they had recently learned, entitled "El Chuchumbé." This is a real song, and the lyrics can be authenticated because the Inquisition transcribed them.

En la esquina está parado	Standing on the corner
un fraile de la Merced	A Mercedarian friar
con los ábitos alzados	Is lifting his habit
enceñando el chuchumbé	Showing his *chuchumbé*[39]

This was not a new song during Hidalgo's time in San Felipe. Several decades earlier, in 1766, the Inquisition had issued an edict that threatened excommunication for anyone who danced or sang the song. "El Chuchumbé" was only one of any number of irreverent and sensual dances that were called by the name *jarabe* (literally "syrup"). The lyrics frequently included profane references to sacred texts and religious rituals, especially mockery of the sacrament of confession.[40] An Inquisition edict dated December 4, 1802, prohibited another jarabe saying it was "so indecent, dissolute, lewd, and provocative, that words fail to express its malignancy and impudence and that both the dancers and the spectators drink in the mortal poison of lust through the eyes, ears, and the rest of the senses." The Holy Office not only banned that particular dance; it also attempted to "prohibit everything similar and comparable in words, actions, and swaying of the hips, with the object of provoking lust even though the song, the title, and the rhythm might vary."[41] These songs and dances were so popular that they were constantly changing shape so that the Inquisition had to be continually banning them. As historian Maya Ramos Smith wrote, "The Jarabe was a favorite target of the attacks by the Church and the sanctimonious, in whose eyes it appeared as the epitome of the most unrestrained sensuality."[42]

One such sanctimonious individual was a Dominican friar, Ramón Casaús Torres, a peninsular Spaniard and one of the most well-known theologians of the time. Passing through San Felipe while Hidalgo was the curate there, Casaús heard stories about the activities at Hidalgo's home and described them as "a scandalous life and gatherings of the uncouth people who eat, drink and whore around in his house."[43] In addition to such general accusations, Casaús reported, more specifically, that he had heard that one of the Hidalgo's vicars had danced while wearing around his neck the holy oils that were used to anoint the sick and dying. Unlike the friar's other accusations, this one turned out to be true. Hidalgo's friend, a lieutenant priest named Martín García de Carrasquedo, confessed: "being a time of smallpox epidemic when I was there as vicar, for that reason I always wore an ampule in the shape of a reliquary around my neck" so that he might be ready when called on to administer extreme unction. If he had danced while wearing this container, he said, "it was not out of hatred or deprecation for the holy oil, but because of my distracted nature and being too much inclined to dancing." No one thought that there was any problem with a priest who danced (as long as he did not have the holy oil with him), and no one accused Hidalgo himself of inappropriate dancing.[44]

MASS MURDERS AND A SOCIOPATH

Serrano's film attempts to humanize Hidalgo by showing his enjoyment of music, dancing, and the theater and makes him more attractive to modern audiences by giving him a sex life. The filmmakers also attempt to mitigate Hidalgo's responsibility for the mass murders of Spanish men during the early months of the rebellion by shifting the blame to another fictionalized character. In the film, the character named "Marroquín" provides the opportunity to show Hidalgo in the rural environment of which he was proud. Hidalgo's father was a hacienda administrator, so Hidalgo and his siblings grew up in the countryside. He learned to speak Otomí, probably by playing with Indigenous children. He and his brothers rode horses and managed cattle from an early age. Later in life, Hidalgo owned several haciendas and raised fighting bulls to pay off his debts.[45] Hidalgo did not need Marroquín to teach him about rural culture.

History tells us that while Hidalgo was living in San Felipe and Dolores, the real Agustín Marroquín was engaging in assorted criminal activities. He was probably born around 1775, but Marroquín only entered the historical record in 1795, when he was jailed. He remained locked up for two years until he escaped while the privy scourers were carrying out the excrement from the jail's latrine. Over the next two years, he stole some oxen and was alleged to have committed robberies, assaults, and a murder, all in the area east and north of Mexico City. Marroquín was arrested again in 1799. He was found guilty of rustling cattle but not guilty of the murder charge, so he spent the next three years in Mexico City's jail. Since he had been a model prisoner this time, Marroquín was released in January 1802, but he soon returned to his life of crime. He robbed and extorted the people of Apam, a town northeast of Mexico City, while carrying on a notorious affair with the wife of an innkeeper there. He committed a highway robbery near San Felipe that was said to have amounted to ten thousand pesos, so it seems possible that

Hidalgo might have heard of Marroquín then. Marroquín was also accused of other robberies, and he later confessed to stealing three thousand pesos in Acaxochitlán, back near his old home in Tulancingo. He escaped after a gun battle in the cemetery there left two men dead. Late in October, he headed farther south and west to Guadalajara, where Marroquín and his band were arrested in the early hours of November 11, 1805, after another shoot-out. This time Marroquín would remain in jail for five years until he was freed when insurgent forces, set in motion by Miguel Hidalgo, freed all the prisoners in the city's jail in November 1810.[46] Historian Eric Van Young concluded:

> As far as Marroquín's personal characteristics are concerned, one has the impression of a man at once devious but ingenuous, charming but inconstant and, on occasion, sadistic, capable of being ingratiating with authorities but prone to challenge authority figures, personally fearless and even reckless, generous and acquisitive, petulant, intelligent, and given over entirely and without conscience to a life of idleness when he could manage it and of undiscriminating crime against individuals and the state whenever his resources dwindled. In short, Agustín Marroquín probably can reasonably be described as a sociopathic personality.[47]

The film's Marroquín seems to enjoy killing, smiling maniacally as he stabs his victims with an *estoque*, the curved sword used by matadors to kill bulls at the end of a bullfight. In contrast, historical evidence tells us that the mass murders of European Spaniards were carried out by slitting their throats, just as animals were killed, or by stabbing them with lances. Such a profusion of blood would have been too shocking for movie audiences, perhaps even more so because the victims were first stripped naked since their clothing was too valuable to be ruined by all that blood. Yet the film makes another misstep. To make an emotional appeal to the audience and to illustrate and emphasize the pathos of separating the families, the male peninsulars are shown waiting in the countryside with their wives and children under a blue sky. Instead, contemporary documentation tells us that only men were taken prisoner since they were Europeans. Their wives and children were Americans, so they were not detained. Every effort was made to keep these executions secret. The Spanish men were taken from their prisons at night, in small groups, and transported to remote locations where they were stripped and killed and their bodies hidden. In the end, Hidalgo admitted that he was responsible for the deaths of 350 Spaniards. Alamán estimated the total was more like a thousand. Marroquín admitted to forty-eight, but even then, he pointed out that he only supervised their executions; he did not murder the men himself.[48]

The idea of taking the peninsular men as hostages was part of the plan from the beginning. Hidalgo and his coconspirator Ignacio Allende took Spaniards

as their prisoners from the first hours of their rebellion. They forced the surrender of the city of Celaya by threatening to slit the throats of those peninsular hostages if the city put up a fight. As they approached Guanajuato,
Hidalgo changed the plan. He wrote a formal letter to the administrator of the
province, Juan Antonio Riaño, a peninsular Spaniard who had been Hidalgo's
friend: "I see the Europeans not as enemies, but only as an obstacle that
obstructs the successful outcome of our undertaking."[49] Instead of threatening to kill the Spanish hostages he already held, as in Celaya, Hidalgo only
demanded that the *peninsulares* be surrendered to him. If the Spaniards were
not turned over to him, Hidalgo threatened that he would use every force he
had to destroy them. Riaño refused. He gathered the Spaniards, many creoles,
and most of their moveable wealth into the city's fortified granary, known
as the Alhóndiga, planning to wait there for the arrival of royalist troops.
The result was a catastrophe. The city's population was enraged and joined
Hidalgo's army in the attack. Once the crowd broke into the Alhóndiga, they
killed every Spaniard they could find. Looting in the city lasted for days.[50]

The bloodbath in Guanajuato does not appear in the film, and the pillaging
is only briefly depicted in a scene that lasts less than thirty seconds. The siege
of Guanajuato was a shocking demonstration of the lower classes' hatred for
the Spanish elite as well as vivid evidence of the indiscipline of Hidalgo's
mass army. Afterward, Manuel Gallegos, a sergeant major in the Valladolid
militia, suggested that Hidalgo and Allende select fourteen thousand men from
among their mass following and take them into the mountains for two months
of military training; they would then continue the war with a more disciplined
and conventional army. Hidalgo rejected the idea. He believed their success

Figure 4.1: The Alhóndiga de Granaditas in Guanajuato, Mexico. (Getty Images)

would be quick so that there was no reason to delay. After all, Guanajuato was regrettable, but Celaya and Valladolid had surrendered without a fight and with only a little looting.[51] Later, other cities, including Guadalajara, would fall to the insurgents with little violence. When confronted by trained royalist troops, though, Hidalgo's army did not fare as well. From Valladolid, Hidalgo and his mass army turned toward Mexico City. They forced a small royalist force to retreat at Monte de las Cruces, but they suffered heavy casualties. A week later, they were decisively defeated by a royalist army at Aculco. Many of those who did not die simply deserted.[52]

Hidalgo returned with a few remaining troops to Valladolid. It was there that the organized murders of Spanish men began, although to call them "organized" is only a way to distinguish them from the hot-blooded massacres of civilians in Guanajuato. Signs of indiscipline characterized these killings as well. Verses circulated that the innocent as well as the guilty would die. But who can say who was guilty and who was not when there were no trials? Some peninsular men were killed even though they had exemptions signed by Hidalgo himself. The first group of forty-one were stripped and killed on the night of November 12–13 before their bodies were dumped into a ravine on the Cerro de Bateas southwest of the Valladolid. Two days later, a second group of thirty-one met the same end on the Cerro de Molcajete west of the city. Once he learned that José Antonio "El Amo" Torres had taken Guadalajara for the insurgents, Hidalgo soon left Valladolid behind. The murders stopped. About a hundred Spanish men remained in prison there.[53]

In Guadalajara, Hidalgo was received with an elaborate ceremony on November 26. He decreed the abolition of slavery and the head tax on Indigenous men. He wrote a manifesto, which was printed and circulated. He granted some more exemptions to peninsular Spaniards. Then Hidalgo met with Allende on December 10 and learned that Guanajuato had fallen to Félix María Calleja, who had allowed his royalist troops to take their own bloody revenge on that city's population. Two days later, the murders of Spaniards resumed in Guadalajara. Every third night for about a month a group of twenty to thirty Spanish men were led from their prison cells into the night. The killings lasted until Hidalgo led his army to confront Calleja's royalist forces at the Puente de Calderon, east of the city. Again, Hidalgo's poorly armed and trained volunteers were defeated by the royalist army. Those who were not killed were scattered. After two months on the run, Hidalgo was captured. He was transported north to Chihuahua, to avoid the risks of conveying him to Mexico City through territory where the population was hostile to the viceregal government.[54]

Nemesio Salcedo, the royalist military commander in Chihuahua assigned Ángel Abella to interrogate and try Hidalgo. Abella's approach was slow, methodical, and relentless, lasting for two and a half days. Abella began in much same way that the Inquisition began its work. He first asked Hidalgo, "Do you know why you are in prison: who apprehended you, where, and what other subjects were apprehended with you, their names and roles with the Insurgents, and their current whereabouts particularly those named Don Ignacio Allende, Don José Mariano Jiménez and Don Juan Aldama?" For the first two days, Hidalgo was loquacious, and his answers were detailed. On the second day, he confessed to the murders in Valladolid and Guadalajara, saying that he regretted his "criminal condescension to the desires of the army composed of Indians and the rabble." By the third day, he gave only short answers.[55] Clearly a feature film does not have time to recount fully these long hours of questioning, so the film condenses the interrogation into three brief scenes that last only about five minutes in total. Hidalgo expresses regret for shedding innocent blood, defends his movement for independence, and denies rebelling against the king. "What king?" he says. The French have replaced the Spanish monarch with Napoleon's "drunken little brother."

The military authorities completed their interrogation by the middle of the day on May 9, but Hidalgo could not be sentenced and executed immediately. Salcedo found himself frustrated by the delays, which ended up postponing Hidalgo's execution for almost twelve weeks. Since Hidalgo was a priest, he had the right to have his fate determined in an ecclesiastical court by judges who were also priests. This did not mean that Hidalgo would be turned over to the Inquisition, but Salcedo did allow Mateo Sánchez Alvarez, the Inquisition's commissioner in Chihuahua, to question him. Hidalgo wrote out his answers to the Inquisition's charges against him. Although the film highlights his interest in comedy, Hidalgo was really much more serious about theology. As Herrejón Peredo concluded, "they may have defeated him at Calderón, but they could not vanquish him in the arena of theology."[56]

In fact, the military authorities in Chihuahua regarded the Inquisition as irrelevant and would not permit Sánchez Alvarez to communicate with his superiors in Mexico City. Instead, Salcedo told Francisco Fernández Valentín, canon of the church in Chihuahua, to perform the formal ceremony to remove Hidalgo from the authority of the Church and make it legal for the military to execute him. Fernández Valentín refused. He explained to Salcedo that he had no authority to do so, citing as his evidence the specific regulation set down by the Council of Trent in the sixteenth century. Then Salcedo wrote to the bishop of Durango, who eventually ordered Fernández Valentín to carry out the ritual. This was depicted in one of the film's first scenes with a lot of shouting and even bloodshed, but the actual derogation ceremony would have been "solemn and grandiloquent" instead. Rather than using a rasp and a knife, Fernández Valentín would have used only his own fingernails to scratch the palms of Hidalgo's hands as a physical demonstration that Hidalgo was no

Figure 4.2: Mexico City's Monument to Independence. (Getty Images)

longer worthy of the holy oil with which he had been anointed when he was ordained as a priest in 1778.[57]

Once he was no longer protected by the Church, Hidalgo was quickly sentenced to death; he was executed the next morning, on July 30, 1811. Hidalgo was allowed to face his executioners, unlike the others who had been shot in the back as traitors. Hidalgo was seated, bound to a chair, with his eyes blind-folded. It took three volleys before he died. Afterward, Hidalgo's body was exhibited in the city's main plaza for a few hours before it was taken inside, where his head was separated from his body, then salted and transported to Guanajuato. There, it was put on display along with the heads of Allende, Jiménez, and Aldama, each in a metal cage on a corner of the Alhóndiga, which had been the scene of so much bloodshed in 1810. There they remained until 1821.[58]

Once Mexico was independent, Hidalgo's head was reunited with his body (which had been buried in the Franciscan convent in Chihuahua), and he was interred in Mexico City's cathedral on September 16, 1823. During the first decades of the independence era, there was controversy about whether to celebrate the anniversary of the date Hidalgo began the war for independence (September 16, 1810) or the date that Agustín de Iturbide entered Mexico City with the victorious army (September 27, 1821). Finally, the celebration of Hidalgo's Grito de Dolores became accepted as the republic's indepen-dence holiday, with the nation's presidents marking the occasion by ringing the bell from Hidalgo's parish church in Dolores, which was brought to Mexico City in 1896. On September 16, 1925, Hidalgo's remains, along with those of Allende, Jiménez, and Aldama, were moved to the Independence Monument (known as *El Ángel*) in the middle of Mexico City's Avenida de la Reforma.[59] The erudite priest who loved music and comedy and who excelled as a theologian was memorialized as the principal hero of the independence movement. Hidalgo's apotheosis was complete.

ADDITIONAL RESOURCES

Alamán, Lucas. *Historia de Méjico desde los primeros movimientos que preparon su independencia en el año de 1808, hasta la época presente*. Mexico: J. M. Lara, 1849–1852.

Beezley, William H., and David E. Lorey, eds. *¡Viva México! ¡Viva la Independencia! Celebrations of September 16*. Wilmington: SR Books, 2001.

Chuchiak, John F., ed. and trans. *The Inquisition in New Spain, 1536–1820: A Documentary History*. Baltimore: Johns Hopkins University Press, 2012.

Hamill, Hugh M., Jr. *The Hidalgo Revolt: Prelude to Mexican Independence*. Gainesville: University of Florida Press, 1966.

Herrejón Peredo, Carlos. *Hidalgo: Maestro, párroco e insurgente*. Mexico: Fomento Cultural Banamex, 2011.

Molière, Jean-Baptiste Poquelin de. *Tartuffe*. Translated by Prudence L. Steiner. Indianapolis: Hackett, 2009.

Pompa y Pompa, Antonio, comp. *Procesos inquisitorial y militar seguidos a D. Miguel Hidalgo y Costilla.* Mexico: Instituto Nacional de Antropología e Historia, 1960.
Ramírez Flores, José. *El gobierno insurgente en Guadalajara, 1810–1811.* Guadalajara: Gobierno de Jalisco, Secretaría General, Unidad Editorial, 1980.
Ramos Smith, Maya. *La danza en México durante la época colonial.* Havana: Casa de las Américas, 1979.
Van Young, Eric. "Agustín Marroquín: The Sociopath as Rebel." In *The Human Tradition in Latin America: The Nineteenth Century*, edited by Judith Ewell and William H. Beezley, 17–38. Wilmington: SR Books, 1989.
Warren, Richard. "Bell of Dolores." In *Iconic Mexico*, edited by Eric Zolov, 40–45. Santa Barbara: ABC-CLIO, 2015.

NOTES

1. Carlos Herrejón Peredo, *Hidalgo: Maestro, párroco e insurgente* (Mexico: Fomento Cultural Banamex, 2011), 305. Unless otherwise noted, all translations from Spanish are my own.
2. Tania Molina Ramírez, "Recrea cinta a un cura pícaro, que se amargó con el tiempo," *La Jornada*, September 11, 2010, 7.
3. Molina Ramírez, "Recrea cinta," 7.
4. See the statement of José Martín García to the Inquisition, June 11, 1811, in Juan E. Hernández y Dávalos, comp., *Colección de documentos para la historia de la guerra de independencia de México de 1808–1821* (Mexico: J. M. Sandoval, 1877), 1:150. The earliest published translation into Spanish appears to be Molière, *El hipócrita. Comedia de Moliere en cinco actos en verso*, trans. D. J. Marchena (Madrid: Alban y Delclasse, 1811).
5. Roger W. Herzel, "Introduction," in *Tartuffe*, Jean-Baptiste Poquelin de Molière, trans. Prudence L. Steiner (Indianapolis: Hackett, 2009), x–xii.
6. Herzel, "Introduction," xii.
7. Herrejón Peredo, *Hidalgo*, 115.
8. Mistranslations in subtitles are a common problem in many films. This is one example. The erroneous subtitle reads: "In the winter he gave blankets to a couple of interns."
9. Lillian Estelle Fisher, *Champion of Reform, Manuel Abad y Queipo* (New York: Library Publishers, 1955), 102; Herrejón Peredo, *Hidalgo*, 240.
10. Herrejón Peredo, *Hidalgo*, 174, 209. On the operation of the Juzgado, see Michael P. Costeloe, *Church Wealth in Mexico: A Study of the "Juzgado de Capellanías" in the Archbishopric of Mexico, 1800–1856* (London: Cambridge University Press, 1967).
11. Paul Ganster, "Churchmen," in *Cities and Society in Colonial Latin America*, ed. Louisa Schell Hoberman and Susan Migden Socolow (Albuquerque: University of New Mexico Press, 1986), 154–56.

12. Herrejón Peredo estimated that Hidalgo's income at his first promotion after Valladolid (to interim priest in Colima) was more than three times his income in Valladolid. His next promotion to San Felipe was not only a more permanent appointment; it was an additional increase to four times what he had made in Valladolid. Herrejón Peredo, *Hidalgo*, 102, 110.

13. Herrejón Peredo, *Hidalgo*, 85, 105, 173–74, 210–11.

14. Herrejón Peredo, *Hidalgo*, 143.

15. Jean-Baptiste Poquelin de Molière, *Tartuffe*, trans. Prudence L. Steiner (Indianapolis: Hackett, 2009), 80.

16. Lucas Alamán, *Historia de Méjico desde los primeros movimientos que prepararon su independencia en el año de 1808, hasta la época presente* (Mexico: J. M. Lara, 1849–1852), 2: 43. On the types of illegitimate children, see Donald Fithian Stevens, *Mexico in the Time of Cholera* (Albuquerque: University of New Mexico Press, 2019), chap. 3. Herrejón Peredo, *Hidalgo*, 415–16, explains who "la Fernandita" really was.

17. Herrejón Peredo, *Hidalgo*, 201. The following paragraphs closely follow Herrejón Peredo's argument.

18. Pedro González, *Apuntes históricos de la ciudad de Dolores Hidalgo* (Celaya, Mexico: Impr. Económica, 1891), 299–300.

19. José M. de la Fuente, *Hidalgo íntimo: Apuntes y documentos para una biografía del benemérito cura de Dolores D. Miguel Hidalgo y Costilla* (Mexico: Tipografía Económica, 1910), 141.

20. Luis Castillo Ledón, *Hidalgo: La vida del héroe* (Mexico: N.p., 1948), 1: 76–77.

21. A few years later, Jesús Amaya said that Josefa Quintana was the daughter of a carpenter. Amaya also claimed to have discovered an earlier illegitimate child of Hidalgo, a boy named Joaquín, born in 1788 to Viviana Lucero in Guanajuato. See Jesús Amaya, *El padre Hidalgo y los suyos: Gene-biografía del héroe, sus antepasados y parientes* (Mexico: Editorial Lumen, 1952), 70–72.

22. "La Familia de Hidalgo y Costilla: Verdad Histórica," *El Imparcial*, no. 383 (October 5, 1897): 2. Herrejón Peredo, *Hidalgo*, 100, points out the factual errors in this article.

23. De la Fuente, *Hidalgo íntimo*, 141; Herrejón Peredo, *Hidalgo*, 415–16, explains who the mysterious passenger really was.

24. Castillo Ledón, *Hidalgo*, 1: 47, 77. Herrejón Peredo, *Hidalgo*, 100, points out this discrepancy.

25. Amaya, *El padre Hidalgo*, 69–70.

26. Castillo Ledón, *Hidalgo*, 1: 47.

27. Herrejón Peredo, *Hidalgo*, 200–201.

28. Herrejón Peredo, *Hidalgo*, 100, 201.

29. John F. Schwaller, "The Inquisition: Spanish America," in *Encyclopedia of Latin American History and Culture*, ed. Barbara A. Tenenbaum (New York: Charles Scribner's Sons, 1996), 3: 282–85.

30. This accusation is a distortion of the Inquisition's record and is mistranslated in the subtitles. In fact, Friar Ramón Casaus told the inquisitors that *someone* once

"had hidden the consecrated Host on the alter, so that the priest who was celebrating the mass would think it had been stolen and the congregation would laugh." Antonio Pompa y Pompa, comp., *Procesos inquisitorial y militar seguidos a D. Miguel Hidalgo y Costilla* (Mexico: Instituto Nacional de Antropología e Historia, 1960), 45.

31. Hidalgo was correct as the Roman Catholic Church made clear when a new translation was made official in 2011. See Daniel Burke, "Did Isaiah Really Predict the Virgin Birth?" https://religionnews.com/2012/12/12/did-isaiah-really-predict-the-virgin-birth/ (consulted May 18, 2022). A corrected translation also proved controversial for Protestants. See Peter J. Thuesen, *In Discordance with the Scriptures: American Protestant Battles Over Translating the Bible* (New York: Oxford University Press, 1999), Chapter 4: "The Great RSV Controversy: Bible-Burning, Red-Hunting and the Strange Specter of Unholy Scripture."

32. Pompa y Pompa, *Procesos inquisitorial y militar*, 9–12, 28–33.

33. Pompa y Pompa, *Procesos inquisitorial y militar*, 73, 105.

34. Pompa y Pompa, *Procesos inquisitorial y militar*, 104–9 with quotations on 108–9.

35. Pompa y Pompa, *Procesos inquisitorial y militar*, 61, 62.

36. Pompa y Pompa, *Procesos inquisitorial y militar*, 105.

37. Herrejón Peredo, *Hidalgo*, 51, 58–62.

38. Herrejón Peredo, *Hidalgo*, 242, 259; Henry Charles Lea, "Hidalgo and Morelos," *American Historical Review* 4, no. 4 (July 1899): 636–51; Fisher, *Champion*, 222–34.

39. For the Spanish transcription, see Sergio Rivera Ayala, "Lewd Songs and Dances from the Streets of Eighteenth-Century New Spain," in *Rituals of Rule, Rituals of Resistance: Public Celebrations and Popular Culture in Mexico*, ed. William H. Beezley, Cheryl English Martin, and William E. French (Wilmington: SR Books, 1994), 31. My translation differs slightly from his.

40. Rivera Ayala, "Lewd Songs and Dances," 31, 37–38.

41. Quoted by Maya Ramos Smith and Patricia Cardona Lang, eds., *Antología: Cinco siglos de crónicas, crítica y documentos (1521–2002)*, vol. 2 of *La danza en México: Visiones de cinco siglos* (Mexico: Consejo Nacional para la Cultura y las Artes, 2002), 119–20.

42. Maya Ramos Smith, *La danza en México durante la época colonial* (Havana: Casa de las Américas, 1979), 46.

43. Quoted by Herrejón Peredo, *Hidalgo*, 162.

44. Quoted by Herrejón Peredo, *Hidalgo*, 162–63.

45. Herrejón Peredo, *Hidalgo*, 35, 49, 115.

46. Eric Van Young, "Agustín Marroquín: The Sociopath as Rebel," in *The Human Tradition in Latin America: The Nineteenth Century*, ed. Judith Ewell and William H. Beezley (Wilmington: SR Books, 1989), 17–38.

47. Van Young, "Agustín Marroquín," 20.

48. Herrejón Peredo, *Hidalgo*, 411–14, 453–54; José Ramírez Flores, *El gobierno insurgente en Guadalajara, 1810–1811* (Guadalajara: Gobierno de Jalisco, Secretaría General, Unidad Editorial, 1980), 107; Van Young, "Agustín Marroquín," 35; Pompa y Pompa, *Procesos inquisitorial y militar*, 234–46.

49. Quoted by Herrejón Peredo, *Hidalgo*, 326–27.

50. Herrejón Peredo, *Hidalgo*, 319, 326–38.

51. Herrejón Peredo, *Hidalgo*, 348–49.

52. Herrejón Peredo, *Hidalgo*, 353–98.

53. Herrejón Peredo, *Hidalgo*, 411–14. A month after Hidalgo left, as a royalist army approached the Valladolid, a mob attempted to murder the remaining Spaniards, but they were not entirely successful. Clergy were able to protect most of these men, and only three were killed.

54. Herrejón Peredo, *Hidalgo*, 480–503.

55. Pompa y Pompa, *Procesos inquisitorial y militar*, 219 (for Abella quotation), 234–36 (for Hidalgo's answer on the murders), 218–48 (for all the questions and answers); Herrejón Peredo, *Hidalgo*, 506–7.

56. Herrejón Peredo, *Hidalgo*, 505–26, with quotation on 523.

57. Herrejón Peredo, *Hidalgo*, 517–26, with quotation on 526. The dispute between Salcedo and the Inquisition continued even after Hidalgo was executed. See Lea, "Hidalgo and Morelos."

58. Herrejón Peredo, *Hidalgo*, 527, 530.

59. Herrejón Peredo, *Hidalgo*, 530; William H. Beezley and David E. Lorey, eds., *¡Viva México! ¡Viva la Independencia! Celebrations of September 16* (Wilmington: SR Books, 2001); Richard Warren, "Bell of Dolores," in *Iconic Mexico*, ed. Eric Zolov (Santa Barbara: ABC-CLIO, 2015), 40–45.

Chapter 5

Passion and Patriarchy in Nineteenth-Century Argentina

María Luisa Bemberg's Camila

Donald F. Stevens

Camila *(1984); produced by Lita Stantic; directed by María Luisa Bemberg; written by María Luisa Bemberg, Beda Docampo Feijoo, and Juan Bautista Stagnaro; color; 105 minutes; GEA Cinematográfica. In nineteenth-century Argentina, Camila O'Gorman (Susu Pecoraro), the strong-willed and romantic daughter in a prominent and wealthy family, shocks her father (Héctor Alterio), the Church, and the government by eloping with a priest (Imanol Arias).*

María Luisa Bemberg's feature film *Camila* is a vivid and provocative introduction to nineteenth-century Argentine history. Based on the true story of Camila O'Gorman, a young woman from a wealthy family who eloped with a Catholic priest named Ladislao Gutiérrez, the film is both a splendid evocation and a pointed criticism of Argentine culture during the Federalist dictatorship of Juan Manuel de Rosas (1829–1852). Intense internecine conflicts between Unitarians and Federalists provide the background for a brilliant illustration of the connections between patriarchal power in the family, the state, and the Church. Bemberg's film is faithful to the style of the period in many of its details as it brings a feminist perspective to the struggle between patriarchy and passion.

Bemberg's denunciation of terrorism and patriarchal authority resonated strongly with an Argentine population just emerging from the brutal tyranny of a military dictatorship. *Camila* was a sensational success, attracting some of the largest audiences in the history of Argentine cinema.[1] It achieved international acclaim as well, including an Oscar nomination for best foreign film.

MARÍA LUISA BEMBERG

Unlike most newly acclaimed filmmakers, Bemberg was neither male nor relatively young; *Camila* was released when she was sixty-two years old. Born into a wealthy Argentine family descended from nineteenth-century German Catholic immigrants, young María Luisa was raised in material comfort but suffered the constraints of social propriety and intellectual stultification. Married at the age of twenty, she gave birth to four children before separating from her husband ten years later. Although divorce was not legal in Argentina at that time, Bemberg was able to reclaim her own name and raise her children with the cooperation of her husband. She found an understanding of her situation in feminist literature, particularly the works of Betty Friedan and Simone de Beauvoir, but her efforts to form feminist groups were stifled by a series of military governments.[2]

Bemberg waited until she had finished raising her children before she turned her attention to making films. Then, she began with a clear vision. She knew that she must tell women's stories from their own point of view, "a bit like a promise to my own gender," in her words. The year she turned fifty, Bemberg directed her first film, a documentary entitled *El Mundo de Mujeres*, and wrote her first feature-length script. Having burst the bounds of traditional family roles, she continued to face the constraints of censorship by the military governments of the 1970s as she developed her craft with a series of scripts and films.[3]

Bemberg's feminism and her focus on Camila as the protagonist provide a distinct perspective. "If a man had directed 'Camila,' I'm sure it would have been a story of a gentle innocent seduced by a libertine priest. My story is about a passionate woman's intellectual and sexual seduction of a man she found morally desirable," she said. In Bemberg's version of the story, Camila is an assertive woman who knows what she wants: passionate love for a man she can be proud of, even if that means defying her father and social conventions. As Bemberg explained, "Camila was a transgressor, she broke the received pattern of Argentine, not to mention feminine, decorum. Not only did she enjoy a love affair with her priest, but her actions fought the paternalistic order—another triangle of family, church and state."[4]

As it happened, Bemberg's own family opposed her plans to film Camila's story, but they could not stop her. In fact, it was her inheritance that made it possible for her to make movies. Bemberg began filming *Camila* (based on a script that she had cowritten) on the day after Raul Alfonsín took power as Argentina's first democratically elected president in eight years. Fortunately for Bemberg, one of Alfonsín's first actions was to eliminate state censorship. Bemberg believed that the previous military regime would never have permitted her to make this film because of opposition from the Catholic Church. In 1912, a short film had been made about the affair of Camila and Ladislao, but every director since then had been forbidden to tell their story.[5]

In the absence of official censorship, the Church could create obstacles, such as preventing Bemberg from using a particular sanctuary she preferred, but ecclesiastical authority was no longer able to block the project. Bemberg's own internalized intellectual restraints had a larger effect on the film. Despite her feminism and the breakup of her marriage, Bemberg had not abandoned Roman Catholicism. She believed it helped her with the Church that in her version of the story, the priest was the pure one, seduced by the romantic Camila. Before she began filming, she voluntarily showed her script to her confessor, who found it acceptable.[6]

Bemberg filmed *Camila* in what she acknowledged to be "a highly romantic style," the better to affect audiences emotionally and viscerally. "Melodrama is a very tricky genre, because at any minute it can turn into something sentimental, which I detest. So it had all those little tricks, such as the handkerchief, the gold coin, the priest who's sick with love, and the thunder when God gets angry. They're all like winks at the audience."[7] When Camila first touches Ladislao during a game of blindman's buff, three dowagers shake their heads in disapproval, a foreshadowing of the social condemnation that will confront their more intimate relationship later. The next time they touch, when Ladislao has succumbed to one of those Bronte-esque fevers that used to result from forbidden passions in romantic novels, Camila is shocked by his carnality.

Vincent Canby described the film as "austere and unsentimental" and recognized that it used "the gestures and mannerisms of romantic fiction for distinctly unromantic ends." Some reviewers, particularly those from conservative perspectives in the *Chicago Tribune*, the *Washington Post*, and the *National Review*, did not recognize her irony and took these allusions for cliches. John Simon, in his generally critical review, recognized that he was limited by his lack of historical perspective. How far did Bemberg's film go beyond what Simon called "mere factual reportage"?[8] What do we really know about the historical Camila O'Gorman?

THE O'GORMAN FAMILY

The film begins with the arrival of Camila's lovesick and demented grandmother, who had been condemned to house arrest.[9] Ana María Perichón de

Figure 5.1: Camila O'Gorman (Susu Pecoraro) first touches Father Ladislao Gutíerrez (Imanol Arías). (Photofest)

Vandeuil had been born on the island of Mauritius in the South Indian Ocean when it was a French possession, known as Île de France. There she met and married Camila's grandfather, Thomas O'Gorman, a native of Ireland, born in county Clare.[10] Camila's father was their first child, born on Mauritius about 1792. A few years later, the government of revolutionary France declared the abolition of slavery. When the official decree arrived in Mauritius in June 1796, an armed crowd confronted the representatives of the French government and forced them to return to Europe without announcing the end of slavery.[11] Camila's grandfather and his father-in-law decided it was time to leave Mauritius for Spanish territory. The family arrived in Montevideo in 1797 on a ship they owned along with twenty-nine enslaved persons. A few months later, they settled in Buenos Aires. In his petition for naturalization, Thomas O'Gorman announced his intention to buy and sell enslaved people since he had "his own ship to go to look for them on the coasts of Africa." Thomas O'Gorman did not limit himself to the market in the Rio de la Plata region; he sold people in Chile and Peru and as far away as Cuba and the United States.[12]

Today, it may be difficult to imagine how important the slave trade was in colonial Buenos Aires and in the first half of the nineteenth century. After the 1850s, massive immigration from Europe changed the demography of the region, but at the end of the colonial period, Blacks made up almost a third of the city's population and about one fifth of them were free. Enslaved and free Blacks worked in many occupations, but they were especially prominent as artisans and household servants.[13]

In the years that followed, both of Camila's paternal grandparents behaved scandalously. When British troops invaded in 1806, the British commander, William Carr Beresford, confiscated 600,000 pesos from the viceregal treasury and used the money to pay Camila's grandfather to provide supplies to his troops. After Argentine militias forced the British to withdraw, Thomas O'Gorman went into exile, abandoning his wife and three children (the oldest of whom, Camila's father, Adolfo, was about fifteen years old at the time). Not long after that, Camila's grandmother began a notorious affair with Santiago de Liniers, the hero of resistance to the British invasion and later interim viceroy. As a result of the scandal, Liniers was eventually forced to send Camila's grandmother into exile in Rio de Janeiro. Liniers was executed in 1810 as a traitor for his resistance to Argentine independence from Spain.[14]

Adolfo O'Gorman y Perichón Vandeuil, Camila's father, married Joaquina Ximenes Pinto in 1818. Camila was the fifth of their six children, named (in order) Carlos, Carmen, Clara, Enrique, Camila, and Eduardo. The older sons, Carlos and Enrique, do not appear and are never mentioned in Bemberg's film. The brothers' absence may be sensed by historians who will wonder why an elite family would apparently send its only male heir, Eduardo, into the priesthood. Who would inherit the wealth that had been so diligently accumulated? Although the film portrays the patriarchal structure of society and the family, it ignores the role of this same power in planning the family's future by shaping the lives of sons as well as daughters. Choice of career was not an individual decision. Fathers and extended family, rather than children alone, made the crucial decisions about access to the family's accumulated capital and whether or not to pursue specialized training for a career in the military, medicine, law, or the Church. Surplus sons who might only weaken the family's patrimony were frequently sent into the priesthood, but rarely would the perpetual celibacy demanded of priests have been an acceptable option for a sole male heir. The patriarchal tradition required sons to carry on the family name.

LADISLAO GUTIÉRREZ

The same structure of patriarchal power would have shaped the career path of Ladislao Gutiérrez. Much less is known about his family background. Since no one has found his baptismal certificate, there is no certainty about the names of his parents or why he was given the name Ladislao. He is described in Bemberg's film as a nephew of the governor of Tucumán, Celedonio Gutiérrez. Historical evidence seems to indicate a closer connection: that

Figure 5.2: Camila reads love letters to her grandmother (Mona Maris). (Photofest)

he was Governor Gutiérrez's illegitimate child.[15] There is no doubt that the governor of Tucumán supported Ladislao, but even the legitimate sons of Argentina's wealthiest and most politically powerful families would have had limited options for a career. Older brothers would inherit the family's land and wealth. Younger sons might make a career of the military or the Church. Because the Gutiérrez family was well connected politically, we may assume that the decision was not Ladislao's alone. Might the preference for the Church over a career in the military indicate a passive and pensive, rather than an active and aggressive nature, or even an ethical opposition to killing, as Bemberg suggests? That question is hard to answer. Because the focus of dramatic and historical attention has always been on Camila, little has been published about Ladislao Gutiérrez and his family. Nevertheless, Ladislao's political connections certainly helped once the decision had been made. Ladislao arrived in Buenos Aires at the age of twenty-three with letters of introduction from his uncle to Governor Juan Manuel de Rosas, the bishop, and to prominent families such as the O'Gormans. He was sheltered for a time in the home of the secretary general of the curate, Dr. Felipe Elortondo y Palacios (who later, after the scandal broke, wrote a long, obsequious apology to Rosas explaining the reasons for and exact extent of his aid to the young priest).[16]

JUAN MANUEL DE ROSAS

Although Bemberg portrays Ladislao as a Jesuit, we know that he was certainly not a member of that order. Governor Rosas always had enjoyed great support from both the clerical hierarchy and the parish priests. Portraits of the governor adorned churches all over the province and were typically placed on the altar itself. Priests were outspoken in support of the "Holy Federal Cause" and denounced Rosas's foes as liberal enemies of religion. When Rosas invited the Society of Jesus to return to Argentina in 1836, some seventy years after they were expelled by Spanish monarch Charles III, he expected their support as well.

The Society of Jesus, however, had a different point of view. After their expulsion from the Spanish empire in 1767, the Jesuits had avoided political entanglements, but Rosas demanded that they demonstrate their support of his regime. He was first frustrated, then furious, to find that they insisted on remaining neutral. Although there is no evidence to support his accusations that the Jesuits were subversive or organizing treason, Rosas accused them of being pro-Unitarian on the grounds that they would not submit to the use of their schools and churches for pro-Federal propaganda. He decreed their expulsion from the Province of Buenos Aires in 1843 (years before Ladislao arrived in the city) and arranged with the governors of other provinces to expel them from all Argentine territory in the following years.[17] Although the cinematic Ladislao attracts the admiration of Bemberg's Camila with his courageous sermon attacking tyranny and asserting the love of God for all men, the situation is purely imaginary. Rosas would not have ignored an outspoken opponent of his regime. His hired assassins would have acted quickly on orders to silence such a person permanently.

CAMILA AND LADISLAO

The courtship of Camila and Ladislao probably took a more conventional course. Camila later described how Ladislao had taken his priestly vows against his own will and that in their view, these vows were invalid as a result. Given that society would not allow them to marry, Ladislao told her, he would take Camila for his partner before God. He visited her every day, gave her gifts, and accompanied her on horseback rides through the forest of Palermo, near Rosas's palace. Camila began spending all her time in the parish church to be near him. "If something was whispered about what the public or the neighbors presumed about this association, no one dared to denounce their relationship as a fact nor was an accusation of dishonor made."[18]

Camila and Ladislao chose to flee on the night of December 12–13, 1847, at the beginning of the Argentine summer. We do not know what was on her mind, but there is circumstantial evidence. Her beloved grandmother had died that month; her father was absent from the city, working on his estancia; and Camila was pregnant. All of the documentation makes it clear that Camila and Ladislao fled on horseback that night. They rode west to Luján before heading north to Rosario, where they arrived at the end of December. There Camila suffered a miscarriage. They remained in Rosario for several weeks until she was well enough to travel again, then they continued north. They ended their flight in the middle of February, in the city of Goya, about nine hundred kilometers north of Buenos Aires. Ladislao, using the name Máximo Brandier, opened a primary school. Camila called herself Valentina Sanz. Four months later, in June, they were recognized by an Irish priest named Michael Gannon. Camila and Ladislao were arrested and held there in Goya for more than a month before they were sent to Buenos Aires, a trip that took twenty-seven days.[19]

Antonino Reyes, who was in charge of the military prison at Santos Lugares, tells us that when Camila and Ladislao arrived there, she appeared worn and disheveled but spoke with ease and simplicity. She announced immediately that she was ill and needed a doctor. Uncovering and distending her abdomen, she said, "Can't you see my condition?" She asked for food but not the meals that were prepared for prisoners. Reyes promised to give her the same food that was served to him. She asked what the governor would do and if he was very angry. She mentioned her friendship with Rosas's daughter, Manuelita. Reyes advised her not to repeat to anyone else what she had told him about the course of the courtship. He recommended that while maintaining this discreet silence, Camila should rely on the reputation of her sex for weakness and she should beg Rosas for clemency. Clearly, Reyes believed during the course of his interview with Camila that she was not telling him a story or displaying the appropriate sort of feminine subordination that was likely to save her life.[20]

Camila's character showed in another way as well. Reyes was reluctant to carry out his orders to keep Camila and Ladislao shackled. He looked for the lightest leg irons in the prison and lined them with cloth before complying. Camila accepted her chains, indicating with assurance and affection tinged with a certain defiance that she would endure that punishment with pleasure, the more so since Ladislao was shackled too.[21] It is important to remember that Camila told these things to her jailer. She was not trying to reduce her responsibility or mitigate the circumstances. Bemberg portrays Camila as strong-willed and romantic, the instigator of the romance, rather than Ladislao's pliable victim. Historical evidence indicates that Bemberg was right.[22]

Camila does appear to have been willful and a true romantic in love with Ladislao. Does this mean that her father was vindictive? Bemberg portrays him as what one reviewer called the original "Pampas ass."[23] In one of the film's first scenes, Camila worries that her father will kill the litter of new kittens she has found, and he does. He keeps his own mother imprisoned in a tower and tries to prevent Camila from visiting her. When Camila and Ladislao flee, Eduardo finds his father in the countryside in gaucho costume supervising the decapitation and evisceration of cattle. Adolfo reacts violently to the news, striking his son. On returning to Buenos Aires, he immediately writes to the governor, denouncing their flight as "the most atrocious act ever heard of in this country." This phrase is a direct quotation from a letter that Camila's father actually wrote to Rosas in the days after the lovers had fled from Buenos Aires.[24] (See text at end of chapter.)

When read carefully, though, a different Adolfo O'Gorman emerges from between the lines, a more appropriate paterfamilias who was less menacing and more sympathetic to Camila. His letter shows Adolfo to be a father attempting to salvage his daughter's and if possible, his own reputation. He would not have regarded these objectives as separable. He could not uphold his family's honor without rescuing his daughter.

The letter is dated December 21, 1847, nine days after Camila and Ladislao disappeared. Even if he was not told that Camila was missing for the first four days (until December 16, as he says in the second paragraph) because he was away on his estancia, Adolfo still waited another five days before informing the authorities. No doubt, he hoped that his daughter would return or could be found and that the matter could be hushed up. In the absence of public scandal, his family's reputation would remain intact. Apparently, it was not possible to maintain secrecy. Julio Llanos, who was among the first to publish many of the letters that the film quotes, suggests that Adolfo only wrote his letter after the governor had already learned of the scandal from his own daughter, Manuelita.[25] It is also possible that the news spread from the family's servants. Bemberg portrays the household staff as stereotypically ignorant but affectionate and loyal flunkies. In contrast, the historian John Lynch reports that Rosas was popular among the large population of Afro-Argentines (many of whom were domestic servants) and that the governor encouraged them to spy on their masters for him.[26]

In his letter, Adolfo clearly denounced Ladislao as the perpetrator of a crime against his daughter and his family. He describes the priest's infraction as the seduction of his daughter "under the guise of religion." Ladislao "stole her away." All of his sentences accuse Ladislao alone, referring to "the preparations he has made," "he is heading inland," "he will cross into Bolivia," "he will not feel secure in the Argentine Republic." Adolfo portrays his daughter as a passive victim and fears that she will grow to accept her captivity. He asks Rosas to send out descriptions of the pair "in every direction to prevent that this poor wretch finds herself reduced to despair, and, understanding that she is lost, she may rush headlong into infamy."

Adolfo keeps Ladislao at a distance, referring to him as "the male individual." He describes his daughter as "the girl" and refers to her as "my youngest daughter," but it is significant that he never divulges her name. In writing about the fugitive lovers in this way, Adolfo was suggesting that his daughter's and family's name could be kept from the public, that Camila could return home without public humiliation. He wrote, as one father to another, with the expectation that Rosas would be able to remedy the situation. Still hoping that the case might be kept from public knowledge, he describes his family as submerged in desolation and joined in begging Rosas to protect them. Adolfo O'Gorman was fulfilling his role as a familial patriarch. As the head of his family, O'Gorman should have protected his daughter from Ladislao. When he failed, O'Gorman appealed to the more powerful father figure, Governor Rosas, to protect both his daughter and family. Camila's father described her as a passive victim, although he must have known better, but he did not denounce or condemn her.

Bemberg also incorporates into her script phrases from a letter written a few days later by Mariano Medrano y Cabrera, the bishop of Buenos Aires. Unlike Adolfo O'Gorman, the bishop did condemn both Ladislao and Camila as *"miserables, desgraciados, y infelices."* The bishop also specifically named Ladislao Gutiérrez, and like Camila's father, he did not divulge her identity, referring to her only as "a young woman from a distinguished family."[27]

If Adolfo had hoped to avoid a public scandal, he was severely disappointed. The descriptions that Rosas sent to all corners of the Argentine Republic contained not only physical descriptions of the fugitives but both of their real names as well. By deliberately publicizing their identities, Rosas advertised the disgrace of the O'Gorman family. Adolfo must have felt the rejection of his private plea as the public repudiation that Rosas intended it to be. It was Rosas who ensured the dishonor of his family, not Camila and Ladislao's actions or Adolfo's letter alone.

It was not until after Rosas publicly divulged the scandal that his enemies used it to attack him. Valentín Alsina, an Argentine exiled in Montevideo, Uruguay, for his opposition to the Rosas dictatorship, published reports in his newspaper, *El Comercio de la Plata*, which brought the scandal international attention. His paper claimed that the Church was distressed only because Canonigo Palacios had loaned an ounce of gold to Ladislao, which he had used to finance their escape. *El Comercio* denounced Rosas for making light of the situation. At Rosas's home at Palermo, "they speak of all this as something amusing, since there they use a free federal language." Meanwhile, *El Comercio* reported that a nephew of Rosas had attempted to follow Ladislao's lead by kidnapping a young woman from another family but he had been prevented in time. The lessons learned at Palermo could not be otherwise, *El Comercio* claimed in a thinly veiled reference to Rosas's mistress, because "the examples seen there and the conversations heard there can bear no other fruits."[28] These examples demonstrate how the flight of Camila and Ladislao was interpreted as a scandal within the traditional patriarchal framework; that is, Alsina and the others did not assert the rights of children to pursue relationships based on their emotions. Rather, they castigated Rosas for his failure to control his subordinates, both in his own family and in the larger society.

As early as January 4, 1848, *El Comercio* denounced the crime of Ladislao in these words: "Is there on earth a sufficiently severe punishment for a man who behaves this way with a woman whose dishonor he cannot repair by marrying her?"[29] Clearly, if Ladislao were not a priest and were able to marry Camila, her family would suffer no disgrace. Ann Twinam has examined hundreds of cases where illicit sexual relations and even pregnancy out of wedlock could be prevented from damaging a family's honor as long as the circumstances were kept from public knowledge.[30] In the understanding of the time, Camila and her family were both victims of a crime perpetrated by the degenerate priest, Ladislao Gutiérrez. Adolfo O'Gorman had failed to protect his daughter. The Church had failed to control its priest. Rosas had failed to prevent the breakdown of hierarchy and subordination. The patriarchal system was exposed as a failure. Within this system, Ladislao's crime is clear enough, but what about Camila? How did she come to be executed as well? Manuel Bilbao concluded, "For Rosas, the true crime of Gutiérrez and Camila was to have mocked his authority, and to have appeared to defy him in the eyes of society."[31]

In the Province of Buenos Aires, Rosas's word was law. There was no other authority, no balance of power, no source of appeal. In 1835, the provincial House of Representatives had voted to give Rosas unlimited power to make and enforce order for a term of five years. He preferred to maintain a pretense of constitutionalism and periodically offered his resignation, but it was only a charade. Woe to anyone who might consider accepting his offer to resign! His minions in the legislature repeatedly begged him to extend his term of unlimited power. Rosas was seriously challenged only during a brief period in 1839–1840 when he used his control of the military and organized bands of assassins to murder anyone who appeared to question his authority. During the rest of his tenure as governor of the Province of Buenos Aires, Rosas used terror more sparingly. He manipulated the House of Representatives, controlled the bureaucracy, and dominated the judiciary. He took a personal interest in a variety of cases, personally examining the evidence and making judgments himself. Lynch describes Rosas as sitting alone at his desk "writing on the files 'shoot him,' 'fine him,' 'imprison him,' 'to the army.'"[32]

The political justification for Rosas's power was classically Hobbesian. Anarchy was the only alternative; only a savage would oppose "The Restorer of Laws." Rosas used symbols and language to terrorize and control the population. It was not enough to accept his rule; everyone had to be an enthusiastic supporter. Rosas demanded obvious and increasing displays of subordination. At first, he revived the use of the heading "Viva la federación" at the top of all official documents. In 1842, he ordered it to be changed to "¡Viva la Confederación Argentina!" and added the more bloodthirsty "Death to the Savage Unitarians!" The slogan was repeated constantly. Night watchmen called out "Death to the savage Unitarians!" before announcing the time each half hour. Supporters tried to outdo one another in their ferocious denunciations of their enemies. Lynch quotes this example from a joint decree of a justice of the peace and a priest: "Stupid fools, the angry people will hunt you through the streets, in your houses and in the fields; they will cut you down by the necks and [make] a deep pool of your blood for patriots to bathe in and cool their rage."[33]

Rosas restored the red emblem as "a sign of fidelity to the cause of order, tranquility and well-being among the people of this land under the Federal system, as a proof and public acknowledgment of the triumph of this sacred cause in the whole republic and a mark of confraternity between Argentines."[34] The governor initially demanded that persons in certain specific occupations and positions wear a red emblem bearing the words "Federation or Death" on the left side of their chests, over their hearts. Included among them were militia and army officers; everyone who received a salary from public funds whether government officials, laymen or priests, professors or students, and practitioners of law or medicine; and finally, "all those who even though they do not receive a salary from the state are regarded as public servants."[35] Eventually everyone was expected to conform, and the Federalist style was extended to other aspects of their appearance. Women as well began to pin the red emblem on their dresses and used only red ribbons in their hair. Men wore red hatbands, waistcoats and jackets, long sideburns, and mustaches. The wrong sort of facial hair was sufficient evidence of political unreliability. One wonders whether Adolfo O'Gorman's description of Ladislao Gutiérrez as having a full beard might bear this sort of symbolic weight. Houses, doors, and furnishings were red. Pale blue and green virtually disappeared from Buenos Aires. This chromatic conformity was not voluntary. It was enforced by gangs of thugs who broke into private homes to destroy property in the offending colors.[36]

Rosas permitted nothing less than complete deference and obedience. As Lynch put it, "'Subordination' was his favorite word, authority his ideal, order his achievement."[37] Exemplary punishment could be meted out to those who defied him. When, in the film, the severed head of Mariano the bookseller appears on the fence outside the parish church, the fiancé of Camila's sister Clara repeats a saying attributed to Rosas that twenty drops of blood shed at the proper moment may prevent the need to spill twenty thousand more. These were Rosas's sentiments.[38] The executions of Camila and Ladislao were meant to warn others not to keep secrets from him, not to doubt patriarchal authority, and not to accept passion as an acceptable guide to choosing a mate. It was a struggle to control children that even in Rosas's own time was being lost.[39]

Bemberg's film insinuates that all patriarchs were, like Rosas, monstrous. The governor remains in the shadows in the film, behind the omnipresent portraits, the universal red ribbons, and the pervasive atmosphere of menace and terror. His flesh may be absent, but his spirit inhabits the body of Camila's father. Later in the film, Adolfo is confronted by his wife and son, who beg him to intercede with Rosas to save his daughter's life. He refuses. He replies bitterly that a daughter who betrays her father does not deserve forgiveness. He is certain that she is not repentant. We have no way of knowing whether this conversation or another like it ever took place.[40] Many people were horrified by what they perceived as a grave injustice, and the execution of Camila played a role in undermining support for the Rosas dictatorship. Even loyal followers such as Antonino Reyes, the jailer who continued to support Rosas even after he was overthrown, regarded the executions as a terrible mistake.

Although Camila told her jailer, Antonino Reyes, that she was a friend of Rosas's own daughter, Manuelita, historians are skeptical. Certainly, they were not close friends. Even forty years later, Manuelita never expressed any remorse about Camila's death.[41] Nevertheless, Manuelita did in fact enjoy a reputation as the "last hope of the unfortunate." Reyes did write a last-minute letter to Manuelita trying to save Camila's life, but Rosas replied that the execution should be carried out the following morning. In addition, he demanded that the prison be surrounded by armed guards and that no one be allowed to enter or leave until the sentence had been carried out. These extraordinary orders indicate that Rosas expected some difficulty in ensuring that the executions would take place in a timely manner.[42] Rosas later claimed, "No one advised me to execute the priest Gutiérrez and Camila O'Gorman, nor did anyone speak to me on their behalf." This assertion was clearly not the case. Rosas contradicted himself in the next sentence, with the admission, "On the contrary, all the leading members of the clergy spoke or wrote to me about this insolent crime and the urgent necessity to make an exemplary punishment to prevent similar scandals in the future."[43]

The Unitarians and other enemies of the dictatorship had taken advantage of the scandal early in 1848, publicly attempting to humiliate Rosas while demanding exemplary punishment for Ladislao Gutiérrez. Later in that year, when the news came that both Camila and Ladislao had been executed, they continued to propagandize against Rosas, claiming that Camila was eight months pregnant and that she had nearly drowned after being forced to drink large amounts of water in a sadistic ritual that they called a "federalist baptism."[44] The question of whether or not Camila was pregnant when she was executed is so thoroughly enveloped in the propaganda against Rosas that we may never be certain. We know that Reyes did not immediately observe that Camila was pregnant but he was nevertheless willing to assert that she was, in his vain attempt to save her life. Certainly, no one who actually saw Camila ever said that she was eight months pregnant, as some reports claimed.[45]

Accounts also differ on whether the firing squad took one volley or more to kill Camila and Ladislao. Reyes, who could not bring himself to supervise their executions in person, recorded that he had the pair buried in a single coffin, with the explanation that their relatives one day might wish to claim their bodies.[46] This statement might appear puzzling until we understand that sequestering the bodies of his enemies after he had had them executed was standard operating procedure for Rosas. He wanted to prolong the suffering of the families of those who had opposed him. (Argentine families who had had their relatives "disappeared" during the military rule in the 1970s certainly understood that anguish.) It was not until Rosas had been defeated and exiled that her brothers were able to retrieve Camila's body from Rosa's estate.[47]

The ending is not a happy one for modern audiences: traditional family values of patriarchal authority and dependent submission triumph over the romantic, utopian family based on mutual affection and individual choice. Bemberg's Camila is a courageous, romantic woman whose defiance of social conventions provokes the vicious retribution of patriarchal authorities, but the film is only one of many interpretations. The existing documentation and literary works based on their stories provide various and often disparate solutions to the multitude of endlessly fascinating questions provoked by the lives of Ladislao Gutiérrez and Camila O'Gorman.

DOCUMENT

LETTER FROM ADOLFO O'GORMAN TO JUAN MANUEL DE ROSAS[48]

VIVA LA CONFEDERACIÓN ARGENTINA!
MUERAN LOS SALVAJES UNITARIOS.

Buenos Aires on 21 December 1847.

Most Excellent Señor:

I take the liberty of addressing Your Excellency by means of this letter, to raise to your Superior understanding the most atrocious act ever heard of in this country; and convinced of Your Excellency's rectitude, I find a consolation in sharing with you the desolation in which all the family is submerged.

Most Excellent Señor, Monday the sixteenth of the current month I was advised at La Matanza (where I reside) that my youngest daughter had disappeared; I instantly returned and have learned that a clergyman from Tucumán named Ladislao Gutiérrez had seduced her under the guise of religion, and stole her away, abandoning the parish on the twelfth of this month, letting it be understood that in the evening he needed to go to Quilmes.

Most Excellent Señor, the preparations he has made indicate that he is heading inland, and I have no doubt he will cross into Bolivia, if possible, since the wound that this act has caused is mortal for my unfortunate family, and the clergy in general; consequently, he will not feel secure in the Argentine Republic. Thus, Señor, I beg Your Excellency to send orders in every direction to prevent that this poor wretch finds herself reduced to despair, and, understanding that she is lost, she may rush headlong into infamy.

Most Excellent Señor, that my presumptuous letter may find you at Lujan, and the state of affliction in which I find myself, both compel me to bring to the attention of Your Excellency these descriptions of the fugitives. The male individual is of average height, thin of body, moreno in color, large brown eyes that bulge somewhat, curly black hair, a full but short beard of twelve to fifteen days; he has two woven ponchos, one black and the other dark with red stripes, he has used them to cover pistols in his saddlebags. The girl is very tall, dark eyes, white skin, chestnut hair, thin of body, and has a front tooth that sticks out a bit.

Most Excellent Señor, deign to overlook the style of this letter. Your Excellency is a father and the only one capable of remediating a case of transcendental importance for all of my family, if this becomes public knowledge. All of them add their pleas to mine, to implore the protection of Your Excellency whose humble servant is

Adolfo O'Gorman.

ADDITIONAL RESOURCES

On Argentine Politics and Society

Andrews, George Reid. *The Afro-Argentines of Buenos Aires, 1800–1900.* Madison: University of Wisconsin Press, 1980.

Halperín Donghi, Tulio. *De la Revolución de independencia a la Confederación rosista.* Buenos Aires: Editorial Paidós, 2000. A history of the period by one of Argentina's great historians.

Lynch, John. *Argentine Dictator: Juan Manuel de Rosas, 1829–1852.* Oxford: Clarendon Press, 1981. The essential biography of Rosas by a distinguished historian.

Sarmiento, Domingo Faustino. *Life in the Argentine Republic in the Days of the Tyrants, or, Civilization and Barbarism.* New York: Gordon Press, 1976. English translation of the classic indictment of gaucho culture and Federalist caudillo Juan Facundo Quiroga and by implication, of Rosas himself. Originally published in Spanish in 1845 as *Facundo.*

Scobie, James R. *Argentina: A City and a Nation.* New York. Oxford University Press, 1978. The classic introduction to Argentine history in English.Shumway, Jeffrey M. *The Case of the Ugly Suitor and Other Histories of Love, Gender, and Nation in Buenos Aires, 1776–1870.* Lincoln: University of Nebraska Press, 2005. Family conflicts in historical context.

Shumway, Nicolas. *The Invention of Argentina.* Berkeley: University of California Press, 1991. Examines the intellectual development of the "guiding fictions" of Argentine nationalism with particular attention to the opposition to Rosas.

Szuchman, Mark D. "A Challenge to the Patriarchs: Love among the Youth in Nineteenth-Century Argentina." In *The Middle Period in Latin America: Values and Attitudes in the 18th-19th Centuries*, ed. Mark D. Szuchman, 141–65. Boulder, CO: Lynne Rienner Publishers, 1989. Lawsuits over choice of marriage partners demonstrate that parents were losing control over their children.

Historical, Literary, and Polemical Works on Camila O'Gorman

Ascasubi, Hilario. *Trobas y lamentos de Donato Jurao, soldado argentino, a la muerte de la infeliz Da. Camila Ogorman [sic] que en compañía del desgraciado Cura Gutiérrez fueron ferozmente asesinados en Buenos Aires por el cobarde carnicero Juan Manuel Rosas titulado Gefe Supremo*. Uruguay: Impreta del Colejio, 1851(?).

Calvera, Leonor. *Camila O'Gorman, o, El amor y el poder*. Buenos Aires: Editorial Leviatan, 1986.

Espejo, Miguel. *Senderos en el viento*. Puebla, Pue., Mexico: Universidad Autónoma de Puebla, ICUAP, 1985.

Fajardo, Heraclio C. *Camila O'Gorman: Drama histórico en seis cuadros y en verso*. Buenos Aires: Imprenta Americana, 1856.

Gorriti, Juana Manuela. "Camila O'Gorman." In *Obras completas*. 4 vols. Salta, Argentina: Fundación del Banco del Noroeste, 1992, 2: 183–90. First published 1865.

Helguera, Luis Ignacio. *Camila y Uladislao: Tragedia en tres actos*. Buenos Aires: Ediciones Amaru, 1991.

Imbert, Julio. *Camila O'Gorman: Tragedia*. Buenos Aires: Talia, 1968.

Kisnerman, Natalio. *Camila O'Gorman: El hecho histórico y su proyección literaria*. Buenos Aires: Universidad de Buenos Aires, Instituto de Literatura Argentina "Ricardo Rojas," 1973.

Llanos, Julio. *Camila O'Gorman*. Buenos Aires: La Patria Argentina, 1883.

Mazzucchelli, Victor Hugo. *Se llamaba Camila y estaba encinta*. Buenos Aires: Ediciones "Mirtgradan," 1972.

Mendoza Ortiz, L. *Camila O'Gorman: Drama histórico, arreglado de la novela de Gutiérrez, del mismo titulo: En 5 actos y en verso*. Barracas al Sud (Avellaneda, Argentina): Imprenta El Censor, n.d.

Méndez Avellaneda, Juan N. *Camila: La antihistoria: Asesinato por partida triple*. Buenos Aires: Editorial Armerias, 2019.

Molina, Enrique. *Una sombra donde sueña Camila O'Gorman*. Buenos Aires: Editorial Losada, 1973.

Olivera, Miguel Alfredo. *Camila O'Gorman, Una tragedia argentina*. Buenos Aires: Emece, 19 59.

Pelissot, Felisberto. *Camila O'Gorman*. Buenos Aires: Las Artes, 1857.

Siri, Eros Nicola. *Rosas y el proceso de Camila O'Gorman (su responsibilidad de gobernante)*. Buenos Aires: N.p., 1939.

White, Anibal. *Camila O'Gorman: Drama histórico mas para ser leido, en tres actos y en verso, de la época de Juan Manuel de Rosas*. Buenos Aires: N.p., 1969.

NOTES

1. More than two million people saw the film in Argentina alone, by far the largest audience of any Argentine film of the 1980s. See Alberto Ciria, *Más allá de la*

pantalla: Cine argentino, historia y política (Buenos Aires: Ediciones de la Flor, 1995), 192.

2. Caleb Bach, "María Luisa Bemberg Tells the Untold: Interview," *Américas* 46, no. 2 (March 1994): 20–27; Carrie Rickey, "'Camila': Argentina's Forbidden Story," *New York Times,* April 7, 1985.

3. Bach, "Bemberg," 22–23.

4. Quoted in Rickey, "'Camila.'"

5. "If I had not my own money I never would have made movies," as quoted in her obituary in *The Times* (London), May 19, 1995; Rickey, "'Camila;'" Estela Dos Santos, *El cine nacional* (Buenos Aires: Centro Editor de America Latina, 1971), 13.

6. Kevin Thomas, "'Camila': Argentina's Star-Crossed Lovers," *Los Angeles Times,* April 25, 1985; "María Luisa Bemberg," *The Times* (London), May 19, 1995.

7. "Pride and Prejudice: María Luisa Bemberg," interview by Sheila Whitaker in *The Garden of Forking Paths: Argentine Cinema,* ed. John King and Nissa Torrents (London: British Film Institute, 1988), 117.

8. Vincent Canby, "'Camila': Story of Love in Argentina," *New York Times,* March 15, 1985; David Beard, "New Vitality in Argentina's Film Industry," *Chicago Tribune,* July 12, 1985; Paul Attanasio, "Doomed 'Camila,'" *Washington Post,* May 3, 1985; John Simon, "Moving Picture Reviews," *National Review,* May 17, 1985.

9. The grandmother, known as "La Perichona," is played by Mona Maris, an Argentine star of fifty-eight Latin American, European, and Hollywood films from the 1920s to the 1940s. Bradley Graham, "In Argentina, Cinema's Time to Shine: After Censorship, a Filmmaking Boom," *Washington Post,* May 4, 1986.

10. An earlier version of this chapter misstated the name and occupation of Camila's grandfather, following Manuel de Vizoso Gorostiaga, *Camila O'Gorman y su epoca, La tragedia mas dolorosa ocurrida durante el gobierno del "Restaurador de las Leyes" estudiada a base de documentación y con opiniones de sus contemporaneos* (Santa Fe, Argentina: Talleres Gráficos Castellvi, 1943), who confused Camila's grandfather Thomas O'Gorman with Michael O'Gorman, an Irish medical doctor who was also living in Buenos Aires and seems to have been a relative of her grandfather.

11. Claude Wanquet, *La France et la première abolition de l'esclavage 1792–1801. Le cas des colonies orientales Île de France (Maurice) et la Réunion* (Paris: Karthala, 1998), 308.

12. Héctor Daniel de Arriba, *Enrique O'Gorman: El policia hermano de Camila* (Buenos Aires: Editorial Dunken, 2017), 12, 17–19.

13. Slavery disappeared gradually between the end of the colonial period and the 1860s. George Reid Andrews, *The Afro-Argentines of Buenos Aires, 1800–1900* (Madison: University of Wisconsin Press, 1980), 4–6, 32, 48–57; Lyman Johnson, "Manumission in Colonial Buenos Aires," *Hispanic American Historical Review* 59, no. 2 (May 1979): 258–79.

14. Marcus de la Poer Beresford, *Marshall William Carr Beresford: 'The Ablest Man I Have Yet Seen in the Army'* (Newbridge, Ireland: Irish Academic Press, 2019), 13; Juan N. Méndez Avellaneda, *Camila: La antihistoria: Asesinato por partida triple* (Buenos Aires: Editorial Armerias, 2019), 10.

15. Héctor Daniel de Arriba, *Cuatro curas y una mujer: Camila O'Gorman* (Buenos Aires: Mis Escritos, 2014), 90–91; Méndez Avellaneda, *Camila*, 15. We do not know enough about the history of child-naming in Argentina, but it is interesting to note that Camila's older brother Carlos named a daughter María Ladislada, with her younger brother Eduardo as the padrino. The child was born on June 27, 1858 (St. Ladislao's day), and baptized in San Nicolás de Bari parish on September 2, 1858. On the history of naming practices in nineteenth-century Mexico, see Donald Fithian Stevens, *Mexico in the Time of Cholera* (Albuquerque: University of New Mexico Press, 2019), chapter 2, "Birthdays, Patron Saints, and Names for Newborns."

16. For a transcript of this letter, see Manuel Bilbao, ed., *Vindicación y memorias de Don Antonino Reyes* (Buenos Aires: Imprenta del "Porvenir," 1883), 348–53; or Natalia Kisnerman, *Camila O'Gorman: El hecho histórico y su proyección literaria* (Buenos Aires: Universidad de Buenos Aires, Instituto de Literatura Argentina "Ricardo Rojas," 1973), 14–17.

17. John Lynch, *Argentine Dictator: Juan Manuel de Rosas, 1829–1852* (Oxford: Clarendon Press, 1981), 185–86.

18. Bilbao, *Vindicación y memorias*, 345–46. This and all subsequent translations from the Spanish are mine.

19. Méndez Avellaneda, *Camila*, 47, 57–63; Arriba, *Cuatro curas*, 99; Héctor Daniel de Arriba, *Presbítero Miguel Gannon: ¿Culpable o inocente?* (Buenos Aires: Editorial Dunken, 2013), 83, 88.

20. Bilbao, *Vindicación y memorias*, 361–62.

21. Bilbao, *Vindicación y memorias*, 363.

22. See especially, Méndez Avellaneda, *Camila*, chapter 11: "El Tema de la Seducción," 81–87.

23. Attanasio, "Doomed 'Camila.'"

24. Transcriptions of the original appear in Julio Llanos, *Camila O'Gorman* (Buenos Aires: La Patria Argentina, 1883), 121; and Kisnerman, *Camila O'Gorman*, 5–6.

25. Llanos, *Camila*, 121.

26. Lynch, *Argentine Dictator*, 119–24. On the importance of Afro-Argentines to the economy of Buenos Aires, see George Reid Andrews, *The Afro-Argentines of Buenos Aires, 1800–1900* (Madison: University of Wisconsin Press, 1980).

27. See the transcript of this letter in Llanos, *Camila*, 122; or Kisnerman, *Camila O'Gorman*, 7–8.

28. Bilbao, *Vindicación y memorias*, 355–56.

29. Bemberg's script quotes this fragment but changes the chronology, moving it from shortly after the lovers fled Buenos Aires to eight months later, after the pair had been arrested and returned to Buenos Aires to await their punishment.

30. Ann Twinam, "Honor, Sexuality, and Illegitimacy in Colonial Spanish America," in *Sexuality and Marriage in Colonial Latin America*, ed. Asunción Lavrin (Lincoln: University of Nebraska Press, 1989), 118–55.

31. Bilbao, *Vindicación y memorias*, 357.

32. Lynch, *Argentine Dictator*, 169.

33. Lynch, *Argentine Dictator*, 178.

34. Lynch, *Argentine Dictator*, 177.

35. Lynch, *Argentine Dictator*, 179.

36. Lynch, *Argentine Dictator*, 177–79.

37. Lynch, *Argentine Dictator*, 125.

38. Lynch, *Argentine Dictator*, 179.

39. Mark D. Szuchman, "A Challenge to the Patriarchs: Love among the Youth in Nineteenth-Century Argentina," in *The Middle Period in Latin America: Values and Attitudes in the 18th-19th Centuries*, ed. Mark D. Szuchman (Boulder, CO: Lynne Rienner Publishers, 1989), 141–65. See also, Jeffrey M. Shumway, *The Case of the Ugly Suitor and Other Histories of Love, Gender, and Nation in Buenos Aires, 1776–1870*. Lincoln: University of Nebraska Press, 2005.

40. I am not aware of any documentation proving that Camila's father approved of her execution, although the accusation that he suggested it to Rosas appears in a number of works.

41. Méndez Avellaneda, *Camila*, 43–44, 92–93.

42. Bilbao, *Vindicación y memorias*, 364–66.

43. Lynch, *Argentine Dictator*, 240.

44. The story that Camila was eight months pregnant seems to have circulated at the time of her death in 1848. Juan Manuel Beruti recorded it in his diary, which was published as *Memorias curiosas*, in the series Senado de la Nación, *Biblioteca de Mayo* (Buenos Aires: Senado de la Nación, 1950), 4: 4076–77. One of the earliest published descriptions of Camila as eight months pregnant and the "federalist baptism" is Hilario Ascasubi, *Trobas y lamentos de Donato Jurao, soldado argentino, a la muerte de la infeliz Da. Camila Ogorman* [sic] *que en compañía del desgraciado Cura Gutiérrez fueron ferozmente asesinados en Buenos Aires por órden del famoso y cobarde carnicero Juan Manuel Rosas titulado Gefe Supremo* (Uruguay: Imprenta del Colejio, 1851[?]), 37, 39.

45. Héctor Daniel de Arriba, *Antonino Reyes: Edecán y carcelero de Rosas* (Buenos Aires: Editorial Dunken, 2016), 111, 116.

46. Bilbao, *Vindicación y memorias*, 367.

47. Arriba, *Antonino Reyes*, 116–18; Méndez Avellaneda, *Camila*, 24–26, 105.

48. Translated by Donald F. Stevens from the Spanish version published in Llanos, *Camila*, 271. The Spanish text also appears in Kisnerman, *Camila O'Gorman*, 5–6.

Chapter 6

In Search of a New Ecology

Ciro Guerra's Embrace of the Serpent in the Age of Climate Crisis

Daniel O. Mosquera

El abrazo de la serpiente (2015) *or* Embrace of the Serpent; *produced by Cristina Gallego; directed by Ciro Guerra; written by Ciro Guerra and Jacques Toulemonde; inspired by the travel accounts and photographs of a German ethnologist Theodor Koch-Grünberg and U.S. American ethnobotanist Richard Evans Schultes; photographed by David Gallego; various production companies and funds; black and white; 125 minutes.* El Abrazo de la serpiente *explores the relationship between an Amazonian healer believed to be the last survivor in his community and two Western explorers whom he encounters and with whom he journeys at different stages of his life over the course of just over three decades. Traveling this region of the Amazon in search of sanative resources while documenting through journals and taxonomies what they witness, the explorers assess their findings and seek restoration while learning of the indigenous healer's knowledge of the Amazon and of his own existential predicaments.*

In September 2019 and January 2020, there were two Amazon-related summits in South America bringing together the nations bordering the basin. The earlier took place in Colombia under the auspices of Iván Duque's government, and the latter was organized by the indigenous leaders and communities of the Brazilian region, as they responded to President Jair Bolsonaro's scornful assault on their and nature's tenuous dominion.[1] After unprecedented fires and subsequent deforestation threatening forest ecosystems in Brazil, Bolivia, Paraguay, and Peru were reported, a new sense of urgency seemed imminent regarding the Amazon's protection. Stupefying blaze images coming from California and joining this tragic repertoire in 2020 only heightened global fears of environmental ruin, with intensified drought, new fires, and heatwaves seen in 2021 in the U.S. West Coast and Siberia; severe floods in various nations; and further deforestation in the Amazon. Still, the Amazon remains earth's precious "breathing gift," as global consensus beckons, its main set of lungs. Throughout the COVID-19 pandemic, media outlets and scientists have reported on the increased plight of Amazonian biomes, referring often to the climate crisis, the need for collective action, and the amplified reality of economic and extractivist pressures in need of cessation or new regulations.[2] Even Pope Francis chimed in with his "Post-Synodal Apostolic Exhortation of the Holy Father Francis, 'Querida Amazonia'" in December 2020, after the Synod held in Rome in October of the same year focused on this region with a restorative vision titled "The Amazon: New Paths for the Church and for an Integral Ecology." How indigenous communities constitute a vital presence and mediation in this process is a topic often curtailed in such considerations, even though they are referred to as custodians of the Amazon and occupy a relatively tangible, if still atavistic, place in global perception. The devastation circulating through a gamut of photographic and filmic registers up until today centers on the land and its resources, revealing a representational quandary common to the modern eye: how do we make visible and acknowledge *as active agents* those who have been systematically expunged from, romanticized, and distorted in our ecological and historical consciousness? How should those communities whose identities continue to be routinely vilified in direct and subtle ways be humanized and historicized? What type of ecological and cognitive justice must we foster and fortify to recognize, not only as sovereign but also as fully sentient and complementary, indigenous ways of knowing and living?[3] By re-creating two historical encounters between Western scientists and Amazon communities, Ciro Guerra's *Embrace of the Serpent* (2015) provides stimulating approaches to these and other questions, as much edifying as they are ontological, animated and existential as they are also paradoxical.

The film is inspired by ethnographic, ethnobotanical, and photographic accounts related to two separate but intersected expeditions to the Amazon— that of German ethnologist Theodor Koch-Grünberg (1872–1924, played by Jan Bijvoet as Theodor von Martius, or Theo) in the early 1900s and that of American ethnobotanist Richard Evans Schultes (1915–2001, played by Brionne Davis as Evan) in the early 1940s. It weaves together a transtemporal saga in which the fictional indigenous character Karamakate, also known in the film as the "world mover," serves at two different stages of his life as guide and window into a vibrant and mutating world as he and Theo and Evan journey together into the Amazon in search of a rare health-giving plant called *yakruna* (the young Karamakate is played by Nilbio Torres and the elder version, by Tafillama-Antonio Bolívar Salvador).[4] Both Theo and Evan manifest a need to document and use this plant to enrich their research and satisfy their scientific curiosity but also to heal maladies each of them suffers. Loosely inspired by the travel journals and graphic records left behind after Koch-Grünberg's and Schultes's journeys, as well as by Guerra's own ethnographic research and artistic vision, the film has been hailed for its striking cinematography and for representing indigenous peoples in a way that according to the director and many film reviews, signals a fresh narrative ethics. In exploring the paradoxes and possible significance of this process, *Embrace of the Serpent* becomes a relevant and timely cinematic intermediation in which the historical filter serves not just to revisit the past but more important, to reposition our perceptions of its relevance, as the film's fictional remapping of an ecologically enigmatic future also suggests. In this sense, Guerra's film enters the Amazon's historiographic arena by rethinking but also echoing questions common to Latin American postcolonial and environmental history while also conveying—not without predictable contradictions—possibilities of renewal and intersection within an imagined ecological order.

THE INSCRUTABILITY OF THE AMAZON AND THE SEARCH FOR A NEW INDIGENOUS SUBJECT

The opening of the film brings viewers before the blurry reflection on the water's surface of a young Karamakate, as his contemplative posture becomes gradually visible. Portrayed as highly attuned to his environment, the young shaman detects a disruption and immediately tenses his countenance. The film cuts to his back, as he probes the river's horizon after hearing the unusual noise, and gradually zooms in within proximity of his neck. The noise was produced by a canoe carrying an ailing von Martius and his indigenous aide Manduca (played by Miguel Dionisio Ramos), who had been instructed by other tribes to seek Karamakate as the sole healer able to provide remedial help.

Audiences from the start of the film discern closely not just the density of the Amazon but also its boundlessness. The reflection of the jungle on the water's surface creates a sense of a mystical, lush opacity that recurs throughout the film, enhanced by dazzling panoramic vistas and dramatic twists that re-create a sense of infinite expanse and the inscrutability of an Amazonia with complex powers. From different perspectives, such tropes have informed our imagination of a region that became the stuff of cinematic ecological excess and mystery, or fragility—a primeval, fertile spectacle waiting to be graphed, here awash in super 35 mm monochromatic wonder at the hands of David Gallego's cinematography. This gateway into the Amazon's enigmatic excess creates a dramatic but strategically piercing counterpoint to the film's historicity, enhanced by the foregrounding of indigenous actors who carry some of the fictional elements on their histrionic and mythicized shoulders alongside the historical and scientific archive that inspires the film.

After the long opening, the credits begin to roll simultaneously with a prolonged reference to the cyclical nature of Amazonian mythology, a close-up sequence of a snake giving birth while also seemingly eating its own offspring, an allusion to the figure of the anaconda outlining Amazonian cosmology, which we will once again see being eaten by a jaguar later in the film. The sequence culminates in one of the small reptiles swimming away in the water, gliding into old Karamakate's presence while he is etching this very mythology on the surface of a big rock. The film's careful narrative parallelism becomes evident, as old Karamakate senses a slight interference, aided by a suspenseful score, and Evan makes his first entrance. Thus, exploration of Amazonian mythology and history resumes through the eyes of the same indigenous shaman, with the recognition that this history, affected by time and colonizing disruption—and like all the main characters in the film—is also in need of restoration.

Historical memory is thus dependent, as the film often insists, on initiation, transmission, and belonging. At this point, the two travelers merge into

Figure 6.1: Young Karamakate, as he leads Theo (Koch-Grünberg) to the healing plant.

Figure 6.2: Older Karamakate with Evan (Schultes), as they search for the yakruna flower.

a metaphoric continuum that owes its narrative structure as much to history (Schultes was inspired by Koch-Grünberg's travel journals) as to cultural memory given that interviewed Amazonian communities that knew or knew of the travelers spoke of them to Guerra as manifestations of the same being.[5] As Camilo Jaramillo Castrillón explains, this fictional amalgamation allowed Guerra the possibility to elude difficulties associated with representing indigenous voices or privileging dominant (Western) evocative structures.[6]

The desire to give indigenous subjects a voice in *Embrace of the Serpent* is paramount, as is the belief that this objective could only be accomplished by magnifying the mythological scope serving as complement to the historical pretext and inspiration. As Guerra explains it, this process was necessary to destabilize and reverse dominant epistemological enclosures:

At the beginning of the project, I wanted to make a historical and anthropologically accurate film. I did extensive, in-depth research on the subject. I structured the script in a way that was *faithful to what really happened* [my emphasis]. But, then, as I started working with the Amazonian communities, I realized that their point of view regarding this story had never been told. That was the real film that I had to do because it's the one film that hasn't been done, that I have never seen, and that would make the film unique and special. In order for the film to be true to that, I had to stop being faithful to the "truth" because, to them [Amazonian communities], ethnographic, anthropological, and historical truths were as fictional as imagination and dream, which for them was [sic] valid. The historical film needed to contaminate itself with Amazonian myth.[7]

The concepts of singularity and cross-pollination underpin Guerra's own assessment of his cinematic artistry. Guerra's own understanding situates indigenous mythology as embodied in their cultural traditions as well as "contaminating" the historical impetus of the story, evoking a critique of historical objectivity, we might associate more aptly with Hayden White's emphasis on the constructedness of historical representation and the production of meaning (e.g., historiography).[8] This approach, he suggests, can reshape our understanding of what constitutes historical truth. In this, *Embrace of the Serpent* follows a corrective representational politics that emphasizes bringing to the indexical forefront indigenous cultural patterns and beliefs. This was reflected in the ascendency of indigenous mythology and languages (Ocaina, Ticuna, Huitoto, and Kubeo are spoken in the film, as are, less frequently, Spanish, German, and Portuguese, and to a lesser degree, Latin) and the leading role of indigenous actors.[9] Equally significant is the belief that by weaving them into historical events and expanding their metaphoric expediency, contemporary audiences (among which are professionals and governments) might change their minds not just about Amazonian ways of life and knowledge traditions but also about the need for their fortification in light of an ecological crisis.

While this intervention serves a dramatic, revisionist, and conceptual purpose, it becomes an opportunity as well to revisit specific episodes in the history of Amazonian exploration, extractivism, and the power relations that inform instances of contact such encounters entail. Thus, returning to well-documented realities of evangelization, the systematic persecution and suppression of indigenous cultures and languages, the enslavement and annihilation of Amazon peoples during the "rubber boom" periods, and the horrifying convergence of all these bookending Koch-Grünberg's and Schultes's expeditions allows a reevaluation of the role of modernity and Western epistemological technologies in contributing to current ecological predicaments and giving form to a historical record the film both complements and tries to disrupt. By interposing young and Old Karamakate's encounters with each traveler in such a way that we can see the evolution of these processes, the film connects past and present, alternatingly. To this is added the presence of Manduca, Theo's indigenous travel partner during young Karamakate's episodes, whose emergence reveals internal conflicts born of previous experiences among native subjects with Western colonial and neocolonial incursions and colonialism's lingering consequences. Identifying him as a sort of "noble savage," Karamakate chides Manduca for submitting to the "whites without a fight" when the latter introduces himself as a "Maloka Bará" tribe member, emphatically separating himself as untainted by a proximity most of which he insists has damaged indigenous lives and cultures. Angry that Theo is wearing a necklace he identifies as belonging to his decimated Cohiuano (fictional) community, he demands an explanation. When Theo clarifies that his necklace was a gift from a Cohiuano shaman, affirming that a few members of his tribe are still alive, bafflement ensues. This brings in a process of mythical construal (a giant tapir emerges as Karamakate reassesses the situation) resulting in a shift of mind and an agreement between Theo and the young shaman that triggers their joint journey deep into the Amazon, first, in search for the sacred plant *yakruna* to cure Theo of his malady and second, for the possibility of reuniting young Karamakate with his people, whom he believed to be extinct.[10]

Knowledge of natural resources, such as rubber or quinine, and the brutal decimation of Amazon indigenous communities circulated before and during the first half of the twentieth century, leaving behind formal registers that drove as much interest in documenting it among diplomats, correspondents, and ethnographers as it did in inciting further exploratory incursions. The paradox of vindicating ethnographic work—of witnessing and chronicling—while conceding or anticipating the real extinction of entire communities is a constant in many records dating back to early colonial times. Echoing Bartolomé de las Casas's sixteenth-century perspective on the destruction of indigenous lives and knowledge, Claude Lévi-Strauss echoed such sentiments while conducting his own research also in the Amazon, near the time of Schultes's travels. Out of Lévi-Strauss's travels and research was born *Tristes Tropiques*, published in 1955, in which the framing of "lost worlds" and the ambiguous nature of anthropological work were further developed.[11] Levi-Strauss highlights yet another paradox in the representation of native communities, this time related to the perception that they are frozen in time and that their cultural evolution is static. In a sense, *Embrace of the Serpent* is an attempt to reconcile denunciation with historical revisionism regarding some of these beliefs and aestheticized, even surrealist ethnography, with alternative epistemologies in such a way that the presaged occurrence of indigenous ethnic and epistemological evanescence is met by a reinterpretation that attempts to show a different, dynamic portrayal. Guerra himself highlights the connection between the threat of vanishing indigenous languages and knowledges and the urgency in capturing their participation in the film as a casting choice of much importance but also, as an opportunity to leave an evocative trace of endurance behind. In speaking about his concerns for the "knowledge being lost," Guerra reveals that while researching, he found a member of the Ocaina tribe, made up of only sixteen people at the time, whose language was about to disappear, and immediately sensed he should play old Karamakate; "that's when I knew the film would be made," he said. Bolívar

Salvador echoes similar concerns when reflecting on the loss of authenticity or belonging among members of his ethnic group, given interethnic mixing or relocation of members to or from other groups or to urban centers like Leticia, the capital of Amazonas state in Colombia, where Bolívar himself has lived.[12] Guerra's film is described as a remedial channel as well given that this character (Bolívar Salvador), who is claimed to have been displaced in real life when young by the second wave of rubber exploitation and to have been ill-treated when acting in a previous film, expresses trust in Guerra's filmic approach.[13] Yet like Koch-Grünberg and Schultes, Guerra is to a degree also another outsider able to ingratiate himself with the Amazonian subjects and derive authentic expressions and schemes of knowledge from them, with the expressed intent to recognize indigenous agency and capture the realistic knowledge their lives encapsulate within the film's fictional reconstruction.

EXTRACTIVISM AND THE AMAZON: A KNOWN HORIZON?

Even in its most altruistic contexts, the exploration of the Amazon regarding the knowledge and resources it holds has been inextricably tied to extractivist interests and desires, understood in their simplest form as the obtaining or recording of a knowledge whose ultimate (and often equivocal) significance resides in that knowledge's outward functions. As Pellegrino Luciano argues when examining the history of quinine, for example, interest in pharmacological uses was consistently driven by empire building and associated with colonial practices.[14] In addition, the studies and insights that explorers produced served to advance science and industry but also the arts. Koch-Grünberg's journeys in the Brazilian-Colombian and Venezuelan Amazon regions from 1903 until his death from malaria in 1924 opened the door to greater investigation, leaving affective traces among the communities he met and inspiring, years later, Schultes's own expeditions, among several others. His interest in indigenous cosmologies fed his professional connection to ethnology and museography and served as background to literary works like Mario de Andrade's *Macunaíma* (1928), which re-creates from an ironic perspective Brazil's multiethnic history.[15] Although some of Koch-Grünberg's audiovisual ethnographic work remains missing or incomplete, in particular in connection to his expeditions in the Brazilian Amazon, and even though he himself dissented from the limits of his assigned responsibilities as a museum "collector," his declared motivations signal tensions between his professional aims and his own anthropological curiosity:

[F]or me, the main objective in my journey was not that of a collector. Frequently delayed by weeks, even months in each village, participating intimately in the lives of indigenous peoples, I intended essentially to cohabit with them and access their life visions, given that the visitor who passes by hastily through the region gains from his research merely fleeting and often false impressions. [cited in Frank, my translation][16]

Embrace of the Serpent emphasizes the caring side of Koch-Grünberg's diverging callings by having Theo feature both his wide knowledge of native lore and his almost consistent deference toward Amazonian beliefs.

Cutting to Theo's last appearance in the latter part of the film and transitioning back from the future when old Karamakate and Evan sit listening to classical music beneath a starry sky—a moment pregnant with metaphysical reverence, as Evan further absorbs Amazonian knowledge—the film's time shift is held together diegetically and extra-diegetically by the music itself and by old Karamakate's spoken lesson to Evan (who sits, blurry, in the background) and to Theo in Evan's past, gluing past and present together and offering a Diogenes-like instruction to self-knowledge that echoes Karamakate's persistent critique of Western utilitarian materialism: "To become a warrior every Cohiuano man must leave everything behind, and go into the jungle, guided only by his own dreams. In that journey, he has to discover, in solitude and silence, who he really is. He has to become a vagabond of dreams. Some

Figure 6.3: Theo Von Martius (Koch-Grünberg) with one of the fictional Amazonian communities he befriends in the film. (Photofest)

get lost and never come back. But those that do, are ready to face whatever may come." When old Karamakate follows this moment with a sequence of ontological questions pertaining to cultural memory—"[W]here are they? Where are the chants that mothers used to sing to their babies? Where are the stories of the elders? The whispers of love? The chronicles of battle? Where have they gone?"—Theo collapses in the dark of the jungle to wake up, delirious and defiant, the next day, breaking with young Karamakate's fiats and in parallel, with the jungle's imperatives. To what extent the historical figures expressed such skepticism or departed from local mandates in their exchanges with indigenous shamans is hard to fathom but can be gleaned partly in the preeminence of their scientific discourses, which stand as epistemologically totalizing and certifying. In the film, Amazonian mythology is designed to subsume and subsequently move aside Western scientific discourses and practices. In the end, the film uses Manduca partly to exonerate Theo of his Western intransigence, as he tries to persuade young Karamakate that Theo's learning of their customs and ultimately of *yakruna* can help to educate "white" folks of Amazonian lives, history, and humanity, a message later echoed by old Karamakate to Evan himself.

Schultes's astonishing research and taxonomic span, on the other hand, opened the door to new learning in the realm of ethnobotany, highlighting the need to understand the Amazon in connection to its inhabitants' cultures. Although his empirical work placed him in the dominion of applied research, his emphasis on conservation echoed Kock-Grünberg's and was genuine and consistent in his diaries and correspondence; his expressions of concern about Amazonian "primitive" communities' well-being emphasized humanitarian but also paternalistic notions of preservation. Fear or anticipation of their disappearance is a constant and justifies the need for greater exploration. Schultes's documented focus on the functional deployment and possible commercialization of his research gave Guerra a pretext to probe, however, the exploitation of natural resources while construing a dramatic space in which Western self-questioning could be expanded and indigenous agency underscored. Schultes's initial journey to the Amazon was inspired by Koch-Grünberg's journals and prompted initially by the U.S. government's search for more durable rubber strains and also by his assiduous interest in psychotropic and medicinal composites, thus, his expressed interest in poisons that could be deployed, like muscle relaxants and anesthetics, in the context of World War II.[17] They all stirred his attraction to Amazonian peoples and their pharmacological knowledge.[18]

Guerra's film highlights some of the conflicts in this fixation with classifying extractable substances, which could result in the manufacture of new compounds in addition to advancing knowledge of Amazonian beliefs, botany, and medicine. Schultes himself identified this double objective in several of his writings, more clearly in *The Healing Forest: Medicinal and Toxic Plants of the Northwest Amazonia* (1990) published with Robert F. Raffauf, a well-known phytochemist who accompanied Schultes and his students in several field trips. In the preface, Schultes explains that the book's goals were, first, to draw an extensive ethnobotanical compendium and second, "to call attention to the distinct possibility that from some of these plants might come new chemical compounds of eventual value to modern medicine and industry," fields where he had already built a rich legacy.[19] Given that his work's objective was also to salvage these societies' pharmacopoeia and native lore—as he terms them—we sense an urgency, also extant in Koch-Grünberg's journals and visible in Guerra's film, that grapples with these internal contradictions. Although references to the dilemma of scientific exploration that *also* seeks the protection of ecological practices are not foregrounded, the film nonetheless exploits them to the benefit of the fictional critique of commercialization and the systemic brutality that accompanied it. Several events mark this preoccupation: the search for *yakruna*, as explained before, a plant believed to be capable of healing the illnesses harming the physical and mental health of both travelers; the revisiting of the Amazon rubber industries and the scars they left on Amazonia's flora and communities through traces both explorers and Karamakate witness and must come to grips with; and the gradual purging of Western epistemological and historiographic tools/practices used to access and record native knowledge. This multipronged trope in many an approach to representing indigenous beliefs and ways of life is enabled by Theo's and Evan's gradual yet obstinately willful shedding of Western taxonomizing conventions, as the two travelers adopt (often by ingestion) native forms of knowing, that is "going native" on the part of Western travelers. This opens the door in Guerra's film to several realities in the human unconscious, manifested in the film's final explorations of psychedelia, and to the possibility of transcending, through access to indigenous knowledge, the limits of Western utilitarianism.

The rubber exploitation remains a traumatic period in Amazonian and world history, memorably captured in the Latin American literary canon by José Eustasio Rivera in *La vorágine* (*The Vortex*, 1924) and denounced vividly by the British consul-general Roger Casement after 1910 in the context of the Anglo-Peruvian Arana Brothers rubber company and its deplorable history in the Putumayo region. Guerra's film references this in several ways, more openly by dramatizing early an encounter between young Karamakate, Theo, and Manduca and an indigenous man tortured, scarred, and maimed as he tries to protect the rubber he has been extracting after Manduca, in anger and recalling his own previous enslavement, spills the collected substance. One of the most compelling episodes in the film, the horror of the rubber exploitation is carved into the forest and on indigenous bodies, ending with the indigenous man asking Manduca to kill him to end his misery. Manduca's reencounter with the reality of rubber exploitation rouses his own memory—having been rescued (purchased) in the past by Theo himself from a rubber plantation—and foretells the next encounter in the journey, this time with an evangelizing mission where the reference to rubber, bringing Christianity and Capitalism together in one single sequence, takes us back to the reforming impulses of the early twentieth-century Colombian president Rafael Reyes (1849–1921) and his civilizational aspirations.

As a political figure, entrepreneur, and military man, Reyes advocated passionately for the grafting of the Amazon to the dynamics of industrial agribusiness and global capital, hoping at the same time to bring modernizing changes to the region while celebrating industry and development as a compound heroic enterprise.[20] The film calls attention to this history by focusing on a sign at the mission where young Karamakate and Theo's expedition makes a stop, memorializing some of Reyes's own ideas and a triumphant and contradictory radicalism that emphasizes the need to eradicate "barbarism" among indigenous peoples, implants Christianity as part of their reeducation, and grafts its institution in indigenous cultural memory as the only path to their survival, the joint forces capable, according to Reyes, of bringing the nation to a new civilizational level. The sign reads: "In recognition of the courage of the Colombian rubber pioneers who bring, while risking their lives and belongings, civilization to the land of cannibal savages, showing them the path of God and His Holy Church. Rafael Reyes, President of Colombia, August 1907." Reyes, nonetheless, acknowledged to some degree in his memoirs, while more in the context of multinational competition for resources, the genocidal circumstances in which rubber was being exploited, though mostly in relation to its Peruvian manifestations.[21]

By connecting the two Western explorers and both versions of Karamakate with the encroachment and settlement in the Amazon of evangelical Christianity through fictional intervention, the film establishes links to the horror associated with its forceful imposition and the rubber exploitation that took place under its wings since the mid-nineteenth century, when the lives of tens of thousands of enslaved indigenous people were sacrificed at the altar of this new industrial compound. The film revisits Christianity as one of the most troubling and ubiquitous Eurocentric colonial instruments modifying Amazonian cultural history, in some instances echoing perceptions that date to the beginning of colonialism in the continent. Although the film approaches realities of cross-cultural identity (Manduca, for instance, represents a hybrid indigenous subject connecting different value systems), it remains married to a rather binomial worldview, of purer or corrupted indigenous subjects within the spectrum of neocolonial power. That Christianity has transformed modern-day indigenous subjectivity is a historical given, with young Karamakate even recalling biblical verses summoned from his novice youth. Less clear is the extent to which some of these identities served strategically the subjectivity spectrum Guerra sought to re-create. For instance, in describing his casting choices, Guerra speaks of "generations that have become so disconnected [from their Amazonian ecosystems]" who "live in a world that is difficult to reach."[22] Implicit in this reflection is per-haps the belief that transformed worldviews under assimilated or neocolonial impacts (such as that of Christianity) give birth to less authentic indigenous cultural expressions. The main argument emphasizes a Christianity whose civilizational impulses result in a deeply perplexing, cultlike liturgical rite of cannibalism witnessed by old Karamakate and Evan after they land in the same mission young Karamakate, Theo, and Manduca had encountered, beholding an act of self-delusion and self-destruction the film prophesies. The reference is to children and their reeducation under evangelical instruction, which young Karamakate questions when speaking with some of the children he meets at the mission, condemning its doctrinal logic and calling attention to its suppressive powers, as the children are punished brutally by a Spanish friar (played by Luigi Sciamanna) when they display indigenous cultural pat-terns or speak Amazonian languages, an influence young Karamakate tries to reverse.

RELIGIOUS COLONIALISM AND EXTRACTIVE EPISTEMOLOGIES

The Christian mission resurfaces in the second expedition, with some of the remaining children now grown into adult devotees who take old Karamakate and Evan prisoner as soon as they arrive. This segment of the film shows an irrational transformation given the bizarre appropriation of Christian lore and ceremonies (some of the indigenous adherents wear burlap *capirotes* similar to those associated with penitents in Catholic confraternity groups and popular rituals) and culminating in an extreme act of cannibalism inspired by a fanatical Messiah figure (played by Nicolas Cancino), staging his own eucharistic sacrifice, who has taken over the congregation from the Spanish missionary by establishing a cultish flock. When hearing from Evan that they are "scientists" looking for sacred plants, this new Messiah declares narcis-sistically in Portuguese, "A única coisa sagrada nesta mata são eu!" ("The only sacred thing in this forest is me!"). Both travelers escape in a context of self-destructive frenzy. Despite the drastic transformation of the mission, its representation is not historically incongruous, signaling yet another layer of neocolonial, anti-ecological fatality befalling indigenous communities.

Students of colonial history will easily identify the inculturation and transcul-turation schemes to which evangelized indigenous communities, and specially children, have been subjected under Christianity since the early sixteenth century, often by force and at times with catastrophic results, as many com-munities and individuals were persecuted and their cultures eclipsed under the yolk of evangelization and the pretext of eradicating "pagan" religions.

News of the reeducation of indigenous communities at the hands of reli-gious institutions and of punishment, even death or self-immolation, is not a thing of the past, however. As we learned in 2021 of the deaths and unmarked graves of thousands of indigenous children in reeducation schools in Canada, the persecution and annihilation of indigenous cultures and bodies has been a pernicious global project for centuries, running parallel with a brutal civi-lizational ethno-Eurocentrism and its attendant modernizing forces.[23] Even Schultes himself complained, alongside some of his coauthors, of the noxious influence Christian Western influences had on indigenous medicinal knowl-edge and not just in the Amazon region, resulting often in the condemnation of ritual substances like peyote.[24]

Abuses by the church and the emergence of rigid evangelical structures or doctrinal swindlers alongside the creation of novel liturgies are borne by history, and references to various eschatological formations in the Americas abound from the sixteenth century to the present regarding the evolution of Christianity. What the film does is further question the universalist claims of Western epistemological practices under the aegis of religious colonialism, reflected in the destruction of indigenous knowledge and ritual practices, which, from the ethnologist's perspective, ought to be first understood, then preserved and deployed for posterity within the framework of scientific analysis and classification as their prevailing epistemological processes of substantiation. Although the film centers here on an undefined northern Amazonian frontier region, its geopolitical remapping is unambivalent in pointing to Colombians as protagonists in this process of genocide, evoking President Reyes's own modernizing ambitions as well. Once Theo, Manduca, and young Karamakate reach what was once the latter's community, they find its members drunken and defiling the *yakruna* flower, soldiers fearful of Colombian invasions, and a mythological (and ecological) bond broken amid disorientation and decadence, fear, and territorial volatility. They all flee in horror as Colombian soldiers invade and gun people down, with Theo and Manduca parting ways permanently with young Karamakate after the latter burns to the ground the desecrated *yakruna* flower tree. It will be his older self's task, in his attempt to question and reposition Evan's acquisitive impulses and procure his own conversion, to find the last remaining mani-festation of the flower with, and for the sake of, Evan. After a short sequence in which a jaguar appears eating a snake, a reference to the myths the film introduced earlier in the film, Theo disappears in the jungle, perhaps a metaphoric reference to his real death of malaria.

Guerra must have been familiar with the documentary *Apaporis: In Search of a River* (Antonio Dorado, 2010), which traced not only Schultes's extensive travels through the Apaporis River basin but also used his disciple and well-known Amazon ethnographer and ethnobotanist Wade Davies, who had also made similar expeditions, to narrate parts of the film. Using archival footage of Franklin Delano Roosevelt's well-known 1942 appeal to the American public to help collect enough used rubber for the war effort against Japan and Germany, the documentary frames the search for rubber as a critical industrial objective. In referencing Roosevelt's address, the documentary expects audiences to discern Schultes's subsequent objectives (in his second expedition, he was commissioned by the U.S. government with finding sturdier rubber strains), which overshadow to a degree the evolving humanitarian impulses engraved in his journals and celebrated by environmentalists and some of the Amazonian communities that still remember him as well as by Dorado's and in a different way, Guerra's own film. *Apaporis* exemplifies a conventional perspective through which indigenous people are spoken for given that the narration is dominated by Wade Davies and the director himself, a documentary that emphasizes the disappearance of indigenous knowledge while celebrating its expert, Western-inspired humanitarian conservation through the actions of explorers like Schultes and Davies. As a critique of both the Eurocentrism implicit in this approach and the dominance of Western epistemological filters in understanding Amazonian history, Guerra's film is an attempt to provide an antithesis to this outlook.

Nonetheless, this parallel critique of colonial and neocolonial forces at work, related to the disappearance and appropriation of indigenous knowledge and Amazon natural resources, on the one hand, and the Western epistemological concepts and tools offered as restorative apertures on the other, leaves an ambiguous trace. The repurposed indigenous Amazonian concept of "chullachaqui" in the film might serve in this context as a strategic goal,[25] fictionalizing Amazonian mythology to reflect a variety of crises each character exemplifies from their own individual conditions. For example, Manduca is called a *chullachaqui* by young Karamakate for having lost his indigenous identity and becoming "other" under Western realities of servility; young Karamakate calls a photographic reproduction of his semblance a *chullachaqui*, construing the indexical product as a disembodied reflection of his real self, a being emptied of his history and humanity; Theo's delirium and inability to rectify his own malady hints at a split state of being; Evan is associated with this state because of his inability to dream and his emphasis, almost until the end, on the extractivist and utilitarian value of indigenous medicinal knowledge; and old Karamakate blames himself for being a *chullachaqui* because of his inability to recall his knowledge of indigenous medicines, feeling empty and bewildered. In the end, to be a *chullachaqui* is to inhabit a disembodied space, alienated from a proper self and unable to inhabit a grounded, congruent universe in which historical memory is part of an embodied, proximate continuum.

First mentioned when young Karamakate meets Manduca as a type of insult to his "colonized" self, the term *chullachaqui* migrates to old Karamakate in the context of having gone adrift and lost his ability to reconstitute the physical and metaphysical contours of the Amazonian interconnected topography he'd embodied. When approached by Evan about his drawings at the start of the film, he explains, "the line is broken, my memories are gone. Rocks, trees, animals, they went silent. Now they are just pictures on rocks." Having learned that Evan is able to make *mambe* (coca leaf powder), a mixture he'd also forgotten how to make, an interdependence is established that compels both men to redraw their journey, as Evan claims to have been told that *yakruna* would help him heal, for he is unable to dream. That Evan and Theo before him used intimate indigenous knowledge to establish trust gives the indigenous informant but also the filmmaker an entry point into a cinematic universe that replicates ethnographic handicraft. The third instance in which the concept of *chullachaqui* emerges explains this process differently, when young Karamakate rejects initially his photographic semblance, calling it his *chullachaqui*, an entity that "only drifts around in the world, empty, like a ghost in time without time" (thus, the prevalence in various film reviews of thinking of this as a type of ghostly double), but then comes to accept it as a way to relate to the white world where his photographic semblance will, with his consent, circulate. The term serves thus to expand the metaphoric universe of the film but also to enable, through fictional extension, a reflective narrative of individual growth we see evolving in Evan's and old Karamakate's trek.

Evan's and Theo's motivations, propelled by accessing and preserving existing indigenous knowledge, place them as men of science with different ontological needs but also as men whose vocations revolve around service not just to that science and its idioms but also to its applications. In Theo's case, *yakruna* may save his life, yet he still must write his journals and collect data intended for Western audiences and interests, and in Evan's case, *yakruna* gives him the opportunity to transcend the limitations of scientific rationality and question or disregard his own utilitarian objectives and as a result, have once again the capacity to dream (the psychedelic sequence we see in the conclusion of the film pays homage to this filter to knowledge). Yet as a memorial seminar at Harvard's Peabody Museum of Archaeology and Ethnology dedicated to Schultes in February 2019 reveals, the celebration of the scientist remains encased in historiographical mythicizing.[26] Here a politics of memory serves to highlight the historical expurgation of indigenous cultures as well as their resistance to that erasure given not only that their knowledge passes from them to the Western travelers but also that it is in the latter where that knowledge finds a legible home. The film adopts a benign, inclusive approach, whereby the Western explorer, particularly in the guise of Evan, not only accesses the knowledge but seems to finally comprehend its transcendence and is left free to decide what to do with this new knowledge. His ability to dream is not only restored but enhanced through the Amazonian medium, enabled by old Karamakate. A sequence more likely to evoke out-of-world, extra-sensorial dimensions of experience, it also includes the return of young Karamakate, who, reminiscent of a cosmic divinity, appears permeated by intergalactic light (a luminescence), which emerges out of his eyes and mouth. By then, the film has allowed Amazonian mythology, as synthetized by Guerra's film, to become a gateway through which Evan emerges, apparently healed and evocative of the same mystical numinescence old Karamakate displayed early in the film when he was surrounded suddenly by butterflies, accompanied by a score that takes us back to the start of the film.

CONCLUSIONS

The tradition of highlighting indigenous purity and celebrating a state of nature in which harmony with all living entities reigns highest is not entirely absent in Guerra's approach to representing Amazonian people. Among different manifestations of this trend, manifest in the early Spanish chronicles and disseminated diversely since then, the concept of the "noble savage" was often used to draw a contrast with European degeneracy and cruelty, not to emphasize an ecological crisis. As such, its deployment served to critique an emergent modernity whose ideological contours confronted Western cultures with their own barbarity. One can argue that despite the existence of multiple ethnographies, the prevalent mindset regarding this figure consistently underscored its invented character. In Guerra's critique of Eurocentrism, the prevalent impulse is to give a cinematic voice and photographic space to the "real" Amazonian indigenous subject to be more authentic, without quite succeeding in extricating the film from the limits of Eurocentrism's representational limits. In other words, Western barbarism not only justifies the purity of the indigenous man but also provokes it.[27]

In justifying this purity, the film employs and re-creates Amazonian mythology. The epilogue indirectly highlights the mistiness this approach evokes, which is mentioned at the beginning of the article: "The diaries are the only known accounts of many Amazonian cultures. This film is dedicated to all the peoples whose song we will never know," it states, interspersed with black and white archival photos of the travelers, the same photos Guerra construed as driving his choice not to make his film in color.[28] This segment in the film's epilogue is not just a reference to inevitable loss and indirectly, to the frequency with which indigenous languages and cultures vanish without a trace but also to their inscrutability and remoteness. The extermination of Amazonian communities and ecosystems through settler colonialism, industrial agriculture, extractivist enterprises, and persistent discrimination or assimilation remains unabated, as recent reports about increased deforestation and the Amazon's becoming a net carbon producer also attest.[29] In spite of organizations such as the Amazon Conservation Team, inspired by the work of Schultes himself, political and economic ambitions driven by modernization and beliefs that any conceivable solutions must be mediated by Western technology and intervention still predominate. Although *Embrace of the Serpent* has done much to bring new attention to the survival of the Amazon, while offering a cinematic platform on which indigenous cultural expressions become more proximate, intelligible meanings related to the politics of representation remain equivocal. On July 2, 2021, the Colombian newspaper *El Espectador* published an article titled, in Spanish, "Carrera contra el reloj para salvar el conocimiento sobre plantas medicinales" (Race against the Clock to Save the Knowledge of Medicinal Plants). Based on a recent study conducted by Rodrigo Camara-Leret and Jordi Bascompte on the connection between language safeguarding and the preservation of medicinal knowledge in indigenous communities in regions that included Northern Amazonia, the main point centers on a dismal projection: the predicted extinction of up to 30% of indigenous languages, which will transform our ability to learn about medicinal knowledge, making their documentation a key priority in preservation efforts.[30] To this dilemma is added the corollary of biodiversity loss due to the climate crisis and extractivist industries, including modern agriculture. Combined, these effects "would substantially compromise humanity's capacity for medicinal discovery."[31] In a compelling way, *Embrace of the Serpent* selectively employs Koch-Grünberg's and Schultes's ethnographic work and the recollection of their presence in the Colombian Amazon to call attention to related dimensions of this predicament but fails to construct a radical, relational politics in which indigenous subjects disrupt prevailing epistemological structures.

What all these perspectives coincide in highlighting is that for such oral traditions to survive, being tightly linked to memory retention and the transmission of knowledge, Western science and technology must continue to play a central role, thus the emphasis on capturing and documenting. Other recent attempts promote similar perspectives, such as those found in two short documentaries, *The Return* (Eriberto Gualinga, 2021), an Amazonian-filmed and-produced documentary, emphasizing indigenous Amazon resilience during the COVID-19 pandemic, and *The Living Forest* (Marc Silver, 2015), mimicking Schultes's ethnobotanical title, which documents members of the same Kichwa Ecuadorian community six years earlier as it made a trek to the Climate Change Conference in Paris to provide an indigenous perspective on climate crisis solutions and to bring attention to the pressures they faced at the hands of oil companies and multinational corporations. In the documentary, the group constructs a canoe, which is transported to Paris from the Amazon and used to sail down the Seine River to spotlight the Sarayacu region as a frontline reality of environmental activism. Indigenous-produced media is prolific and well known, although its circulation is limited to local settings and international festivals, for the most part.

Celebrated for its nomination to the Oscars in 2015 for Best Foreign Language Film, after winning the Art Cinema Award at the Cannes Film Festival, plus other accolades, *Embrace of the Serpent* received almost universal acclaim. Four years after the film's release, Netflix released *Frontera verde* (*Green Frontier*, 2019) an eight-series part ethnography, part detective thriller that takes us deep into Amazon territory and the urban settlements that dot the crossroads between Brazil, Perú, and Colombia, bringing us also into visual contact with various indigenous communities and their mythologies. The first episode was directed by Ciro Guerra. Some of the actors appearing in *Embrace of the Serpent* reappear in the Netflix series. The most prominent among them is perhaps Miguel Dionisio Ramos, who played Manduca and who had been part in 2008 of a docu-fiction directed by Gustavo de la Hoz, *Mangutangu aru ngoechiga* (The Origin of the Tikuna People), to which Ramos belonged.

There is no lack of attention given to the Amazon, as we can see, and spaces continue to open for different types of representation and self-representation given that indigenous communities have for years fostered the production of their own media. We must ask a question that Ella Shohat and Robert Stam tackled in *Unthinking Eurocentrism: Multiculturalism and the Media* (1994) regarding the complexity of a corrective representational politics that attempts to offset the lasting, even lethal, impact of negative stereotypes. As they concluded, what is needed is a radicalization in the kind of multiculturalism that is evoked: "What is missing . . . is a notion of ethnic relationality and community answerability. . . . In this sense a radical multiculturalism calls for a profound restructuring and reconceptualization of the power relations between cultural communities."[32] As Santasil Mallik argues, both precredits and postcredits featuring young and old Karamakate, respectively, are demarcated by close-up shots of an anaconda giving birth to its offspring. In his view, this signals an emphasis on the regenerative forces that constitute Amazonian cycles.[33] In spite of the epilogue, the film privileges a notion of regeneration that pertains to Evan's (Schultes's) evolution and restoration rather than the Amazon's from the compound perspective of its inhabitants. Even though *Embrace of the Serpent* elaborates a critique of Eurocentrism and compellingly offers an alternative epistemological and ecological order, these goals remain subordinate to a vulnerable, vanishing Amazonian horizon in need of Western scientific recognition and intervention. In this sense, the foregrounding of Amazonian mythology serves a purpose that stops at the threshold of a radical relational politics. Reading through the web page dedicated to the Amazonian Travels of Richard Evans Schultes, and in honor of his work, a project created by the Amazon Conservation Team, striking images of two superimposed photos of Schultes's travels evoke this disconcerting narrative.[34] In the image on "Tab 1, Putumayo: Sacred Plant," for example, three indigenous subjects appear in the upper portion of the photo as spirits watching over or watermarking a foregrounded Schultes while he examines a plant on the ground. The composition of the superimposed images in this and other tabs renders indigenous historical subjectivity static, ghostly, mythologized, an apparition hazily visible, while the scientist is seen in action yet contemplative, embodied. An indigenous presence framed as ethereal watches over him, sanctions his mission. In ways I hope to have clarified in this essay, our perception of the Amazon remains mired in similar constructions, as does to a degree, despite all its supporting attributes and critically activist historical revisionism, *Embrace of the Serpent*.

ADDITIONAL RESOURCES

Camara-Leret, Rodrigo, and Jordi Bascompte. "Language Extinction Triggers the Loss of Unique Medicinal Knowledge," *PNAS* 118, no. 24 (2021). A thorough, data-supported recent study of the connection between language maintenance and epistemological traditions regarding the diffusion and preservation of medical knowledge among indigenous communities, including the Amazon's.

Castrillón Jaramillo, Camilo. "La sensatez del conocimiento: saber, poscolonialidad y crítica ambiental en *El abrazo de la serpiente* de Ciro Guerra," *Revista Canadiense de Estudios Hispánicos* 43, no. 3 (Spring 2019): 579–601. A Spanish-written, congratulatory, albeit also critical, view of *Embrace of the Serpent*'s decolonizing, environmentalist perspectives.

Clifford, James. *The Predicament of Culture: Twentieth Century Ethnography, Literature, and Art*. Cambridge, MA: Harvard University Press, 1988. An insightful and critically reflexive view of the recording and construction of cultural difference from the perspective of ethnography.

Dorado, Antonio, dir. *Apaporis: In Search of a River*, 2010, DVD. Documentary film that traced not only Schultes's extensive travels through the Apaporis River basin relying on Schultes's disciple and well-known Amazon ethnographer and ethnobotanist Wade Davies to qualify Schultes's work and influence and narrate parts of the film.

Guillén, Michael. *"Embrace of the Serpent*: An Interview with Ciro Guerra." *Cineaste* 41, no. 2 (2016). An extensive interview with the director of the film, in which cinematic and artistic choices are discussed alongside the film's historiographic and ethnographic foundations.

Koch-Grünberg, Theodor. *Del Roraima al Orinoco*. Caracas: Ernesto Armatano, 1981. Ethnographic journals in Spanish translation encompassing Koch-Grünberg's travels in Amazonia and the Orinoco region.

Martínez Pinzón, Felipe. "Héroes de la civilización. La Amazonía como cosmópolis agroexportadora en la obra del General Rafael Reyes." *ACHSC* 40, no. 2 (2013): 145–77. The article analyzes the discourse of appropriation of the Amazon territory set forth by President, General, and entrepreneur Rafael Reyes (1849–1921) in speeches, lectures, travel diaries, and autobiographical memoirs.

Nugent, Stephen L. *The Rise and Fall of the Amazon Rubber Industry: An Historical Anthropology*. New York: Routledge, 2017. A recent historical account examining the dramatic rise and fall of the rubber industry. The book contests several held assumptions about the connections between extraction of natural rubber by indigenous and peasant laborers in Amazonia, international trade, and capitalist industry.

Pinchot, Ryan Bradley, and Matías Martínez Abeijón. *Dándoles Más de Lo Que Pidieron: La Justicia Epistemológica En El Abrazo de La Serpiente de Ciro Guerra*. Cleveland State University, 2017. Master's thesis and one of the most comprehensive, attentive Spanish-written analyses of *Embrace of the Serpent*.

Rouch, Jean. *Ciné-Ethnography*. Edited and translated by Steven Feld. Minneapolis, MN: University of Minnesota Press, 2003. Jean Rouch's chronicles, interviews, and reflections on the use of film as ethnography. This remains one of the most insightful compendia on the politics of filmic representation, besides offering pioneering and critical intuition about photographic media and anthropology.

Schultes, Richard Evans, and Robert F. Raffauf. *The Healing Forest: Medicinal and Toxic Plants of the Northwest Amazonia*. Dioscorides Press, 1990. One of Schultes's most extensive anthologies of his life's work, including fifty years of field research in the Northwest Amazon.

Shohat, Ella, and Robert Stam. *Unthinking Eurocentrism: Multiculturalism and the Media*. New York: Routledge, 1994. One of the most illuminating historical and theoretical approaches to representational politics in media and cinema in Latin America, analyzing prevalent structures of Eurocentric hegemony in our understanding and representations of diverse cultures and subjectivities.

NOTES

1. Since his election, Bolsonaro has been one of the most vocal public figures expressing his public disdain for indigenous peoples, evoking well-known nineteenth-century mandates to civilize or exterminate them. See Luís Jaime Acosta, "Amazon Countries Sign Forest Pact, Promising to Coordinate Disaster Response,"

Reuters, September 6, 2019; Adriaan Alsema, "Bolsonaro Cancels Trip to Colombia for Amazon Summit," *Colombia Reports*, September 4, 2019; "Raoni e filha de Chico Mendes anunciam aliança contra 'retrocessos' de Bolsonaro," *Folha de São Paulo*, January 5, 2020; "Amazon Nations Meet in Indigenous Hut at Colombia over Forest Protection," *Deccan Chronicle*, September 7, 2019; "The resistance continues: Amazon Indigenous Leaders Gather to Launch 2020 Activities," *Green Peace*, January 30, 2020; and Tom Phillips, "Jair Bolsonaro's Racist Comment Sparks Outrage from Indigenous Groups," *The Guardian*, January 24, 2020.

2. As I write this, new reports have emerged of new fires, deforestation, and urban encroachment in the Brazilian Amazon, anticipating intensified disruption in global weather patterns. See Jake Spring, "Scientists Warn of Bad Year for Fires in Brazil's Amazon and Wetlands," *Reuters*, May 27, 2021; Tomasso Protti, "Amazonia: Life and Death in the Brazilian Rainforest," *The Guardian*, June 4, 2021; and Flávia Milhorance, "Deforestation in Brazilian Amazon Hits Highest Annual Level in a Decade," *The Guardian*, August 20, 2021.

3. Several events since 2020 in Latin America reveal how disparate and conflicting such processes of recognition are, from the hemispheric questioning and removal of colonial symbols in public spaces and the choice of 17 indigenous elected members out of 155 helping to rewrite the Chilean constitution and the recent election of the Mapuche woman, Elisa Loncón, as president of the Chilean Constitutional Convention, to the racism, even from government officials, confronting indigenous communities. Consider such examples as President Jair Bolsonaro's comments about indigenous people, the racist comments describing "minga" expressions of collective effort in Colombia by indigenous communities and the rise in social media of extremist and racist beliefs about indigenous and rural people in the context of the election of Pedro Castillo in Perú, today part and parcel of Latin American social media history, among others.

4. According to Ciro Guerra, Karamakate also means "he who tries." This interpretation resonates with his role in the film connecting and guiding the two travelers. See Michael Guillén, "Embrace of the Serpent: An Interview with Ciro Guerra," *Cineaste* 41, no. 2 (Spring 2016).

5. Michael Guillén, "*Embrace of the Serpent*: An Interview with Ciro Guerra." Unless able to read German, see Koch-Grünberg's Spanish translation of his travel journals through the Northern Amazonia and the Orinoco region, *Del Roraima al Orinoco*, 3 vols. (Caracas: Ernesto Armatano, 1981).

6. "La sensatez del conocimiento: Saber, poscolonialidad y crítica ambiental en *El abrazo de la serpiente* de Ciro Guerra," *Revista Canadiense de Estudios Hispánicos* 43, no. 3 (Spring 2019): 579–601.

7. As quoted by Michael Guillén, "Embrace of the Serpent: An Interview with Ciro Guerra," *Cineaste* 41, no. 2 (Spring 2016), https://www.cineaste.com/spring2016/embrace-of-the-serpent-ciro-guerra.

8. See Hayden White, *The Content of the Form: Narrative Discourse and Historical Representation* (Baltimore: John Hopkins University Press, 1990).

9. See interview with Bolívar Salvador on YouTube to hear an indigenous perspective on the making of the film: https://youtu.be/yBAwxIG4D-s.

10. Like *yakruna*, *Maloka*, *chullachaqui*, and *Cohiuano* are also invented or repurposed terms in this context, part of Guerra's creative license in the film.

11. In the "Prologue," Lévi-Strauss says: "It was more convenient, and more soothing for the European conscience, to treat [eyewitness accounts] as exaggerations ascribable to the naivete or boastfulness of adventurers than to gauge the extent of the massacres by these reports. By the time the voyages of scientific exploration and ethnographic research began in the nineteenth century, the illusion was firmly established that the condition of the Indian communities at that time was the same as it had been in the age of discovery. Travelers and scientists endorsed it." *Saudades do Brasil: A Photographic Memoir* (Seattle: University of Washington Press, 1994), 12.

12. Interview with Tiapuyama (Antonio Bolivar): https://youtu.be/yBAwxIG4D-s. Bolívar Salvador mentions sixty members, roughly, a different demographic number from that evoked by Guerra. Note that here he is called "Tiapuyama" and not "Tafillama," as his native name appears elsewhere.

13. Guillén, "Embrace of the Serpent: An Interview with Ciro Guerra."

14. "When Quinine Was King: A Note on the Global Ecology of Health," *Practicing Anthropology* 37, no. 2 (Spring 2015), 31.

15. Telê Ancona Lopez, "O macunaíma de Mário de Andrade nas páginas de Koch-Grünberg," *Manuscritica* no. 24 (2013), 151–61.

16. Erwin Frank, "Objetos, imagens e sons: a etnografia de Theodor Koch-Grünberg (1872–1924), *Boletim do Museu Paraense Emílio Goeldi* 5, no. 1 (2010): 153–71.

17. See Schultes's 1990 recorded interview for direct reference to these goals as well as to his emphasis on salvaging "primitive" societies' pharmacological knowledge before its complete disappearance: https://youtu.be/1lxtn7zbQfw. The film construes Evan's search for new rubber strains with *yakruna* in the context of World War II, when he tries to stop old Karamakate from turning the last flower into "caapi."

18. More specifically, Schultes was sent by the Rubber Development Corporation, a subsidiary of the Office of Economic Warfare. See Ryan Bradley Pinchot, *Dándoles Más de lo Que Pidieron: La Justicia Epistemológica En* El Abrazo de La Serpiente *de Ciro Guerra* (Cleveland, OH: Cleveland State University, 2017), 16.

19. *The Healing Forest: Medicinal and Toxic Plants of the Northwest Amazonia* (Portland: Dioscorides Press, 1990), 9.

20. Felipe Martínez Pinzón, "Héroes de la civilización. La Amazonía como cosmópolis agroexportadora en la obra del General Rafael Reyes." *ACHSC* 40, no. 2 (2013): 145–77; see also Stephen L. Nugent, *The Rise and Fall of the Amazon Rubber Industry: An Historical Anthropology* (New York: Routledge, 2017).

21. Gina Paola Sierra, "La fiebre del caucho en Colombia," *Revista Credencial* (October 2011).

22. Guillén, "Embrace of the Serpent: An Interview with Ciro Guerra."

23. First discovered at the Kamloops Industrial School, which had opened in 1890, remaining in operation until 1978, the center was first run by the Catholic Church until the Canadian federal government took it over in the late 1960s. As Sarah Beaulieu—a specialist in ground-penetrating radar who has been leading forensic research—suggests, "this investigation has barely scratched the surface, covering just under two acres of the total 160-acre residential school site," Paula Newton, *CNN*,

July 16, 2021. In a recent op-ed, Luis Guzmán argues, echoing indirectly and ironically Immanuel Kant's famous analogy of humanity as a crooked timber, that in these realities "La barbarie occidental se ejerce a la sombra del árbol de la civilización. No es inconsistencia en la aplicación de ideales; es estrategia de destrucción y exterminio camuflada bajo esos mismos ideales" ("Western barbarism is deployed in the shadow of the tree of civilization. It is not inconsistency in applying its ideals [but] an extermination and destruction strategy concealed underneath those very ideals" (my translation), "La barbarie civilizada," *Diario Criterio*, July 17, 2021. Guzmán's reflections speak to a racist structure manifest most recently in President Jair Bolsonaro's public comments about Amazonian communities, among others.

24. Richard Evans Schultes, Albert Hoffman, and Christian Rätsch, *Plants of the Gods: Their Sacred, Healing, and Hallucinogenic Powers* (Rochester, VT: Healing Arts Press, 1996), 114, 121, 146.

25. Among several Amazonian cultures, "chullachaqui" refers to a spirit or entity often perceived as destructive, responsible for creating disorientation and false perception, as it often assumes the guise of others. In Guerra's film, the concept expands to deploy ideas related to existential alienation, loss of memory and identity, or doubling, as in the German concept of doppelgänger. See Guillén, "Embrace of the Serpent: An Interview with Ciro Guerra."

26. See Mark Plotkin's lecture "The Amazonian Travels of Richard Evans Schultes, February 20, 2019, https://youtu.be/vBqQ2SQuq68.

27. Luís Guzmán, personal communication, June 27, 2021.

28. Guillén, "Embrace of the Serpent: An Interview with Ciro Guerra."

29. Ane Alencar and Ariadne Esquivel Muelbert, "The Amazon Is Now a Net Carbon Producer, but There's Still Time to Reverse the Damage," *The Guardian*, July 19, 2021.

30. Juliana Jaimes, "Carrera contra el reloj para salvar el conocimiento sobre plantas medicinales," *El Espectador*, July 2, 2021; Jaimes's report is based on Rodrigo Camara-Leret and Jordi Bascompte's study "Language Extinction Triggers the Loss of Unique Medicinal Knowledge," *PNAS* 118, no. 24 (2021).

31. Jaimes, "Carrera contra el reloj para salvar el conocimiento sobre plantas medicinales," 4.

32. *Unthinking Eurocentrism* (London: Routledge, 1995), 47.

33. "The Native Eye: Re-Embracing the Serpent with 'Chullachaqui,'" *Bright Lights Film Journal*, June 15, 2017.

34. See "The Amazonian Travels of Richard Evans Schultes," https://www.amazonteam.org/maps/schultes/en/.

Chapter 7

History, Autobiography, and Truth in Euzhan Palcy's *Rue Cases-Nègres*

Mohamed Kamara

Rue Cases-Nègres [Sugar Cane Alley] *(1983): produced by Jean-Luc Ormières; directed by Euzhan Palcy; written by Euzhan Palcy, based on the novel by Joseph Zobel; color; 103 minutes; NEF Diffusion, Orca Productions, SU.MA.FA. José (Garry Cadenat) lives with his grandmother (Darling Légitimus) on a plantation in Martinique. Her determination and his resilience and intelligence enable him to escape from oppressive sugarcane fields.*

Euzhan Palcy's 1983 eponymous cinematic rendition (*Rue Cases-Nègres [Sugar Cane Alley]*) of Joseph Zobel's[1] 1950 autobiographical novel, *La Rue Cases-Nègres*, opens with a series of sepia-colored still images (most of which, if not all, are postcards) depicting early 1930s Martinique.[2] Why open the film with these images that freeze a place and people in time? Does Palcy do this to assuage, in advance, the viewer's concerns vis-à-vis what might appear to be the preeminence of a political message over historical accuracy or autobiographical truth in her film? Or is she framing the debate regarding historical accuracy, noting that history can be represented in various ways, in specific dates and in artifacts fixed in time or in dynamic stories that portray the zeitgeist of a people over a certain time span? Or is she simply alerting the viewer to the possibilities (and traps) inherent in the representation of what we refer to as historical truth and fact?

In what follows, I propose an analysis of Palcy's *Rue Cases-Nègres* that allows us to view the film as a specific kind of history, a specific way of doing history, one that complicates and challenges received notions of the how, what, and why of history. In the process, I hope to illuminate Palcy's

133

ethnographic and historiographic project, especially as it relates to the life and times of Blacks and other historically marginalized peoples.

FILM SUMMARY

Rue Cases-Nègres focuses on its two main characters, the eleven-year-old José Hassam (played by the affable Garry Cadenat) and his grandmother, M'man Tine (played by the endearing Darling Légitimus). In the absence of his parents, José becomes the complete ward of his grandmother, a laborer in the sugarcane plantations of rural Martinique, less than a century after the definitive abolition of slavery by France. Together with other black plantation workers and their families, they live in Black Shack Alley, a place Sylvie Kandé labels "the politico-cultural ghetto where the West Indian working classes strive to survive"[3] and "a topography of oppression."[4] M'man Tine works harder than appropriate for her age so she can put her gifted grandson through school, seeing in education the surest way out of the cane fields. When José passes his high school entrance examination and heads to the capital, Fort-de-France, on a partial government scholarship, M'man Tine leaves their home in Black Shack Alley in Petit-Bourg and heads to the capital with her ward, where she does laundry to support him. When José wins a full scholarship thanks to his impressive performance in school, M'man Tine returns to Black Shack Alley, where she dies shortly after. There are many other important characters in the film, including Médouze (played by the impressive Douta Seck), the son of an enslaved African who participated in the abolitionist insurrection leading to the end of slavery. Médouze, through his folktales and stories about Africa and slavery, becomes a link between José's Martinique and the Africa of his ancestors. He is the equivalent of the West African griot, master of the word and guardian of memories.

SOME KEY DIFFERENCES BETWEEN
THE FILM AND THE NOVEL

A cinematic rendition of a literary re-creation from memory and imagination, Palcy's *Rue Cases-Nègres* is several degrees removed from Zobel's *La Rue Cases-Nègres*, in time, space, content, and such other considerations as gender, class, and race. Beyond the evident divergences, there are significant narrative, philosophical, and thematic differences between the film and the novel, a few of which are worth highlighting here.

Whereas in Zobel's novel, José's mother is alive and later plays a crucial role in her son's life, in Palcy's film, we are told Délia died (leaving only a bowl behind and of course, her son).[5] The roles of M'man Tine and Délia are combined into one person, M'man Tine. Also, the character of Léopold (José's friend) in the film is an amalgam of two characters in the novel: Georges Roc (Jojo) and Raphael, which allows Palcy to engage the question of class and race conflict through a single character, further underscoring the intersection between the two.

While in the novel the reader, like José, can only imagine what lies within and behind the walls of white homes (since José enters none of them), in the film, we see the inside of Léopold's house in Petit-Bourg as well as that of Carmen's boss in Fort-de-France. This enables Palcy to juxtapose the privilege of white life and the abject material poverty of Blacks.

In both novel and film, José is accused by his teacher of having plagiarized his essay about Médouze and the cane fields. The matter remains unresolved in the book. In the film, however, two important things happen that are absent in the book. First, José defends himself vigorously against the accusation, even planning to bring the matter up with the school principal. In so doing, he asserts his humanity, courage, and agency even in the face of possible retaliation. Second, his teacher realizes his mistake, apologizes, and recommends José for a full government scholarship.

In part three of Zobel's novel, José spends a good amount of time visiting and talking about the Fort-de-France waterfront. Given the preponderance of the sea in the popular imaginary of Martinique as a tourist mecca, a French outpost in the Caribbean where metropolitan French citizens go to drown the stress accumulated from their metro-boulot-dodo life, it is significant that Palcy barely shows the sea in the film.

Palcy's film, like Zobel's novel, is not the typical bildungsroman, which tends to focus on the main character while using all others as props. Her choice of a community and not the individual for the title of her film, as Zobel did for his novel, makes *Rue Cases-Nègres* "a collective, generic autobiography."[6] If Zobel's novel is mostly José's story (told entirely from his perspective), Palcy's film comes across as the story not only of José but also of Black Shack Alley. True to her predilection for the collective, Palcy opens and closes her film with the laboring community of Black Shack Alley. As Carolyn Durham observes, "Palcy significantly alters Zobel's narrative of the escape of an exceptional individual by adding a final crowd scene that marks in song the solidarity of the community of Martinique and its collective revolt against colonialist oppression."[7] It is fitting that the last words we hear as the film closes are the following from José: "Tomorrow I return to Fort-de-France, and I will take my Black Shack Alley with me."

EUZHAN PALCY

Renowned film director, writer, and producer, Euzhan Palcy was born in 1958 in Gros-Morne, central Martinique. After completing her studies on the island, she went to France to study drama and literature, before switching to film studies at the Ecole normale Supérieure Louis-Lumière in Paris,[8] where she was a student of Jean Rouch, a pioneer of cinema verité and cinematic ethnofiction. One of the most important influences on Palcy was fellow Martinican and cofounder of the Négritude movement, Aimé Césaire. Of him, she said: "My first godfather was Aimé Césaire. He taught me everything I know politically, philosophically, my history."[9] Palcy returned to Martinique to work in television, during which time she made *Rue Cases-Nègres*, her first feature. Palcy was the first Black woman to be produced by a major Hollywood studio for her 1989 *A Dry White Season*. Thanks to *Rue Cases-Nègres,* she became the first Black director to win a Silver Lion award (Venice, 1983) and a César award (Paris, 1984). The film also won a FESPACO award (Ouagadougou, 1985).

Deciding at age ten to become a filmmaker to help tell the story of Black peoples, Palcy's small but impressive corpus[10] reveal "an engaged and engaging change agent."[11] Her vision of Martinique is antipodal to the touristy Martinique, "un morceau de la France sous les Tropiques" (a bit of France in the Tropics).[12] Alain Ménil labels this Martinique the place of the three Ss, "sea, sex, and sun."[13] Palcy's Martinique is the Martinique of everyday Martinicans, the Martinique of "la densité palpable du quotidien" (the palpable density of everyday life).[14] She realized even as a little girl in Gros-Morne that the best way to tell the people's story of Martinique is to go back in time and return to the present with usable nuggets relating to the lived experiences of Blacks in slavery and colonization.

A PENCHANT FOR HISTORY

According to an Igbo proverb, "a man who does not know where the rain began to beat him cannot say where he dried his body." A cursory glance at Euzhan Palcy's œuvre reveals how Palcy's reflex as a filmmaker is forged in historical consciousness. She realizes that until we can fully appreciate the significance of historical events, we cannot expect to move into the future in a meaningful way.

Palcy's preference for stories grounded in deep history is quite conspicuous in her filmography. The vast majority of her films, if not all, are inspired by and crafted through the lens of specific historical events. For example, for *A Dry White Season*, she went undercover to interview perpetrators and victims alike of the Special Branch, the hit squad of the South African apartheid police.[15] *The Killing Yard* is based on the 1971 Attica prison uprising in New York. *Ruby Bridges* is inspired by the story of Ruby Bridges, the six-year-old who became the most iconic figure of the American desegregation crisis of the 1960s.[16] As we shall see in due course, all the major themes of *Rue Cases-Nègres* (including race, class, gender, and education), a film inspired by an autobiographical novel, are depicted from a decidedly historical perspective.

HISTORY, MEMORY, REPRESENTATION, AND THE TRUTH QUESTION

In the introduction to his English translation of Zobel's novel, Keith Warner notes thusly: "After all, the novelist is not a historian in the true sense of the word, nor is he a sociologist. How then can one accept what he says about his society and milieu without the nagging feeling that it is severely, and quite understandably, biased?"[17] Warner is reacting to Zobel's claim that even though his novel was inspired by Richard Wright's *Black Boy* (1945), "everything in it is autobiographical" even if "the story was patterned after [his] own aesthetics of composition."[18] Palcy could say the same about her film, patterned after her own aesthetics of cinematography: choice of subject matter, camera angles, color, dialogue, sound, editing. And so on. Furthermore, historical facts are just raw materials. What one includes or omits, how one does this, and when in the narrative train, are all a matter of choice that has as much to do with "the truth" or facts as it does with the time and place of its telling as well as with the ideology, intention, resources, and temperament of the teller.

In a sense, every representation is fictitious! We can only imagine what really happened and in representing it from our imagination, more or less distort it. All histories are recounted in the present, and the present has its demands that cannot be ignored. If it is true that "the historian establishes verisimilitude rather than objective truth,"[19] the maker of fictional films (or documentaries) cannot honestly claim absolute objectivity and should not be expected to be absolutely objective. The question then becomes, why do we represent historical truth, or facts, the way we do? Not only can we not know or remember everything that happened; our remembrance and recounting of things past are by nature and necessity selective. They are also subjective, which makes them more or less unreliable. History is not an artefact, or a golden nugget, to be sanitized, neatly packaged, and bequeathed to subsequent generations. It is a dynamic entity that pulsates in the memory of those who lived or inherited it. Because history does not belong to any one person or group and because it is thought, understood, and lived differently by different people, it benefits from being reviewed, revised, and rewritten as and whenever new truths and memories are unearthed or whenever old ones are engaged with fresh eyes.

In the remainder of this chapter, we shall discuss some of the key themes in Palcy's film, while showing how the filmmaker's engagement with them is anchored in her understanding of history as a process and as a means to an end.

EDUCATION AS KEY TO FREEDOM

The ultimate goal of any education project is to assure the continuity of a given society through the transmission of its history, ethos, culture, and civilization from one generation to the next. A good education is holistic because it foregrounds its conscious and not-so-conscious, material and spiritual, and its moral and intellectual values. Edouard Glissant summarizes this concept quite well in his *Caribbean Discourse*:

> the technical development of the individual, that is, his ability to play a role in
> society that in practical terms is no more or no less a long-term investment; the
> general molding of the individual, that is, his cultural, emotional, and intellec-
> tual equilibrium, without which no human being would know how to 'play his
> role' in society, and without which, furthermore, there would be no society to
> plan its objectives or to fulfil them more or less.[20]

The French school was central to France's colonial *mission civilisatrice*, the self-granted vocation of bringing light and progress to the dark corners of the world. The primary goal of colonial education was two pronged: (1) spread knowledge of French and French culture and civilization to the mass of the colonized and (2) mold, from that mass, a distinct class of individuals inten-tionally beholden to the French colonizer and thoroughly estranged from their own people and society. It was an assimilationist program of erasure by which France sought to absorb the cultures and resources of other peoples into its black hole of self-aggrandizement. Brazilian philosopher of education, Paolo Freire, calls this kind of education system the pedagogy of the oppressed,[21] and Césaire characterizes it as a "parody of education."[22]

Palcy engages two forms of education in *Rue Cases-Nègres*: formal French education provided at the brick-and-mortar schools and the informal education provided by Médouze. The distinction between the two regarding their form and substance is made unequivocally clear in the film.

In the movie, the French education meted out to the students is alien to their lived experience, a point Sheila Petty reiterates thusly:

> [T]he film also illustrates the absurdity of a French curriculum ill suited to Martinican experience. In a later sequence, Mr. Roc, the teacher, faces two lines of students outside the schoolroom as he instructs them to remember that he will quiz them on glaciers the next day. Depicted in a long shot that emphasizes the tropical architecture of the school, the reference to alpine glaciers seems almost comically misplaced.[23]

Later on in the film, the dictation component of the scholarship exam José and other kids take features an excerpt from Alphonse Daudet's bucolic *Lettres de mon moulin* (*Letters from My Windmill*, 1869). There is nothing in the curriculum portrayed in the film that talks about the life of Martinican Black or indigenous peoples.

Deftly juxtaposed with this out-of-place education are the educational interventions of Médouze, which are portrayed as more holistic, practical, and relevant to José's reality. The knowledge Médouze dispenses to José is historical (about slavery), technical (art as seen in his carving of the figurine during one of the sessions with José,[24] the medicinal quality of plants, for example), and general (about creation and the place of humans in it).

There are two major educational sessions involving Médouze and José. In the first, Médouze offers a primer on slavery. He talks about how his own father and his uncle and aunt were captured in Africa and brought to the Caribbean. By connecting the larger experience of slavery to his own life, Médouze brings real urgency to that history for José, who is nearly a century removed from it. Médouze then proceeds to the specific story of the Martinican slave insurrection of May 20, 1848, the last of slave revolts before the abolition of slavery on the island.[25] By narrating this particular instance of marronage (slave uprising) in which his father participated, Médouze is not only countering the colonizer's narrative of the subservient Black incapable of thought, planning, and heroic action; he is also memorializing all slave revolts before and after it in the Americas.[26]

In the second session, Médouze focuses on creation and the natural environment. In keeping with African cosmogony and animism, he insists on the sacredness, interconnectedness, and complementarity of all telluric forces. He tells José that everything in creation has its secrets and we must not interfere with creation: "no one should meddle with life." He further notes that "water and fire are not enemies"; they are instead complementary. Finally, he teaches José that creation takes care of its own affairs, thus alluding to a higher power that will eventually mete out justice by rectifying the imbalance caused by human greed and hubris as exemplified in slavery, colonization, and other forms and instances of evil.

These two diametrically opposed visions of education (French and Afrocentric) are bound to collide in the student. The collision occurs in high school in Fort-de-France. When José expresses his agency by writing an essay about Médouze and the sugarcane fields, hence about his own life and experiences in Black Shack Alley, he is accused of plagiarism. "Ironically," notes Durham, "José is accused of stealing (from the) French, not when he slavishly imitates the highly structured system of written expression into which he is being deliberately indoctrinated, but on the single occasion on which he dares to produce an original and authentically black text."[27] We must add that José's narrative is also an intensely personal one.

As it turns out, in the new world created by the French, French education becomes the key to survival. Mr. Roc, the schoolteacher in Petit-Bourg, tells his pupils to inscribe in the middle of the first page of their exercise book (to be read each morning) the sentence "Learning is the key that opens the second door[28] to our freedom."[29] The primary school certificate (Certificat d'Études Primaires), the first documentation of achievement in colonial education, literally stands between a life of backbreaking work in the sugarcane fields and a relatively decent life.

Orality as a vehicle for the transmission of historical and practical knowledge inherited from prior generations takes center stage in Palcy's philosophy of education and history. In addition to the full-blown stories he recounts to José, Médouze tells the boy riddles and proverbs. With other elements of folklore, such as songs, chants, and proverbs, as well as the traditional combat dance (also known as *laghia* and *danmyé* in Martinique, similar to the Brazilian capoeira), in the evenings after work in the plantation, Euzhan Palcy gives us a full range of oral expressive culture in Black Shack Alley. Oral literature, for example, not only helps explain phenomena and define a society; it also equips members of a given society with the tools essential for their survival. Africans on the continent and in the diaspora, not unlike other peoples, use their folklore to edify, to amuse, and to ensure cultural cohesion, integrity, and continuity. Through oral praxis, Africans and people of African descent are able to inscribe themselves in history and in their social, physical, and metaphysical environments. By privileging orality in her film, Euzhan Palcy became one of the early proponents of the use of orature as a source of historical knowledge.[30]

RACE, CLASS, AND GENDER

Rue Cases-Nègres is the story of how race, class, and gender intersect within a colonized space. Euzhan Palcy deploys many strategies to elucidate her purpose in the film. As Durham notes, *"Rue Cases-Nègres* uses such conventions as standard shots and framing, so-called 'natural' color, and continuous editing to force Western spectators to see beyond their neocolonialist vision of Martinique as an exotic and luxurious vacation paradise to the reality of its history both of racist exploitation and of native resistance to that oppression."[31] Through her use of postcard images; sepia tones; and depiction of characters, their attitudes, and actions, the filmmaker discredits racial mythologies while decrying their real life consequences.

The postcard was, for at least the entirety of the twentieth century, the most iconic memento of contact among peoples and cultures. It was the medium preferred by vacationers, tourists, and visitors to a particular place, usually unfamiliar to them, to memorialize their visit and to share their vision of the place with those left behind at home. Like all artifacts of human civilization, postcards have a history, and this history is steeped in the colonialist project:

> The postcard, a turn-of-the-century invention of French colonialism, literally reproduces the colony and colonized people as a succession of "pretty pictures," a source of local color and exotic clichés, that replaces indigenous reality with the prejudices and phantasms of the colonized themselves, even as it exposes the voyeurism that characterizes colonialist society as a whole. By the immobility of their subjects, the still photographs epitomize colonialist domination of the native people and culture of Martinique; and the falseness of the "color" in these shots, tinted in a shade of greenish-yellow, reveals the artificiality of this self-reflective mise-en-scène of colonialist exoticism.[32]

Colonial postcards are about ideology, conquest, and domination. By fixing their subjects in time and space, the colonizer is exempt from the hard and essential task of knowing them as full humans equal to them. In this light, therefore, it makes sense that Palcy opens her film the way she does. Proceeding almost in the classic French argumentative style of "thèse-antithèse-synthèse," she deftly dissects and dismantles the racist myth of the exotic, docile Black, devoid of any complexity. While the image on the postcard may contain some element of truth, it certainly does not offer the full picture. Palcy undertakes an incursion into this artefact to search for more solid truths about the Caribbean experience in history lying beneath the surface. The filmmaker then reemerges and proceeds to showing the dynamic reality of her people and their daily struggles for survival as well as their agency, even within the context of cultural and socioeconomic disenfranchisement.

Martinican society has historically been characterized by a three-tier stratification system, with whites (including *békés*, descendants of the early white European settlers, many of whom were slaveholding families) at the top, mulattos in the middle, and the majority Blacks at the bottom of the ladder. The family of José's friend, Léopold, offers a complex perspective on the question of race and class. Léopold's father is white, while his mother, Honorine,[33] is a mulatto. Léopold's parents forbid their son to speak creole and to associate with José, "the little barefoot nigger who cannot even speak French."[34] While for the father, the interdiction could be a clear-cut case of his racial superiority complex, for the mother, there is a more practical, class motivation. The rejection of her blackness vis-à-vis her son seems born out of genuine love for her son and a concomitant desire on her part to protect him from the harsh fate reserved for unassimilated Blacks in a French-dominated society. And we must not forget that M'man Tine, though to a lesser extent than Léopold's mother and the cinema clerk in Fort-de-France,[35] has also imbibed the discourse of French superiority as seen in the scene where she forbids José from eating with his fingers: "a well brought up child uses a spoon." Her concern, like Léopold's mother for her son, is for her grandson to rise above the station designated for Blacks in Black Shack Alley. She recognizes that assimilating a certain degree of Frenchness will improve her grandson's prospects for upward social mobility.

By juxtaposing white-dominated spaces and black spaces (Léopold's house in Petit-Bourg and that of Carmen's bosses in Fort-de-France, for example), Palcy renders visible race and class distinctions in Martinique, with their accompanying mannerisms and material manifestations. The death of Léopold's father and the refusal of Mr. de Thorail to transfer his family name to his son,[36] which pushes Léopold to run away, allow Palcy to introduce another element into the race–class question. Léopold's reappearance at the end of the movie as a whistleblower, under arrest for attempting to show the defrauding of plantation workers by white owners, causes the viewer to wonder: Is Léopold's rebellion against race or against class? In the context of Palcy's film, it becomes nearly impossible, even unnecessary, to separate one from the other.

The insertion of American-born French entertainer and activist Josephine Baker into the plotline of the film, through the song "J'ai deux amours: mon pays et Paris" (I have two loves; my country and Paris), which she performed in 1930 in Paris, adds another layer to the race question, in addition to providing us a specific historical reference to Paris of the interwar years. This historically accurate reference to Baker allows Palcy, among other things, to expand the scope and trope of race relations and tensions well beyond the borders of Martinique. As Gerise Herndon suggests, the "choice of Baker rather than a white singer refers to the discourses of exoticism and primitivism as well as multiple layers within the discourse of racial mythology."[37] A light-skinned Black American woman in Paris demonstrates her willingness and ability to negotiate the treacherous terrain of race and politics by playing the part of the exotic and primitive Black woman, among many other roles in her adopted country of France.[38] Additionally, the 1920s and 1930s saw not only an influx of Black American intellectuals and artists looking for a reprieve from American anti-Black racism; they also witnessed the creation of the Negritude[39] movement.

It is easy to think that José is the main character of *Rue Cases-Nègres*. Upon a closer look, however, we see how much M'man Tine dominates the narrative. Outside of the fact that she is José's biological grandmother, there really is no José without M'man Tine. She is the visible and invisible hand that pulls the strings that make her grandson move physically, morally, and psychologically. Even when she is not there physically with José (when she is in the fields or on a trip alone, for example), the old woman is present in José's every moment and thought. Furthermore, no adult male figure is present in M'man Tine's life to try to dominate her. Not even the colonial system of oppression and the legacy of slavery that she and other Blacks have to endure can make her flinch. When José is denied a full scholarship, M'man Tine realizes she must make a greater sacrifice so her grandson can go to school ("They don't know I am a fighting woman!" she says).

By crystallizing all parental responsibilities in M'man Tine, Palcy achieves two things. First, she highlights the importance of grandparents, especially grandmothers, in Black societies. Second, she elevates M'man Tine to the status of a self-sacrificing matriarch. M'man Tine's role as a strong Black woman in the face of tremendous social and financial headwinds is reminiscent of Lena Younger (Mama) in Lorraine Hansberry's *A Raisin in the Sun* (1959). What Hansberry said of "Mama" can be applied to M'man Tine:

> The Black matriarch incarnate: The bulwark of the Negro family since slavery; the embodiment of the Negro will to transcendence. It is she who, in the mind of the Black poet, scrubs the floors of a nation in order to create Black diplomats and university professors. It is she who, while seeming to cling to traditional restraints, drives the young on into the fire hoses and one day simply refuses to move to the back of the bus in Montgomery.[40]

Unlike in the novel where M'man Tine cedes responsibility for José to her daughter when the boy goes to Fort-de-France to attend school, M'man Tine in the movie lives until it is clear her grandson no longer needs her financial support; it is as if the battered old woman has willed herself to stay alive just for that.

THE FILMMAKER AS ACTIVIST AND EDUCATOR

Trica Danielle Keaton provides the following assessment of Palcy and her work: "Her films, if not the entirety of Palcy's career, illustrate that this pioneering artist is not simply a filmmaker but also is an activist, that is, one who has sought to exercise her craft in the interest of social justice and institutional memory."[41] Euzhan Palcy refuses the title of "réalisateur engagé" (activist filmmaker).[42] She prefers the moniker of educator when she says, "[f]ilmmakers have a very important responsibility because we are educators."[43]

Being an educator and being an activist are not necessarily mutually exclusive. While she may not like the label of activist, Euzhan Palcy is by any stretch of the imagination an activist filmmaker, and an intentional one to boot. An activist is someone who, driven by their perception of things and a desire to change the status quo, does something that moves people to see themselves in a new light, and perhaps do something to change their condition.[44] In all the interviews she has given, Palcy has described her work as attempts on her part to do two specific things with her career: serve as a spokesperson for the downtrodden and right the wrongs in and of history. In one of her most recent interviews, she reiterates this point when she quotes a line from Aimé Césaire's *Cahier d'un retour au pays natal* (*Notebook of a Return to My Native Land*, 1939): "My mouth shall be the mouth of those calamities that have no mouth, my voice, the freedom of those who break down in the prison holes of despair."[45] In a much earlier interview, Palcy stated, "I'm just someone who is trying to make a difference, and over the years, I've been trying to rectify something that had been very badly done, that perhaps had not been done: to bear witness to an injustice."[46] This deeply felt obligation and urgency to tell oft-ignored stories pushed her specifically to make the documentaries on young Martinican dissidents of the 1940s[47] and on Aimé Césaire. "I wanted to do justice to those people, and also because they were old and dying,"[48] she said of the dissidents and of Césaire who was eighty-one when the documentary was released and would pass away fourteen years later, she said, "I am glad I caught him at the time."[49]

In her role as filmmaker, Palcy even sees a calling higher than simply bearing witness to an injustice: "I must take my camera to *restore the roots* and *heal the wounds of history*, bring life back."[50] With this ardent desire to restore balance to a seriously traumatized world, it is no surprise that she dedicates *Rue Cases-Nègres* to oppressed and dispossessed peoples everywhere: "pour toutes les rues cases-nègres du monde" (For all the black shack alleys of the world).[51]

THE FILMMAKER AS HISTORIAN
AND ARCHAEOLOGIST

To be an effective educator, one must have a personal stake in the educational project, and one must be a knowledgeable historian. And to be a knowledgeable historian, one has to be willing to do the hard work of excavating buried treasures from the debris left behind by oppressive and universalizing histories. From the starting point of her own ignorance guaranteed by the colonial education system—"Nobody told me my history, my people's history, at school"[52]—Euzhan Palcy has to become an archaeologist for herself and others: "I learned it by digging and looking for it."[53] Palcy's identity as a Black Caribbean woman makes her job all the more meaningful. She says: "being a black filmmaker from the Caribbean, also a kind of anthropologist or archaeologist. I am always digging, trying to look for the truth, for the memory of the past, to find out who we are, where we come from, and what we can offer."[54] The work of unearthing the past of her people is not enough; Palcy has to be an architect and engineer who must utilize her findings as raw material to design and build living and accessible resources for the edification of her people and the memorialization of their experiences.

BY WAY OF CONCLUSION

When *Rue Cases-Nègres* was released in 1983, Euzhan Palcy was a young female activist making a film based on a book written by a man who disavowed any intentional political activism in his book. In her essay on the film, Herndon notes that:

> Palcy's auto-ethnographic impulse to retell her own history through the medium of film and to represent black Martinicans is a political move by a "Third World" artist that functions to displace the racial mythologies of exoticism and primitivism and to appropriate power. The film shows that the master's tools can indeed be used to dismantle the master's house.[55]

Why make a movie based on a book that was already revolutionary by any standard, especially three decades after that book's publication? One could imagine at least two motivations for this. First is the need to pay homage to Joseph Zobel as an elder in the annals of efforts for the recuperation of the dignity of the Black race. Second, as a student of African and African diaspora history, Palcy knows the importance of continuing the work of teaching new generations the vital history she was not taught when she was a child. For a project of this magnitude and urgency, namely, telling the story of those

Frantz Fanon referred to as the "wretched of the earth,"[56] what better way to do it than through film!

Donald Stevens's claim that "[f]ilms have an emotional impact and a popular appeal that is usually missing from professional scholarship"[57] makes sense. Other qualities of film make it an attractive medium to Palcy. That it is possible to compress hundreds of pages and centuries of history into a few hours makes films more appealing and accessible to a much larger number of people. Furthermore, whereas reading seems to be a more solitary event, the cinema is a community experience. So in keeping with the aesthetics and praxis of orality, and seeing the representation of Black Shack Alley (all the black shack alleys of the world) as a collective project undertaken from the perspective of the downtrodden and the forgotten, *Rue Cases-Nègres* qualifies as effective history because it is beautiful and true.

ADDITIONAL RESOURCES

Bernabé, Jean, Patrick Chamoiseau, and Raphaël Confiant. *Éloge de la créolité / In Praise of Creoleness*. Translated by M. B. Taleb-Khyar. Paris: Gallimard, 1993. A long essay by three contemporary Martinican writers arguing that Creoleness (a blend of distinct African, Asian, and European heritages) is the true Caribbean identity, not any part of the sum total.

Capecia, Mayotte. I Am a Martinican Woman *and* The White Negress: *Two Novelletes by Mayotte Capecia*. Translated by Beatrice Stith Clark. Pueblo Colorado: Passeggiata Press, 1998. Mayotte Capecia infuriated her compatriot, Frantz Fanon, so much by her rejection of her Blackness that Fanon wrote a scathing review of her work and complex in his first book, *Black Skin, White Masks*.

Césaire, Aimé. *Discourse on Colonialism*. Translated by Joan Pinkham. New York: MR, 1972. One of the most lucid and biting criticisms of colonialism and its supporting ideologies.

Fanon, Frantz. *Black Skin, White Masks*. Translated by Richard Philcox. London: Pluto, 2008. A text that focuses on the question of Blackness. What does it mean to be Black in an age dominated by whiteness?

————. *The Wretched of the Earth*. Translated by Constance Farrington. New York: Grove Press, 1968. Arguably the most widely read and referenced text on decolonization and its immediate aftermath.

Glissant, Édouard. *Caribbean Discourse: Selected Essays*. Translated J. Michael Dash. Charlottesville: University Press of Virginia, 1989. A series of essays on various aspects of Caribbean identity.

Okpewho, Isidore. *African Oral Literature: Backgrounds, Character, and Continuity*. Bloomington: Indiana University Press, 1992. An in-depth analysis of the trajectory, uses, and usefulness of African oral literature, also known as orature.

Palcy, Euzhan, dir. Césaire, Aimé, et al. *Aimé Césaire: A Voice for History = Une Voix Pour L'histoire*. JMJ Productions, 2006. This three-part documentary on the life and career of Aimé Césaire is also an excellent introduction to the modern history of Martinique.

Zobel, Joseph. *Black Shack Alley*. Translated by Keith Q. Warner. Boulder/London: Lynne Rienner, 1996. An English translation of the novel on which Palcy's film is based.

NOTES

1. Joseph Zobel was born in 1915 in Rivière-Salée, southern Martinique. His father, mother, and grandmother worked for the same white family, owners of a sugarcane plantation. With the parents mostly unavailable, Zobel was raised by his grandmother. After earning his baccalaureate, he stayed and worked in Fort-de-France for a few years before heading to France for further studies. Upon Léopold Sédar Senghor's encouragement, Zobel moved to Senegal, where he lived and worked for many years. He eventually relocated to France, where he continued his intellectual output until his passing in 2006. Zobel wrote many novels, including *Diab'-là* (1947), *La Rue Case-Nègres* (1950), *La Fête à Paris* (1953), and *Les Jours immobiles* (1978), and short story collections, including *Le Soleil partagé* (1964), *Laghia de la mort* (1978), *Et si la mer n'était pas bleue* (1982), *Mas Badara* (1983), and *Gertal et autres nouvelles, suivi de Journal, 1946–2002* (2002), as well as poetry, including *Incantation pour un retour au pays natal* (1964), *Poèmes de moi-même* (1984), *Poèmes d'Amour et de Silence* (1994), and *Le Soleil m'a dit* (2002). Zobel was also the recipient of prestigious awards, including Chevalier de la Légion d'Honneur (1998) and the Grand Prix du Livre Insulaire (2002).

2. Before Columbus "discovered" the island in 1502 during his fourth voyage to the so-called New World, what became known as Martinique was occupied first by Arawaks, then by Caribs, both groups coming from South America. Occupied in the name of France in 1635, Martinique was a slave island until 1848, when slavery was abolished for the second and final time. Thereafter, Martinique was a French colony until it became an overseas department of France (département d'outre-mer, or DOM) in 1946. In December 1959, within the backdrop of a fraught economic and social situation, a small altercation between a French man and a Martinican turned into a full-blown riot. Three young men were killed, and many more were wounded after French security forces opened fire on demonstrators. The situation quickly degenerated, eventually leading to the creation of the pro-independence organization, OJAM (Organisation de la Jeunesse Anticolonialiste de la Martinique). The leaders of OJAM asserted that "under the hypocritical mask of departmentalization, Martinique is a colony . . . economically, socially, culturally, and politically dominated by France." They proclaimed, "The authenticity of the Martinican and Antillean personality owing to a peopling different from that of France . . . the right for Martinicans to govern their own affairs" and asked "the Guadeloupean and Guyanese people to work together to free their country and for a common future," quoted in Gesner Mencé, *L'Affaire de l'OJAM ou le 'complot du Mardi-Gras'* (Martinique: Editions Désormeaux, 2001), 50.

3. Sylvie Kandé, "Renunciation and Victory in 'Black Shack Alley,'" trans. Kwaku Gyasi, *Research in African Literatures* 25, no. 2 (1994): 35.

4. Kandé, "Renunciation and victory," 40.

5. The father is not mentioned at all in the film.

6. Kandé, "Renunciation and victory," 35.

7. Carolyn Durham, "Euzhan Palcy's Feminist Filmmaking: From Romance to Realism, From Gender to Race," *Women in French Studies* 7 (1999): 163.

8. "Biographie d'Euzhan Palcy," accessed July 25, 2021, https://riviere-salee.fr/la -ville/culture/biographie-euzhan-palcy/.

9. Euzhan Palcy, interviewed by Aaron Hunt, "Misfortunes That Have No Mouth: A Conversation with Euzhan Palcy," accessed July 28, 2020, https://mubi.com/ notebook/posts/misfortunes-that-have-no-mouth-a-conversation-with-euzhan-palcy.

10. Palcy's filmography includes the following: TV series: *Les Mariées de l'Isle Bourbon* (*The Brides of Bourbon Island*, 2007), *La messagère* (*The Messenger*, 1975); documentaries: Parcours de dissidents (*The Journey of the Dissidents*, 2006), *Aimé Césaire: une voix pour l'histoire* (*Aimé Césaire: A Voice for History*, 1994), and Comment vont les enfants? (*How are the Kids?*, the "Hassane" episode, 1990); and features: *The Killing Yard* (2001), *Ruby Bridges* (1998), *Siméon* (1992), *A Dry White Season* (1989), and *Rue Cases-Nègres* (*Sugar Cane Alley*, 1983).

11. Trica Danielle Keaton, "Euzhan Palcy: Creative Dissent, Artistic Reckoning," Palimpsest: A Journal on Women, Gender, and the Black International 1, no. 1 (2012): 120.

12. Aimé Césaire, "La Martinique Telle Qu'elle Est," *The French Review* 53, no. 2 (1979): 183–89. My translation.

13. Alain Ménil, "'*Rue Cases-Nègres*' ou les Antilles de l'Intérieur," *Présence Africaine* no. 129 (1er Trimestre, 1984): 101.

14. Ménil, "*Rue Cases-Nègres*," 101. My translation.

15. Euzhan Palcy, interviewed by Hunt.

16. Ruby Bridges was immortalized in Norman Rockwell's 1964 painting, *The Problem We All Live With*.

17. Keith Q. Warner, "Introduction," in *Black Shack Alley*, trans. Keith Q. Warner (Boulder/London: Lynne Rienner, 1996), xiii.

18. Warner, "Introduction," xiii.

19. Quoted by Donald Stevens in the introduction to this volume, 6.

20. Edouard Glissant, *Caribbean Discourse*, trans. Michael Dash (Charlottesville: University of Virginia Press, 1989), 174.

21. Paulo Freire, *Pedagogy of the Oppressed*, trans. Myra Bergman Ramos (New York: Continuum, 2000).

22. Aimé Cesaire, *Discourse on Colonialism*, trans. Joan Pinkham (New York: Monthly Review Press, 1972), 20.

23. Sheila J. Petty, *Contact Zones: Memory, Origin, and Discourses in Black Diasporic Cinema* (Detroit: Wayne State University Press, 2008), 76.

24. José takes the figurine with him everywhere.

25. In Zobel's novel, unlike in Palcy's movie, where the enslaved fight for their own freedom, Médouze's father and other slaves flee their plantations upon receiving news of their emancipation.

26. For example, the Martinican slave revolts (1678, 1710, 1822, 1831, and 1833), the Amistad revolt (1839), and the Haitian Revolution (1791–1804), arguably the most successful slave insurrection in history.

27. Durham, "Euzhan Palcy's Feminist Filmmaking," 157.

28. The key to the first door being the slave insurrections (together with other abolitionist efforts) that led to the legal end of slavery. The need for a second liberation shows the inadequacy of the first, as the story Médouze recounts about his father eloquently demonstrates: "I ran so much. . . . I think I ran all around Martinique. When my feet refused to go on, I looked ahead and behind, I saw I was back to the cane fields. We were free, but our bellies were empty. The master had become the boss. So, I stayed like other blacks in this cursed country." It seems real liberation for Blacks is a dream deferred.

29. Aphorisms about the liberating power of education appeared in many different places where Blacks have suffered slavery and colonization. For example, George Washington Carver is believed to have said, "Education is the key to unlock the golden door to freedom." Of the primary school certificate, the highest a colonized subject could get in the early days of French colonization of Black Africa, Amadou Hampaté Bâ wrote, "That bit of parchment—one of its corners crossed by the French stripes—was a miraculous key, an 'open sesame'; *The Fortunes of Wangrin*, trans. Aina Pavolini Taylor (Bloomington: Indiana University Press, 1987), 8.

30. The late Amadou-Mahtar M'Bow, director of UNESCO for thirteen years, deplored the erstwhile rejection by European scholars of African orature as a viable source of African history: "Although the *Iliad* and *Odyssey* were rightly regarded as essential sources for the history of ancient Greece, African oral tradition, the collective memory of peoples which holds the thread of many events marking their lives, was rejected as worthless." Amadou-Mahtar M'Bow, "Preface," *General History of Africa IV: Africa from the Twelfth to the Sixteenth Century* (Berkeley: University of California Press, 1984), xvii.

31. Durham, "Euzhan Palcy's Feminist Filmmaking," 154.

32. Durham, "Euzhan Palcy's Feminist Filmmaking," 156.

33. Unlike Honorine, who rejects her blackness, the filmmaker unapologetically embraces hers: "I'm a mixed blood person, I have African blood, European blood, Asian blood, but the one that I cherish most is the African one, because it is the one that is the most degraded, most insulted on the screen and all walks of life; it's the one I will kill and die for without any hatred for anybody" (Euzhan Palcy, interviewed by Hunt). Palcy's statement reminds us of the opening line of the essay *In Praise of Creoleness*, "Neither Europeans, nor Africans, nor Asians, we proclaim ourselves Creoles," Jean Bernabé, Patrick Chamoiseau, and Raphaël Confiant, *Éloge de la créolité / In Praise of Creoleness*, trans. M. B. Taleb-Khyar (Paris: Gallimard, 1993), 75.

34. My translation.

35. The young Black movie clerk despises being Black because according to her, Blacks are doing nothing to dispel the myth of their insufficiencies as a race. When

José points out the illogicality of her statement, she quips, "Except for my color, I am not black." The clerk reminds us of Mayotte Capétia, the young Martinican métisse woman and author of *Je suis Martiniquaise* (1948) and *La Négresse blanche* (1950), who openly expressed her preference for the white race.

36. He says, "It is not for Léopold; it is a white man's name, not a mulatto's." My translation.

37. Gerise Herndon, "Auto-Ethnographic Impulse in '*Rue Cases-Nègres*,'" *Literature/Film Quarterly* 24, no. 3 (1996): 264.

38. Josephine Baker moved to France in 1925 and became a French citizen in 1937. She was also a humanitarian and a French anti-Nazi resistance hero. French President Emmanuel Macron decided in August 2021 to reinter Baker's remains at the Panthéon in November 2021. This honor will make Baker the first Black woman and the sixth woman to be buried at the same place containing the remains of such French figures as Voltaire, Victor Hugo, Marie Curie, and Simone Veil.

39. Léopold Sédar Senghor (Senegal), Aimé Césaire (Martinique), and Léon-Gontran Damas (French Guyana) founded the cultural and literary movement of Négritude (a word first used by Césaire in the 1934–1935 Black student review, *l'Étudiant noir*. Négritude was founded as a reaction to the Eurocentric notion rife during the colonial period that Blacks had no history, no culture, no civilization, no literature. Senghor defined the term as "l'ensemble des valeurs de la civilization noire" ("The sum total of the cultural values of the black world"), Léopold Sédar Senghor, *Ce que je crois: Négritude, Francité et Civilisation de l'Universel*." (Paris: Bernard Grasset, 1988), 136.

40. Quoted in Margaret B. Wilkerson, "'A Raisin in the Sun': Anniversary of an American Classic," *Theatre Journal* 38, no. 4 (1986): 447.

41. Keaton, "Creative Dissent," 117.

42. John West and Dennis West, "Euzhan Palcy and Her Creative Anger: A Conversation with the Filmmaker," *French Review* 77, no. 6 (May 2004): 1194. My translation.

43. West and West, "Euzhan Palcy and Her Creative Anger," 1194.

44. Euzhan Palcy, interviewed by Hunt, "Every time I do a masterclass I tell [the students] that they can create a 'revolution' with films."

45. Aimé Césaire, *The Complete Poetry of Aimé Césaire*, trans. James Arnold and Clayton Eshleman (Middleton: Wesleyan University Press, 2017), 27.

46. Keaton, "Creative Dissent," 121.

47. *Parcours de dissidents* tells the story of thousands of young Martinicans who decided on their own, in response to General de Gaulle's June 18, 1940, radio appeal, to join in the fight for French liberation.

48. Keaton, "Creative Dissent," 127.

49. Ibid.

50. Euzhan Palcy, interviewed by Hunt. My italics.

51. The viewer sees this line at the start of the movie.

52. Euzhan Palcy, interviewed by Hunt.

53. Ibid.

54. West and West, "Euzhan Palcy and Her Creative Anger," 1194.

55. Herndon, "Auto-Ethnographic Impulse," 266.

56. Frantz Fanon, *The Wretched of the Earth*, trans. Constance Farrington (New York: Grove Press, 1968).

57. Stevens, "Introduction," 2.

Chapter 8

From Gap Year Hijinks to a Collectivist Awakening

Che Guevara's Motorcycle Diaries *in Fact and Fiction*

Thomas C. Field Jr.

Diarios de Motocicleta *(2004): produced by Michael Nozik, Edgard Tenembaum, and Karen Tenkhoff; directed by Walter Salles; written by José Rivera, based on the books by Ernesto "Che" Guevara and Alberto Granado; color; 126 minutes; FilmFour, South Fork Pictures, Tu Vas Voir Productions. A young medical student (Gael García Bernal) and his friend (Rodrigo de la Serna) set off by motorcycle on a road trip.*

Few genres of film and literature are more compelling than the coming-of-age story. This is even truer when the subject is a transformational historical figure from a seemingly run-of-the-mill background. Clearly fitting into this category is *The Motorcycle Diaries*, a film by Brazilian director Walter Salles, which is based on the true story of how a slightly boorish white boy from an aristocratic, blue-blooded Argentine family became the most celebrated (and despised) revolutionary of the twentieth century. As the film and its source material suggest, before there was "Che" Guevara, guerrilla commander and Cuban diplomat, there was Ernesto Guevara de la Serna, an asthmatic country club kid born into Argentina's once swaggering, pre-depression bourgeoisie. And at first glance, there is little in Guevara's childhood or family background that would have suggested this boy would eventually travel the world, commanding Third World liberation armies consisting mainly of black, mulatto, mestizo, and indigenous guerrilla fighters.

Enter *The Motorcycle Diaries*, a Bildungsroman tracing Ernesto Guevara's seven-month trek across South America in early 1952, during which the over-protected Ernestito embraced a post-adolescent identity known for sporting fury and a devil-may-care sense of adventure. Traveling alongside his child-hood friend Alberto Granado, the epic journey cleared ideological space for Guevara's impending secondary transformation in the late 1950s and 1960s, during which time he became a committed revolutionary who led rebel guer-rilla columns in Cuba, Congo, and Bolivia, where he was summarily executed at thirty-nine years of age.

After describing the 1952 journey across South America as history, this chapter concludes with an analysis of the shortcomings of Salles's uneven film adaptation of *The Motorcycle Diaries*. On the one hand, the film warmly embraces the Argentines' spirit of adventure, their penchant for hijinks in the hospitable Chilean south, and their discomfort with the injustices of poverty displayed alongside breathtaking Andean and Amazonian landscapes in northern Chile and Peru. On the other hand, the adaptation takes liberties beyond the editorial omissions necessary to cut a 100,000-word diary into a two-hour feature film. Moreover, its false vignettes and anecdotes seem sys-tematically chosen to construct an almost infallible Ernesto Guevara, at the undeserved expense of nearly everyone else in the film. Sadly, this advances an individualist message that is diametrically opposed from the collectivist one revealed in Guevara's written diary.

BEFORE THE MOTORCYCLE

In trying to locate special characteristics of Ernesto Guevara's life that might have represented a Road to Damascus moment, there are several earlier candidates that could conceivably compete with the converting power of the journey described in *The Motorcycle Diaries*.[1] Born in 1928, Ernestito was raised surrounded by the adventure of the countryside, beginning with his first year of life on a two-hundred-hectare yerba matée plantation in the borderland backwater of Misiones. Subsequently, after a couple of years on a family shipyard near Buenos Aires, Guevara's asthma forced the family to relocate to the idyllic, rural resort town of Alta Gracia about forty kilometers southwest of Argentina's third city, Córdoba. There Ernestito was mostly homeschooled by his brilliant and iconoclastic mother, Celia de la Serna, a fiercely anticlerical liberal, who taught him French and a love of progressive literature until truant officers pressed her to enroll Ernesto in formal educa-tion. Here, the exceptionalism to Guevara's very early life diminishes signifi-cantly, at least until young adulthood.

After attending middle school in Alta Gracia, Ernestito Guevara began busing—and occasionally hitchhiking—to an inclusive public high school in Córdoba. Despite being scions of Argentine elites, both Ernesto Sr. and Celia harbored democratic ideals rather typical of late 1930s bohemian liberals. These were the days of the Popular Front, in which it was not uncommon for Córdoba's tiny handful of Communist Party members—including Celia's sister Carmen—to be tactically embraced by anti-fascist liberals like the Guevaras. During this period as a young adolescent in the late 1930s, Ernesto Jr. adopted a keen interest in the Spanish Republican cause, a military curiosity rather than a political one, much like how a precocious young boy in Virginia or Pennsylvania might become interested in the flags and bugles of the civil war. After the Republican defeat in 1939, the hospitable Ernesto Sr. and Celia frequently hosted liberal, and occasionally leftist, refugees from fascist Spain. Meanwhile, with Argentina remaining neutral into World War II, Ernesto Sr. helped run a branch of Acción Argentina, an anti-fascist information ring that reported signs of Axis activity and propaganda to a frequently indifferent Argentine government.

One would have to strain to interpret any of these experiences as particularly unique in post-depression Argentina, or anywhere else in the world for that matter. Aside from the preadolescent homeschooling, which is not known for forging Communist revolutionaries, Ernestito lived a fairly normal childhood for a country (club) boy in a downwardly mobile depression-era family. His parents bickered; his father struggled to provide, financially and emotionally. The apolitical Ernestito Guevara found solace in friendships, adventure, and chasing girls. Pretty typical stuff. To the extent he started keeping a journal at age seventeen, according to one biographer, Guevara's writings initially addressed run-of-the-mill bourgeois concerns as "hysteria, sexual morality, faith, justice, death, God, the devil, fantasy, reason, neurosis, narcissism, and morality." A couple of years later, however, when the family moved to Buenos Aires, Guevara enrolled in medical school and began to engage in more sustained analysis of the anticolonial writings of Jawaharlal Nehru. By the time he turned twenty-one in 1949, his notebooks included a nascent and growing interest in Lenin's adaptation of Marxism toward a political project that would soon coalesce into a Third World nonaligned movement.[2]

That was when the summer travels began, starting with a solo trip to Argentina's northwest mountains in early 1950 on a bicycle outfitted with an aftermarket four-stroke Ducati Cucciolo engine. After stopping in Córdoba to see family, the young Guevara puttered north to visit a childhood friend and rugby coach, Alberto Granado, who now worked as a biochemist at a leper colony a few hours north in San Francisco de Chañar. After that, Guevara had his sights set on Bolivia, but he got only as far as Salta and Jujuy before it was time to return home and continue medical school. Still, he had seen the first of many leper clinics Alberto's profession would take him to over the next two years, and he was exposed to what is known in Argentina as the "Indian North." In these ways, his two-month motorized bicycle trip served to whet Ernesto's appetite for more experiences and adventures. As he recorded at the time, while taking "breaks at midday to study medicine under a tree . . . my flesh was weak and cried out for a mattress, but my spirit was willing and the ride went on."[3]

Shortly after he returned to Buenos Aires, the twenty-two-year-old boy began dating an old acquaintance, one of the more sought-after daughters of old Córdoba money, María del Carmen "Chichina" Ferreyra. At the time passing through his third year at medical school, Ernesto Guevara still had his eye on the quintessentially liberal goal of individual achievement. "I wanted to be successful, as everyone does," Guevara later recalled of this period, adding that "I was, as we all are, a product of my environment."[4] From this point until they broke up two years later, Guevara spent as much time as possible at his girlfriend's hacienda club, swimming and riding horses. He dreamed, as he later admitted, of becoming a bourgeois scholar–doctor, albeit one with liberal sensibilities, a social conscience, and a long-standing identification with the poor and the weak.

Leaving Chichina behind in early 1951, Ernesto Guevara attempted to outdo his motorized bicycle trip with an austral summer in the Argentine merchant marine. This experience would introduce him to the Caribbean, but it was ultimately unfulfilling. For someone who wanted to become acquainted above all with the masses, Ernesto was frustrated that his time was spent almost entirely at sea, with precious little time at port when they stopped briefly in Brazil, Venezuela, and Trinidad. When Guevara returned to Buenos Aires to finish his fourth and penultimate year of medical school, he decided to ensure that his last medical school summer would be one he would never forget. While visiting Chichina in October 1951, Ernesto Guevara plotted an epic journey with his old friend Alberto Granado, one that would soon take Ernestito Guevara from the Atlantic to the Pacific, from the Andes to the Amazon, and from the Southern Cone to the Caribbean.

LIBERATION, FROM ARGENTINA TO CHILE

Remarking fifty years later on the "absurdities and craziness" of her father's infamous 1952 trip across South America, Ernesto Guevara's daughter identified the journey as an important waypoint in the future revolutionary's process of maturation not just "as a human being" but also "as a social being." Similar words come from Hilda Gadea, Guevara's first wife, who later characterized the "tremendous adventure" as having been crucial to transforming this essentially bourgeois individualist into a curious young man, ready to explore the collectivist implications—dangerous for a boy of his background—of his "growing sense of a Latin American identity."[5] To be sure, the journey immortalized in the book and film, *The Motorcycle Diaries*, represented Ernesto Guevara's declaration of independence from the bourgeoise liberalism of his privileged youth.

Barely out of earshot from his parents and friends on the Argentine pampas in mid-January 1952, Ernesto Guevara declared himself alienated from the political bankruptcy of the Argentine middle classes, where liberals (such as his parents) and even doctrinaire leftists (such as his aunt) had found themselves allied with the oligarchy, decidedly on the other side of history from the country's nationalist masses. Yet the politically homeless Guevara was still unwilling to fully rebel against his family by embracing Argentina's proworker nationalist government, headed since the mid-1940s by the quasi-fascist Colonel Juan Perón. This meant that when it came to oligarchic/bourgeois anti-Peronism (which included the doctrinaire left) and working-class Peronism, Guevara found himself "as remote from one as from the other." Aware that "the world I left for dead behind me . . . [was] mocking the so-called liberation I sought," the now rootless Guevara threw caution to the wind and embarked on a journey toward "[d]istant countries, heroic deeds, and beautiful women." By the time he returned to Argentina seven months later, "[t]he person who wrote these notes [had] passed away."[6]

Contrary to Guevara's later reputation as a swashbuckling man of action, the first thing one notes when reading *The Motorcycle Diaries* is the young man's prosaic skill and his profoundly romantic disposition. "Readers of this book will not be well versed about the sensitivity of my retina," he began, admitting that they "will not be able to check what is said against a photographic plate to discover at precisely what time each of my 'pictures' was taken." Adding with a mixture of humility and arrogance that "you can either believe me, or not; it matters little to me," Guevara closed his introduction by saying that "I'll leave you now, with myself, the man I used to be."[7] Particularly lyrical are his "lovesick" passages on leaving Chichina in early January, at the Miramar oceanside a couple hours south of Buenos Aires: "My head rested in the lap tying me to this land, lulled by everything around. The entire universe drifted rhythmically by, obeying the impulses of my inner voice. . . . And then, for the last time, I heard the ocean's warning. Its vast and jarring rhythm hammered at the fortress within me and threatened its imposing security." Moved in opposing directions by the Atlantic's contradictory siren calls, Guevara rejected the security of Miramar. Realizing that "my destiny is to travel," Guevara embraced adventure and departed the beach club with his "bohemian" friend, Alberto Granado.[8]

Just before crossing into Chile a month later, Guevara experienced one of the most important catalysts in his quest for independence from the Argentine bourgeoisie: a breakup letter from Chichina, whose elite parents were unimpressed with Guevara's proposals to eventually embark with their daughter on a life of vagabondary. "I read and reread the incredible letter," Guevara wrote to himself, adding that "[j]ust like that, all my dreams of home, bound up with eyes that saw me off in Miramar, came crashing down for what seemed like no reason." Though glossed over in the film, the event meant his political homelessness was now accompanied by a personal "feeling of profound unease," just as Guevara spiritually and physically "bid farewell to Argentine soil." Realizing that he was now at "a kind of crossroads," Guevara noted that he was symbolically "looking to the future, through the narrow band of Chile and to what lay beyond." What had begun as an adventurous gap year now had the potential to lead Ernesto Guevara toward a much profounder personal transformation.[9]

Spending late February among the genteel and hospitable southern Chileans, Guevara and Granado experienced little in the way of political awakening. Here, they honed their skills as moochers, not difficult among the generous multicultural societies of Osorno, Valdivia, and Temuco. By the time their motorcycle broke down in Los Angeles—after an incredible number of crashes, miraculously without human victims—the two Argentines had become known, true in Granado's case, for being specialists in what was for the Chileans an exotic disease: leprosy. Welcomed as middle-class bohemians in police stations and firehouses, Guevara and Granado had plenty to eat and drink and were never without a roof over their heads. Aware that their warm reception was partially due to their membership in a particular race and class, the travelers were nonetheless wary of how things would now go without a motorcycle. "To a certain extent we had been knights of the road; we belonged to that long-standing 'wandering aristocracy' . . . No longer. Now we were just two hitchhikers with backpacks." Saying goodbye to their lives as "motorized bums," Guevara and Granado thumbed it to the Chilean capital city of Santiago on the last day of February, half excited that "the next stage seemed set to be more difficult, as 'bums without wheels.'"[10]

With the motorcycle portion of their journey over, the two traveling Argentines were now better placed to come into contact with regular people, especially the poor and working class, whose suffering inspired in the middle-class Ernesto Guevara some of his first considerations regarding the virtues of collectivism. While failing to catch a twice-yearly boat from nearby Valparaíso to Easter Island, where the young men had hoped to see a legendary leper colony, Guevara visited the home of a sick woman he had recently met. In his heart still harboring individualist dreams of a medical profession, here Guevara was struck by the doctor's "complete powerlessness" when facing "the injustice of a system" that forced this woman to become "a purely negative factor" within her hardworking family. Such is the "profound tragedy circumscribing the life of the proletariat the world over," Guevara mused, in a test of his growing—albeit still inchoate—employment of socialist terminology, adding with disdain that private medical financing leaves sick members of the working class not only physically miserable but also despised by their family members, "who resent their illness as if it were a personal insult to those who have to support them."[11]

While stowing away on a cargo ship to the northern Chilean port of Antofagasta, a brazen adventure omitted from the film adaptation, Guevara discovered that nonstop travel was not only his destiny but his "true vocation . . . to move for eternity along the roads and seas of the world . . . not setting down roots in any land." The two Argentines then hitchhiked up to see Chile's infamous Chuquicamata copper mine, whose (North) American managers told them, without amusement, that "[t]his is not a tourist town." Particularly moving for Guevara was his roadside encounter with a Communist mine worker, who had been expelled from the camp and was leaving with his wife to find work farther into the mountains "where the climate is so bad and the living conditions so hard that you don't need a work permit and nobody asks you what your politics are." For Guevara, who remained skeptical of Communism at this point in his life, the suffering miner's "mysterious, tragic air" symbolized "a living representation of the proletariat in any part of the world." Still unsure of the wisdom of this worker's chosen political solution—"the red blaze that now lights up the world"—Guevara nonetheless lamented "that they repress people like this." Putting aside the question of whether "collectivism, the 'communist vermin,' is a danger to decent life," Guevara posited that "the communism gnawing at his entrails was no more than a natural longing for something better, a protest against persistent hunger transformed into a love for this strange doctrine." Revealing a deeper curiosity in communism than ever before, Guevara finally asked himself if things were really better "over there," in the countries of the socialist camp. "So they say," the bourgeois twenty-three-year-old responded, before adding his persisting doubt, "I don't know."[12]

Still without a clear political ideology—he remarked at this time that the Chilean political scene was, like Argentina's, "confusing"—Ernesto Guevara's intense identification with the poor only deepened over the coming weeks as he and Granado hitchhiked to another mining camp (also on strike) and eventually to the Peruvian border in late March. Yet one aspect of Guevara's future worldview had emerged with increasing clarity. To liberate the Latin American working classes, "the poor, unsung heroes . . . who die miserably in one of the thousand traps set by nature to defend its riches," it would be necessary for countries like Chile "to shake its uncomfortable

Yankee friend from its back, a task that for the moment at least is Herculean, given the quantity of dollars the United States has invested and the ease with which it flexes its economic muscle whenever its interests appear threatened."[13]

AWAKENING, IN PERU AND BEYOND

For the bulk of their remaining voyage, from late March until late June, Guevara and Granado explored the varied geography and demographics of Peru. For two middle-class *gauchos*, they were immediately struck by rural Peruvians' excitement about the Argentine government of Colonel Juan Domingo Perón, "where the poor have as much as the rich and the Indian isn't exploited or treated as severely as he is in this country." Not letting on that they came from anti-Peronist backgrounds, Guevara and Granado played along, "embellishing to our hearts' desire the *capo*'s exploits, filling the minds of our listeners with stories of the idyllic, beautiful life in our country." Not mentioned in the film, here the young men learned about the socialist ideology undergirding Peru's largest mass party, *Alianza Popular Revolucionaria Americana* (APRA; American Popular Revolutionary Alliance), and they both demonstrated a steady awakening toward collectivism and away from the bourgeois liberalism of their childhoods. While Ernesto Guevara remained as skeptical of *aprismo* as he had been of Argentine nationalism, by the end of the journey he was joking to his anti-Peronist mother that Granado seemed to have taken the locals' views to heart and now "believes he is Perón's natural heir."[14]

In terms of specifics, Guevara and Granado sailed on Lake Titicaca, spent an emotional week exploring the Incan ruins around Cuzco, made a moving visit to a highland leper colony at Huambo, and then spent seventeen days observing operations at a leprosy hospital in Lima. On Titicaca in late March, Guevara waxed lyrical on the "once rebellious Aymara race who had held the Inca armies in check," only to be "brutalized by modern civilization." In "evocative" Cuzco during early April, he mused at length on the "anguished Indian . . . untouched by a conquering civilization" yet also representative of "a civilization that has long since passed." And at the shockingly underfunded Huambo leper colony in mid-April, Guevara and Granado learned that advances at Peru's most important leprosy clinics were thanks to the work of a renowned leprologist in Lima, Dr. Hugo Pesce, who put them up in his leprosy hospital when they reached the Peruvian capital on May 1. Spending almost three weeks observing Pesce's work and dining daily at his home, Guevara was struck that the "expert leprologist . . . welcomed us with extraordinary kindness for someone at the head of such a well-respected

Figure 8.1: Ernesto Guevara's travels, December 1951 to August 1952. (SEH Mapping)

medical unit." During this formative period, Guevara learned that Pesce was not only a "fascinating conversationalist" but also an embattled member of Peru's Communist Party. Unlike Guevara's encounter with the Communist mine worker in Chile, which provoked intense musings about the relative benefits of liberalism versus collectivism, Guevara described his warm friendship with Pesce as being important from a purely "scientific perspective." Ernesto Guevara was no longer a bourgeois liberal, but he was clearly not yet prepared to embrace Marxist collectivism.[15]

From Lima, the Argentines set out for another one of Dr. Pesce's leper colonies, this one deep in the Amazon jungle. This required taking a cargo truck up to the headwaters of the Ucayali, where they boarded a riverboat—La Cenepa—that took six days to take them down to the Amazonian wonderland of Iquitos. Fueled by constant adrenaline injections to keep his asthma at bay, a weakened Guevara engaged in what was likely his journey's only sexual adventure, with a female riverboat passenger who "seemed rather easy" and eventually "showed sympathy for my pathetic physical state." Guevara wrote that the encounter "penetrated dormant memories of my preadventurer life," taking his mind to Chichina's country club, where she was likely now "whispering her strange, composed phrases to some new suitor." It was one of his few moments of fleeting doubt during the long trip: "My eyes traced the immense vault of heaven; the starry sky twinkled happily above me, as if answering in the affirmative to the question rising deep within me: 'Is all of this worth it?'"[16]

After a five-day wait in Iquitos, on June 6 the journeyers boarded the Amazon riverboat *El Cisne*, which took two days to reach the San Pablo leper colony. There the young Argentines spent almost two weeks observing conditions facing six hundred patients and seventy healthy employees, who were "lacking basic amenities . . . like electricity during the day, a refrigerator, or even a laboratory." Through a set of strong relationships not depicted in the film, Guevara and Granado were moved by the hospitality shown them by such a humble collection of humanity, sick and healthy alike. On Guevara's birthday, June 14, the colony threw a massive party with "a delightful, huge meal . . . [and] a lot of the Peruvian national drink, *pisco*." It was here that Ernesto Guevara delivered a short toast that revealed his awkward intermediate ideological waypoint between liberal individualism and Communist internationalism. Reflective of a sort of bourgeois racial nationalist, Guevara declared that "the division of [Latin] America into unstable and illusory nations is completely fictional. We constitute a single mestizo race, which from Mexico to the Magellan Straits bears notable ethnographic similarities." The future revolutionary still had a long way to go before he would embrace Marxist-Leninism and, with it, the distinct version of pan-racial Third Worldism that would later become associated with Ernesto "Che" Guevara.[17]

After making a brief visit to the Amazonian indigenous community of Yaguas, Guevara and Granado rode a handmade raft, the *Mambo-Tambo*, down to Leticia, Colombia, where they raised enough money coaching the local soccer team to catch a cargo plane out of the Amazon to the Colombian capital. After a week in early July at a leprosy hospital in Bogotá, they submitted themselves to repeated police checkpoints on a bus trip to the Venezuelan capital of Caracas. Both countries struck Guevara as suffering "more repression of individual freedom . . . than in any country we've been to," yet young Ernesto Guevara displayed no interest in getting involved despite the fact that "a revolution may be brewing [in Bogotá]." He wrote his mother on July 6 that "it's suffocating here," adding that "[i]f the Colombians want to put up with it, good luck to them, but we're getting out of here as soon as we can." Throughout this period, which is not included in the film, Guevara was hassled by Colombian and Venezuelan police over a knife he had been carrying since Argentina. Leaving his friend Alberto Granado to take up a job at a leprosy colony south of Caracas, Guevara bought a plane ticket home to finish medical school in Buenos Aires.[18]

Not included in either the book or film were Ernesto Guevara's experiences in Miami, Florida, where he spent an unplanned two-week layover due to airplane mechanical troubles. His biographers have pieced together a lonely and difficult period, during which the destitute young man got around the sweltering city on foot while staying with a distant relative.[19] In lieu of a report from Miami, Guevara concludes his diary with a moving and rather prescient experience in a mountain village just outside Caracas, where he met an old European refugee from fascism. Predicting that "[t]he future belongs to the people," the old man warned that the masses' impending revolt "will cost many innocent lives . . . those unable to adapt—you and I, for example—will die cursing the power they helped, through great sacrifice, to create." In case his prophesy was not clear enough, the man looked directly at Guevara and said, "you will die with a clenched fist and a tense jaw, the epitome of hatred and struggle. . . . [Y]ou are not aware of how useful your contribution is to the society that sacrifices you." Ernesto Guevara's reaction to this speech was to resign himself to a sacrificial fate: "I see myself, immolated in the genuine revolution . . . proclaiming the ultimate *mea culpa*." Yet Guevara, still without a clear political ideology, was sure of one thing: "when the great guiding spirit cleaves humanity into two antagonistic halves, I would be with the people. . . . I, eclectic dissembler of doctrine and psychoanalyst of dogma, howling like one possessed, will assault the barricades or the trenches, will take my bloodstained weapon and, consumed with fury, slaughter any enemy who falls into my hands." All that remained, for the rebellious Ernesto Guevara, was a cause.[20]

INDIVIDUALISM IN WALTER SALLES'S
THE MOTORCYCLE DIARIES

In Ernesto Guevara's written diary, the young Argentine described himself as having been being moved by the spirited generosity and confident kindness of the regular people all around him, including his devoted friend Granado, easygoing Chilean firefighters, brilliant Peruvian leprologists, and kindhearted nuns. Finding something inspiring in nearly everyone he met, Guevara saw himself as being saved from bourgeois ambition by these imperfect yet noble masses, who taught him the value of collectivism and pointed him toward some yet-to-be-defined mass politics. Unfortunately, the film's Ernesto Guevara frequently liaises with helpless souls and angry scoundrels, each of whom stand in holy judgment—saved or condemned—by Guevara who seems to float above the South American muck. Within this false dialectic, a fictitious Ernesto Guevara doubles down on the individualist, do-gooder spirit that sent him on the road in the first place.

A central reason the film fails to reveal the transformation away from individualism that took place in the life of Ernesto Guevara at this time is its deafening silence on the political valence of his travels through early 1950s Latin America. This is particularly strange since Guevara's diary includes frequent (albeit subtle) references to his rejection of bourgeois liberalism (represented by his family's activism in the middle-class reformist Radical Party) and his nascent interest (tepid curiosity at this point) in the mass enthusiasm he witnessed for collectivist politics. His fictional encounters with the poor at no time betray the intense hope they frequently expressed to him in real life, during which they hailed specific anti-liberal ideologies such as Argentine Peronism, Peruvian *aprismo*, and international Communism. The kind, brilliant Dr. Hugo Pesce is presented as an upstanding citizen, not the Communist Party member he was, and his recommendation of the writings of *indigenista* José Carlos Mariátegui includes no mention of the latter's lifelong adherence to Marxist analysis and politics. In the film, Dr. Pesce's recommendation letter helps Granado secure a job at a leper colony in the Caribbean; in real life, Pesce's leftist politics provoked suspicion in the police states farther north.[21]

The film's one mention of collectivist politics, Guevara's encounter with a Communist mine worker in northern Chile, is presented in reverse fashion from how it actually occurred. The film audience is led to believe that the worker seeks a job in the Chuquicamata mining camp, having fled random police repression, presumably for merely being a member of the Communist Party. In reality, the worker had just been *expelled* from Chuquicamata, where leftist miners like him were leading strikes against the stinginess of their (North) American owners. In the film, Guevara and Granado are kicked out of the mining camp after *Guevara* expresses pity for the *working* miners and demanding that a foreman give them water; in reality, Guevara was welcomed by the foreman for an extensive tour, during which the *foreman* expressed sympathy for the *striking* miners and condemned the bosses—the "[i]mbecile gringos, losing thousands of *pesos* every day in a strike so as not to give a poor worker a few more *centavos*." The next day, the Argentine travelers admired another group of striking leftist workers at the Magdalena mine, who were "celebrating the victory of the people's cause a little prematurely by getting plastered." Later, they bonded with yet another group of combative workers over a game of soccer, followed by a massive feast. Compare this with the film, in which the poor are universally depicted as miserable and weak, requiring salvation from an outsider like Guevara. Needless to say, the film includes not a single shot of the mining camp's "blond, efficient, and arrogant managers," as described in Guevara's diary.[22]

If the film unnecessarily elevates young Ernesto Guevara by prostrating the poor masses of South America, it also clumsily sanctifies him by vilifying his dear friend Alberto Granado. In the diary, Guevara describes Granado as a model traveling companion, patient with Ernestito as he bid farewell to his girlfriend in Miramar and respectful of the fifteen dollars she gave Guevara to buy her a swimsuit in Miami. In the film, Granado is an insufferable rogue, mocking Guevara's first true love (and his asthma), demanding they leave Miramar immediately, then insisting repeatedly (six times) that he cough up her money. The film's Granado consistently second guesses Guevara's cunning decisions, lies while Guevara is honest to everyone they meet, sneaks off to bed with a pair of friendly Chilean sisters while Guevara cares for the sick, and gambles to raise money for an Amazonian prostitute when Guevara once again refuses to hand over Chichina's money. In reality, the two best friends were a brilliant team, occasionally defrauding their hosts in a joint effort to stay housed and fed. While Guevara cared for the sick, Granado liaised not with easy girls but with local Chilean doctors. And it was Guevara, not Granado, who engaged in an adventure, apparently *pro bono*, with the riverboat seductress.

Of all the film's moments of irreverence toward the actual history of the 1952 journey, the most striking is its bizarre reversal of reality at the leper colony at San Pablo, Peru. Following its pattern of depersonalizing everyone around Guevara, the film disparages the colony's kind, selfless workers and prostrates its bold, spirited patients. Contrary to real life, in which the colony's workers and patients live essentially together across the Amazon River from the village of San Pablo, the film version of the colony is divided by the enormous river into separate quarters for the healthy and the sick. This scandalizes the fictitious Guevara, who stands in harsh judgment over the arrogance of these imaginary doctors and nurses whose real-life dedication and kindness provided profound inspiration to Guevara. The true Ernesto Guevara was deeply moved when a joint band of healthy and leprous musicians, including one fingerless accordion player with sticks strapped to his hands, rang in his twenty-fourth birthday celebration on June 14, 1952. In the film, Guevara is put off by what is falsely depicted as a segregated, "healthy-only" birthday party. Determined "to celebrate my birthday on the other side," the fictional Guevara makes a dramatic (and supposedly dangerous) late-night swim across the river near the film's finale, embracing the lepers while the colony's white-frocked employees gaze in horror from the other side of the river.[23]

As a result of these editorial decisions, the film version of *The Motorcycle Diaries* fails to depict the precise transformation that occurred in Ernesto Guevara de la Serna in 1952. The film begins with Guevara and Granado already expressing devotion to "this grand continent," which they plan to explore to the tip of Venezuela, and it suggests that the trip served chiefly to inject in Guevara a liberal awakening to the plight of the poor. In reality, the opposite occurred. Far from starting as Latin American nationalists (or even regionalists), the two boys' goal was to reach the *United States*, yet they fell in love with South America in the process. Ernesto Guevara had already inherited a social conscience from his parents, yet his experiences in Chile and Peru taught him the limits of liberalism to solve the masses' collective problems. In the film, Guevara concludes his trip in Caracas, bidding Granado farewell and expressing morosely that "something happened" to him on the long trip, "something I'll have to think about for a long time." In realty, his trip ended with Guevara in Miami, broke and miserable, and it did not take him long to figure out what had happened to him. In his diary's final chapter, omitted from the film, Guevara resolved to embark on a quest to identify a political cause that would give him the chance to fight, collectively, with the masses: "I feel my nostrils dilate, savoring the acrid smell of gunpowder and blood, the enemy's death; I steel my body, ready to do battle, and prepare myself to be a sacred space within which the bestial howl of the triumphant proletariat can resound with new energy and hope."[24]

Whatever the filmmakers' motivation for presenting such a toned-down and sterilized version of Guevara's coming-of-age experience, the film nonetheless leaves audiences with two accurate lessons regarding the future revolutionary's transitional politics during this period. By the end of the trip, Guevara had indeed become a Latin American nationalist, which was a temporary (and rather awkward) waystation on his journey toward Communist internationalism, pan-racial Third Worldism, and fierce antagonism toward what he saw as U.S. economic and political imperialism.[25] Alongside the film's attractive landscapes, one identifies in the fictitious Guevara profound indignation toward poverty and a still inchoate desire to do something about it. According to this rather limited metric, the film's editorial choices and aesthetic appeal combine to land an emotional, if historically unsatisfying, punch.

DENOUEMENT AND CONCLUSION

By the time Ernesto Guevara returned to Buenos Aires for his final semester of medical school in late 1952, he was no longer the liberal Ernestito, but neither had he become the collectivist "Che." As one of his more observant biographers wrote, "breaking with [his mother] Celia and the entire family in the midst of a highly polarized [Argentine political] situation was . . . inconceivable."[26] Yet for Guevara, foreign travel offered liberation from his bourgeois background, and it meant a growing desire to commune with the masses. In the words of the historian Paulo Drinot, these wanderings illustrate the process by which a "young, petulant, and not very insightful Argentine of no great historical interest . . . was to turn from the moth of Ernesto Guevara into the butterfly of Che."[27]

Given his intense spirit of adventure, Ernesto Guevara would not remain long in the no-man's-land between middle-class individualism and popular collectivism. Shortly after completing his degree in early 1953, Guevara set out again, this time for Bolivia, where he witnessed the unfolding of that country's revolutionary nationalist agrarian reform.[28] Staying on the move through Peru, Ecuador, and Central America, the rebellious young man temporarily found a possible cause in Guatemala, where the Communist Party was helping to organize another land reform program, this time with the support of a democratically elected leftist president, Colonel Jacobo Arbenz. Amid the many Latin American exiles living and working in Arbenz's 1950s Guatemala, Guevara met his first wife, the revolutionary Peruvian left *aprista* Hilda Gadea. Here, his only complaint was President Arbenz's unwillingness to arm the masses and employ violence to defend what Guevara called the most "democratic" country in the Americas, facing a CIA-organized counterrevolution.[29]

Fleeing to Mexico after the 1954 coup d'état, which had been organized and launched by the U.S. Central Intelligence Agency, Guevara and Gadea married and eventually grew close to a group of revolutionary Cubans. This included Fidel Castro and his Communist brother Raúl, who had just been released from prison two years after leading the attempted July 26, 1953, uprising against the Fulgencio Batista dictatorship. Ernesto Guevara had engaged in almost no political activity up to that point, but the twenty-seven-year-old was profoundly impressed by Castro's charisma as well as his organizational prowess. He had just revealed to his mother, with whom his relationship deepened during these years, a dangerous inkling that members of the Communist Party "deserve respect" and that "sooner or later I will join the Party myself." With Castro's arrival, Guevara finally identified a permanent cause worthy of his restless nature and remarkable bravery. After training with Castro's 26th of July revolutionary movement and suffering a brief period of arrest and rough treatment by Mexican authorities, Guevara disembarked with Castro and eighty-one other rebels aboard the *Granma*. They landed at the foot of the future guerrilla base in the Sierra Maestra mountains, where Guevara became known as "Che" due to his frequent use of the Argentine slang word—similar to "man" or "dude"—which is used to attract a friend's attention or express surprise.[30] Quickly rising to become a commander of one of the most important columns of the rebel army, Che Guevara led the taking of Cuba's second city, Santa Clara, all but sealing the revolution for the rebels. He then assumed a number of posts in the revolutionary government, including the head of the agrarian reform and then the central bank. Also becoming Cuba's informal envoy to liberation movements in Africa and Latin America, Che Guevara eventually commanded rebel columns in Congo and then in Bolivia. It was in the latter effort that Guevara perished on October 9, 1967, after being captured and executed by members of Bolivia's counterguerrilla Second Ranger battalion, which had just been inaugurated by the U.S. Defense Department.

In mid-1960, while still basking in the success of the Cuban revolution eighteen months earlier, "Che" Guevara told a group of Cuban medical students that his travels across South America had taught him that it was futile to aspire to solve poverty or alleviate misery through solitary "personal triumph." Conceding that he had begun his journey as an individualist, "a child of my environment," Guevara described his steady realization that "the individual effort, the purity of ideals, the desire to sacrifice an entire lifetime to the noblest of ideals means naught if that effort is made alone . . . against hostile governments and social conditions that do not permit progress." As he described it, the Andean and Amazonian encounters helped him realize that if one really wishes to become "a revolutionary doctor," or any other kind of professional, "there must first be a revolution . . . an entire people mobilized."[31] Following his travels around South America, Ernestito Guevara was no more, and his human canvas had been cleared for the construction of "Che."

ADDITIONAL RESOURCES

Anderson, Jon Lee. *Che Guevara: A Revolutionary Life*. New York: Grove Press, 1997.

Castañeda, Jorge G. *Compañero: The Life and Death of Che Guevara*. New York: Knopf, 1997.

Cupull, Adys, and Froilán González. *Canto Inconcluso*. Quito: Sur Editores, 2009.

Drinot, Paulo, ed. *Che's Travel's: The Making of a Revolutionary in 1950s Latin America*. Durham, NC: Duke University Press, 2010.

Gadea, Hilda. *Mi Vida con el Che*. Lima: Comisión Organizadora de los 50 Años de la Gesta Heróica del Che, 2017.

Granado, Alberto. *Con el Che por Sudamérica*. Buenos Aires: Editorial Marea, 2013.

Guevara, Ernesto Che. *The Motorcycle Diaries: Notes on a Latin American Journey*. Melbourne: Ocean Press, 2003.

Taibo II, Paco Ignacio. *Guevara, Also Known as Che*. New York: St. Martin's Press, 1997.

NOTES

1. Unless otherwise noted, early Guevara biographical notes are taken from a combination of sources: Jon Lee Anderson, *Che Guevara: A Revolutionary Life* (New York: Grove Press, 1997), 3–94; Jorge G. Castañeda, *Compañero: The Life and Death of Che Guevara* (New York: Knopf, 1997), 3–55; Paco Ignacio Taibo II, *Guevara, Also Known as Che* (New York: St. Martin's Press, 1997), 2–24; and Adys Cupull and Froilán González, *Canto Inconcluso* (Quito: Sur Editores, 2009), 29–66.

2. Anderson, *Che Guevara*, 38.

3. Guevara, quoted in Taibo II, *Guevara*, 15.

4. Guevara, quoted in Taibo II, *Guevara*, 13.

5. Aleida Guevara March, "Preface," and Aleida March, "Preface to the First Edition," in Guevara, *The Motorcycle Diaries*, 2–4.

6. Ernesto Che Guevara, *The Motorcycle Diaries: Notes on a Latin American Journey* (Melbourne: Ocean Press, 2003), 32, 38–40. Though not enamored by Perón, Guevara liked to shock his parents by occasionally expressing sympathy with the followers of the populist colonel. Moreover, as a child he took no part in middle-class (conservative, liberal, or left) activism against the nationalist regime. Regarding his jesting comments about Peronism, see page 51, for example.

7. Guevara, *The Motorcycle Diaries*, 32.

8. Guevara, *The Motorcycle Diaries*, 36–37, 45.

9. Guevara, *The Motorcycle Diaries*, 53–55.

10. Guevara, *The Motorcycle Diaries*, 56–66. Guevara began remarking on his whiteness when entering Argentina's indigenous southeastern highlands (page 43), and these comments would continue throughout the remainder of his trip, especially when passing through indigenous regions of northern Chile and Peru.

11. Guevara, *The Motorcycle Diaries*, 70.

12. Guevara, *The Motorcycle Diaries*, 75–81.

13. Guevara, *The Motorcycle Diaries*, 80, 89.

14. Guevara, *The Motorcycle Diaries*, 91, 95, 154. Regarding Guevara's hesitance to fully embrace *aprismo*, see also Paulo Drinot, "Awaiting the Blood of a Truly Emancipating Revolution: Che Guevara in 1950s Peru," in *Che's Travel's*, 97–98.

15. Guevara, *The Motorcycle Diaries*, 97, 107, 122, 133–40.

16. Guevara, *The Motorcycle Diaries*, 138–44.

17. Guevara, *The Motorcycle Diaries*, 146–49.

18. Guevara, *The Motorcycle Diaries*, 149–60.

19. Anderson, *Che Guevara*, 93–94; Castañeda, *Compañero*, 54.

20. Guevara, *The Motorcycle Diaries*, 163–65.

21. Guevara said that Pesce's letter was of limited use in Colombia since he "plays the same position as Lusteu," an Argentine footballer known for his skill on the left wing. Guevara, *The Motorcycle Diaries*, 156.

22. Guevara, *The Motorcycle Diaries*, 78–79, 83.

23. The actual Guevara did swim across the Amazon after an afternoon of fishing on the other side. Yet it merited little more than annoyance since it took two hours and the colony's chief leprologist "had no desire to wait so long" for his return. Guevara, *The Motorcycle Diaries*, 150.

24. Guevara, *The Motorcycle Diaries*, 165.

25. Omitted from the film was the racial portion of his speech where Guevara toasts the "notable ethnographical similarities" of Latin American *mestizaje*. Guevara, *The Motorcycle Diaries*, 149.

26. Castañeda, *Compañero*, 35.

27. Paulo Drinot, "Introduction," in *Che's Travels*, 2.

28. Ann Zulawski, "The National Revolution and Bolivia in the 1950s: What Did Che See?" in *Che's Travels*, 182–83. Zulawski notes that Guevara was as ambivalent toward Bolivia's version of revolutionary nationalism as he had been toward Peru's and Argentina's.

29. Cindy Forster, "'Not in All of America Can There Be Found a Country as Democratic as This One': Che and Revolution in Guatemala," in *Che's Travels*, 216–22.

30. Eric Zolov, "Between Bohemianism and a Revolutionary Rebirth: Che Guevara in Mexico," in *Che's Travels*, 263–70. According to Zolov, "Guevara's meeting with Castro in July 1955 changed everything." According to the *Real Academia Español*, "che" is used "to call someone, detain them, or attract their attention, or to express astonishment or surprise."

31. Guevara, "Appendix: A Child of My Environment," in *The Motorcycle Diaries*, 167–68.

Chapter 9

Kidnappings of Diplomats and Revolutionary Politics in Authoritarian Brazil

The Tale of Two Films, Four Days in September *and* Marighella

James N. Green

O Que É Isso, Companheiro? (1997) *or* Four Days in September; *produced by Lucy and Luiz Carlos Barreto; directed by Bruno Barreto; written by Leopoldo Serra; loosely based on the book* O que é isso, companheiro? Um depoimento *(What's This, Comrade? A Testimonial) (1979) by Fernando Gabeira; color; 110 minutes; RioFilme, Miramax. A semi-fictionalized version of the 1969 kidnapping of the U.S. ambassador in Rio de Janeiro by two Brazilian urban guerrilla organizations that demanded the release of fifteen political prisoners in exchange for his freedom.*

Marighella (2019); *produced by Andrea Barata Ribeiro, Bel Berlinck, and Wagner Moura; directed by Wagner Moura; written by Wagner Moura, Felipe Braga, and Erez Milgrom; based on Mário Magalhães,* Marighella *(2012), color; 155 minutes, O2 Filmes. In the aftermath of the 1964 Brazilian military coup d'état, Carlos Marighella breaks with the Brazilian Communist Party and founds an urban guerrilla organization in an attempt to overthrow the military regime until he is ambushed and assassinated by the state's repressive apparatus in late 1969.*

In early September 1969, two Brazilian revolutionary organizations kidnapped Charles Burke Elbrick, the U.S. ambassador stationed in Rio de Janeiro, and held him captive for four days. In exchange for his release, they demanded that the military government, which had come to power in 1964, disseminate a revolutionary manifesto to be published in newspapers and read on radios and televisions throughout the country (see the document at the end of this chapter). They also threatened to execute the ambassador if the armed forces didn't immediately free fifteen political prisoners and ensure that they arrived safely in a third country.[1]

The idea for this action originated with a group of militants, based in Rio de Janeiro, who had mostly broken from the dissident youth wing of the Brazilian Communist Party (BCP) because they considered that it had failed to offer effective resistance to the military takeover and subsequent authoritarian rule. Shortly before the kidnapping, they assumed the name Movimento Revolucionário 8 de Outubro (8th of October Revolutionary Movement, MR-8), which referenced the date that Che Guevara, the Argentine revolutionary and leader of the Cuban Revolution, had been assassinated in Bolivia in 1967 while organizing a rural guerrilla movement in that country. Recognizing their logistical military inexperience, they joined forces with members of Ação Libertadora Nacional (National Liberating Action, ALN), a similar communist dissident group in São Paulo, to carry out the sequester. After tense negotiations between the military and the urban guerrillas, the Brazilian government freed fifteen imprisoned revolutionaries from different organizations and flew them to Mexico, where they promptly held a press conference denouncing the torture of political detainees in Brazil.[2] In turn, Elbrick was released, suffering only a slight head wound inflicted when he was captured.

Almost thirty years later, Brazilian director Bruno Barreto captured the drama of this revolutionary action in a film with the English title *Four Days in September*. It featured a Brazilian cast, with U.S. actor Alan Arkin starring as Elbrick, and was one of five 1998 Oscar finalists for Best Foreign Film. Loosely based on the Brazilian best seller, *O que é isso companheiro? Um depoimento (What's This, Comrade? A Testimonial)*, which Fernando Gabeira, one of the participants in the kidnapping, wrote while in exile, the film's release in Brazil provoked a lively and intense debate among members of the "Generation of 1968," including former members of MR-8 who had planned and executed the sequester.[3] Critics both challenged the historical accuracy of the film and questioned its underlying premises.[4]

Two decades later, Brazilian director Walter Moura completed a feature-length film about Carlos Marighella, the founder of ALN, who was actually hiding underground in Rio de Janeiro when the kidnapping of the U.S. ambassador took place in that city in September 1969.[5] Marighella was a left-wing political prisoner in the 1930s and early 1940s, a Communist Party congressman between 1946 and 1948, and a long-term leader of the

Figure 9.1: The fifteen political prisoners released and flown to Mexico in exchange for the freedom of U.S. Ambassador Charles Burke Elbrick in September 1969. (Iconografia)

BCP before he left to form the ALN. Without Marighella's previous knowledge, Joaquim Câmara Ferreira, another veteran Communist and the ALN's second-in-command, known by the code name Toledo, approved and participated in the sequester, a decision that Marighella later criticized.

The film *Marighella* focuses largely on the last years of the film's namesake—from his disillusionment with the BCP after the 1964 coup d'état and the formation of the largest armed struggle organization in Brazil until the guerrilla leader's assassination in November 1969 in an ambush by the government's repressive apparatus. *Marighella* was completed on the eve of the 2018 presidential election of Jair Bolsonaro, the far right-wing former army captain who has publicly defended the righteousness of the 1964 military takeover and the dictatorship's use of torture on oppositionists, including former President Dilma Rousseff, herself a veteran of the armed struggle and victim of torture in the early 1970s. The polarized political climate that lingered after the 2018 election, bureaucratic tie-ups with ANCINE (the Brazilian government film agency), and COVID-19 pandemic film-viewing restrictions in Brazil forced Moura to hold back *Marighella*'s commercial release for two years. However, even before its first public debut in Brazil, Bolsonaro's supporters attacked the film, arguing that it promoted terrorism. Right-wing forces also used bots to drive down its ratings on internet sites about the film even though it hadn't yet been released.[6] No doubt, *Marighella*, as was the case with *Four Days in September*, will provoke controversies and debates among filmgoers and critics. The two films, which overlap at times in representing actual historical events, including real-life characters written into the plot, and in portraying two of them in both films, offer distinct but in some ways similar, and sometimes, problematic versions of the revolutionary times of the 1960s in Brazil when thousands of radicalized youth and others picked up arms to challenge military rule.

THE HISTORICAL CONTEXT

Before analyzing elements of the two films, it is essential to understand the historical context of the period in which they are set, namely, the sociopolitical upheavals that took place in Brazil and throughout Latin America in the aftermath of the 1959 Revolution in Cuba; national liberation struggles that unfolded in Algeria, sub-Saharan Africa, and Vietnam; and the Cultural Revolution that broke out in the People's Republic of China. These processes inspired a generation of students and others in Brazil and elsewhere to imagine the possibilities of successful revolutionary transformations, which would overcome long-term socioeconomic inequalities. In Brazil in the early 1960s, a politically mobilized youth, especially middle-class, mostly white, university students, embraced Marxist ideologies and joined left-wing organizations that promised a pathway toward this revolutionary change.

The 1964 military coup d'état that overthrew the government of moderate reformist President João Goulart further radicalized a sector of the politicized student movement influenced by the Brazilian Communist Party and other left-wing groups. Dissident sectors of the BCP considered that the Party's decision to retreat underground and regroup rather than militarily resist the armed forces' seizure of power was an abdication of its historical obligation to lead a revolutionary resistance to the new regime. Among the dissenters, Carlos Marighella led rebellious forces in the state of São Paulo, where he had considerable influence among Communist Party youth. In 1967, he definitively broke with the BCP and founded a new organization whose strategy was to prepare a rural guerrilla movement that would topple the regime. However, to implement this plan, his group carried out urban guerrilla actions, such as bank robberies, bombings, arms expropriations, and targeted assassinations. Rejecting the centralizing organizational structure of the BCP, Marighella also encouraged autonomous initiatives by different armed units. Although accurate statistics are unavailable, at its height the ALN perhaps had two thousand or so militants and supporters. Other breakaway groups from the BCP, such as the MR-8, as well as new organizations largely founded by radicalized students from other political backgrounds, also came into being throughout the country. During the same period, the pro-Maoist Communist Party of Brazil sent dozens of militants to an area of the Amazon rainforest to mingle among the local rural population and prepare a rural guerrilla movement.[7]

While this accumulation of revolutionary militants and an accompanying underground infrastructure were taking shape, 1968 in Brazil proved to be a landmark year, as it was across the globe. Students took to the streets to mobilize against the military regime; wildcat strikes challenged the military's economic and labor policies; intellectuals and artists criticized censorship; and left-leaning politicians questioned arbitrary rule. As a result, the military decided to crack down on all opposition forces, including the revolutionary organizations that were carrying out or preparing to carry out armed actions against the dictatorship and its supporters. On December 13, 1968, the military regime issued Institutional Act No. 5, which closed Congress, suspended the political rights of many politicians and public figures, increased censorship, and gave the green light for state agents to torture oppositionists. With legal avenues of protest cut off, more radicalized students opted to join the emergent revolutionary organizations to confront the regime with arms. But by the end of 1969, the repressive apparatus set in place by the dictatorship, as well as the widespread use of torture to extract information from militants in order to dismantle organizations and discourage collaboration, cut off easy recruitment to underground groups fighting the regime. Although an estimated five thousand people, 20% of whom were women, joined clandestine armed struggle groups in this period as militants or close supporters, by 1974, the military regime had managed to decimate all of these revolutionary organizations through systematic imprisonment, assassination, or forced exile.[8]

That same year, Ernesto Geisel, the fourth of five generals to preside over the military regime as president, announced a gradual liberalization process (*distensão*). This slow-motion return to civilian rule would take eleven years and would accelerate at times due to electoral victories of the legal opposition; economic instability; and a resurgence of student demonstrations, labor strikes, and other mobilizations against the regime's policies. In 1979, the Congress approved an amnesty law that released most political prisoners (but not those who had been involved in armed actions in which people died), reduced sentences for those tried in abstentia, and lifted restrictions on exiles, allowing thousands to return to civilian life. The law, however, included a provision that would be interpreted as a ban on any prosecution of state agents involved in torture or other serious human rights violations.

During this period of political liberalization and the end of censorship, former participants in revolutionary movements, especially former exiles, published their memoirs about their time underground. Several were best sellers. Fernando Gabeira's book, first published in 1979, was reprinted dozens of times in its first two years on the market. Alfredo Sirkis's work,

Figure 9.2: The last known photo of Carlos Marighella before he was killed in an ambush in November 1969. (Iconografia)

Os carbonários: memorias de uma guerra perdida (*The Carbonarios: Memories of a Lost War*), which came out in 1981, was also an overnight success. Sirkis wrote about his involvement in the sequesters of the German and Swiss ambassadors in June and September 1970, respectively, in which urban guerrillas obtained the freedom of 110 political prisoners in exchange for the release from captivity of the two foreign envoys.[9] In 1992, the book was an inspiration for the popular TV series *Anos rebeldes* (*Rebel Years*), which portrayed the urban guerrilla movement in a relatively favorable light. The program was produced by mega-media conglomerate TV Globo, which, ironically, during the most repressive years of the dictatorship had enthusiastically supported the military regime and condemned militants of the armed struggle as terrorists.[10]

For a new generation of youth, which I call "Generation 77," that joined mobilizations against the military regime during the late 1970s and early 1980s, these works responded to a curiosity about what had actually taken place a decade previously, when information channels had been under strict censorship. Gabeira's lively narrative presented an almost comical account of the innocence and foibles of a tiny band of young, idealistic rebels engaged in daring but naive efforts to topple the regime. In his testimonial, as he subtitled the original edition of his work, implying its historical accuracy from his perspective, Gabeira leads the reader to understand that he came up with the idea of kidnapping the U.S. ambassador and wrote the guerrillas' revolutionary manifesto. In the early 1980s, Gabeira also became a public figure and media star for embracing feminism, gay rights, and environmental issues and for criticizing conservative attitudes among the Brazilian left. Sirkis's story of his escapades as a high-school-student-turned-revolutionary evoked a similar sense of the noble but foolish endeavors of those who, as the book's subtitle states, "lost" the war.

In the 1990s, new historical works on the military regime sparked a series of debates about the nature of the armed struggle in Brazil. Were sectors of the left justified in taking up arms against a regime that had declared its legitimacy through the very act of illegally seizing power in the name of a "revolution"? Was the armed struggle an effort to turn radical mobilizations against the military regime into a process that would lead to a socialist revolution, as had taken place in Cuba, or was it merely a democratic resistance designed to return the country to the rule of law without a radical restructuring of the socioeconomic and political order? Did actions of the guerrilla movements in which civilians were harmed or killed and individuals assassinated for allegedly being "enemies of the people" represent one side of an evil dichotomy in which its opposing forces, namely, the armed forces and the police apparatus, were equally culpable for their participation in the repression, torture, and disappearance of oppositionists?[11]

DEFENDING THE GUERRILLA MOVEMENT

While the two films under consideration do not directly address all of these issues, both make the case that the armed struggle was a legitimate response to the 1964 coup d'état and the regime set in place thereafter. *Four Days in September* begins with black-and-white photos of the easygoing life in Rio de Janeiro in the early 1960s, with a version of the international bossa nova hit "The Girl from Ipanema" playing gently in the background. Suddenly, this tranquil scene is interrupted by a black slide explaining: "In 1964, the democratic government of Brazil is overthrown in a military coup." It is followed by another informing viewers: "In 1968, the military junta that governs the country suspends all civil rights and freedom of the press. . . . The jails are filled with political prisoners, the streets with demonstrators." Chants of the slogans "The people united will never be defeated" and "Down with the dictatorship" provide the soundtrack for vintage footage of downtown Rio during the March of 100,000 in June 1968 against military rule. Historical aerial shots of demonstrators fade into a scene of students, whom the viewer will soon understand are the film's young revolutionary protagonists, carrying a banner. Police then attack student protesters, who resist by hurling rocks, again melding actual footage of street battles of 1968 with simulated "authentic" participation of the film's characters. The images convey a clear message. After unsuccessfully demonstrating peacefully and ineffectively resisting repression, those opposing the regime had only one option: resorting to more radical measures. It is also the director's signal that the events are based on historical facts, even though, as we shall see, many are loosely applied to fit the film's narrative.

In *Marighella*, the illegitimacy of the 1964 regime and the protagonist's radicalization begin immediately in the aftermath of the coup, when the Communist Party leader resists arrest during a police roundup of targeted oppositionists. (Marighella later wrote a book, *Why I Resisted Prison*, explaining the reasons he decided to fight back against the regime instead of retreating underground as the Party leadership had ordered its members to do.[12]) Like *Four Days in September*, *Marighella* begins with black-and-white footage of the early sixties, which also suggests that the story is based on historical facts. However, unlike the action film on the kidnapping of the U.S. ambassador, which dates the resistance to the regime as taking place after the failure of student mobilizations in 1968, in *Marighella* citizens already resist the new regime in 1964 by throwing rocks at the tanks rolling through the streets of Rio de Janeiro. This is an important distinction, as Marighella and other revolutionary groups had actually begun organizing the guerrilla movement and carried out armed actions prior to Institutional Act No. 5 in

December 1968, whereas the more popular narrative about opposition to the dictatorship, which is explicitly articulated in *Four Days in September*, argues that only when legal channels were shut down at the end of 1968 did students and others with no other options resort to armed actions to overthrow the regime. (In what seems to have been a technical error of those editing *Marighella*, an opening title informs the viewer that the first scene, in which the ALN seizes military arms from a train, took place in 1964 when in fact it happened four years later, inadvertently leaving one to assume that immediately after the coup, Marighella was collecting weapons for the struggle.) In either case, in 1967 Marighella founded the ALN in order to launch a guerrilla movement, defeat the dictatorship, and inaugurate a process leading to an anti-imperialist, anti-feudal, nationalist and democratic government, as was the program of the ALN,[13] or as the joint statement with the MR-8 published at the end of this article promised, to end "the regime of the great exploiters and with the constitution of a government that frees the country's workers from this situation in which they find themselves."

From this point on, *Four Days in September* portrays a perspective in which both sides—the revolutionaries and the torturers—are equally guilty of excesses. But at the end of the day, the guerrilla leaders are the coldhearted fanatics. On the other hand, Henrique, the head of the security force, who is trying to identify the guerrillas' whereabouts, is a sensitive man haunted by his involvement in torture. He even expresses regrets about the whole endeavor: "We opened a Pandora's box. We shouldn't have done it. Things got out of control." Although it is possible that during the dictatorship some members of the repressive forces might have had second thoughts about their work, the choice to have Henrique indulge in such ruminations makes him a compassionate character and perhaps an exception to the rule. Moreover, while short scenes of state violence convey to filmgoers that the military regime is involved in heinous gross violations of human rights, Ambassador Elbrick is kind and reasonable, even understanding of the guerrillas' motivations. He personally opposes the military regime and distances himself from official U.S. policy that supported the 1964 military coup. He is perhaps the most sympathetic character in the film.

By contrast, in *Four Days in September*, Virgílio Gomes da Silva, known by the code name Jonas, who serves as the guerrilla commander of the action, promises to kill any comrades who fail to follow orders. At one point, he aggressively and inexplicably threatens the ambassador with execution. He later sets up a situation in which Gabeira's character, Pablo, whom he seems to irrationally hate, will be forced to assassinate the ambassador should the Brazilian government not meet the guerrillas' demands. In using Gomes da Silva's alias (Jonas), which the real-life revolutionary used while participating in the kidnapping, the filmmakers imply that this was the actual way he comported himself during the kidnapping. Yet in a series of essays written by participants in the event, this portrayal of Jonas's actions during the sequester is contradicted by his former comrades.[14] Similarly, Toledo, the code name for Joaquim Câmara Ferreira, the political leader of the sequester, is portrayed as a die-hard Communist who is callous and distant and dedicates his free time sullenly listening to a recording of the *Internationale*, the revolutionary anthem adopted by the Soviet Revolution. Again, by using the character's actual underground alias, the filmmakers suggest that this was the essential nature of Toledo, diminishing the possibilities for empathy with him. Both figures personify a malevolent and out-of-control revolutionary left.

These two historic figures are portrayed quite differently in *Marighella*. In real life, Virgílio Gomes da Silva, named Jorge in the film, who was one of millions of the hard-working poor, migrated to São Paulo in the 1950s from the Brazilian Northeast seeking a better life and eventually finding employment as a factory worker. He became a union activist and member of the Communist Party, leaving with Marighella in 1967 to found the ALN. Franklin Martins, another participant in the kidnapping, described him as having been "brave and determined, tranquil and attentive, enthusiastic but with his feet on the ground" during the action.[15] These characteristics stand out in the character of Gomes da Silva as he is depicted in *Marighella*. He is dedicated both to his family and to the revolutionary cause and suffers a brutal death at the hands of torturers. Far from the enraged maniac that appears in *Four Days in September*, his commitment to the revolution comes from his hard-life experiences as a poor migrant and worker. His final words, based on the testimony of political prisoners who overheard his torture sessions from his cell and reproduced in the film, were "you are killing a Brazilian." *Marighella* also humanizes Joaquim Câmara Ferreira, known as Branco in the film, who is intelligent, kind, reasonable, and affectionate, even after he and Marighella sharply disagree over Toledo's participation in the kidnapping, which Marighella predicts will lead to increased surveillance and repression. Gomes da Silva and Câmara Ferreira are three-dimensional characters with emotions and motivations for their revolutionary choices. They are self-aware agents of their own destinies, rather than foolish fanatics with misplaced strategies for changing the world.

While portraying Jonas and Toledo as caricatured irrational zealots in *Four Days in September*, the filmmakers choose to make Henrique, the intelligence officer and torturer, a complex character. He has insomnia because of his work. When challenged by his girlfriend about whether he is involved in torture, he explains: "Either you torture them right away and they confess where they last met, or there is no progress in your investigation. That's the logic of the guerrilla movement. If you don't torture them, they win. And if you do, they still win. They accuse you of being barbaric. It's total hypocrisy, but it works. It really works." While apparently feeling some compassion for his victims, he ultimately justifies the use of state-directed violence: "Most of them are innocent kids with big dreams. Kids being used by dangerous scum. And if they get into power, there won't just be torture, but many executions." In short, torture is a political necessity to avoid revolutionary terror in an imagined future order of a victorious revolutionary left. Although formally speaking, both sides are represented as evil forces fighting each other, Jonas and Toledo are stock characters engaged in a fanatic endeavor with no noticeable ambivalence about their mission, and Henrique is humanized in what are almost tender and intimate conversations with his girlfriend. Similarly, Elbrick and his wife have a warm and intimate partnership, and he is considerate and reasonable in his interactions with the revolutionary captors.

In *Marighella*, Wagner Moura is less ambiguous in his portrayal of Lúcio, the police investigator trying to track down the ALN leader. The character seems largely inspired by the historical figure Sérgio Paranhos Fleury, the head of the São Paulo State Department of Political and Social Order, a notorious torturer also involved in extrajudicial executions of indigents and Afro-Brazilians suspected of having committed crimes. Lúcio is relentless: sadistic in his treatment of detained revolutionaries and their supporters, including Dominican friars who offered logistical help to the ALN, yet calm and cozy at home with his wife and young daughter as he watches the reading of the revolutionary manifesto on the television after the kidnapping of the U.S. ambassador. He elicits no sympathy and is clearly the wicked foil to Marighella's jovial demeanor, compassion for his colleagues, and revolutionary dedication.

WASHINGTON'S CULPABILITY AND REVOLUTIONARY TERRORISM

Lúcio is also allied with Bob, a representative of the U.S. government, who joins him in the pursuit of the guerrillas. There is near consensus among historians about the role of the Kennedy and Johnson administrations in assisting the Brazilian military in planning the 1964 coup d'état. In 1962, Kennedy gave U.S. government officials the green light to support the Brazilian armed forces should they decide to oust the democratically elected government of João Goulart. Two years later, Johnson authorized the deployment of arms and ammunition and the aircraft carrier *Forester* and support vessels to Brazil to intervene in the coup should armed resistance to the military takeover result in a civil war.[16] In part, the decision of the Brazilian Communist Party not to mobilize its members and the reluctance of Goulart to oversee a bloodbath of his supporters meant that the covert U.S. action, known as Operation Brother Sam, could be called off.[17] Under the advice and guidance of U.S. ambassador Lincoln Gordon, who operated in Brazil from 1962 until 1966 when he became the Assistant Secretary of State for Western Hemispheric Affairs, Johnson immediately recognized the new government and authorized crucial financial assistance to ensure the economic stability of the new regime.[18] In 1969, President Richard Nixon continued to support the dictatorship after its crackdown on all opposition through the unlimited power contained in Institutional Act No. 5, receiving the third four-star general-president Emílio Garrastazu Médici at the White House in December 1971. At the same time, across the street in Lafayette Park, the mother of a recently released Brazilian political prisoner who had been arrested and tortured the previous year, joined a small cluster of clergy and anti–Vietnam war activists to protest political repression in Brazil.[19]

Thus, there is a logic among revolutionaries to want to hold the U.S. ambassador and his government accountable for their role in supporting the dictatorship. Yet in *Four Days in September*, when the guerrilla fighters interview Elbrick during his detention about the U.S. role in backing the regime, including CIA interference in domestic affairs, the ambassador denies any knowledge of its actions and states that he is personally against torture. This was precisely the position taken by Ambassador Gordon, his predecessor, who similarly disassociated himself from and claimed innocence about any information that the Brazilian government was committing gross violations of human rights.[20] On the other hand, *Marighella* leaves no room for doubt about official U.S. complicity in supporting the dictatorship. The character Wilson Chandler, representing Charles Chandler, a military officer studying in Brazil who was accused of complicity in supporting the regime, offers a speech to Brazilian military officers about the importance of tracking down the guerrillas. When he is killed in front of his son by ALN militants in a political assassination, Bob offers U.S. aid to support Lúcio and the state repressive apparatus to capture the guerrillas.

In this regard, *Marighella* doesn't back away from the fact that ALN used the language of revolutionary terrorism to justify its cause. Soon after his death, Marighella became famous throughout Europe for his writings, which were censored in France in 1970 and then published in Great Britain in 1971. His work, *For the Liberation of Brazil*, includes "The Handbook of the Urban Guerrilla Warfare," which Marighella completed in June 1969 while living underground and directing the efforts of the ALN. In the introduction, Marighella states: "My object is to recruit as many supporters as possible. The words 'aggressor' and 'terrorist' no longer mean what they did. Instead of arousing fear or censure, they are a call to action. To be called an aggressor or a terrorist in Brazil is now an honor to any citizen, for it means that he is fighting, with a gun in his hand, against the monstrosity of the present dictatorship and the suffering it causes."[21] In another document on guerrilla tactics, his position is unequivocal: "The tactic of revolutionary terrorism and sabotage must be used to combat the terrorism used by the dictatorship against the Brazilian people."[22]

Nor does *Marighella* hide from the fact that the ALN carried out bombings of U.S. government offices and "revolutionary executions," such as the aforementioned killing of Charles Chandler. In the film, one of the militants involved in the action gets cold feet after the killing. Paralyzed with confusion, he is captured by the police. Under torture, he reveals the ALN safe house, leading to a raid and the death of several comrades. The underlying message seems to be that had he not had second thoughts about the act of "revolutionary justice," he might not have been arrested and his comrades might not have died.

Marighella also tries to convey a linkage between the revolutionary movement in Brazil and other national and international insurgencies. The film's opening scene is an action-packed assault on a train to expropriate arms, likely inspired by the successful ALN action to capture the monthly payroll of a railroad company in August 1968. On the overlaying soundtrack, Chico Science raps, "Long Live Zapata! Long Live Sandino! Long Live Zumbi! Antonio Conselheiro. All of the black panthers, Lampião, your image and likeness. I am sure they too will sing someday."[23] The funk rock and maracatu fusion of the music and the eclectic choice of insurgent figures from Mexican and Nicaraguan revolutionaries to a rebellious slave leader, a millenarian religious figure, African American militants, and a Brazilian rural bandit send the message that the urban guerrillas' fight is not frozen in time but rather part of a longer international struggle for social justice of the most marginalized and oppressed.

VIEWERS' EMPATHY AND HISTORICAL ACCURACY

As might be expected given the fact that the film is a biopic, throughout *Marighella* the lead character is portrayed as a noble person. He has loving, intimate scenes with Clara, his partner, who painfully declines to join him in the armed struggle but supports the revolutionary cause. He also has a close relationship with his son, Carlos Jr., whom he desperately misses while living underground. In the midst of the 1964 military coup, the father abandons security precautions to take his son to the beach, and four years later, he almost risks capture in arranging a clandestine meeting with him. While in hiding, he tapes a tender message for his son, explaining why they have to be separated and why he has sacrificed time with his offspring in order to make the world a better place for him. In return, Carlos Jr. corrects his teacher who has classified the 1964 military takeover as a "revolution" and states in the classroom that it was a coup. He is beaten up by his classmates when they discover his parentage. In addition, he warns his father of an impending ambush when Marighella drives to Salvador to see his son, which happens to take place during the kidnapping of the U.S. ambassador (when in actuality Marighella was in hiding in Rio de Janeiro at the time). In spite of all adversities, Marighella forges on, realizing that the struggle might lead to his death.

The racial representation of Marighella also plays an important part in the film. Film director Moura made a conscious choice to cast Jorge Mário da Silva, known by his stage name as Seu Jorge, a dark-skinned Afro-Brazilian actor and musician, in the main role, even though Marighella was the light-skinned son of a descendant of enslaved Africans and Italian immigrants. Mobilizations in recent years by Afro-Brazilian activists and their allies have denounced hegemonic ideas that the country is a racial democracy. They have also criticized that notions of race are organized around a color hierarchy that favors lighter-skinned over darker-skinned people. Casting Seu Jorge in the film's main role seems to be a conscious statement that centers Afro-Brazilians in the radical resistance to the dictatorship although in actuality the revolutionary movement, including its leadership, was mostly composed of middle-class European-descendant youth. Still, this choice seems to be the affirmation of a new way of understanding race in Brazil in which increasingly large numbers of people of mixed African, European, and/ or Indigenous descent identify as Black to emphasize their African ancestry.

Feature-length films based on historical events inevitably are forced to amalgamate characters, shift chronologies, and play with the facts in order to produce a succinct artistic production that is legible to the audience. A film cannot be a lengthy historical tome with long-winded introductions, extensive argumentation, and voluminous footnotes. So certain factual flaws in film are understandable if not forgivable. Nevertheless, for the record, in *Four Days in September*, Fernando Gabeira (Paulo) did not come up with the idea of the kidnapping, nor did he write the revolutionary manifesto. Vera Silvia Magalhães (René), one of the members of the team involved in bank robberies and the kidnapping, did not sleep with the person in charge of the U.S. embassy's security to learn information about the daily routine of the ambassador. As Magalhães commented in an interview with the author of this essay over fifteen years ago, "I didn't need to, men are so naïve and easily manipulated."[24] The two female characters in the film are based on Magalhães. However, Andréia, the hardened female commander of the MR-8 curiously donning a military cap, making her into a ridiculous figure, has little real-life resemblance to the sole female leader of the MR-8. In fact, although Magalhães participated in the abduction, no women stayed in the house with the ambassador. So much for the sex scene between Andréia and Pablo during those tense four days in September, although Magalhães and Gabeira were for a time a couple after the kidnapping while in exile. Similarly, no women participated in the ALN's railroad payroll heist. Nonetheless, women did play leadership roles in many of the revolutionary organizations of the period, including participating in armed actions. Finally, in *Four Days in September*, one must simply discount incomprehensible elements in the plot, such as Paulo's improbable stalking of Henrique and listening in on his conversations or the security chief's climbing a telephone pole to surveil the revolutionary's hideout as well as the improvable induction scene of new recruits at the beginning of the film.

One major flaw in both movies is the failure to fully capture the isolation that the guerrillas had from the general population. Although a taxi driver expresses his enthusiasm about the gutsy kidnapping of the U.S. ambassador to Pablo, and Brazilians listen carefully to the broadcasting of Marighella's declarations when the guerrillas manage to splice into public airwaves and presumably read the printed version that the left-wing newspaper editor published, there is only a slight indication in a short scene between Pablo and Andréia that they are cut off from the people, immediately before their arrest. Lúcio is more explicit in *Marighella* in explaining the government campaign to transform the revolutionaries into dangerous terrorists. The dictatorship was, indeed, very successful in ensuring popular support through government propaganda, censorship, domination of media, and an expanding economy so that the guerrillas had few opportunities to convey a positive message to the population. While the daring escapade of kidnapping the diplomatic representative of the most powerful country in the world might have elicited some temporary sympathetic sentiments toward these urban revolutionaries, they were largely ephemeral.

Still, both films end with an upbeat scene, even though soon after the release of the fifteen political prisoners, most of those involved in the kidnapping were arrested, tortured, or killed by the military regime and two months after the abduction of the U.S. ambassador, Marighella was assassinated in São Paulo. Nevertheless, in the final scene of *Four Days in September*, jailed revolutionary survivors of the sequester gather in front of an airplane to be flown to Algeria after the release of the kidnapped German ambassador in June 1970 in exchange for the freedom of forty political prisoners. The scene is filmed in black-and-white to simulate historical footage and is reminiscent of the iconic image of thirteen of the fifteen prisoners from the kidnapping of the U.S. ambassador posing for a photographer in front of a plane just before they are flown to freedom. In the film, there is joy and relief to see who has survived and will be allowed to leave the country, marred only by the solemn image of Andréia being brought to the scene in a wheelchair, temporarily crippled by her torturers. In *Marighella*, after the ALN leader is ambushed and killed by the police, the final scene shows one of the female guerrilla fighters, whom Marighella ordered to leave operations in the city, arriving at a rural church where a priest greets her. They enter the building and open a box containing arms. She picks up a machine gun, handles it carefully, and then stares into the camera. The significance is clear: the struggle continues. The press kit for the film is also unambiguous: "his [Marighella's] ideals live on through the young revolutionaries who continue his fight."[25] In other words, the film's last scene is not just an allusion to those youth who continued the struggle as ALN militants until the organization was dismantled by 1974. It also pays homage to a new generation that had recently mobilized to resist the authoritarian Bolsonaro government not necessarily for a socialist revolution but certainly for democracy and social justice. This theme of revolutionary dedication is reinforced after the major credits for *Marighella* are flashed onto the screen. In what looks like a film outtake, five ALN guerrilla fighters, the core of Marighella's group but without their leader present, hold hands in a tight circle and enthusiastically sing the Brazilian national anthem. One phrase rings out as particularly appropriate: "But if thou raise the strong mace of justice, thou will not see that son of thine fleeing from battle, nor do those who love thee [Brazil] fear their own death." There is determination, joy, and pride in the way they show passion for their country. Rather than crazed terrorists or foolish youth, they are loyal patriots who are fighting for a noble cause.

DOCUMENT

The following declaration, written by Franklin Martins, was released on September 4, 1969, after U.S. Ambassador Charles Elbrick was sequestered by two revolutionary organizations.[26]

Revolutionary groups today detained U.S. Ambassador Charles Burke Elbrick, bringing him to an unnamed location in the country where they are holding him captive. This act is not an isolated episode. It adds to the innumerable revolutionary deeds already carried out: bank robberies that raise funds for the revolution and return what the bankers take from their employees and from the people; occupations of [army] barracks and police stations, where weapons and ammunition are obtained for the fight to bring down the dictatorship; invasions of prisons, during which revolutionaries are freed so that they can return to the people's struggle; explosions of buildings that symbolize oppression; and the execution of hangmen and torturers.

In reality, the abduction of the ambassador is just one more act of a revolutionary war that advances every day and that initiated its rural guerrilla stage just this year.

With the kidnapping of the ambassador, we want to show that it is possible to defeat the dictatorship and exploitation if we arm ourselves and organize. We will appear where the enemy least expects us and disappear immediately, weakening the dictatorship and causing terror and fear among the exploiters, hope and certainty of victory among the exploited.

In our country, Mr. Elbrick represents the interests of imperialism that, allied with the big bosses, landowners, and national banks, maintains a regime of oppression and exploitation.

It was this alliance's interest in gaining even more wealth that created and maintained the salary squeeze, the unjust agrarian structure, and institutional repression. The kidnapping of the ambassador is therefore a clear warning that the Brazilian people will not let [the exploiters] rest and at every moment will unleash upon them the weight of their struggle. Let it be known to all that this is a struggle without truce, a long and hard fight that does not end with the exchange of one general in power for another, one that only finishes with the end of the regime of the great exploiters and with a constitution of a government that frees the country's workers from this situation in which they find themselves.

We are in Independence Week. The people and the dictatorship commemorate [the occasion] in different ways. The dictatorship promotes public events and parades, sets off fireworks, and posts propaganda. With [these displays], the dictatorship does not commemorate anything; it seeks to throw sand in the eyes of the exploited, establishing a false happiness with the objective of hiding the life of misery, exploitation, and repression in which we live. How can you hide the obvious? Can you hide from the people their own misery when they feel it in the flesh?

During Independence Week, there are two commemorations: that of the elite and that of the people, that of those who organize parades and that of those who kidnap the ambassador, a symbol of exploitation.

The life and death of the ambassador are in the hands of the dictatorship. If it meets two requirements, Mr. Elbrick will be released. Otherwise, we will be forced to fulfill revolutionary justice. Our two requirements are:

a) The release of 15 political prisoners. There are 15 revolutionaries out of thousands who suffer torture in prisons across the country, who are beaten, and who suffer from the humiliations imposed by the military. We are not demanding the impossible. We are not demanding the restitution of the lives of countless fighters murdered in prisons. Those will not be released, of course. They will be avenged one day. We only demand the release of these 15 men, leaders of the struggle against the dictatorship. Each of them is worth a hundred ambassadors, from the people's point of view. But a U.S. ambassador is also worth a lot from the standpoint of dictatorship and exploitation.

b) The publication and reading of this message, in its entirety, in the main newspapers, radio and television stations across the country.

The 15 political prisoners must be taken by special plane to a specific country—Algeria, Chile, or Mexico—where they will be granted political asylum. No reprisals should be attempted against them, under penalty of retaliation.

The dictatorship has 48 hours to respond publicly whether it accepts or rejects our proposal. If the answer is yes, we will release the list of 15 revolutionary leaders and wait 24 hours for their transport to a safe country. If the answer is negative, or if there is no answer within that period, Mr. Burke Elbrick will be executed. The 15 comrades must be released, whether they are condemned or not: this is an "exceptional situation." In "exceptional situations," the jurists of the dictatorship always come up with a formula to resolve things, as was recently seen in the rise of the military junta.

The talks will only start with public and official declarations from the dictatorship that it will comply with the requirements.

The method will always be public on the part of the authorities and always unforeseen on our part. We want to remember that deadlines are non-extendable and that we will not hesitate to fulfill our promises.

Finally, we want to warn those who torture, beat and kill our comrades: we will not accept the continuation of this heinous practice. We are giving the last warning. Whoever goes on torturing, beating and killing, should be on alert. Now it's an eye for an eye, a tooth for a tooth.

National Liberating Action (ALN)
8th of October Revolutionary Movement (MR-8)

ADDITIONAL RESOURCES

Green, James N. *Exile with Exiles: Herbert Daniel, Gay Brazilian Revolutionary.* Durham, NC: Duke University Press, 2018. Biography of a medical student turned guerrilla leader who after living in exile for eight years, returns to Brazil to become a leading spokesperson for people living with HIV/AIDS.

Huggins, Martha K., Mika Haritos-Tatouros, and Philip G. Zimbardo. *Violence Workers: Police Torturers and Murderers Reconstruct Brazilian Atrocities.* Los Angeles: University of California Press, 2002. Study of Brazilians who participated in torture during the military dictatorship.

Langland, Victoria. *Speaking of Flowers: Student Movements and the Making and Remembering of 1968 in Military Brazil.* Durham, NC: Duke University Press, 2013. Political history of the Brazilian student movement and its opposition to the military dictatorship.

Marighella, Carlos. *For the Liberation of Brazil.* Translated by John Butt and Rosemary Sheed. Introduction by Richard Gott. Harmondsworth, England: Penguin Books, 1971. A collection of writings and articles by urban guerrilla leader Carlos Marighella, initially published in France in 1970 soon after his death and subsequently issued in English.

Sattamini, Lina Penna, *A Mother's Cry: A Memoir of Politics, Prison and Torture under the Brazilian Military Dictatorship,* trans. Rex P. Nielson and James N. Green, introduction by James N. Green, and epilogue by Marcos P. S. Arruda. Durham, NC: Duke University Press, 2010. A passionate account of a mother's ordeal trying to get her son, a political dissident, released from prison.

Serbin, Kenneth P. *From Revolution to Power in Brazil: How Radical Leftists Embraced Capitalism and Struggled with Leadership.* Notre Dame, IN: University of Notre Dame Press, 2019. The study of the political and life trajectories of members of the National Liberating Action, the revolutionary organization founded by Carlos Marighella.

Skidmore, Thomas E. *The Politics of Military Rule in Brazil, 1964–85.* New York: Oxford University Press, 1988. A comprehensive political and economic history of the Brazilian military dictatorship.

NOTES

1. Interviews with the participants in the action and those released from prison can be found in Silvio Da-Rin, *Hércules 56: O seqüestro do embaixador americano em 1969* (Rio de Janeiro: Jorge Zahar, 2007).

2. Juan de Onis, "Freed Brazilians Charge 'Tortures' by Regime," *New York Times,* September 9, 1969, 8.

3. Fernando Gabeira, *O que é isso, companheiro? Um depoimento* (Rio de Janeiro: Editora Codecri, 1979).

4. Essays and newspaper articles criticizing the film were collected and published in Daniel Aarão Reis, et al., *Versões e ficções: O sequestro da história* (São Paulo: Editora Fundação Perseu Abramo, 1997).

5. The film *Marighella* relied heavily on Mário Margalhães, *Marighella: o guer-rilheiro que incendiou o mundo* (São Paulo: Companhia das Letras, 2012).

6. "Após ação coordenada anti-'Marighella,' IMDB apaga críticas ao filme," *Veja*, February 18, 2019.

7. For a comprehensive analysis of the armed struggle in Brazil, see Jacob Goren-der, *Combate nas trevas* (São Paulo, SP: Editora Atica, 1999).

8. Marcelo Ridenti, *O fantasma da revolução Brasileira* (São Paulo: Editora da UNESP, 1993), 197.

9. Alfredo Sirkis, *Os carbonários: memorias de uma guerra perdida* (São Paulo: Globo, 1980).

10. João Robert Martins Filho, "The War of Memory: The Brazilian Military Dic-tatorship According to Militants and Military Men," *Latin American Perspectives* 36, no. 5 (2009): 89–107.

11. The most important work that raised these questions is Daniel Aarão Reis, *A revolução faltou ao encontro—Os comunistas no Brasil* (São Paulo: Brasiliense, 1990).

12. Carlos Marighella, *Porque eu resisti à prisão* (Salvador: São Paulo-SP Editora Brasiliense, 1995).

13. Carlos Marighella, *For the Liberation of Brazil*, trans. John Butt and Rosemary Sheed, with an introduction by Richard Gott (Harmondsworth, England: Penguin Books, 1971), 19–27.

14. Reis et al., *Versões e ficções*.

15. Franklin Martins, "As duas mortes de Jonas," originally published in *O Globo* on May 10, 1997, and reprinted in *Versões e ficções*, 119.

16. See Chapter 1 in James N. Green, *We Cannot Remain Silent: Opposition to the Brazilian Military Dictatorship in the United States* (Durham, NC: Duke University Press, 2010).

17. Phyllis Parker, *Brazil and the Quiet Intervention, 1964* (Austin: University of Texas Press, 1979).

18. Ruth Leacock, *Requiem for Revolution: The United States and Brazil, 1961–1969* (Kent, OH: Kent State University Press, 1990).

19. Lina Penna Sattamini, *A Mother's Cry: A Memoir of Politics, Prison and Tor-ture under the Brazilian Military Dictatorship*, trans. Rex P. Nielson and James N. Green, introduction by James N. Green, and epilogue by Marcos P. S. Arruda (Dur-ham, NC: Duke University Press, 2010).

20. See Ralph Della Cava, "Torture in Brazil," *Commonweal* 92 (April 24, 1970): 1, 135–41; his exchange with Lincoln Gordon, "Letter to the Editor," *Commonweal* (August 7, 1970): 378–79, 398; and Ralph Della Cava's "Reply": 398–99.

21. Marighella, "Handbook of Urban Guerrilla Warfare," in *For the Liberation of Brazil*, 62.

22. Marighella, "Guerrilla Tactics and Operations," in *For the Liberation of Brazil*, 112.

23. Chico Science, "Monólogo ao pé do ouvido," *Da lama ao caos* (1994).

24. Vera Sílvia Magalhães, interview with author, July 17, 2003, Rio de Janeiro, tape recording.

25. *Marighella* press kit, accessed June 30, 2021, https://static1.squarespace.com /static/5d821cf67566a2183227d7c8/t/5e6095ad9f9a545c227a5256/1583388258410/ MARIGHELLA+-+Press+Kit.pdf.

26. James N. Green, Victoria Langland, and Lilia M. Schwarcz, eds., "The Kidnapping of the U.S. Ambassador," in *The Brazil Reader: History, Culture, and Politics,* second edition (Durham, NC: Duke University Press, 2019), 457–59.

Chapter 10

"If You Don't Cheat, You'll Face Defeat"

La Ley de Herodes, *Corruption, and Authoritarianism in Mexico*

Jürgen Buchenau and Madison Green

La Ley de Herodes (1999) *[Herod's Law]; produced by Luis Estrada; directed by Luis Estrada; written by Luis Estrada, Jaime Sampietro, Fernando León, and Vicente Leñero; color; 122 minutes; Bandidos Films, Alta Vista Films, Fondo para la Producción Cinematográfica de Calidad (FOPROCINE), Instituto Mexicano de Cinematografía (IMCINE). Appointed interim mayor of an impoverished and isolated village, Juan Vargas (Damián Alcázar) learns how the Mexican political system really works.*

La Ley de Herodes (*Herod's Law*), Mexico's most famous political satire, challenged the ruling Partido Revolucionario Institucional (PRI, or Institutional Revolutionary Party) on the eve of the party's first-ever defeat in a presidential election in 2000. Claiming the mantle of the Mexican Revolution, three iterations of an official revolutionary party had enjoyed a virtual monopoly on power since 1929. The film is set during the presidency of Miguel Alemán Valdés (1946–1952). Mexicans remember the Alemán era as a time when the ruling elite sold out its revolutionary ideals and cast its lot with authoritarianism and corruption. *La Ley de Herodes* draws even stronger parallels to its own time. A tumultuous decade, the 1990s featured the sale of state-owned assets, the integration of Mexico into the North American Free Trade Agreement (NAFTA), the Zapatista Rebellion of 1994, the assassination of a presidential nominee, and a serious financial crisis. The major themes of *La Ley de Herodes* include corruption, authoritarianism, the drawbacks of modernization, and the government's disregard for poor and indigenous Mexicans.[1]

The film draws effective parallels between two periods marked by retrenchment from reform and generational change.[2] During and after World War II, the ruling party distanced itself from the populist program of General Lázaro Cárdenas, whose administration (1934–1940) had nationalized the oil industry and parceled out 49 million acres to landless campesinos. The Alemán years also witnessed the transition from a generation of revolution-ary generals to the *licenciados*, or college graduates.[3] Following the collapse of the economy in the 1982 debt crisis, a succession of neoliberal govern-ments similarly distanced themselves from the neopopulist presidencies of Luis Echeverría Álvarez (1970–1976) and José López Portillo (1976–1982). Echeverría revived Cárdenas's policies seeking national control of resources and land reform, and López Portillo parlayed an oil boom into state assis-tance for Mexican workers. Presidents Miguel de la Madrid (1982–1988) and Carlos Salinas de Gortari (1988–1994) amended the nationalist provisions of the revolutionary Constitution of 1917, sold off state-owned businesses to private investors (and often, cronies), and curtailed government assistance to the poor. The new ruling generation held not only undergraduate degrees from Mexican universities but also graduate degrees from top institutions in the United States.[4]

The film is not based on a true story. Its protagonists are fictitious, as is the village of San Pedro de los Saguaros, located in an unnamed state. As political satire, *La Ley de Herodes* works through hyperbole and allegory. The film's characters appear irredeemable, with few possessing any identifiable virtues. They inhabit a forbidding political and social landscape where bad deeds are rewarded and good deeds get punished. The director, Luis Estrada, was thus able to produce the first Mexican movie to criticize the PRI directly. In many ways, *La Ley de Herodes* did for film what Carlos Fuentes's famous *La muerte de Artemio Cruz* had done for the Mexican novel almost four decades earlier.[5]

PLOT SUMMARY

When the mayor of San Pedro de los Saguaros attempts to flee the village with funds he has extorted from the population, an angry mob pursues him, and a campesino kills him with a machete. The state's governor is preparing a run for president in 1952 and cannot afford a scandal. As an interim replace-ment, Secretario de Gobierno "Licenciado López" appoints Juan Vargas, a junkyard operator and low-level member of the PRI. The initial dialogue between Vargas and the second in command in the state government sets up the party's expectations:

> López: I'm going to be straight with you, Vargas! As you know well, modernity has finally arrived in our country. We need to implement the revolutionary ideals and . . . the words of our president, Miguel Alemán: help the country move forward, put an end to corruption and, above all, the chaos of a few malcontents. There are a few officials who do not understand that they need to serve the country. They . . . enrich themselves at the people's expense. The country needs true patriots, people like you.
> Vargas: Thank you, sir.
> López: I'm going to need your help.
> Vargas (laughs): You tell me whom to kill.
> López: No, no, no, Vargas, times have changed.

Vargas and his wife, Gloria, arrive in the village with good intentions, promising to bring "progress and social justice" to a poor indigenous village with no electricity. But there are only seven pesos in the municipal treasury. Moreover, the true authorities are the local physician, "Doctor Morales"; the priest; and Doña Lupe, the owner of a brothel. Unable to exert any authority, Vargas returns to López to ask him to send money. On the way there, his car breaks down, and a blond norteamericano, Robert Smith, stops to lend a hand. Smith asks for 100 dollars as payment and reaches under the hood to reconnect a cable. Vargas asserts that his status as a mayor means that he is good for the money.

But extracting more money proves impossible. López has no intentions of sending any money to the village, and when Vargas asks to be switched to a different village, he exclaims, laughing:

> Ah, hell! . . . You turned out way smarter than I thought. No! No way, it's your turn with "Herod's Law." Either you get fucked, or you get screwed. . . . Sit down, I will help you out. Here is a book of federal and state laws.
> Vargas: Do I have to read all of it?
> López: No, no, no, Varguitas. This is so you have a budget! If you know how to use it, you'll know how to get something out of everyone, between fines, taxes, licenses . . . use it at your convenience, and everything will be set. Remember, in this country, if you don't cheat, you'll face defeat.[6]

When Vargas points out that the inhabitants do not respect authority, López takes a pistol out of his desk and says: "Here you go. Go ahead, dude, take it. If someone threatens you with a machete, point the pistol at him, and you'll see how no one will be in your way." He adds: "it is all here in this little book, whether the executive, legislative, or judiciary branch, you are it. The supreme authority of San Pedro . . . or whatever the hell it is called."

This lesson inaugurates Vargas's rapid descent into corruption and violence. He accepts a bribe from Doña Lupe and visits the brothel's sex workers. He learns how to use the law to wring money out of the poor inhabitants. Vargas and Smith join in a corrupt partnership that promises to bring electricity but only has a single electrical pole to show for its efforts. Vargas makes a deal with the priest, who is willing to trade confessional secrets for payments toward the purchase of an automobile. His only opposition is Morales, a member of the opposition Partido Acción Nacional (PAN) and longtime mayoral candidate, who demands the closure of the brothel. When Doña Lupe's bodyguard beats up Vargas in response to his tactics, the protagonist shoots both of them. He frames the local drunk, Filemón, for the murders, extracting a confession that Filemón acted on Morales's orders. En route to prison, Filemón reveals to Vargas that he knows the truth. Vargas kills him and dumps his body in a ravine. When he finds Gloria—who is aware of his escapades in the brothel—in bed with Smith, he beats her and keeps her chained to a bed. Vargas learns from the priest that Morales has sexually assaulted his teenage maid, which allows him to drive the doctor out of the village. The departure of the only local opposition figure drives Vargas toward delusions of grandeur. He extracts taxes and fines at will, jails those who refuse to pay, and even writes his own laws, including one that sets the mayoral term at twenty years and allows up to four consecutive reelections.

A bloody dénouement concludes this fast-paced film. López arrives on the run with his second-in-command, appropriately named "Tiburón" (shark), having engineered an assassination attempt on President Alemán's nephew, who has predictably secured his uncle's support for the PRI gubernatorial nomination. When López learns just how much money Vargas has extracted from the villagers, he wants all of it. But Smith and Gloria Vargas have escaped with all of his wealth, leaving only a note and a U.S. flag. An angry Vargas kills Tiburón and López, only to confront a throng of irate campesinos carrying torches. He escapes by climbing up the electrical pole, and government forces come to his rescue. The closing scene finds Vargas in Congress as the hero who has killed López, the enemy of the Alemán family and the Mexican nation. Vargas exhorts the other deputies to make sure that the PRI will stay in power forever. Meanwhile, in San Pedro de los Saguaros, a new mayoral couple have arrived in the exact same fashion as Vargas and Gloria had.

THE FILM AS COMMENTARY ON THE 1940S

This political satire portrays PRI rule in the 1940s, a regime that claimed to represent the aspirations of the Mexican Revolution for democracy, land reform, and social justice but in fact applied the brakes on the social reforms of the Cárdenas era. It offers several critiques of the Alemán years. First and foremost is the authoritarian structure of Mexican political life as well as the PRI's cynical portrayal of its revolutionary antecedents. Second, the movie highlights the prevalence of corruption on all levels. Third, it lambastes the program of import-substitution industrialization (ISI), which featured deepening dependence on the United States. Finally, *La Ley de Herodes* shows the enduring chasm between Spanish-speaking and indigenous Mexico.

The film introduces the audience to an authoritarian, top-down political system. The PRI system left state governors at the whim of the president, who ruled without any accountability and chose his successor in what Mexicans know as a *dedazo*, or finger point.[7] Similarly, local leaders obeyed the dictates of the governor. The methods of this hierarchical rule included coercion through military and police force and persuasion through budgetary allocations. Yet the film also offers harsh criticism of the opposition. For all of his posturing about the need to close Doña Lupe's brothel, Morales has secrets in his own past that he would prefer to keep buried. We also see authoritarian structures in Vargas's conflicted relationship with the priest, keeper of the villagers' secrets through the Sacrament of Confession and almost equally covetous of material benefits. Their uneasy coexistence symbolizes the rapprochement between church and state after decades of conflict that culminated in the devastating Cristero War (1926–1929).

Paul Gillingham and Benjamin Smith have called this system a *dictablanda* (soft dictatorship), a term that elicits unfortunate comparisons to Augusto Pinochet's description of his own military dictatorship in Chile beginning in 1973.[8] The Peruvian novelist Mario Vargas Llosa famously labeled the PRI state the "perfect dictatorship,"[9] a term Morales references during a dinner meeting of all power brokers that stands as the most substantial political discussion in the film. Whether a *dictablanda* or a perfect dictatorship, the Alemán presidency appeared to usher in the *pax priista*, the period between 1946 and 1968 that historians long considered a period of relative social quiescence and PRI dominance.

Yet we now know that the *pax priista* was not such. The period 1946–1948 included two agrarian rebellions and one abortive coup.[10] There were more top military officers in 1953 than there had been in 1942.[11] In the Alemán years, the PRI was not yet as authoritarian as the film describes. At the state and local levels, party primaries featured a process that Gillingham calls *auscultación.* The term describes the action of a stethoscope listening to internal organs, but it is used here in the sense that the party hierarchy attempted to take the temperature of the grass roots.[12] In a new book, Gillingham aptly states that the PRI could be an "adornment to rather than a bulwark of the state"[13] and depicts the crafting of "unrevolutionary Mexico" as a contested process. The 1952 election to replace Alemán featured Miguel Henríquez Guzmán, who mounted a strong challenge to the PRI on a platform to restore the Cardenista push for agrarian reform. Recent scholarship has demonstrated the deep history of the popular effervescence that led to the massacre of hundreds of protesters at Tlatelolco Square in October 1968.[14] PRIista Mexico was a system in motion, not in stasis. Although the PRI was the dominant party, the party and the state were not the same thing.[15]

The twin metaphors of the law book and the gun suggest that authoritarianism goes hand in hand with corruption. Corruption is a concept often used to stereotype Latin America as a region of lawlessness and self-enrichment. As one Argentine journalist put it, "corruption in Latin America is not merely a social deviation, it is a way of life."[16] Although the revolutionaries who overthrew Porfirio Díaz in 1910 aimed to get rid of the grand corruption of the dictator's cronies, the revolution ushered in a series of new ruling factions that abused their access to power and wealth in a similar way as Díaz's group had done.[17]

For example, Filemón's roadside killing evokes the Huitzilac massacre. On October 3, 1927, an army unit murdered a presidential candidate, General Francisco R. Serrano, and thirteen of his supporters on their way to prison in Mexico City. The deed occurred on the orders of President Plutarco Elías Calles and General Álvaro Obregón, Mexico's former president and candidate in the July 1928 presidential elections.[18] Historian Alan Knight has defined corruption as "the use of political power and office in ways that are geared to some individual or collective self-interest and that are illegal and/or considered corrupt, improper, or self-serving," distinguishing peculation, or "government at the service of graft," from systemic corruption, or "graft at the service of government."[19]

Like the *políticos* of the Alemán years, Vargas illustrated both of these types. He used his office for personal financial gain, and he also kept himself in power by striking illicit deals with individuals who could be helpful to his ambitions. As Morales chided him during the dinner featuring the leadership of San Pedro de los Saguaros: "Please, licenciado! The government is in the hands of a gang of thieves, and the worst is your boss, [Miguel Alemán]. You are an example of the class of rascals that rules over us. Since you got here, you have done nothing else than extort anyone who will let you."

La Ley de Herodes offers scathing commentary on Alemán's economic policies. The official memory labels the 1940s and the two succeeding decades the "Mexican Miracle" structured by ISI and the expansion of food production. The state fostered ISI, which followed four decades of slow industrialization during the late Porfiriato and the revolutionary decades, by financing prioritized industrial projects and mobilizing domestic capital. Inspired by the writings of the Argentine economist Raúl Prebisch, the accelerated industrialization program sought to wean Mexico from its dependence on imported industrial items. Vargas's failed promise to bring electricity to San Pedro de los Saguaros represents Alemán's incomplete program of modernization. The need for capital goods and investments to build the new industries, as well as the importance of U.S. tourism and remittances from Mexican American workers, meant an ongoing reliance on the United States. Although Mexico featured high growth rates for two decades, skyrocketing debt with high interest rates ultimately led to the financial crisis of 1982, which wiped out half of the country's middle class, led to massive capital flight, and sent the peso into a tailspin.[20]

The film critiques the PRIista economic policies represented in Vargas's assertion that he will bring "modernity" to San Pedro de los Saguaros. The electrical pole in the middle of the village symbolizes the empty promises of the government but also saves the protagonist's life during the insurrection. Smith absconds with Vargas's ill-gotten gains, with Gloria in tow. The film thus assails the deleterious effects of industrialization on the countryside, Mexico's dependence on the United States, and the connection between the program of industrial development and widespread corruption.

Finally, *La Ley de Herodes* slams the government for abusing the indigenous population. Vargas's paternalistic assertion that he has come to bring modernity to San Pedro de los Saguaros implies that the indigenous inhabitants need modernity. In fact, however, one of their greatest and most painfully obvious needs is to get rid of oppressive and corrupt jefes like Vargas, who do nothing to lift them out of poverty. The postrevolutionary Mexican state—and the PRI in particular—claimed to act on behalf of the poor and in particular, the indigenous population. This claim was particularly cynical because of a state-sponsored Hispanicization campaign that went by the name of *indigenismo*. Dating back to the thought of the anthropologist Manuel Gamio and the rural education campaign of Obregón's Secretary of Public Instruction, José Vasconcelos, *indigenismo* sought the "redemption" of the more than 15% of the population that spoke a language other than Spanish as their primary idiom.[21] However, this redemption involved an appreciation of Mexico's rich indigenous past rather than the present, which featured racist assimilationist policies focused on erasing contemporary indigenous culture in favor of Mexican national culture. Vargas never even makes an attempt to understand the culture of the people, considering them irredeemably backward. In a revealing phrase, he tells the villagers: "you are poor because you want to be!"

However evocative this statement is, *La Ley de Herodes* does not transcend Vargas's perspective. In the film, the indigenous villagers are either passive or violent; Filemón is an end-stage alcoholic; and none of them appear interested in working for a better future, either for themselves or collectively. Aside from their periodic revolts, they appear as objects rather than subjects of history.

THE FILM AS COMMENTARY ON THE RECENT PAST

The film is even more important for the director's interpretation of the recent past than its portrayal of the Alemán years. Contemporary themes echo in *La Ley de Herodes*: the impact of neoliberalism; indigenous revolt; and the political bankruptcy of the PRI, including the use of violence to remove dissident voices. The film connects these themes to portray a regime more authoritarian and corrupt than its ancestor of the late 1940s.

Both the opening scene and the village's rebellion against Vargas near the end of the movie remind the Mexican viewer of the 1994 Zapatista Rebellion in Chiapas, which featured an indigenous uprising against the "benefits of modernization" squelched by federal authorities. Specifically, the Zapatista Rebellion targeted NAFTA, which took effect on January 1, 1994, promising to bring investments and material improvements.[22] While NAFTA did attract basic industries to Mexico—at least in the short term, until these same industries fled to countries with even lower wages and benefits—it also benefited multinational corporations at the expense of the poor and particularly, the indigenous communities. NAFTA accelerated the sale of Mexico's state-owned companies.[23] In the film, Smith represents NAFTA, and neoliberalism in general, in addition to U.S. influence. Smith's flight with Vargas's ill-gotten gains symbolizes the free-trade agreement and neoliberalism as a theft of national resources. Of course, the fact that Smith leaves town in the company of Vargas's wife makes a highly problematic point—as if Mexican women were such a "resource," objects to be exploited and "exported."

The film also reflects the legacy of two fraught presidential transitions that shattered whatever public trust the PRI had remaining. In postrevolutionary Mexico, a president is elected for six years and can never be elected to that office again. Throughout the reign of the PRI, the outgoing president played an outsized role in picking the party's candidate in the next election (i.e., the next incumbent). In Alemán's days, the future president was usually the powerful Secretario de Gobernación, the Secretary of the Interior, in charge of the police and public safety as well as relations with the state governments. In the case of Carlos Salinas de Gortari and his successor, Ernesto Zedillo, the *dedazo* pointed at someone with an economics degree from a U.S. university and with experience heading the Secretariat of Planning and Budget, the same cabinet post also held by Miguel de la Madrid, the president before Salinas (1982–1988).

In the late 1980s, the PAN and the left-leaning Partido de la Revolución Democrática (PRD) launched strong challenges to the PRI. Founded in 1938 in part to coalesce the Catholic opposition, which was barred by the constitution from forming an expressly clerical party, the PAN embraced the PRI's economic program but demanded a political opening, just like Morales did in the film. In 1989, the PAN won its first state governorship and two years later, its first senatorial election at the federal level. Estrada's left-leaning perspective does not consider the PAN a genuine alternative, as evidenced by Morales's own hypocrisy and the fact that his wife sleeps with everyone she can in the village. Represented perhaps by the eternal "secretary" of the village, the bilingual Carlos Pek, the PRD split from the PRI to strike out in a different direction. Like the PRI, it drew justification from the revolution, but it cast its lot with the poor and opposed authoritarianism and corruption. The party was founded by Cuauhtémoc Cárdenas, the son of the most popular president of the revolutionary generation.[24] In the July 1988 election, PRI candidate Salinas faced a Cárdenas, who bore the first name of the last Mexica emperor as well as the PAN's well-funded Manuel Clouthier. He also confronted a population that had borne the brunt of the brutal 1982 financial crisis, which resulted in a decline in real incomes of approximately 50%, capital flight, and a sharp decline of the peso—not to mention the aftermath of the 1985 earthquake in Mexico City, which highlighted PRI mismanagement and corruption.

Although postelection returns indicated that Salinas had lost, the computers tabulating the election results crashed twice under mysterious circumstances, and the PRI candidate emerged as the winner. The phrase *se cayó el sistema* (the system has crashed) held a double meaning: "for the ordinary citizen, it was not the computer network but the Mexican political system that had crashed."[25] *La Ley de Herodes* perfectly expresses popular frustrations with the perennial rule of the PRI cynically defended by party leaders. As Vargas tells Morales: "In this country, we respect the vote. It is not our fault that the people always vote for my party." What the popular mood did not capture at the time was that the fraudulent elections left the PRI hopelessly split between an old guard hoping to keep control and a democratizing faction. After 1988, the demise of the party's hegemony was only a matter of time.[26]

In March 1994, less than four months before the next presidential election, a gunman killed Luis Donaldo Colosio, the PRI presidential candidate whom Salinas had handpicked. The day before, Colosio had given a speech attacking authoritarian rule and calling for meaningful political reform and dialogue with the Zapatistas.[27] His murder remains unsolved. To replace Colosio, Salinas tapped Ernesto Zedillo, a man considered one of his puppets. This time, the PRI candidate won easily. But in September 1994, an assassin shot Salinas's brother-in-law, José Francisco Ruiz Massieu, who was in line to become majority leader in the Chamber of Deputies. After the suspect testified that he had been paid for the murder, authorities arrested Salinas's brother, Raúl, as the one responsible for this crime.[28] The film's final scenes, including the attempt on Alemán's nephew and the killings of López and Tiburón, evoke the high-profile murders of 1994.

Beginning in that crucial year, missteps deepened the crisis of the government. In December, the freshly installed Zedillo administration allowed the overvalued peso to "float" against the U.S. dollar, and the currency crashed. Zedillo also decided to confront the Zapatistas through military force before reversing course several times in a series of unsuccessful attempts to suppress the rebellion. Vargas's triumph over his adversaries presages a similar pattern: the authorities win in the end, but the people keep resisting.

The Zedillo administration marked the end of PRI dominance. Unlike Salinas, Zedillo expressed his full commitment to a democratic transition. He viewed fair and free elections and a multiparty democracy as an essential component in the restructuring of Mexico. In 1996, an Electoral Reform established a federal electoral institute that oversaw elections independent of government control. In July 2000, the victory of PAN candidate Vicente Fox finally broke the ruling party's streak of seventy-one uninterrupted years in power.[29]

THE END OF CENSORSHIP AND THE
FILM AS A POLITICAL AGENT

Democratization amidst the trials and tribulations of Zedillo's administration provides the immediate context for the making of Estrada's masterpiece. Just as many other Mexican films, *La Ley de Herodes* confronted difficulties after its production in 1999 and its official release in February 2000. Mexico's long history of censoring cinema and other forms of media extends further back than the PRI's authoritarian government. Censorship was a cooperative effort among different governmental institutions, the Catholic Church, and the public via unions created by citizens who worked within the film industry. *La Ley de Herodes'* commentary on the past and present provoked an adversarial response from the PRI, the failure of which showed the deterioration of the government's authority over cinema. Apart from its historical and social commentary, *La Ley de Herodes* therefore also offers important insights into the legal, political, and cultural framework of censorship at the turn of the millennium.

Censorship of film dated back to the Mexican Revolution in the 1910s and specifically, to the Censorship Decree of dictator Victoriano Huerta in 1913.[30] Huerta's decree prohibited scenes containing "attacks on authorities, other people, morality, good manners, peace and public order, or any depiction of unpunished crime or misconduct."[31] It established the groundwork for future administrations to police aesthetics and morality in film, a new medium considered a powerful tool to shape the hearts and minds of malleable citizens. Huerta ushered in a new age of state oversight, protecting public morality from racist stereotypes in international film and negative characterizations of its government, language, and culture both internationally and domestically. In 1919, President Venustiano Carranza established the Council of Censorship under the purview of the Secretaría de Gobernación, the powerful Ministry of the Interior.[32]

Beginning in the 1920s, state-sponsored film, art, and other media served as tools to diffuse a nationalist ideology that defined the mestizo and institutionalized the revolution and its promises of modernity. Extending through the golden age of Mexican cinema in the 1940s, this era reflects a shift in focus from public morality to an effort to use film to promote the image of the party and the revolution, especially under Cárdenas and his successor, Manuel Ávila Camacho (1940–1946). Cárdenas delegated the administration of censorship law to the Dirección General de Información (DGI) and created a slate of subordinate offices under the DGI's scope to levy fines and approve final edits of films before distribution to theaters. Ávila Camacho instituted the broad strokes of the system that Estrada knew in the 1990s, featuring a carrot and a stick. The carrot was a Banco Cinematográfico responsible for funding production and distribution. The stick consisted of the categorization of films via a rating system.[33] A new Dirección General de Cinematografía regulated cinema by blocking the distribution of films on a variety of grounds, including attacks on a citizen's private life; immorality; and the advocacy of crime, vice, or disruptions of the public order and peace.[34] Under these guidelines, directors did not dare criticize the government and army and refrained from displaying nudity, drunkenness, disorderly behavior, or domestic violence—all significant features of *La Ley de Herodes*. Aside from the film's political content, it therefore also sent an aesthetic message to the effect that modern film would tell all rather than hide behind a veneer of public morality.

Film scholar Daniel Chávez observed two phases of transition in the next three decades in which opposition to censorship grew incrementally. During the first phase (mid-1950s to late 1960s), filmmakers used allegories and metaphors to voice political frustration in film. Chávez called the second phase (the 1970s and early 1980s) the era of "denunciatory realism"—a time when directors continued to employ allegories while pushing the boundaries of what was acceptable in film.[35] During the decades before the release of *La Ley de Herodes*, the PRI created a complicated system for defining and enforcing censorship laws that required the support of different bureaucracies and the cooperation of the film community for enforcement.

The last three PRI regimes changed film drastically by means of neoliberal economic policies that eventually privatized funding of the film industry. The repeated economic shocks in the 1980s and 1990s led to a dramatic reduction of Mexican films while Hollywood movies crowded the market.[36] In 1983, the de la Madrid administration founded the Instituto Mexicano de Cinematografía (IMCINE), which employed economic rather than outright censorship. IMCINE took advantage of neoliberal funding cuts to make itself the prime benefactor of Mexican cinema, an entity that "subsidized, sponsored, and censored Mexican film."[37] Directors also continued to practice self-censorship by avoiding controversial topics that were political in nature, not to mention the RTC film rating that limited audiences by setting an age restriction for films deemed to contain content not suitable for children. They were mindful of the example of Julio Bracho's *La Sombra del Caudillo*. Based on a 1930 novel by Martín Luis Guzmán, this film criticized the Mexican government and army and in particular, the events culminating in the abovementioned 1927 Huitzilac massacre. It was not released to the public until 1990. In 1989, Jorge Fons's *Rojo Amanecer* also faced issues with IMCINE because of its metaphorical critique of the army and its participation in the Tlatelolco Massacre, which claimed hundreds of lives on October 2, 1968. However, IMCINE allowed the screening of the movie in 1990. These films illustrated the type of economic and political roadblocks confronting films like *La Ley de Herodes*. Further liberalization occurred under IMCINE Director Ignacio Duráns, a Salinas de Gortari appointee, who allowed filmmakers to procure private funding for their projects. Designed to save money, the move gave filmmakers some leverage with regard to IMCINE and the state. At the same time, the PRI's authority over film production and distribution with the help of mass media declined. These developments gave Estrada the space to produce his controversial film.

Nonetheless, Estrada had to fight the agency to actually show his movies in Mexican theaters. Having staked 60% of the film budget, or US$900,000, IMCINE director Eduardo Amerena tried his best to use this stake to make sure most Mexicans would not actually be able to see *La Ley de Herodes*. In anticipation for the advanced preview of the film planned for the Festival de Cine Francés in Acapulco in November 1999, the agency claimed Estrada's film would not exhibit due to technical issues, but when two stars of the film, Damián Alcázar and Leticia Huijara, publicly complained to the press about the sudden cancellation, their narrative shifted and the agency claimed that the film would not screen because it had not yet received an RTC rating and stamp of approval.[38] As Estrada recalled, IMCINE rejected the film three times. The director was offered a briefcase full of money but refused the bribe. According to Estrada, Amerena told him to postpone the release of the film by a few months so that it would not affect the presidential elections. Amerena relented but still put obstacles in the way of *La Ley de Herodes*. On December 3, 1999, he allowed showings of the film in two Mexico City theaters, the Cineteca Nacional and the Centro Nacional de los Artes, with minimal advertising: there were no movie trailers or posters to advertise its screening in the two small theaters. News of the release spread mostly through word of mouth throughout the city, and citizens rushed to view the forbidden film before it was taken away once again.

Acting against legislation that guaranteed films produced with any government funding a minimum run of fifteen days, Amerena tried to end showings after just one week. Furious, Estrada asserted that Amerena's actions amounted to closet censorship. He accused IMCINE of withdrawing his film so quickly that the Mexican public would not notice it and thus provoked a prolonged lawsuit that would have remained unresolved until after the 2000 elections.[39] As Estrada recalled: "I lived through the whole process terrified and thought about leaving the country, but resolved to make three phone calls . . . to Vicente Leñero (writer and journalist); María Rojo of the PRD, the president of the Culture Commission in the Chamber of Deputies, and correspondent journalists. . . . The next day, it was international news, and they spoke to the Government to find out why they wanted to stop a movie."[40]

Bad press from abroad at last foiled the government's obstructive efforts. The president of the Consejo Nacional para la Cultura y las Artes (CONACULTA), Rafael Tovar y de Teresa, looked for an amicable compromise. He insisted that "censorship no longer exists in the political language of the Mexican republic" and accused Amerena of creating the conflict. According to Tovar, "all the wrong decisions were made within the institution over which [Amerena] presides." A few days later, Amerena stepped down from his position. A functionary opposed to Amerena stated: "I believe that it is one of the best films produced in this country. I am proud to have worked on it." Under the agreement Tovar negotiated, IMCINE withdrew as the majority investor, making Estrada the sole owner of the film and obliging him to pay back IMCINE for its investment at an annual interest rate of 5.5%. Estrada was also free to exhibit the film wherever he wanted. The publicity caused by the botched attempt at censorship only succeeded in attracting further attention. For example, Robert Redford invited Estrada to present the film at the Sundance Festival in Park City, Utah, the following January. In the words of the president of the Sociedad General de Escritores de México, Víctor Hugo Rascón Banda, "we are living a moment in which cinema cannot be censored, repressed, or canned as happened in other *sexenios*."[41]

Thus, paradoxically, the failed attempt at censorship highlighted the political opening of a system lambasted in the film as authoritarian and corrupt. Unlike *La Sombra del Caudillo*, *La Ley de Herodes* only faced a slight delay. The durable authoritarian institutions and practices that the film attacked with so much justification had begun to buckle.

CONCLUSION

Estrada's own statements after the release of *La Ley de Herodes* indicate his intention to transcend the politics of the presidential campaign and provide a more general commentary. According to a March 2000 story in the *Los Angeles Times*, Estrada first thought of producing such a film in December 1994, when he watched his savings evaporate overnight in the peso crisis. Estrada suggested that reality itself created his black comedy: "The best comedy ever made in Mexico has come from politicians, with their absurdity, their madness, their excesses. . . . I tried to write it as a fable, a dark comedy without a moral." Referencing government pressure to change the ending so that Vargas was not rewarded with a seat in Congress, Estrada explained: "The real problem is that the system actually rewards the corruption. . . . There is impunity in Mexico."[42] Such corruption was not news by any means to Mexican viewers. Said Estrada sarcastically: "No one will walk out of the theater and declare, 'Oh my, there is corruption in my country.' . . . The fact is that reality is much more impressive than anything you could show people in a movie."[43]

Three years later, Estrada doubled down on this perspective in an interview, calling the corruption of a seventy-year-old regime "no longer just a political problem, but a problem of everyday life." Moreover, Estrada asserted that the contamination of the political system persisted even after the party's defeat. "I decided to make a fable about power and the extreme consequences of ambition to keep it. . . . To tell the story, I opted for the tone of a black comedy, very Mexican, but also very Latin." In his view, "cinema can be a mirror that reflects our concerns."[44]

This important film has remained influential decades after its release. As an artifact of Mexican history and culture, it marked an era of transition aside from its status as the first national movie to openly blame the PRI for corruption and violence. First, its release served as an early warning for what was to come from the election that finally unseated the PRI. The film itself wrote the epitaph for a crumbling authoritarian system while simultaneously serving as a sign of an unprecedented level of freedom of speech and a new democratic era in Mexican politics. Second, *La Ley de Herodes* was not the last film that faced censorship. Film scholar Misha MacLaird argues that the transition to democracy did not mark the abolition of censorship but rather, a transition from direct to indirect censorship, which occurs throughout production and is primarily economic in nature.[45] Thus, *La Ley de Herodes* symbolized a greater level of freedom of speech and the end of direct censorship but not the end of censorship per se. In 2014, Estrada made yet another movie critical of the PRI, *La Dictadura Perfecta*. The title referenced Vargas Llosa's abovementioned characterization of the PRIista system. *La Dictadura Perfecta* heavily criticized the media for favoring PRI candidate Enrique Peña Nieto, whose victory had returned the PRI to power in 2012.[46] Third, the film helped usher in a new era of Mexican film at the turn of the millennium. According to the journalist Julia Preston, the release of *La Ley de Herodes* also "drew attention to the recent revival of Mexican-movie making, in which a younger generation of directors and producers, including Estrada, thirty-seven, are restoring the vitality and momentum to an industry that had seemed virtually paralyzed."[47] Estrada and other directors inaugurated the *nuevo cine Mexicano*, an era that featured internationally renowned movies such as *Amores Perros* and *Y tu mamá también*.

La Ley de Herodes was a sensation at its initial release in 1999 and again after its second release in 2003 and remains relevant both nationally and internationally today. In a February 2020 article in *El Universal*, Estrada recalled stopping by a village while filming in the desert. One of the villagers inquired: "Licenciado, are you the one from *La Ley*? We see it every Saturday in the canteen of my buddy."[48] Because many who lived through the authoritarian regime into a transition toward democracy remain alive to this day, Estrada's film serves as a reminder of lived experiences and a reality not easily forgotten. This particular film is set in a distant past of the 1940s during the presidency of Alemán, but it also speaks to the frustrations of the recent past in the last two decades of the twentieth century. The film remains relevant as a reminder of the living memories of those who experienced the rule of the PRI firsthand—whether the inhabitants of the fictional San Pedro de los Saguaros or the more than four hundred students killed in Tlatelolco Square on October 2, 1968. *La Ley de Herodes* is important in political, aesthetic, and cultural terms and will remain a testament to PRIista Mexico for decades to come.

ADDITIONAL RESOURCES

Alexander, Ryan M. *Sons of the Revolution: Miguel Alemán and His Generation.* Albuquerque: University of New Mexico Press, 2016.

Chávez, Daniel. "The Eagle and the Serpent on the Screen: The State as Spectacle in Mexican Cinema," *Latin American Research Review* 45, no. 3 (2010): 115–41.

Esquivel-King, Reyna M. "Mexican Film Censorship and Regime Legitimacy, 1913–1945." PhD diss., Ohio State University, 2019.

Fuentes, Carlos. *La muerte de Artemio Cruz.* Mexico City: Fondo de Cultura Económica, 1962.

Garrido, Luis Javier. *La ruptura: la corriente democrática del PRI.* Mexico City: Grijalbo, 1993.

Gillingham, Paul. *Unrevolutionary Mexico: The Birth of a Strange Dictatorship.* New Haven, CT: Yale University Press, 2021.

Gillingham, Paul, and Benjamin T. Smith, eds. *Dictablanda: Politics, Work, and Culture in Mexico, 1938–1968.* Durham, NC: Duke University Press, 2014.

Little, Walter, and Eduardo Posada-Carbó, eds. *Political Corruption in Europe and Latin America.* London: Palgrave, 1996.

MacLaird, Misha. *Aesthetics and Politics in the Mexican Film Industry.* New York: Palgrave Macmillan, 2013.

Newcomer, Daniel. *Reconciling Modernity: Urban State Formation in 1940s León, Mexico.* Lincoln: University of Nebraska Press, 2004.

Osten, Sarah. "Out of the Shadows: Violence and State Consolidation in Postrevolutionary Mexico, 1927–1940." *The Latin Americanist* 64, no. 2 (2020): 169–99.

Padilla, Tanalís. *Rural Resistance in the Land of Zapata: The Jaramillista Movement and the Myth of the Pax Priísta, 1940–1962.* Durham, NC: Duke University Press, 2008.

Pascual Gutiérrez, Iris. "Cincuenta años de historia de México: El cine como fuente, agente, y relato histórico en Luis Estrada, 'La Ley de Herodes' (1999)" in *¿Qué es el cine? IX Congreso Anual de Análisis Textual,* edited by Mercedes Miguel Borras, 1011–22. Valladolid, Spain: Ediciones Universidad de Valladolid, 2018.

Pensado, Jaime M. *Rebel Mexico: Student Unrest and Authoritarian Political Culture During the Long Sixties.* Stanford, CA: Stanford University Press, 2013.

Rath, Thomas R. *Myths of Demilitarization in Postrevolutionary Mexico, 1920–1960.* Chapel Hill: University of North Carolina Press, 2013.

Velasco, Salvador. "*Rojo Amanecer* y *La Ley de Herodes*: cine político de la transición Mexicana." *Hispanic Research Journal* 6, no. 1 (2005): 66–80.

Zolov, Eric. *The Last Good Neighbor: Mexico in the Global Sixties.* Durham, NC: Duke University Press, 2020.

NOTES

1. This film has been the subject of frequent discussion in the scholarly literature as in the examples from the notes that follow. Strikingly, the one existing book on Mexico's political cinema since 1968, a Spanish-language edited volume, does not analyze it. Adriana Estrada Álvarez, Nicolas Défossé, and Diego Zavala Scherer, *Cine político en México (1968–2017)* (New York: Peter Lang, 2019).

2. Salvador Velasco, *"Rojo Amanecer* y *La Ley de Herodes*: cine político de la transición mexicana," *Hispanic Research Journal* 6, no. 1 (2005): 76–77.

3. Ryan M. Alexander, *Sons of the Revolution: Miguel Alemán and His Generation* (Albuquerque: University of New Mexico Press, 2016).

4. For a comparison of Cardenismo and neopopulism in the 1970s, see Amie Kiddle and María Olín Muñoz, eds., *Men of the People: Populism in Modern Mexican History* (Tucson: University of Arizona Press, 2010). For the importance of "generations" in Mexican politics, see also the work of Roderic Ai Camp and particularly, *Political Recruitment Across Two Centuries: Mexico, 1884–1991* (Austin: University of Texas Press, 1995).

5. Carlos Fuentes, *La muerte de Artemio Cruz* (Mexico City: Fondo de Cultura Económica, 1962).

6. In the original: "Él que no tranza, no avanza."

7. Jorge Castañeda, *Perpetuating Power: How Mexican Presidents Were Chosen* (New York: New Press, 2000).

8. Paul Gillingham and Benjamin T. Smith, eds., *Dictablanda: Politics, Work, and Culture in Mexico, 1938–1968* (Durham, NC: Duke University Press, 2014).

9. Mario Vargas Llosa, "México es la dictadura perfecta," *El País*, September 1, 1990.

10. Tanalís Padilla, *Rural Resistance in the Land of Zapata: The Jaramillista Movement and the Myth of the Pax Priísta, 1940–1962* (Durham, NC: Duke University Press, 2008); Thomas Rath, *Myths of Demilitarization in Postrevolutionary Mexico, 1920–1960* (Chapel Hill: University of North Carolina Press, 2013), 94.

11. Rath, *Myths of Demilitarization*, 91.

12. Gillingham and Smith, *Dictablanda*, 155.

13. Paul Gillingham, *Unrevolutionary Mexico: The Birth of a Strange Dictatorship* (New Haven, CT: Yale University Press, 2021), 3.

14. Jaime M. Pensado, *Rebel Mexico: Student Unrest and Authoritarian Political Culture During the Long Sixties* (Stanford, CA: Stanford University Press, 2013); Eric Zolov, *The Last Good Neighbor: Mexico in the Global Sixties* (Durham, NC: Duke University Press, 2020).

15. Gillingham, *Unrevolutionary Mexico*.

16. Walter Little and Eduardo Posada-Carbó, eds., *Political Corruption in Europe and Latin America* (London: Palgrave, 1996), 10.

17. See, for example, Jürgen Buchenau, *Blood in the Sand: The Sonoran Dynasty in Revolutionary Mexico, 1910–1934* (Lincoln: University of Nebraska Press, forthcoming).

18. Sarah Osten, "Out of the Shadows: Violence and State Consolidation in Post-revolutionary Mexico, 1927–1940," *The Latin Americanist* 64, no. 2 (2020): 169–99.

19. Alan Knight, "Corruption in Twentieth-Century Mexico," in *Political Corruption in Europe and Latin America*, 220, 227.

20. Enrique Cárdenas, "The Process of Accelerated Industrialization in Mexico," in *An Economic History of Twentieth-Century Latin America*, ed. José Antonio Ocampo Cárdenas and Rosemary Thorpe (New York: Palgrave, 2000), 3: 176–204.

21. Manuel Gamio, *Forjando patria: pro nacionalismo* (Mexico City: Porrúa, 1916).

22. Now renegotiated as the United States-Mexico-Canada Trade Agreement (USMCA).

23. Nora Lustig, *Mexico: The Remaking of an Economy*, second ed. (Washington, DC: Brookings Institution, 1998).

24. Luis Javier Garrido, *La ruptura: la corriente democrática del PRI* (Mexico City: Grijalbo, 1993).

25. Enrique Krauze, *Mexico: Biography of Power: A History of Modern Mexico, 1810–1996*, trans. Hank Heifetz (New York: Harper Collins, 1998), 770.

26. Roderic Ai Camp, "Democratizing Mexican Politics, 1982–2012," in *The Oxford Encyclopedia of Mexican History and Culture*, ed. William H. Beezley (New York: Oxford University Press, 2018), 390–92.

27. Luis Donaldo Colosio, Speech at the Monumento a la Revolución, Mexico City, March 6, 1994, accessed May 12, 2022, https://www.excelsior.com.mx/nacional/este-fue-el-discurso-de-colosio-el-6-de-marzo-de-1994/1303105.

28. See also Iris Pascual Gutiérrez, "Cincuenta años de historia de México: El cine como fuente, agente, y relato histórico en Luis Estrada, 'La Ley de Herodes' (1999)," in *¿Qué es el cine? IX Congreso Anual de Análisis Textual*, ed. Mercedes Miguel Borras (Valladolid, Spain: Ediciones Universidad de Valladolid, 2018), 1011–22.

29. Camp, "Democratizing Mexican Politics," 393.

30. Reyna M. Esquivel-King, "Mexican Film Censorship and Regime Legitimacy, 1913–1945," PhD diss., Ohio State University, 2019.

31. Misha MacLaird, *Aesthetics and Politics in the Mexican Film Industry* (New York: Palgrave Macmillan, 2013), 45. Also see Esquivel-King, "Mexican Film Censorship and Regime Legitimacy," 24–25.

32. Esquivel-King, "Mexican Film Censorship and Regime Legitimacy," 26.

33. Esquivel-King, "Mexican Film Censorship and Regime Legitimacy," 27–29.

34. Álvaro Vázquez Mantecón, "La censura en el cine Mexicano de los años cuarenta," *Revista Fuentes Humanísticas* 16, no. 28 (2004): 171–72.

35. Daniel Chávez, "The Eagle and the Serpent on the Screen: The State as Spectacle in Mexican Cinema," *Latin American Research Review* 45, no. 3 (2010): 115–41.

36. MacLaird, *Aesthetics and Politics in the Mexican Film Industry*, 81–82.

37. Judith A. M. Costello, "Politics and Popularity: The Current Mexican Cinema," *Review: Literature and Arts of Americas* 38, no. 1 (2005): 31–38.

38. MacLaird, *Aesthetics and Politics in the Mexican Film Industry*, 45.

39. "Cinta incómoda: La controversial producción mexicana 'La ley de Herodes,' que involucra al partido en el poder vence a la censura," *La Opinión* (Los Angeles), December 18, 1999.

40. "La Ley de Herodes: La película que aguantó sobornos y presiones," *El Universal*, February 18, 2020.

41. "Cinta incómoda," *La Opinión*.

42. Quoted in "Mexico's Government Becomes the Reluctant Star of the Show," *Los Angeles Times*, March 7, 2000.

43. "Art Imitates Life in a Scathing Film on Mexico Leaders," *Christian Science Monitor*, March 20, 2000.

44. "The Law of Herodes Comes to the Cinemas," *El Nuevo Herald* (Miami), June 20, 2003.

45. MacLaird, *Aesthetics and Politics in the Mexican Film Industry*, 45.

46. "Se estrena 'La Dictadura Perfecta,' una mirada a las entrañas del poder," *La Jornada*, October 15, 2014.

47. Julia Preston, "Standing Up to Censors, Mexican Film Finds Its Voice," *New York Times*, December 16, 1999.

48. "La Ley de Herodes: La película que aguantó sobornos y presiones," *El Universal*, February 18, 2020.

Chapter 11

National Politics, Intimate Labor

The Work to Sustain Middle-Class Households in Alfonso Cuarón's Roma

Susie S. Porter

Roma (2018): produced by Alfonso Cuarón; directed by Alfonso Cuarón; written by Alfonso Cuarón; black and white; 135 minutes; Esperanto Filmoj, Pimienta Films. Cleo (Yalitza Aparicio) is a live-in domestic worker in a middle-class home in Mexico City.

Alfonso Cuarón's *Roma* draws on the experiences of the director growing up in the 1970s in the middle-class *colonia* (neighborhood) of the same name. The story plays out with one foot in the past and one in the future. The past, for middle-class families in colonia Roma, was one of prosperity. During the postwar economic boom, referred to as the Mexican miracle, the middle class grew in both size and the benefits it enjoyed: employment, privileged access to education and social services, a growing number of consumer products, and modern urban amenities. Over the course of the film, the details of daily life accumulate and as they do, provide a window onto middle-class urban life in the years 1970–1971. The narrative centers on Cleo, a fictionalized character inspired by Liboria Rodríguez, the live-in domestic worker employed in Cuarón's childhood household.[1] Cleo works in the middle-class household of Sofia and her husband, Antonio. Sofia is a university-educated, stay-at-home mother of four children: Pepe, Sofi, Toño, and Paco.[2] Antonio works at the Mexican Institute of Social Security (Instituto Mexicano de Seguro Social, IMSS). The family's life is shaped by consumer culture: high and low, national and international, radio, television, music, cinema, and travel. The

family also consumes the labor of Cleo and Adela, live-in domestic workers of indigenous descent, and Ramón, the chauffeur. The politics of the era
hover at the edges of daily life for middle-class Mexico City residents.

The future, as foretold in the film, emerges from the unequal distribution
of the fruits of the economic boom and the unwillingness of the Mexican
government to respond democratically to protest against such inequalities.
Stalled economic growth, increased inflation, and growing personal and
national economic debt led middle-class Mexicans to shift their consumer
habits, social relations, and politics. The generation that came of age in the
late sixties and early seventies questioned family structures, gender relations,
cultural practices, and the political status quo. For Cuarón, there are two
significant wounds to the psyche of Mexico City residents: the massacre at
Tlatelolco (1968) and *el halconazo* (1971). Roma opens between these two
events. Cuarón's reference to wounds to the psyche can be understood as the
middle-class realization that they were not immune from state violence. The
federal government had long deployed police and extra-legal forces against
working-class and rural Mexicans, but the exercise of state violence in 1968
and 1971 shattered the middle-class perception of immunity from political
repression.

Several aspects of Cuarón's technique, especially film choice, camera
angle, and mis-en-scene, contribute to a narrative in which history and social
context are integral to the plot. Taking the advice of collaborator, Director
Emmanuel Lubezki, Cuarón chose to shoot the film in digital, 4K black and
white, to allow for wide shots that put individual characters on a similar
plane with context. "Go 65 and wide," Lubezki encouraged him.[3] *Roma* is
largely filmed on the *x*-axis, perpendicular, contributing to the sense that "the
camera becomes almost like a consciousness revisiting the story." The choice
gave historical time period a role in the film. The choice to film in black and
white was also strategic; however, Cuarón cautions, "It's not a vintage black
and white. It's a contemporary black and white." (For comparison, recent
black-and-white films with themes of social inequality and politics include
Temporada de Patos [Fernando Eimbcke, 2004] and *El Violín* [Francisco
Vargas, 2004]). Cuarón's comments invite the viewer to reflect on both history and contemporary Mexico. During the 1970s, poor and working-class
Mexicans of indigenous descent subsidized the middle-class family and
lifestyle; government repression of protest reinforced that inequality. *Roma*
invites the viewer to consider both the history and persistence of social
inequality as well as the limits on political participation. In yet another interview, Cuarón remarked that *Roma* "forced me to confront the clash between
the memory I had of events and places with the reality of those places."[4] The
viewer too may consider what contributes to the unreliability of memory, both
individual and collective.

THE MAKING OF THE MIDDLE CLASS, 1940–1970

Between 1940 and the mid-1960s, the Mexican middle class grew both in size and in the material benefits it enjoyed.[5] The period, referred to alternatively as the Mexican miracle or the golden age of capitalism, saw a 6.4% per annum growth rate and at 2.5%, low inflation. State control of key resources and infrastructure and increased land under production encouraged economic development. A world preoccupied with war created de facto protectionism for Mexican industry, while demand for Mexican raw materials remained high. Industrial development and the expansion of the professions in both the public and private sectors provided jobs for the middle class. The federal government invested in education, social services, and urban improvements, most of which tended to benefit the middle class. For example, federal expenditures favored the National Autonomous University of Mexico (UNAM) over the National Polytechnic Institute (IPN). In 1940, 70% of UNAM students identified as middle class, while the IPN served working-class students, a trend that persisted in subsequent decades.[6] Mexico City residents saw their city grow and change. The population more than doubled between 1950 and 1970. While the Torre Latinoamericano, built in 1956, reached upward forty-five floors into the sky, suburbs spread out horizontally across the valley. In efforts to address overcrowding, in 1964 the government inaugurated the Nonoalco-Tlaltelolco housing complex near the city center. Hoping to ameliorate increasing traffic, on September 4, 1969, Mexico City mayor Alfonso Corona de Rosal (1966–1970) oversaw the opening of a new metro system.[7]

At the same time, Mexico began a not-so-slow shift from a predominantly rural to a predominantly urban country. Federal agricultural policy favored large commercial interests over small private and collectively held ones, forcing many people to abandon their homes and livelihoods to migrate to cities in search of work. President Manuel Ávila Camacho (1940–1946) used the 1942 agrarian code to further restrict land reform and to encourage the growth of large commercial farms. President Miguel Alemán (1946–1952) provided direct subsidies to large-scale agricultural interests while depriving *ejidatarios* (members of an ejido, collectively held land) of credit. Large commercial agricultural interests increased their economic power and land holdings in the countryside, and small corn producers suffered. What could profitably be grown shifted, leading farmers to grow less corn for people and more sorghum for pigs. The thriving ranching industry sent truckloads of beef to Mexico City, driving past growing numbers of malnourished children in the countryside. With limited employment options in the countryside, growing numbers of people sold their land or left the ejido and migrated to the city in search of work. While expanding manufacturing (7% annually) provided jobs, so too did the service economy: house cleaner, childminder, gardener, chauffeur, and street vendor, for example.⁸

In *Roma*, a family excursion to the country estate of wealthy friends to celebrate the New Year hints at the history of the divergent experiences of middle-and upper-class Mexico and that of the rural working class. The lives of servants and the served play out as the former cater to the latter but in other ways, are largely separate. The elite families speak English, mount trophy kills on the wall, and listen to *Jesus Christ Superstar* on the record player. They drink whisky. Downstairs, domestic workers, groundskeepers, and agricultural workers drink pulque from clay cups. There is hushed talk about whether a dead dog was a response to elite land seizures. An unexplained fire threatens the festivities. The next day, a group of domestic workers take the children on a walk through unplowed fields. Cleo comments that they will walk toward the folds (*falda*) of a nearby mountain. The children, urban creatures that they are, are confused by her way of describing the natural environment. A reference to Cleo's mother having lost her land falls on deaf ears. Behind these references lies a fraught history. During the 1960s and 1970s, the federal government enacted programs to if not ameliorate poverty, at least quell protest. Gustavo Díaz Ordáz (1964–1970), despite leading a conservative government, distributed 12.6% of Mexican land to peasants, though much of that land was unproductive (President Lázaro Cárdenas [1934–1940] had distributed 9.6%, a significant portion of it productive land). However, in 1971 President Luis Echeverría Álvarez (1970–1976) declared agrarian reform as "dead," and continued land takeovers were met with brutal state-sponsored violence.⁹

Growing numbers of people left the countryside and moved to cities where, faced with high real estate prices, they built on unclaimed or inexpensive land. An 80% decline in ejidos in the Federal District opened land for squatters' settlements or *ciudades perdidas* (lost cities). Land developers pocketed profits without fulfilling commitments to provide infrastructure and green space. Dirt roads came into being under the feet of residents' daily coming and goings. People built homes with no formal address and fashioned homemade connections to the electrical grid. They spent inordinate amounts of time in tasks like fetching water, throwing away garbage, and walking to public transportation. People invented entrepreneurial ways to generate income, from childcare to casket sales, haircuts to wedding dresses. Children made toys out of what was on hand, young people shared comic books and played music on a borrowed radio or old guitar, and adults found entertainment in conversation or perhaps, as in the film, watching daredevil acts that cost a few coins thrown in the hat as it passed around. Politicians entertained as well, arriving with tricolor banners and bullhorn, leaving behind freshly painted walls emblazoned with political slogans, free trinkets, and a handful of empty promises. Residents of one such *ciudad perdida*, Ciudad Nezahualcóyotl, began organizing in the 1960s and became an official municipality in 1964. In 1970 Ciudad Nezahualcóyotl appeared in the national census for the first time (when it was home to 580,436 inhabitants). Throughout the 1970s, residents continued to mobilize for formal land titles, pressed for developers to fulfill commitments to provide infrastructure, and held the government to promises for health and human services.[10]

The benefits of the Mexican miracle had been obtained on the backs of the majority. By 1970, 60% of the nation's 50.7 million people lived in cities where they faced significant shortages of housing, running water, and minimum nutrition. Between 1960 and 1970, the housing shortage in Mexico nearly doubled (from 13.7 million to 22 million units). According to the Mexican government, only 24% of the population lived in adequate housing. Fully half of the population lived in informal or squatter settlements. Between 1970 and 1980, the percentage of youth between ages four and sixteen who completed primary school dropped from 10% to 5%.[11] Cautious studies estimated that in 1975, 35.5 million people (65% of the total population) or 90% of the rural population and 19% of the urban population did not have access to sufficient daily nutrition. Forty-three percent of deaths in Mexico in the mid-1970s were due to poverty (malnutrition, disease, and a lack of access to clean water, adequate housing, and health care, for example). Most of those deaths were children.[12]

RECONSTRUCTED MEMORY AND GENERATIONAL CHANGE: CONSUMER CULTURE AND FAMILY RELATIONS

Cuarón forms part of a long tradition of remembering and reimagining colonia Roma. The neighborhood has been built and rebuilt as memory; representation; and a collection of streets, buildings, markets, and parks. Roma has served as the setting for the film *Los Olvidados* (Luis Buñuel, 1950) and for fiction: Arturo Azuela Arriaga, *Manifestación de Silencios* (1979); Luis Zapata Quiroz, *El Vampiro de la Colonia Roma* (1979); and Carlos Fuentes's "cuarteto narrativo," *Agua Quemada* (1980). In *Las batallas en el desierto* (1979), also set in colonia Roma, José Emilio Pacheco writes: "I remember, and I don't remember."[13] For his part, Cuarón sought to reconstruct his memory in part through consumer goods. *Roma*, Cuarón says, is a sensory experience. "There was no screenplay at first. I wasn't going to write one. I wanted to start by recreating the sensory part of it."[14] Cuarón and his team bought up consumer goods from the era: furniture, clothing, home appliances, board games, and cars. A World Cup (1970) poster appears on a bedroom wall. The poster, designed by Lance Wyman, draws on Huichol and pre–Colombian-inspired motifs and transforms them into bold, geometric patterns. The children scatter toys to and fro. The house ebbs and flows from being a mess to meticulously cared for as Cleo travels the house picking up things and putting them away. The family is portrayed in the film as enjoying new luxuries, but they also had to economize. Early in the film, there is a long scene where Cleo walks slowly throughout the house turning off lights to save electricity.

By the 1950s, middle-class Mexicans enjoyed a growing range of new consumer goods. Children ate Kellogg's Corn Flakes and Choco Krispies for breakfast and Gansito prepackaged baked goods as an after-school snack. A 1950s Coca-Cola advertising campaign to paint the country red and white reached the growing middle class, who more and more frequently raised a bottle of Coke "hecho en México." By the 1960s, Ford Motor Company, which initiated production in Mexico in 1925, beamed advertisements for the Galaxie through televisions and into middle-class homes. The 1960s saw the rise of Telesistema Mexicano led by empresario Emilio Azcárraga, Rómulo O'Farril, and former president Miguel Alemán. Shows like *I Love Lucy* and *The Lone Ranger* appeared alongside *Sendas Prohibidas*, a Mexican soap opera that first aired in 1958. The masked Professor Zovek appeared on television in the 1970s, offering an alternative spirituality.[15] As children watched television, outside, the knife sharpener, sweet potato and tamale vendors, a military-style band, and stray dogs filled the city soundscape.

Mexico City offered entertainment along cultural and class divisions. Cleo, with no private space of her own, goes to a matinée that serves as background for a date with Fermín. By 1970, the Golden Age of Mexican cinema had long petered out and old subtitled films like *Le Gran Jeu* (France, Robert Siodmak, 1954) filled the Mexican silver screens. When Cleo exits the theater, the audience sees and hears the sounds of vendors filling the stairs and blocking entry to the building. They sell soap bubbles, rubber punching balls, puppets, little baggies of snacks, and whistles. To populate the scene, Cuarón took care to replicate the ethnic stratification that relegates indigenous and dark-skinned Mexicans to the informal economy.[16] In contrast, when Cleo accompanies the children to the theater, the crowd outside the newly built "Las Américas" cinema is taller, whiter. The boys sneak a peek at risqué magazines as their father hurries past with his girlfriend. Once inside, the screen is filled with an astronaut floating in space, echoes of *2001: A Space Odyssey* (Stanley Kubrick, 1968) and *Gravity* (Alfonso Cuarón, 2013).

Class divisions shaped the evolution of youth culture as well. New generations of music evolved, from English-language covers, to *la onda chicanca*, to Spanish-language Mexican rock and roll, largely coming from those living on the socioeconomic margins and eventually embraced by the middle class. Such was the case, for example, of Perro Fantástico out of Nezahualcóyotl City. The Valle de Bravo rock festival (September 12, 1971) drew upward of two hundred thousand people to the small resort town on Lake Avándaro. The cultural tone of the event with, for example, the appropriation of the Mexican flag and the performance of songs titled "Marihuana" and "We Got the Power" provoked a backlash. The government stopped giving airtime to musical groups associated with the movement. Recording companies canceled contracts.

Roma captures a transitional moment in the history of middle-class family in Mexico City. The film is situated to reflect on older models of middle-class family life, patriarchal norms, and the division of household labor. Women's workforce participation had increased to 17 to 20 percent in 1970. Middle-class families like the one in *Roma* were likely to include 4.3 family members, the father working outside of the home and the mother, perhaps university educated, dedicated her time to raising children.[17] If in 1950 sociologist José E. Iturriaga praised the federal government for its investments in programming that benefited the middle class and traditional family and gender roles, by the 1970s sociologists became more skeptical of both traditional family norms and whether the middle class benefited at all from federal policy. According to sociologist Gabriel Careaga Medina (1941–2004), middle-class Mexicans defined success by marrying well, owning a car and a home in a good neighborhood, and taking annual vacations to national and finances permitting, international destinations. By the early 1970s, however, all this had become nothing more than "aspirations and unattainable dreams."[18] Echoing the antiauthoritarian tendencies of his generation, Careaga leveled a full-throated critique of the middle-class family, describing it as consisting of an absent father, a "possessive and slightly hysterical" stay-at-home mother, and resentful children. He lamented middle-class alienation from authentic sexuality: women lived small lives, and husbands continued to have extramarital affairs, a modernized version of the second household (*casa chica*).[19] In *Roma*, the children learn gender hierarchies at the breakfast table, exchanging insults like "don't be a girl" (*niñita*).

The critiques made by Careaga come together in an early, extended scene of the film *Roma*, when the father takes great pains to park the Ford Galaxie. His dreams of consumption barely fit within the material reality of his narrow patio turned garage. Antonio plays classical music on the radio and smokes Drake cigarettes. He is neither fully visible nor fully knowable—a critique of 1970s fatherhood. As he parks, the car headlights shine on the family. The patio/garage also serves as a dog pen, and the car runs over dog poop. Antonio exits the car by the passenger seat because the space is so small, yells for someone to clean up the mess, and with little emotional fanfare enters the house. Cleo silently enters the scene to clean up. In another scene, a less-expensive Volkswagen Beetle sits on the street and serves as the back-drop for the moment when Antonio walks away from the family (see Figure 11.1). Cleo holds Pepe as he watches his mother attempt to hold on to his father. Later in the film, the mother, now more cynical of the promises of middle-class family life, drives the Ford into the patio, shearing off parts of the car. As she rediscovers herself and claims her independence, she buys a new, smaller car.

Meanwhile, Cleo walks. She walks to the movies, to a food stand, and to a hotel. Cleo also runs, through the streets and into traffic after the children and into the ocean, even though she cannot swim, to save the children to whom she dedicates the hours of the day but who are not hers. With her labor, Cleo subsidizes middle-class lifestyle and gender norms: she cooks and cleans; launders and irons pants and shirts, carefully stacking them on paper-lined shelves; and tucks children into bed at the end of the day. In ways typical of domestic workers, Cleo's job includes integrating herself into the intimate spaces of the lives of her employer, respecting their personal habits in ways that also acknowledge her subservience: where she lingers and for how long; where she sleeps and where she works; the words she can speak, to whom and in what language, ever attentive to power dynamics between herself, the man of the house, the woman of the house, and the children. Never alone and yet not at home. Following Cleo up to the rooftop where she does laundry, Pepe tries to engage Cleo in a game of make-believe shoot-'em-up. Cleo resists and

Figure 11.1: Intertwined regimes of emotional labor, minute 34:21. (Carlos Simonte/ Netflix)

then, on her own terms, lies down on her back to stare at the sky. Pepe lies down on his back next to her, and the two share a moment of quiet intimacy (see Figure 11.2). It is a chilling scene for those who remember news reports that former President Carlos Salinas de Gortari (1988–1994), when a boy, shot and killed a twelve-year-old girl employed in his home as a domestic worker. When interrogated, his mother, Mrs. Salinas de Gortari, did not even know the young woman's last name. The homicide was never prosecuted.[20]

The Mexican middle-class standard of living has historically been subsidized by the low-wage labor of domestic workers. Throughout the late nineteenth and early twentieth centuries, roughly a third of the women engaged in paid labor did so as domestic workers.[21] Women from poor communities, often indigenous, with little formal education worked in food preparation, laundry, housecleaning, and eldercare and childcare. The work is not regulated by contract but rather, verbal agreements. In 1970, the few laws that regulated domestic work went unenforced. Domestic workers did not have access to IMSS or retirement benefits, living at the whim of employers for vacation, holiday, and sick days off. Employer–employee relations depended on the employer and could range from benevolent to demeaning, racist, and/ or sexually abusive. Racist, sexist, and classist stereotypes reinforced the perception of this work as unskilled, expressed in belittling terms such as "muchacha" (girl). As middle-class women entered the workforce in growing

Figure 11.2: Echoes of the past, dangerous intimacies, minute 12:35. (Carlos Simonte/ Netflix)

numbers, their access to the labor of poor women allowed them to maintain larger families. It also allowed them to avoid difficult conversations with husbands and other family members about personal responsibility for household labor. In 1970, as service sector employment expanded, the percentage of women employed in domestic labor declined to 25%. At the same time, the occupation became increasingly feminized: in 1910 women were 79% of domestic workers, and in 1990 they had become 96%. Historically, wages were nominal, often paid in the form of housing and food, which also made workers available to their employer twenty-four hours a day. Over the course of time, women have been less likely to be live-in workers (52% in 1994).[22]

THE CLASS DIVIDES OF POLITICAL REPRESSION

The Party of the Institutionalized Revolution (PRI), in power from 1929–2000, had relied on a growing economy, political patronage, repression, and electoral fraud to maintain power and contain political discontent. While middle-class Mexicans benefited from an expanding economy, jobs, and political patronage, working-class and rural Mexicans long faced violence when they organized to defend their rights. A federal counterinsurgency network included the General Directorate of Political and Social Investigation (est. 1918), Federal Security Directorate (est. 1947), Research Division for the Prevention of Crime, and the Second Section of Military Intelligence. The government sent in the military to subdue striking railroad workers (1959) and at Teléfonos de México and Mexicana Airlines (1960). A combination of military, paramilitary, and police forces infiltrated student groups, broke up student protests, and arrested working-class students in Mexico City in the 1950s and again in 1961. During the late 1960s and early 1970s, the government also developed three paramilitary groups—The Falcons (*los halcones*), the White Brigade, and the Olympia Battalion—to infiltrate what it deemed threatening social movements, including those organized by students.[23]

The PRI engaged in a campaign against insurgents in rural Mexico during the 1960s and 1970s. Decades of federal policy supporting commercial agriculture at the expense of small farmers led some of the latter to organize to defend their rights. During the "Dirty War," Mexican government soldiers raped, murdered, tortured, and destroyed entire villages to weaken both legal and armed opposition. Because Mexico had no large-scale truth commission, as in other countries, some facts remain hidden. Nevertheless, conservative estimates of the number of "disappearances" (extrajudicial murder) hover around 1,200. In 1962, federal police murdered Rubén Jaramillo and family members to put an end to decades of organizing sugarcane workers and small landowners in Morelos.[24] In 1974, government forces killed (or forced the suicide of) Lucio Cabañas, a former teacher and founder of the Poor People's Party (1967–1974) in Guerrero. High levels of state-perpetuated violence, the legalization of left-wing political parties in 1978, and amnesty and release of some political prisoners led to a decline in political mobilization on the left.[25] Of those who did not take up arms or become politically active, some migrated to Mexican cities or farther north to the United States. The Bracero program (1942–1964) deepened preexisting migration networks that continued to flourish. As long as most of the atrocities perpetrated by the Mexican government occurred in the countryside, state control of the Mexican national press meant that Mexico City residents remained ignorant or felt such abuses were out of their hands.

If the PRI had maintained power in part through repression of dissent in the countryside, by the late 1960s, it began to lose its control over urban middle-class political dissent. The summer of 1968 saw signs of student discontent with government interference in school politics and the increasingly authoritarian tendencies of the government. Students were also frustrated that while widespread poverty persisted, the state spent lavishly on projects like the Olympic Stadium (1952). As the Olympic host, the eyes of the world would be on Mexico, providing the opportunity for student organizers to amplify their voice. On October 2, 1968, thousands of students gathered in the Three Cultures Square in Mexico City's Tlatelolco housing complex. Government snipers positioned on rooftops opened fire. People scattered. Some ran for side streets, and others sought cover in the stairwells of apartment buildings. Soldiers positioned on the edge of the plaza fired into the crowd. The government never admitted to the number of dead, which ran in the hundreds. Newspaper reports served up alternating stories of dissolute youth run amok and of a regrettable but supposedly necessary militarized response. Many Mexico City residents accepted a narrative of foreign influence (Cuba or U.S. CIA). It took at least a decade for a counternarrative to emerge that understood 1968 as the beginning of what some considered a democratic opening. In the meantime, the state steam cleaned the blood off the pavement, buried archival evidence behind privacy laws and bureaucracy, and offered government jobs to promising young men (primarily). Some of those former student activists would eventually seek ways to influence government policy from within the regime, while others contented themselves with a steady job and a house in colonia Roma.[26]

The tensions created by this system reached a breaking point that had not fully penetrated the consciousness of middle-class children like those portrayed in the film. Indeed, the film may reflect the way many Mexico City residents experienced political events. Cuarón told *Variety* in an interview that as a child, he had been oblivious to the political, racial, and social conditions unfolding around him. In one scene at the breakfast table, the radio chatters in the background, and one of the boys reports about a man shot and killed in the streets. The boy seems unaware of the implications of such an event. The adults in the room dismiss the comment, and the children remain pleasantly oblivious to the mounting acts of violence. The family is confronted with state-sponsored violence only serendipitously when the women of the family go shopping to purchase a crib.

In an act of re-presentation of memory, Cuarón recreates a photograph he had seen of people looking down from a furniture store on the June 10, 1971, Corpus Christi, on a massacre known as *el halconazo*. Up on the second floor of the store, people peruse furniture and household items available for purchase on layaway. Below, a growing crowd of students and police fill the streets. The protest brought together students from the IPN and UNAM. Class differences between the students at different institutions of higher education had shaped their activism. Whereas working-class IPN students had since the mid-1950s protested dwindling government support (housing, food subsidies, scholarships) and increased government meddling in student governance, UNAM students had been more hesitant to protest the federal government until the 1968 Tlatelolco massacre. In 1971, IPN students again demonstrated in the streets of Mexico City; they were joined by students from UNAM and local high schools. In response, the government called on a paramilitary force known as the *halcones*. The force had been organized by Mexico City Sub-director of General Services Manuel Díaz Escobar, who had recruited disenfranchised male youth and with the support of the CIA, trained them in the martial arts. Armed with bamboo sticks and knives and intending to pass as a rival student group, they collaborated with police and the army, and together attacked and killed dozens of demonstrators. Some estimate 120 people died.[27]

In addition to the terrible human cost of *el halconazo*, the event had a lasting impact on the student movement, which moved underground. The Corpus Christi massacre appears in the film *El Bulto* (Gabriel Retes, 1992) as the beginning of a moment of social amnesia. When the government began to decommission paramilitary groups like the *halcones*, many went on to work with drug cartels.[28] In *Roma*, the *halconazo* sequence, coming toward the end of the film, leaves political context implicit. Cleo, Sofia, and the grandmother are clearly shocked that such violence might intrude on their lives. Young people, fleeing armed *halcones*, burst into the store. Cleo's water breaks and drips to the floor. After a frantic car ride, with the grandmother crying and praying in the back seat, they arrive at an IMSS hospital that is inundated with injured people. Cleo's delivery serves as a metaphor for the post-1968/1971 period.

FEMINISM, 1970–1971

The film *Roma* weaves together the story of women's relationships in a middle-class household, women of radically different circumstances. In one sequence, Sofia, fed up with her now-estranged husband, approaches Cleo and tells her, "No matter what they tell you, we women are always alone." It is a lesson that Cleo already knows. When Cleo learns she is pregnant, Sofia's display of sympathy, while not implausible, is historically unlikely. The idea that Sofia and Cleo, because they are both women, share a similar condition, is fraught. The experiences that might have brought Cleo to such knowledge are very different from those of Sofia. The film does, however, speak metaphorically to a moment of coming to consciousness for some middle-class women.

Roma is set during shifts in women's education, workforce participation, and feminism. Several scenes speak to the ways women were caught up in an era of significant change (see Figure 11.3). The years 1950–1970 saw women marry later (the age of women when the largest number worked outside of the home was fifteen to nineteen in 1950 and twenty to twenty-four in 1970) and have smaller families (a more significant decline began in 1976 when birth control was increasingly available). Women's enrollment in higher education grew so that by the 1970s, they made up 19% of university graduates. In 1970, 17% of women worked outside of the home and tended to be

Figure 11.3: An era of change for women, minute 35:25. (Carlos Simonte/Netflix)

concentrated in the tertiary sector: food preparation, elementary and pre-school instruction, social work, nursing, and as domestic workers in private homes. While growing numbers of women were employed in clerical work, administration, and the professions, the upper echelons of those fields contin-ued to be dominated by men. These factors contributed to women, especially middle-and upper-class women who had access to the press, to critique the status quo and reignite the feminist movement in Mexico.[29]

At the time during which the film is set, women's right to vote was less than twenty years old. While the Mexican constitutions of 1857 and 1917 had not explicitly prohibited women from voting, male politicians blocked their efforts to do so. Early generations of feminists tested their right to vote and to be voted into office in the 1930s, but it was not until 1953 that the federal government granted women's suffrage. The first generation of women was elected to the Senate for the XLIV–XLV Legislative Session (1955–1958).[30] In 1970 the number of women senators remained the same. The first female governor, Griselda Alvarez of Campeche (1913–2009) took office in 1979 and served until 1985. All key opposition and labor leaders were men, even in cases where most of a union's members were women. María Elena Vázquez Nava, as Minister of the Comptroller General, was the first woman to serve on the presidential cabinet (1988–1994). Alongside women engaged in for-mal politics, by the 1970s a new generation of feminists organized.

As a middle-class movement, feminism in Mexico (and elsewhere) emerged as a result of many different cultural trends. Youth across the globe were inspired by the Cuban Revolution (1959), anti-colonial movements in Africa, and protests against the Vietnam war. While roughly equal numbers of young men and women participated in the 1968 movements in Mexico, women did not have the same opportunity to exercise leadership as men. That inequality fueled women's questioning and exploration of the ways "the personal is political." They formed consciousness raising groups to discuss motherhood, the double shift (paid labor outside of the home and unpaid labor in the home), subordination within and outside of the home, and sexuality. The new wave of Mexican feminism was characterized by the appearance, coalition, dispersal, and disappearance of multiple groups. Among the more notable, in 1964 a group of women who had been members of the Communist Party established the National Union of Mexican Women (Unión Nacional de Mujeres Mexicanas, UNMM), dedicated to the rights of women as mothers, workers, and citizens. In 1971 the newly formed Women in Solidarity and Action (Mujeres en Acción Solidaria, MAS) protested at the Monument to Mothers on Mother's Day, and the Homosexual Liberation Front (Frente de Liberación Homosexual, FLH) fought legal and social discrimination and advocated for sexual education that included homosexuality. Public figures included Nancy Cárdenas, a writer and theater director and an early figure to publicly declare her sexual identity as lesbian.

On September 20, 1970, Rosario Castellanos published "Cassandra in *Huaraches*: The Liberation of Women, Here" in *Excélsior* magazine and two weeks later, Martha Acevedo published "Our Dream, on the Precipice," in *La cultura en México*, the weekly magazine for *Siempre!* Both articles reflected on the fiftieth anniversary of women's suffrage in the United States and in the case of Acevedo, living at the time in California, on the Women's Strike for Equality. Castellanos in particular sought to understand women's rights within the specificity of Mexican realities. One of those realities was the way poor and indigenous women subsidized the middle-class women's lifestyle and she argued, complacency. Castellanos wrote, "To be a parasite (which is what we are, not victims) is not without its attractions. But when national industrial development obliges us to get a job in a factory or an office, and at the same time continue to care for children and the home, and how we look, and social life, and etc., etc., etc., then the lightbulb will go on. When the last maid disappears, that maid who is the cushion upon which our conformity rests, only then will the furious rebel emerge."[31] In 1971 Castellanos published the short story "Cooking Lessons," a masterful critique of middle-class married life and sexuality, comparing her body, in the hands of her husband, to a raw piece of meat meant to serve his appetite. Despite such perceptive analysis on the part of women like Castellanos and Acevedo, the women's movement of the 1970s did not, for the most part, bridge class and ethnic lines.

Women employed as domestic workers began their own collective organizing in the twenty-first century. In 1995 Mixe Xaam Cultural Expression formed to defend the labor and human rights of indigenous domestic workers in Mexico City. From this organization, Lorena Gútierrez Gútierrez led founding of the Indigenous Women's Domestic Worker Collective (est. 2011) in Mexico City. In 2000, Marcelina Bautista Bautista founded the Center for Support and Training of Domestic Workers.[32] The CACEH played a central role in hosting the fourth and sixth Congress of Domestic Workers of Latin America and the Caribbean, held in Mexico City in 2001 and 2012. CACEH collaborates with the National Union of Domestic Workers (Sindicato Nacional de Trabajadores y Trabajadoras del Hogar, est. 2015). The Mexican government ratified the International Labour Organization–facilitated Domestic Workers Convention in 2011. Recent films have taken up the topic of female domestic workers in private homes and the hospitality industry.[33]

Women's experiences of pregnancy, childbirth, and reproductive health also appear in the film *Roma*. During the presidency of Luis Echeverría (1970–1976), the Mexican government launched a family planning program. With gains in the sphere of public health and a drop in child mortality, international development agencies identified overpopulation as a national problem. The Mexican government, seeking to ameliorate poverty, considered family planning an effective way to redirect public conversation about the redistribution of wealth to a discussion over a woman's right to control her own body. So while in 1951, Mexican scientist Luis Miramontes had synthesized norethisterone, the active ingredient in the first safe, effective oral contraceptive, it was not until 1973 that birth control was made a national priority and replacing the pro-natal General Law of Population (1947), the right to family planning was added to the Constitution. The Catholic Church was adamantly opposed to such initiatives. Many men protested their wives' using contraceptives because they perceived it as a threat to their capacity to control women's sexuality. Despite such opposition, the federal government initiated a campaign to reach women directly through, for example, telenovelas (soap operas) that portrayed families with fewer children as being more prosperous. The birthrate declined rapidly so that on average women had 2.21 children. With access to birth control in the mid-1970s, some women increased their economic participation and social activism.[34]

Women's right to choose an abortion became a central demand of the feminist movement. It is estimated that in the 1970s, somewhere between 800,000 and 1.2 million illegal abortions took place every year and that more than 10,000 women died due to complications. As in many cultures, interrupting a pregnancy had long been considered a woman's prerogative, one that however, by the mid-nineteenth century had become increasingly medicalized and regulated. In Mexico, the Juárez Code (1871), grounded in the desire to control female sexuality, classified the termination of a pregnancy as a crime distinct from homicide. In 1931, reform-minded feminists recognized the economic impact of the lack of access to an abortion and pushed for legal revisions so that women were not culpable of a crime if an abortion was conducted in response to conception caused by rape. In the 1970s women, many of them university graduates from wealthy and middle-class families, organized around the right to an abortion. It was a practical and symbolic demand. In practical terms, the right to control one's body was a powerful rallying cry for women who had spent decades subjected to their reproductive functions and only partially in control of their own sexuality. Symbolically, the demand gave voice to the desire for bodily self-defense in the face of male violence. In December 1979, Congress considered but ultimately rejected a bill calling for the legalization of abortion. Mexico City legalized abortion in the first trimester of pregnancy in 2007.[35]

CONCLUSION

In *Roma*, director Alfonso Cuarón immerses the viewer in a reflection on history and contemporary Mexico. Between 1940 and 1960, the Mexican federal government supported models of economic growth that benefited industrial production and commercial agriculture. Through federal investment in infrastructure, changes to legal codes to put the brakes on land reform and to support industrial development, the so-called Mexican miracle, transformed the country. The middle class expanded in both size and the benefits it enjoyed, from increased consumption to world-class education and health services. Many middle-class families, as an economic unit and a set of social relations, were subsidized by the physical and emotional labor of poor, indigenous women. *Roma* is set during the years 1970–1971, when that model began to unravel and middle-class Mexicans, especially youth, questioned the status quo. Faced with such questioning, the Mexican government responded with violence, as was the case with Tlatelolco (1968) and *el halconazo* (1971). The film is also a meditation on changing gender roles and women's relationships. By 1970, growing numbers of women attended university and worked outside of the home. As Rosario Castellanos so poignantly portrayed in "Cooking Lessons," many middle-class women did not use that university education to pursue a profession but rather, remained outside of the workforce. The film *Roma* is set just as, in some sectors, women began to critique male privilege in the home, the workplace, and the law. Racial and class inequalities remained at the heart of many households. It was not until the late 1990s that Mexico City domestic workers made significant organizational advances. Changes in gender relations did not elicit similar modes of state violence as did organizing in rural Mexico, shantytowns, and among urban youth. However, state acquiescence to pervasive private and public acts of male violence has contributed to a pandemic of violence that affects women across class, ethnic identity, and sexual orientation.

ADDITIONAL RESOURCES

Blum, Ann. *Domestic Economies: Family, Work, and Welfare in Mexico City, 1884–1943*. Lincoln: Nebraska University Press, 2010.

Chant, Silvia. *Women and Survival in Mexican Cities: Perspectives on Gender, Labour Markets and Low-Income Households*. Manchester: Manchester University Press, 1991.

Davis, Diane. *Urban Leviathan: Mexico City in the Twentieth Century*. Philadelphia: Temple University Press, 1994.

Lenti, Joseph U. "Revolutionary Land Reform and Its End in Mexico," *Oxford Online Encyclopedia*, 8. https://doi.org/10.1093/acrefore/9780199366439.013.595.

Muñoz, María L. O. "Indigenous Mobilizations and the Mexican Government during the 20th Century," *Oxford Online Encyclopedia*, https://doi.org/10.1093/acrefore/9780199366439.013.30.

Olcott, Jocelyn. *International Women's Year: The Greatest Consciousness-Raising Event in History*. New York: Oxford University Press, 2017.

Padilla, Tanalís. *Rural Resistance in the Land of Zapata: The Jaramillista Movement and the Myth of the Pax Priísta, 1940–1962*. Durham, NC: Duke University Press, 2008.

Pensado, Jaime. *Rebel Mexico: Student Unrest and Authoritarian Political Culture during the Long Sixties*. Stanford, CA: Stanford University Press, 2013.

Soto Laveaga, Gabriela. "Shadowing the Professional Class: Reporting Fictions in Doctors' Strikes." *Journal of Iberian and Latin American Research* 19, no. 1 (Summer 2013): 30–40.

Stephen, Lynn. *Zapotec Women: Gender, Class, and Ethnicity in Globalized Oaxaca*. Durham, NC: Duke University Press, 2005.

Vaughan, Mary Kay. *Portrait of a Young Painter: Pepe Zuñiga and Mexico City's Rebel Generation*. Durham, NC: Duke University Press, 2014.

Walker, Louise. *Waking from the Dream: Mexico's Middle Classes after 1968*. Stanford, CA: Stanford University Press, 2018.

Zolov, Eric. *Refried Elvis: The Rise of Mexican Counterculture*. Oakland: University of California Press, 1999.

NOTES

1. At age thirteen, Liboria Rodríguez migrated from small-town Oaxaca to Mexico City in search of work.

2. Cleo (Yalitza Aparicio), Adela (Nancy García), Sofia (Marina de Tavira), Antonio (Fernando Grediaga), Pepe (Marco Graf), Sofi (Daniela Damesa), Toño (Diego Cortina Autrey), and Paco (Carlos Peralta).

3. Anne Thompson, "Cuarón Tells Lubezki How He Filmed 'Roma'—Even One Quiet Shot Needed 45 Camera Positions," *Indie Wire* (interview of Emmanuel Lubezki and Alfonso Cuarón), December 14, 2018, accessed March 26, 2020, https://www.indiewire.com/2018/12/roma-emmanuel-lubezki-alfonso-cuaron-cinematography-1202028167/.

4. Keziah Weir, "Alfonso Cuarón on Roma and the Mexico City of his youth," *Vanity Fair*, November 9, 2019.

5. Sara Minerva Luna Elizarrarás, "Modernización, género, ciudanía y clase media en la ciudad de México: debates sobre la moralización y la decencia, 1952–1966," tesis para optar por el grado de doctora en historia, Universidad Nacional Autónoma de México, 2017, p. 39.

6. Jaime Pensado, *Rebel Mexico: Student Unrest and Authoritarian Political Culture during the Long Sixties* (Stanford, CA: Stanford University Press, 2013), 21.

7. Amanda M. López, "Mexico City Metro and Its Riders," Oxford Research Encyclopedia of Latin American History, 2018, https://doi.org/10.1093/acrefore /9780199366439.013.456.

8. Joseph U. Lenti, "Revolutionary Land Reform and Its End in Mexico," *Oxford Online Encyclopedia*, 2018, https://doi.org/10.1093/acrefore/9780199366439.013 .595.

9. Lenti, "Revolutionary Land Reform," 8.

10. On the decline of urban ejidos, see Lenti, "Revolutionary Land Reform," 8. In 1970, 32% of Ciudad Nezahualcóyotl homes had running water; 40% had sewage connections; and 60% had electricity. By 1971 the government had built some subsidized supermarkets (CONASUPO). Margarita García Luna Ortega and Pedro Gútierrez Araluz, *Nezahualcóyotl: monografía municipal* (Mexico: Gobierno del Estado de México, 1999), 72–80.

11. COPLAMAR, *Necesidades esenciales en México*, vol. 2 (México: Siglo XXI, 1982), 23–40.

12. Francisco Alba and Joseph E. Potter, "Population and Development in Mexico since 1940: An Interpretation," *Population and Development Review* 12, no. 1 (1986): 47–75; COPLAMAR, *Necesidades esenciales en México*, vol. 1, 90–97, 125. On housing and services, see COMPLAMAR, *Necesidades esenciales en México*, vol. 3, 32–54. On mortality rates and causes, see COPLAMAR, *Necesidades esenciales en México*, vol. 4, 57–112. See also Peter Ward, *Welfare Politics in Mexico: Papering over the Cracks* (London: Allen and Unwin, 1986), 16–22.

13. Emilio Pacheco, *Las batallas en el desierto* (México: Ediciones Era, 1981), 9.

14. Mike Reyes, "Road to Roma: 12 Things We Learned from Netflix's Roma Documentary," *Cinema Blend*, published February 23, 2020, accessed March 28, 2021, https://www.cinemablend.com/news/2490564/camino-a-roma-things-we -learned-from-netflixs-roma-documentary.

15. Zovek also appeared in the film *The Incredible Professor Zovek* (1972) directed by René Cardona and starring Germán Valdés.

16. *Road to Roma* (Cuarón, 2020).

17. José E. Iturriaga, *La estructura social y cultural de México* (Mexico: Instituto Nacional de Estudios de la Revolución Mexicana), 67. México. Instituto Nacional de Estadística, Geografía e Informática (INEGI), *IX Censo General de la población*, 1970. On women's workforce participation, see Gabriela Vázquez, Robert McCaa, and Rodolfo Gutierrez, "La mujer mexicana económicamente activa: ¿son confiables los microdatos censales? Una prueba a través de censos y encuestas. México y Estados Unidos, 1970–1990," *Papeles de población*, n.25 (2000): 151–77. According to Brugeilles, in the 1970s women had an average of 7 children and 2.4, by 2000. Carole Brugeilles, and Olga Lorena Rojas, "Análisis del comportamiento diferencial de la práctica anticonceptiva por sexo, origen social y educación en la población urbana de México," *Estudios demográficos y urbanos* 35, no. 2 (2020): 293–332. See also Judith Zubieta-Gracia y Patricia Marrero-Narvaez, "Participación de la mujer en la educación superior y la ciencia en México," *Agricultura, sociedad y desarrollo* 2, no. 1 (2005): 15–28.

18. Gabriel Careaga, *Mitos y fantasias de la clase media en México* (México: Joaquín Moritz, 1974), 69.

19. Careaga, 1974, 75.

20. Alberto E. de Aguilar, "Jugando a la guerra tres niñitos 'fusilaron' a una sirvienta," *Excélsior*, December 18, 1951, 1.

21. Ignacio Rubí Salazar, coord., *El trabajo doméstico en México. La gran deuda social* (México, Secretaría del Trabajo y Previsión Social, 2016), 17.

22. Mary Goldsmith, "De sirvientas a trabajadoras. La cara cambiante del servicio doméstico en la ciudad de México," *Debate feminista* 17 (1988): 85–96.

23. Jorge Luis Sierra Guzmán, "Armed Forces and Counterinsurgency: Origins of the Dirty War (1965–1982)," in *Challenging Authoritarianism in Mexico: Revolutionary Struggles and the Dirty War, 1964–1982*, ed. Fernando Herrera Calderón and Adela Castillo, 182–97 (New York: Routledge, 2021); Pensado, *Rebel Mexico*, 21.

24. Sierra Guzmán, "Armed Forces and Counterinsurgency," 182–97.

25. Adela Cedillo, *Challenging Authoritarianism in Mexico: Revolutionary Struggles and the Dirty War, 1964–1982* (New York: Routledge, 2012); Alexander Aviña, *Specters of Revolution: Peasant Guerrillas in the Cold War Mexican Countryside* (New York: Oxford University Press, 2014), 158.

26. The state investigated many middle-class citizens that it considered a political threat, for example, medical doctors in 1964–1965; see Gabriela Soto Laveaga, "Shadowing the Professional Class: Reporting Fictions in Doctors' Strikes," *Journal of Iberian and Latin American Research* 19, no. 1 (Summer 2013): 30–40. For journalistic reports on the Tlatelolco massacre, see Nora E. Jaffary, Edward W. Osowski, and Susie S. Porter, eds., *Mexican History: A Primary Source Reader* (Boulder, CO: Westview Press, 2010), 385, 389–98.

27. Pensado, *Rebel Mexico*, 34, 127, 236.

28. Sierra Guzmán, "Armed Forces and Counterinsurgency," 83.

29. INMUJERES, 4, 7; Gina Zabludovsky, "Las mujeres en México: trabajo, educación superior y esferas de poder," *Política y Cultura* 28 (2007): 9–41; Orlandina de Oliveira, "La participación femenina en los mercados de trabajo urbanos en México: 1970–1980," *Estudios demográficos y urbanos* 4, no. 3 (1989): 465–93; INMUJERES, "Las Mexicanas en el trabajo," 2003; Orlandina de Oliveira y Brígida García, "Expansión del trabajo femenino y transformación social en México: 1950–1987," *México en el umbral del milenio* (México: El Colegio de México, 1990), 360.

30. *Senadoras de México, 1958–2012* (México: Senado de la República/INMUJERES, 2003), 27. María del Carmen Araiza López, Marcelina Galindo Arce (Chiapas), and Margarita García Flores (Nuevo León), Remedios Albertina Ezeta (State of México); Guadalupe Ursúa Flores (Jalisco), María Guadalupe López Bretón, Aurora Navia Millán, and Aurora Ruvalcaba Gutiérrez served in the XLVIII–XLIX Legislative Session (1970–1976).

31. Translations of article titles are mine. For the originals, see Rosario Castellanos, "La liberación de la mujer, aquí," *Debate feminista* 12 (1995): 351–54; Martha Acevedo, "Nuestro sueño está en escarpado lugar," *Debate feminista* 12 (October 1995): 355–70. For an analysis of Castellanos's feminism, see Marta Llamas, "Rosario Castellanos en sus propias palabras," *LiminaR*, vol. XV, no. 2 (2017): 35–47.

32. See https://caceh.org.mx/.

33. In Spanish, the organizations are Expresión Cultural Mixe Xaam, Colectivo de Mujeres Indígenas Trabajadoras del Hogar, and Centro de Apoyo y Capacitación para Empleadas de Hogar, CACEH. For further information, see http://empleadasindigenas .blogspot.com/search/label/%C2%BFQuienes%20somos%3F; *Roma vista por trabajadoras del hogar* (AJ+ Español (Al Jazeera) with the Center for Support and Training for Household Employees, CACEH, 2019); Lorenza Gutiérrez Gómez, "Mujeres indígenas trabajadoras del hogar," *Revista de derechos humanos-defensor* 1 (2012): 19–23; Natalia Flores Garrido, "Entrevista a Lorenza Gutiérrez Gómez, fundadora del Colectivo de Mujeres Indígenas Trabajadoras del Hogar (COLMITH), México D.F.," *Aletheia: revista de la maestría en historia y la memoria y de la FaHCE* 5, 9 (2014): 1–20. Films include *Hilda* (Andrés Clariond, 2014), *Muchachas* (Juliana Fanjul, 2015), *La Camarista* (Lila Avilés, 2018).

34. Karina Felitti, "En sus propias palabras: Relatos de vida sexual y (no) reproductiva de mujeres jóvenes mexicanas durante las décadas de 1960 y 1970," *Dyanamis* 38, no. 2 (2018): 333–61.

35. Edward Cowan, "Mexican Families Are Wary of the Birth Control Clinic," *New York Times*, November 27, 1975, 12. Alan Riding, "Mexican President Unexpectedly Opposes Legalization of Abortion," *New York Times*, December 17, 1979, 4. Marta Llamas, "El feminismo mexicano y la lucha por legalizar el aborto," *Política y Cultura* 1 (otoño 1992): 9–22. As of July 2020, four states allow for an abortion.

Chapter 12

"How Historical Are You Trying to Be?"

Romero

Kevin Coleman

Romero *(1989); produced by Ellwood Kieser; directed by John Duigan; written by John Sacret Young; color; 105 minutes; Paulist Pictures. Archbishop Oscar Romero (Raúl Julia) is transformed from a quiet ally of the oligarchy to an advocate for El Salvador's poor.*

The last three years of Oscar Romero's life, precisely the period covered by the Hollywood film *Romero* (1989), are abundantly documented. As Archbishop of San Salvador from 1977 to the moment he was assassinated in 1980, crucial moments of his life were recorded on audiocassette tapes, by television cameras, and in still photographs. His writings—four long pastoral letters and hundreds of homilies, bulletins, and press releases from the Office of the Archbishop—are published in seven volumes that add up to some 3,500 pages. His audio diaries, which he privately dictated into a tape recorder, narrate a nearly day-by-day account of his activities from March 1978 to four days before he was shot. His homilies, too, were recorded for posterity. During the last three years of his life, Romero had become one of the only trusted sources of information about what was going on in the country. El Salvador's wealthiest families owned the major press outlets and together with the military dictatorship, which had ruled since 1932, exercised extreme censorship. In the late 1970s, the newspapers and television stations created wall-to-wall coverage of "communist" priests, "terrorist" insurgents, and soldiers sacrificing themselves for the fatherland. The makers of *Romero* had these sources—his audio diaries, the recordings of the homilies, the photographs, and the television interviews—available to them as they conducted research to write the script, design the scenes, and deliver their lines on camera. Romero, we might say, wrote the first draft of the history depicted in this movie.

Amidst the repression, Romero dedicated a substantial portion of his long Sunday homilies to reporting on the facts of the previous week. He provided details on who had been killed, including their names, ages, where they were murdered, and who the likely perpetrators were. He knew these details because he had established the Office of Legal Aid in the Archdiocese of San Salvador to investigate political violence. With no other place to turn for help, the families of people who had gone missing or whose bodies were found dismembered came to this office with photos of their loved ones. Romero's homilies were then broadcast across the country via the diocesan radio station, YSAX. Not only can we listen to the original audio recordings of those homilies; we can also read oral history interviews with some of the ordinary Salvadorans who relied on them to figure out what was going on in their country.

The final recording of Romero captured the moment he was killed. In his homily on March 24, 1980, in the small church at the Hospital of Divine Providence, where he lived, we can listen to Romero speak his very last words:

> By Christian faith we know that at this moment the host of wheat becomes the body of the Lord who offered himself for the redemption of the world, and that the wine in this chalice is transformed into the blood that was the price of salvation. May this body that was immolated and this flesh that was sacrificed for humankind also nourish us so that we can give our bodies and our blood to suffering and pain, as Christ did, not for our own sake but to bring justice and peace to our people. Let us therefore join closely together in faith and hope at this moment of prayer for Doña Sarita and ourselves.

The assassin's shot rings out. Brief silence, then pandemonium. Moments later, a photographer snapped pictures of Romero lying dead on the altar, blood welling from his mouth, nose, and ears. Carmelite nuns in white habits are on their knees, some with their hands on him, others with their foreheads pressed to the polished stone floor. This scene is faithfully reconstructed in the final moments of *Romero*, the film.

Just four days after the sniper (whose name we still do not know) killed Romero with a single .22 caliber round to the chest, the Hollywood writer and director John Sacret Young cut out a news article on the assassination from the *Los Angeles Times* and sent it with a handwritten note to Father Ellwood

"Bud" Kieser: "This could make a fascinating movie of the week."[1] Upon receiving the note, Kieser called Young to say that he was intrigued. Would Young be interested in writing the script for a movie on Romero? The two had worked together on *Insight*, a half-hour television series that sought to convert nonbelievers and that Kieser directed for twenty-three years.

Each man already had the measure of the other. "John had an unconventional approach to the world of the spirit and a love-hate relationship with the Catholic Church," Kieser later wrote. "An Episcopalian by background, he had majored in religious studies at Princeton. Looking like the linebacker he once was, he liked to bait me, playing skeptic and cynic; but in talking to him, I got the feeling that was a cover for something much deeper. He snorted at the externals of religion but constantly wrestled with its inner core."[2] Young, in turn, recalled: "Bud was formidable, literally and figuratively a giant in my life, and not mine alone. He was six feet seven inches tall, looked young even when he wasn't with a 1950s brush/wave of light brown hair. He wore glasses and hearing aids, and was both literally and figuratively deaf. He heard only what he wanted to hear."[3]

Just a few months after receiving the movie-of-the-week suggestion from Young, Kieser discovered that a Jesuit named James Brockman was working on a biography of Romero. As editor in chief of *America*, a monthly magazine published by the Society of Jesus in the United States, Brockman was one of the key conduits between the Jesuits in San Salvador and the order's large community in North America. On the ground in El Salvador, this group of priests worked daily to commemorate the loss of Romero. Brockman's biography, and especially the contacts that he made in El Salvador while doing research for the book, became sources for the script that Young would write.

After much struggle, the film was released in 1989, not on broadcast television but in theaters. Paulist Pictures, which Father Kieser headed, produced the film with a budget of $3,500,000, much of it raised from appeals to Catholic nonprofit organizations in the United States. *Romero* was filmed entirely on location in a village just outside of Cuernavaca, Mexico. The producers were from Hollywood; the director's team was Australian; the actors were Latino, white, and Mexican. The story was Salvadoran.

Romero faithfully depicts the significant events and factors at play in late Cold War El Salvador: the conflict between Church and State; divisions within the Catholic Church; the alliance between the oligarchy and the military; stolen elections and brutal state-backed repression; the organizing work of priests and lay Christian leaders with peasant communities; occasions where ordinary citizens sought refuge from state repression by hiding in Catholic churches. The film accurately portrays these weighty historical moments. It gets other things right as well: garbage dumps and lava fields where death squads and soldiers left the mutilated bodies of those they

Figure 12.1: Original movie poster for *Romero* (1989). (Author's collection.)

suspected of subversion; the effort that ordinary people made to understand the root causes of poverty and exclusion in El Salvador; the kidnapping, carried out by left-wing insurgents, of a government minister from a wealthy family; the letter Romero sent to President Jimmy Carter, requesting that the United States stop providing military equipment and advisors to El Salvador; and the connection between anti-Indigenous racism and the refusal of the wealthiest Salvadoran families to support initiatives that would benefit the country as a whole. The movie is also good on the details. Romero did indeed have a close relationship with his driver, Salvador Barraza, a humble shoe salesman. He wore horn-rimmed glasses, which look like the pair that Raúl Julia wore on screen, and a red miter emblazoned with *"Sentir con la Iglesia."* Black and white photographs of the disappeared, which appear on walls and in photo albums at several points in the film, were important to the work of *Romero*'s Office of Legal Aid. As a film, *Romero* gets all of this history right, and masterfully so.

The movie is decidedly Catholic not only in its subject matter but also in its production. It was made by Paulist Priests, a Roman Catholic missionary order dedicated to evangelizing to non-Catholics. The Paulists produced it with $288,000 in financial support from the U.S. Conference of Catholic Bishops and a $100,000 loan from the Raskob Foundation.[4] *Romero* is what Hollywood would call a biopic and what historians of early Christianity would recognize as a martyrdom narrative.

The official movie poster, those artifacts of the late 1980s that measured 39 x 27 inches, has Romero (Raúl Julia) in his white alb and green stole, symbolizing that he is serving in his official liturgical function. He looks directly at the viewer and is set within the outline of a gold cross. Behind him are the faithful (we can make out the face of Barraza, the friend who drives him to Aguilares and who gave him a new pair of shoes after he was installed as archbishop). So Romero and his flock are on the cross, which makes this image a crucifix, explicitly associating Romero and other Salvadorans with Christ. Between the viewer and Romero, the barrels of two rifles diagonally intersect, giving us a visual shorthand for his persecutors: the state as represented by its military-grade weapons. Two captions attempt to secularize, to mute ever so slightly the overtly religious imagery: "In defense of the poor he fought with the only weapon he had . . . *the truth*" and *"ROMERO*—A true story of a modern hero." But Romero's truth, the images on the poster insist, was Christian, and his heroism was that of Christian martyrs. Yet as historians of early Christianity remind us, the veracity of martyrdom stories is far outstripped by the intensity of belief in a myth of persecution that continues to mobilize white evangelicals in the United States.[5]

ROOT CAUSES, 1932–1977

Romero starts with only a black screen and the thud-thud of a military heli-copter. As the opening credits appear in a red typeface, the din of a crowd can be heard through the chopper's blades. Viewers are then located in a specific time and place: "EL SALVADOR. February, 1977." A man addresses the crowd—"It happened in 1932, *La Matanza*"—and then, a cut from the black screen to a close-up of the speaker, a clean-shaven political candidate in a sportscoat: "It happened in the election of 1945 and 1950. It happened in the *one candidate election of 1962*." The camera cuts from the speaker to the crowd supporting him in an urban center strung with political banners, then to armed soldiers and plainclothes intelligence operatives watching the assembly from balconies nearby. "It happened in the election when the winners kept changing even though the voting was long since completely done. And now, 1977, and this time, we will not stand for it anymore. We will occupy this plaza until there is a true election, a *free election*." The crowd chants "freedom, freedom." A colonel in dark sunglasses looks on and gives orders through a two-way radio. From the flat rooftop of an adjacent building, four men train telephoto lenses on the participants in the rally, putting them in the crosshairs of the camera's viewfinder. Soldiers protect the photographers as they click away. Rather than ensuring open political debate and the expansion of liberty, the repressive forces of the state are figured here as curtailing both.

This lesson in forty-five years of Salvadoran history is condensed into less than a minute of screen time—it is also historically accurate. The Salvadoran military ruled for nearly fifty years, from 1931–1979, longer than in any other country in Latin America or the Caribbean; moreover, El Salvador only began its transition to democracy after the signing of the Peace Accords in 1992.

Agrarian capitalism in El Salvador played an important role in the consolidation of conservative authoritarian rule. Up until the end of the nineteenth century, the country's Indigenous peasantry worked communal landholdings (*ejidos* and *tierras comunales*). But with the global coffee boom of the early twentieth century, large landholders began to change laws to "modernize" agriculture, ejecting subsistence farmers from land held in common and placing them onto small, privately owned plots. Those peasants, now without land to sustain themselves, became rural wage laborers on the expanding coffee estates, which by the late 1920s, brought in 90 percent of El Salvador's income from exports.[6]

By the early 1930s, rural workers had a long list of grievances. They could remember a time of prosperity, and they knew when they lost their land to the coffee elite. As the state repressed a growing leftist labor movement, militancy increased, setting in motion a dynamic of polarization that ended catastrophically. In January 1932, despite being outmatched, the Salvadoran Communist Party reluctantly launched an insurrection. The insurgents controlled six towns and villages for just one day and killed less than twenty civilians, each of whom was a political target.[7] In response, the military regime of General Maximiliano Martínez sent soldiers on a two-week rampage through the countryside of western El Salvador, where they killed around 10,000 people, most of whom were Nahua Pipil. This is *La Matanza*, which the politician in the opening scene of the film is referring to.

While the first wave of enclosures was precipitated by the coffee economy, the second, which began after World War II, was brought on by the expansion of the cotton, sugarcane, and cattle export industries. The privatization of communal lands resulting from coffee cultivation for foreign markets had been softened by placing subsistence farmers onto their own small parcels and by absorbing them into a new labor market, but this second wave of enclosures cut peasants off from their smallholdings without offering the safety valve of employment.[8] The military continued to enforce the interests of large-scale agrarian capitalists at the expense of the peasantry. Although junior officers occasionally promised economic reforms in bids to oust their superiors in the armed forces and to garner the support of the general population, such promises, including the major land reform proposal of Colonel Arturo Molina (1972–1977), were scuttled by landed elites, who called on the military to suppress mass movements that demanded free elections and concrete measures to address the problem of landlessness, and the grinding poverty and exploitation that resulted from it. As in the opening scene to *Romero*, the film emphasizes a lack of democracy without explicitly thematizing why the oligarchy and the military were intent on subverting the will of the Salvadoran people. Without an understanding of the underlying causes of poverty in El Salvador, principally a landless peasantry, the violence depicted may strike viewers as senseless.

ROMERO'S CONVERSION AFTER THE DEATH OF RUTILIO?

The film depicts Romero undergoing a transformation, from "a mouse of a man" into a courageous hero. Early in the movie, a young priest (Tony Plana) who works with the poor, affectionately says to Rutilio Grande (Richard Jordan): "Tilio, you should be the one taking Archbishop Chávez's place." As they banter about who should be the next archbishop, one of the priests declares: "The worst would be Romero." Moments later, we get a contrasting view, as two conservative bishops delight that Romero was selected. "He's a good compromise choice—he'll make no waves," the military vicar says.

The point that these two scenes make—about the way that progressive clergy viewed Romero as a spiritualist who ran interference for the status quo and the church hierarchy who saw Romero as a safe bet in tumultuous times—is true to how he was perceived in early 1977. In both the film and in an influential, though hotly contested, body of scholarly literature, the impetus for a dramatic change in Romero was the assassination of his friend, the Jesuit Rutilio Grande.

In the early 1970s, Romero had a public conflict with the progressive wing of the church in El Salvador. The Jesuits there had begun to reshape their pedagogy in accord with the recommendations made by the Conference of Latin American Bishops at the 1968 meeting in Medellín, Colombia. At one of their high schools, teachers sent the students, most of whom hailed from the upper classes, into shantytowns to study the realities that those communities faced. In the diocesan newspaper *Orientación*, Romero denounced the Jesuits as "certain pedagogues" of "a false liberating education." He railed against the "demagogy and Marxism" in "the pamphlets and literature, of known red origin, spread in a certain school."[9] A couple years later, a study published in *Estudios Centroamericanos*, a social scientific journal run by the Jesuits, found that under Romero's editorship, the diocesan periodical *Orientación* "criticizes injustice in the abstract but criticizes methods of liberation in the concrete."[10] This pastoral rift between the native-born Romero and the Spanish-born Jesuits was suddenly overcome as each side mourned the loss of Grande. Like Romero, Grande was a Salvadoran priest who lived and worked where he was born; like the Basque Jesuits, Grande was himself a member of the Society of Jesus and a liberationist.

The cinematic rendering of the murder of Grande adheres to the historical record. On March 12, 1977, Grande was accompanied by seventy-two-year-old Manuel Solorzano and sixteen-year-old Nelson Lemus in his Volkswagen Safari. As they were leaving town, they stopped to pick up three children. Minutes later, the group was ambushed by gunmen waiting on banks alongside the road and a small pickup truck that had been following them since they left Aguilares. They put twelve bullets into Father Grande, penetrating his jaw, neck, skull, pelvis, and lower back. The three children in the back were spared and later recounted what they had seen.[11]

In the film, when Romero arrives at the wake for Grande and his companions, he sees their bloodied bodies and turns inward. As he processes their deaths, he overhears the two priests who had doubted him emphatically say: "the archbishop must speak." At that point, Romero decides that the church will mourn them in a single Mass of unity at the cathedral. This decision to cancel parish masses angered a few of his fellow bishops, who tell Romero, "you cannot do that, force everyone to go to the same Mass." In the on-screen funeral homily, Romero addresses those gathered at the cathedral steps, as well as those huddled around their radios listening to a Mass broadcast across the country: "This is a moment to gather from these deaths, for all of us who remain on pilgrimage . . . the liberation that Father Grande preached was a liberation rooted in faith. And because it is so often misunderstood, for it, Father Rutilio Grande died."

In fact, the clergy of San Salvador, and not Romero, requested the single Mass, known as the *misa única*, to be concelebrated by the priests of the archdiocese in the cathedral. This daylong meeting took place immediately after Grande's funeral. Those in favor of a single Mass argued that one sector of the church was being persecuted because of its fidelity to Vatican II and that the rest of the church needed to publicly gather in solidarity around these priests and their bishop. Those opposed claimed that a single Mass would be interpreted as a political provocation and would prevent some of the faithful from receiving holy communion.[12] Romero was initially wary of the idea. He faced intense resistance not only from within his divided conference of bishops but also from Papal Nuncio Emmanuel Gerada, who demanded that Romero reverse the decision.[13] Romero resented that his local pastoral authority was being undermined by the Vatican's ambassador, and against the nuncio's wishes, the Single Mass was successfully celebrated. One hundred thousand people were there to mourn in community.

While there is no doubt that Romero changed after Rutilio Grande was murdered, the nature of that change, and whether it was sudden or gradual, is disputed. By tracking how the filmmakers committed to the interpretation of a radical religious conversion, we will see how this became the accepted account of Romero, even though it is at odds with what Romero himself regarded as an evolution in his pastoral approach. The "Road to Damascus" interpretation, we will also see, conflicts with the historical record and a new wave of scholarship on Romero.

Three years after Romero was killed, Father Bud Kieser, the "deaf Don Quixote," and John Sacret Young, the future writer and director of *China Beach*, sat next to each other on a plane from Los Angeles to San Salvador. They had secured press credentials from a Catholic magazine and *Rolling Stone*, and their trip was timed to coincide with the pastoral visit of Pope John Paul II.[14] Over several days, the two moviemakers interviewed the key historical protagonists: U.S. Ambassador Deane Hinton; the Jesuits at the Central American University (UCA); military leaders; bishops; priests; and the family of Salvador Barraza, Romero's friend and driver. Romero's first biographer, James Brockman, had given them this list of people to visit and the local office of Catholic Relief Services set up their appointments.[15] At night, Young struck up friendships with photojournalists, including Susan Meiselas, whose forehead was lanced by camera equipment after the army stopped their bus en route to see John Paul II, and John Hoagland, a

Newsweek photographer who was deliberately shot by a Salvadoran soldier with an M-60 machine gun supplied by the United States.[16] (The last six frames in Hoagland's camera, photojournalists later discovered, recorded the moment he was killed.) On March 10, they attended a cocktail party at the Sheraton Hotel in San Salvador; the theme for the evening was "Analysis of the latest political events in El Salvador and their impact on private enterprise."[17] The guest of honor was Major Roberto D'Aubuisson, the intellectual author of the assassination of Romero.

A few days before the gala at the Sheraton, Kieser and Young ate breakfast with Ignacio Ellacuría, a Jesuit theologian of historical reality at the UCA. Young's handwritten notes from the meeting are revealing: "R. fearful *of communism*, when R. accused them [the Jesuits] already dangerous."[18] Kieser and Young then met with theologian Jon Sobrino and the Jesuit Provincial, César Jerez. Young took note of the appearance of the two priests. Sobrino, he scrawled in his notebook, "brown pants + shirt, double-knit blue shirt, pen in pocket, smokes, heavy-rimmed glasses, ½ open zipper, seam gone on pocket, 2" black belt." Jerez, Young observed, was "balding slightly, grey hair, tinted glasses, fresh white shirt, blue seersucker, black shoes, silver computer watch. Uptown." The two priests described Romero as a "very concrete man." Jerez then recounted to Kieser and Young a private conversation that he had with Romero when the two of them were in Rome together after the assassination of Rutilio Grande.

As they were walking along the Via della Conciliazione, Jerez recalled prompting Romero to open up to him: "Tell me how you've changed."[19] According to Young's shorthand notes, Jerez recalled Romero's response:

> Remember I am the son of a poor family (proud of that) and I went to seminary & I was separated from my roots & then I came back & worked as a parish priest. Then I was made bishop & I was told to get back in touch with people but I was still scared & still [afraid] of Apostasy. Children dying from—poisoned—what they drinking & Apostasy doing nothing about it & then I become archbishop & then Rutilio killed (& his face illuminates) & then I saw my way had [to be] the way of Rutilio.[20]

The narrative arc is complete. Romero went from a scared priest who had forgotten his roots to a man who was converted by the sight of poor children and the murder of his friend Rutilio Grande.[21] He then had the courage to stand with the poor and courageously defy the oligarchy that exploited them and the military and paramilitary forces that terrorized them. This was the story that Kieser and Young would tell.

In late April 1985, Kieser wrote to Brockman: "At long last, we have completed the screenplay on Archbishop Romero." "I would very much like you to read it over," Kieser requested, "and give me your feelings on the truthfulness of our portrayal of the Archbishop and the changes he went through."[22] These, then, are the basic standards toward which Kieser and Young aspired: a truthful portrayal of Romero and his conversion from traditionalist to embattled archbishop defending the poor and persecuted.

Brockman's initial reply to Kieser was a brief acknowledgment that he had received the screenplay. In the week since it had arrived, Brockman had "looked it over once." But he was uncomfortable with it—"the first reading is rather jarring for me"—and asked one question: "how historical are you trying to be?"[23] It wasn't that Brockman required a strictly historical account of Romero, but rather he wanted to know where the producer and writer drew the line between accurately representing Romero and creating a character in a Hollywood film.

Six days later, Brockman was back at his typewriter, composing a three-page letter with his evaluation of the 1985 screenplay by John Sacret Young. In his response to the screenplay, Brockman flagged four issues: the portrayal of the Jesuits, Romero's conversion, Romero as a bookworm, and the need to convey that this is not a "rigidly historical" account. There remained, however, a bigger issue: "Does the spiritual depth of Romero come through?" That, he wrote, "is my chief concern."

Highest on Brockman's list of "other difficulties with the script as it is now" was the prominence accorded to the Jesuits:

> The Jesuits of Central America have suffered much from stereotyping and defamation. One of the canards is that they manipulated or exerted undue influence on Romero. I'm afraid that the position given to the Jesuit provincial in the script furthers that misconception, to neither Romero's nor their benefit. No Jesuit was as close to Romero as Villez is made to be. His closest advisers were Msgr. Urioste, Fabian Amaya, and Jesus Delgado, all diocesan priests. I can see the dramatic reasons for emphasizing the character of Rutilio Grande, but his prominence in the film calls for de-emphasizing other Jesuits, lest Romero appear surrounded and dominated by Jesuits.[24]

Brockman was presciently attuned to the dangers that the Jesuits were facing in Central America. Four years after he wrote this letter, an elite group within the U.S.-backed military would assassinate Ellacuría, along with five other Jesuits who taught at the Central American University. To eliminate witnesses, the soldiers also killed their cook and her daughter. (Sobrino happened to be at a meeting in Thailand and thus escaped the fate of his colleagues.) Brockman concluded his critique of the screenplay's depiction with a request: "Please don't add to the problems of the Central American Jesuits."

As a historian by training, Brockman had gone through the available primary source documents and disagreed with his Jesuit brothers who were trained as theologians. He doubted that Romero had undergone a radical conversion but felt that for dramatic reasons, that could be part of the movie. In his letter to Kieser, Brockman cast doubt on the conversion narrative: "He refused the gift of a fine house when he became archbishop; this was before Rutilio's death and before his supposed change of life."[25]

Rather than interpreting Romero's transformation as a sudden spiritual transformation, recent scholarship emphasizes the way that he was in constant conversion, seeking at every step to discern what he should do in light of the church's authoritative teachings—the Gospel, Ambrose of Milan, *Rerum Novarum* (1891), *Quadragesimo Anno* (1931), *Gaudium et Spes* (1965), *Populorum Progressio* (1967), and John Paul II's 1979 address to the Latin American bishops in Puebla, Mexico.[26] Romero repeatedly drew upon these texts in his homilies and pastoral letters. One historian has even argued that the popular understanding of Romero as a reactionary priest who suddenly became the voice of the Salvadoran people is a myth, one initially propagated by the Jesuits Ellacuría and Sobrino, as they struggled to understand how the bishop who had once denounced them as "communists" unexpectedly shifted to working with them.[27] Between 1977 and 1980, Romero found himself as the head of a church whose progressive elements were being systematically and brutally murdered. In response to the new political dynamic of a country hurtling toward civil war and with the increased pastoral responsibility that came with being the archbishop, Romero gradually summoned the courage to denounce wrongs and to work for a more just distribution of created goods.

DESTRUCTION OF THE TABERNACLE IN AGUILARES

In the film, the military rolls into the town of Aguilares, brutalizes the townspeople, and sets up barracks inside the local church. Romero arrives in Aguilares and walks (with Salvador Barraza trailing behind him) into the church and tells the soldiers: "We are here to remove the Blessed Sacrament while the town is occupied." A soldier replies, "This is a barracks." Romero insists, "We are here to take care of the Eucharist." A blond, pock-faced soldier then turns his back on Romero and opens fire on the altarpiece, blowing the crucified Jesus's plaster head off. The tabernacle is destroyed. The tabernacle is an ornate box that holds the wafers that have been transformed during Mass into the consecrated Eucharist, which Catholics believe is not a mere symbol of the body of Christ but his actual flesh and bones. Thus, within Catholic theology, to shoot the tabernacle is to shoot Christ. With that, the soldier turns around, points his gun at Romero, and orders him to get out.

Romero leaves the church, gets to his car, and hesitates, looking at the poor gathered in the plaza. He steels himself and reenters the church, walking past the soldiers. He goes down on his hands and knees and begins picking up the hosts scattered behind the table of the altar. The soldiers put their boots on his back, pushing him to the ground. Romero gets back on his feet and walks out with the hosts clasped in his hands.

Moments later, Romero dons his liturgical garments, then walks toward the church. Local priests and parishioners join him in procession. He addresses the reassembled congregation, with armed soldiers among them, from the altar: "We are here today to retake possession of this church building and to strengthen all those who the enemies of the church have trampled down." Soldiers hang their heads. "You should know that you have not suffered alone, for you are the church, you are the people of God, you are Jesus in the here and now." Among the parishioners, the camera finds Lucia (Lucy Reina) listening devoutly. The two priests with whom she works in Aguilares are also listening; later in the film, one of these priests will be tortured and killed, and the other will take up arms in frustration with the ways that their nonviolent attempts at change have been brutally repressed. In a subsequent scene, Lucia will be snatched from her bed in the middle of the night and brutally murdered. Romero continues to address the people assembled in the reclaimed church: "He is crucified in you, just as surely as he was crucified 2,000 years ago on that hill outside of Jerusalem. And you should know that your pain and suffering, like his, will contribute to El Salvador's liberation and redemption."

The filmmakers went to great trouble to get this scene right. In January 1988, Father Kieser traveled to El Salvador with John Duigan, the director of the film, and Roger Ford, the production designer. The three visited several churches, marketplaces, and political rallies and went out at night in San Salvador. They went to the chapel at the hospital for cancer patients where Romero was assassinated and to the cathedral where his body was entombed. Ford took photographs in El Salvador and used them to design the set for the scene in which the soldier destroys the tabernacle.

When it came time to shoot the film, Ford found a church in a small town outside Cuernavaca. The church had a big arch near the altar. He recalls, "I thought that what we could do—because we weren't going to shoot up the altar—was to put a flat behind the arch, in front of the altar, and build our own altar. That way, we could have two or three altars; we could shoot the thing up without harming the real church." A member of Ford's design team then managed to get a crucifix and unconsecrated hosts. They built the glass cabinetry with "sugar glass," which looks like real glass. The special effects people planted explosive charges, "bullet hits," all over the place. During the take, they let off the mini-explosives so that they punched holes in the plasterwork. From there, the camera cut to the guy shooting the gun. Ford explains, "It all comes together in a perfectly safe way, where no one gets harmed and no sacrilege occurs."[28]

Is this scene historically accurate? Yes, largely so. In the late 1970s, the military shot up the Catholic church in Aguilares and riddled the tabernacle with bullets. The screenwriter and producer relied on Brockman's account, which was based on contemporaneous information published by the Archdiocese of San Salvador in a bulletin and Romero's May 23, 1977, letter to Colonel Arturo Molina (1972–1977). Brockman himself "saw the bullet-riddled tabernacle a year later and spoke with parishioners."[29] From these distinct sources, he reconstructed what happened:

> Romero tried to go to Aguilares himself to see the situation and to remove the Blessed Sacrament from the church, which the soldiers were using as a barracks. The army would not let him pass, and he then sent the chaplain of the Guardia Nacional. The guardsmen arrested the chaplain and kept him prisoner for an hour. Soldiers shot open the tabernacle and strewed the hosts on the floor.[30]

The movie simplifies actual events without changing their basic contours. In the film, Romero gets through the military checkpoint and personally witnesses the desecration, which he works to repair. In historical fact, soldiers really were using the church in Aguilares as a barracks, and they did shoot up the tabernacle. Romero attempted to get to the town, but the military stopped him.[31]

Beyond Brockman's account, other reports of the events in Aguilares were also available to the scriptwriter. In July 1977, the U.S. Congress House Subcommittee on International Organizations held hearings on religious persecution in El Salvador. Thomas E. Quigley of the United States Conference of Catholic Bishops testified:

> On Sunday, June 12, together with several thousand others I participated in a solemn mass of reparation in the Metropolitan Cathedral in San Salvador. The service of reparation, not the first of its kind, was held to atone for the sacrileges committed by the security forces when they raided Aguilares May 19 and 20, broke open the tabernacle of the church and strewed the consecrated hosts over the floor.

Quigley noted that this act of symbolic reparation, timed as it was for the feast of Corpus Christi, focused on both "the wanton desecration of the sacrament in Aguilares" and on "the sacredness of the human person, the men, women, and children of Aguilares."[32]

Romero's words are also the basis for this distinctively Catholic moment in cinema. In the actual homily of June 19, 1977, in Aguilares, Romero began:

"It is my job to gather up the assaults, the bodies, and all that the persecution of the church leaves in its wake. Today I have come to gather up in this church and in this profaned convent a destroyed tabernacle and above all else a people that has been disgracefully humiliated and sacrificed."[33] In the historical Romero's reading of the military's siege of Aguilares and the desecration of its church, an image of liberation emerges. He tells those who had not yet fled the region: "You are the image of the Divine One who has been pierced, the one of whom the first reading speaks in prophetic, mysterious language. That figure representing Christ nailed on the cross and pierced by the lance is the image of all those people who, like Aguilares, have been pierced and violated."[34] The theology of this image is clear: God made humankind in His own image. As the military persecutes the poor of Aguilares, it is killing God and His creation. The repression worked—within a few years, most of the Catholics of Aguilares had fled and less restive converts to evangelical Protestantism had moved in.

ROMERO AND THE GENRE OF CHRISTIAN MARTYRDOM

Toward the end of the film, Romero is alone in the bleak landscape where Rutilio Grande was killed. Wandering in the desert, Romero is depicted on-screen as speaking to God: "I can't.. . . . You must. . . . I'm yours. . . . Show me the way." Between "I can't" and "You must," there seems to have been an epiphany about what he must do. In uttering "I'm yours" and "Show me the way" at precisely the place where Grande, Solorzano, and Lemus were gunned down (three crosses on the shoulder of the road mark the spot), Romero accepts that he may be killed. The plot is thus the culmination of God's will intertwined with Romero's choices.

It was scenes such as this that made movie critics hostile to *Romero*. "The end of the movie is rife with parallels to Christ's martyrdom," a reviewer in the *Chicago Tribune* wrote, "Romero turning card-playing soldiers out of a church, asking God's guidance in a Gethsemane-like cemetery, assuring his flock that 'If they kill me, I shall arise in the Salvadoran people.' *Romero* is film as veneration and that, more than anything else, stifles it."[35] Variations on this line of critique—that *Romero* is not a good film because it is not art and is, instead, what scholars of early Christianity would call a "martyrdom narrative"—were made by a least a dozen reviewers, including Roger Ebert and Gene Siskel.[36]

As a devout Christian who sought to be faithful to church teachings, Romero modeled himself on the one he regarded as his savior, Jesus Christ. There is thus a generic aspect to both Romero's life and to the film based on that life. Romero was imitating other Christian martyrs, and so *Romero*, as a film, repeats the conventions of Christian martyrdom stories. Nevertheless, Romero the historical figure and *Romero* the movie deviate from this genre. In the prototype, the "victorious victim" always dies at the hands of non-Christian tyrants.[37] But the story of Romero is historically significant precisely because it strays from this convention. In the early 1980s, nearly every Salvadoran was a practicing Christian. The members of the oligarchy and the military were devout Catholics, and prominent bishops continued to publicly oppose Romero even as their priests were being killed. The most historically significant fact about the assassination of Romero was that he was killed by his fellow Christians for following, as carefully as he could, the principles of Christianity. It was this faith that led him not only to denounce direct violence but also to advocate for land reform.

A recurrent theme in Romero's diary was the attacks that he and other clergy suffered from their fellow prelates. On September 13, 1979, Romero spoke the following words into his cassette recorder:

> The morning newspapers, *Diario de Hoy* and *La Prensa*, carried a full-page text of the homily of Bishop Aparicio gave in San Vicente last Sunday. It is a strong condemnation of his priests. He says that he cannot defend them and almost accuses them himself, exposing them to possible assassination. He says that the priests who have been killed were purged by the left and that there are priests committed to the left who cannot pull back without the left killing them. We have met with other priests who are very angry about such dangerous accusations.[38]

Months earlier, Bishop Pedro Aparicio had attacked the Jesuits and Romero while they were in Puebla at the Conference of Latin American Bishops. Newspapers, he said in his diary, "published a statement by Bishop Aparicio in which he blames the Jesuits for the violence in El Salvador and accuses them of having come to Puebla to defend the archbishop's position."[39] Romero skipped a press conference in Puebla because Aparicio's statements were creating public division. The Jesuits, meanwhile, sent a letter to Aparicio asking him to cease and desist.[40] Through his false claims against those within the church who were accompanying El Salvador's poor, Aparicio put their lives in danger.

But direct violence is only part of the story, the part that grabs attention. The other part, the part that the movie *Romero* only gives us glimpses of, is the structural violence of poverty. At the heart of Romero's preaching, theologian Matthew Philipp Whelan has argued, was the belief that "creation is a gift given for common use."[41] In 1975, for instance, Romero detailed the plight of coffee harvesters in a weekly periodical published by the Archdiocese of

San Salvador; as he advocated for seasonal laborers on coffee farms, Romero quoted from the Pastoral Constitution of the Catholic Church: "'Whatever the forms of property may be, . . . attention must always be paid to this universal destination of earthly goods' (*Gaudium et Spes*, no. 69).'"[42] This same axiom about creation would lead him to challenge large landholders not to hoard what God gave to be shared in common. In a country where the vast majority of the population was Catholic, the military and the oligarchy selectively targeted those who worked closely with the oppressed to claim their share of what was already theirs. As part of a strategy of counterinsurgency, the United States made modest proposals to modify land tenure systems that had concentrated vast tracts of fertile land in the hands of very few families. Yet the Salvadoran oligarchy characterized even these limited reforms as communist assaults on private property, liberty, and free enterprise. Romero, to quote Whelan, was "not arguing for the abolition of private property, as communism did, but rather for justice in the distribution of land."[43] Romero was killed during the rollout of land reform. The former president of the National Association of Private Enterprise (ANEP), which led the charge against agrarian reform, allegedly paid the sniper about $200.

Romero was killed by his fellow Christians as part of a struggle for access to land that stretched back to the late nineteenth century and was violently punctuated by the massacre of 1932 and the civil war that erupted in the wake of his death. By adhering closely to church teachings, Romero exposed contradictions within his own society and within the church he served. The principles that he espoused led to his death at the hands of his coreligionists. That's the scandal. The film succeeds—as a historical biography and at least according to its critics, as cinematic art—to the degree that it resists inscribing Romero within a standard narrative of martyrdom and instead grapples with the ways that he defied the genre.

ADDITIONAL RESOURCES

Brockman, James R. *Romero: A Life.* Maryknoll, NY: Orbis, 1989. Revised edition of *The Word Remains: A Life of Oscar Romero.* Maryknoll, NY: Orbis, 1982.

Eisenbrandt, Matt. *Assassination of a Saint: The Plot to Murder Óscar Romero and the Quest to Bring His Killers to Justice.* Oakland, CA: University of California Press, 2017.

López Vigil, María. *Piezas para un retrato.* San Salvador: UCA Editores, 1993.

Morozzo de la Rocca, Roberto. *Oscar Romero: La Biografía.* Milano: Editorial San Paolo, 2015.

Sobrino, Jon. *Monseñor Romero.* San Salvador: UCA Editores, 1989.

Whelan, Matthew Philipp. *Blood in the Fields: Oscar Romero, Catholic Social Teaching, and Land Reform.* Washington, DC: Catholic University of America Press, 2020.

Primary Sources

An online collection of primary source materials on Romero can be found at the Archbishop Romero Trust (http://www.romerotrust.org.uk). This website features digitized versions of the original analog audio recordings of his homilies and audio diaries, as well as English translations of his work, galleries of photographs and videos, and a comprehensive (though somewhat dated) list of the secondary theological and historical literature.

Romero, Óscar A. *Homilías Monseñor Óscar A. Romero.* 7 volumes. Edited by Miguel Cavada Diez. San Salvador: UCA Editores, 2005–2009.

NOTES

1. Ellwood E. Kieser, *Hollywood Priest: A Spiritual Struggle* (New York: Doubleday, 1991): 302.

2. Kieser, *Hollywood Priest,* 303.

3. John Sacret Young, "The Pope of Pacific Palisades," 1 (draft manuscript, cited with permission), Private archives of John Sacret Young.

4. Kieser, *Hollywood Priest,* 108.

5. Kyle Smith, *Collectors of the Dead* (Oakland, CA: University of California Press, forthcoming); and Candida Moss, *The Myth of Persecution: How Early Christians Invented a Story of Martyrdom* (New York: HarperOne, 2013).

6. For an overview of the modern history of El Salvador and the key historiographical debates, see Erik Ching, "El Salvador," *The Oxford Handbook of Central American History,* June 2020, 10.1093/oxfordhb/9780190928360.013.20.

7. For a recent study of the 1932 massacre, see Jeffrey L. Gould and Aldo A. Lauria-Santiago, *To Rise in Darkness: Revolution, Repression, and Memory in El Salvador, 1920–1932* (Durham, NC: Duke University Press, 2008).

8. Matthew Philipp Whelan, *Blood in the Fields,* 57–58.

9. Brockman, *Romero: A Life,* 48.

10. Brockman, *Romero: A Life,* 49.

11. Thomas M. Kelly, *When the Gospel Grows Feet: Rutilio Grande, SJ, and the Church of El Salvador: An Ecclesiology in Context* (Collegeville, MN: Liturgical Press, 2013), xiii–xiv.

12. Brockman, *Romero: A Life,* 13.

13. Archbishop Oscar Romero, *A Shepherd's Diary* (London: Catholic Fund for Overseas Development, 1993), 23–24.

14. Kieser, *Hollywood Priest,* 303; John Sacret Young, "The Pope of Pacific Palisades," 3; for "deaf Don Quixote," see Young, 8.

15. Kieser, *Hollywood Priest,* 303.

16. Young, "Pope of Pacific Palisades," 4.

17. Invitation from the "Asociación Salvadoreña de Egresados de Master de INCAE," March 10, 1983. Private archives of John Sacret Young.

18. John Sacret Young, "Notes on meeting with Ignacio Ellacuría," March 7, 1983. Private archives of John Sacret Young.

19. Young, "Notes on meeting with Jon Sobrino and César Jerez."

20. Young, "Notes on meeting with Jon Sobrino and César Jerez." A decade later, the story of this conversation between Jerez and Romero would be published by María López Vigil, *Piezas para un retrato* (San Salvador: UCA Editores, 1993), 164–65.

21. For an early scholarly version of this argument, see Ignacio Martín-Baró, "El liderazgo de Monseñor Romero (un análisis psico-social), Venue of publication unknown 36, no. 389 (1981): 152–72, accessed July 1, 2021, https://www.uca.edu.sv/coleccion-digital-IMB/articulo/el-liderazgo-de-monsenor-romero-un-analisis-psicosocial/.

22. Kieser to Brockman, April 29, 1985, DePaul University Special Collections and Archives: Rev. James Brockman, S.J. papers, box 32.

23. Brockman to Kieser, May 7, 1985, Brockman papers, box 32.

24. Brockman to Kieser, May 13, 1985, Brockman papers, box 32.

25. Brockman to Kieser, May 13, 1985, Brockman papers, box 32.

26. In *Blood in the Fields*, Whelan traces how Romero's commitment to land reform in El Salvador emerged from his fidelity to Catholic social teaching and further demonstrates how that commitment occasioned Romero's martyrdom.

27. Roberto Morozzo della Rocca, *Primero Dios: Vida de Monseñor Romero*, trans. David Salas Mezquita (Buenos Aires: Edhasa, 2010), 185–95.

28. Oral history interview with Roger Ford, May 19, 2020.

29. Brockman, *Romero: A Life*, 31. For Brockman's sources on the desecration in Aguilares, see p. 259, endnotes 107 and 108. For a similar case, see Romero's comments: "In the village of La Junta, there had been a sacrilegious robbery of the Blessed Sacrament, and we went to celebrate an act of atonement," *Shepherd's Diary*, 120.

30. Brockman, *Romero: A Life*, 31.

31. Further corroboration of these events can be found in a letter Romero wrote on December 27, 1977, to Cardinal Eduardo Francisco Pironio, describing the profanation of the tabernacle in Aguilares; see Morozzo della Rocca, *Primero Dios*, 200.

32. *Religious Persecution in El Salvador: Hearings Before the Subcommittee on International Organizations of the Committee on International Relations*, House of Representatives, July 21 and 29, 1977 (U.S. Government Printing Office, 1977), https://books.google.ca/books?id=2DROAAAAMAAJ&pg=PA4&lpg=PA4&dq=aguilares+desecrations&source=bl&ots=UayPj_Z-a9&sig=ACfU3U2Wsm8XXAQ949GxFP-KLR6aPQAkLg&hl=en&sa=X&ved=2ahUKEwiw-4fj9tjoAhUKCc0KHXO8DBgQ6AEwAHoECAsQKA#v=onepage&q=aguilares%20desecrations&f=false.

33. *Homilías: Monseñor Óscar A. Romero*, Tomo I, 149; and Romero, "A Torch Raised on High," June 19, 1977, Archbishop Romero Trust, accessed June 28, 2021, http://www.romerotrust.org.uk/homilies-and-writings/homilies/torch-raised-high.

34. *Homilías*, Tomo I, 150. For another firsthand account of these events, see Jon Sobrino's reflections on accompanying Romero that day in Aguilares; *Archbishop Romero: Memories and Reflections* (Maryknoll, NY: Orbis Books, 1990), 26.

35. Steinmetz, Johanna. "Veneration Stifles Story of the Man in *Romero*," *Chicago Tribune*, September 8, 1989.

36. Roger Ebert, "*Romero*," movie review and film summary, September 8, 1989, accessed October 9, 2019, https://www.rogerebert.com/reviews/romero-1989; Gene Siskel, "*Romero*'s Heart in Right Place, but Drama Missing," *Chicago Tribune*, September 8, 1989.

37. Michal Beth Dinkler, "Genre Analysis and Early Christian Martyrdom Narratives: A Proposal," in *Sibyls, Scriptures, and Scrolls*, ed. Joel Baden, Hindy Najman, and Eibert Tigchelaar (Leiden: Brill, 2017), 327.

38. Romero, *Shepherd's Diary*, 328.

39. Romero, *Shepherd's Diary*, 146.

40. Romero, *Shepherd's Diary*, 149. Reuters, "Three Bishops Walk Out," *New York Times*, February 14, 1979, A4.

41. Whelan, *Blood in the Fields*, 36.

42. Quoted by Whelan, *Blood in the Fields*, 69.

43. Whelan, *Blood in the Fields*, 4.

Chapter 13

Salvador

Oliver Stone's Odyssey through the First Year of El Salvador's Civil War

Erik Ching

Salvador *(1986): produced by Oliver Stone and Gerald Green; directed by Oliver Stone; written by Oliver Stone and Richard Boyle; color; 122 minutes; Cinema '84, Estudios Churubusco Azteca, Hemdale. Photojournalist Richard Boyle (James Woods) travels to El Salvador to report on the civil war.*

Oliver Stone's *Salvador* (1986) was the first of a very small number of feature-length films set in El Salvador during its civil war (1980–1992). It is a frenetic exploration into the year 1980–1981, which marked the beginning of the war that ravaged the country for the next twelve years. *Salvador* revolves around the experiences of its central protagonist, Richard Boyle, a down-on-his-luck journalist looking to rejuvenate his career by going to a global hotspot in search of a big story. The Boyle character is based on the real-life Richard Boyle (1942–2016), a reporter/photojournalist who indeed had lived and worked in El Salvador in the late 1970s and early 1980s. He and Stone cowrote the script for *Salvador*, and Stone planned initially to have Boyle play himself in the lead role. Any analysis of *Salvador* has to be viewed through the lens of the collaboration between Stone and Boyle and the extent to which Stone relied on Boyle for his information about El Salvador. Stone didn't set out to make a film about El Salvador. Rather, he wanted to make a film in which he could critique U.S. foreign policy during the Cold War, inspired in no small part by his own tour of duty in Vietnam in 1967–1968.

He settled on El *Salvador*'s civil war as his subject matter after a happenstance meeting with Boyle. Ultimately, *Salvador* is less about El Salvador and more about Boyle and Stone.

SALVADOR, THE FILM

Oliver Stone's *Salvador* (1986) is a feature-length film set in El Salvador during a decisive one-year period in that nation's history—February 1980 to January 1981. That year was bookended by the assassination of the nation's archbishop, Oscar Romero, by a right-wing death squad in March 1980 and the launch of the leftist guerrilla army's "Final Offensive" in January 1981. The Offensive failed, and the country was plunged into a brutal twelve-year civil war that cost upward of seventy-five thousand lives and resulted in more than one million displaced persons, all in a nation roughly the size of Massachusetts with a population of five million. El Salvador's civil war was one of the most intense geopolitical hotspots of the Cold War; only Egypt and Israel received more direct U.S. financial aid in the 1980s than did El Salvador.[1]

When Oliver Stone decided to make *Salvador* in 1985, his career was at a turning point. He aspired to be a film director, but the first two films he directed, *Seizure* (1974) and *The Hand* (1981), were critical and commercial failures. He was forty years old, nearly two decades out of film school, and he had a newborn son. His professional success to date was as a writer, which included, among other accomplishments, the script for *Scarface* (1983). In choosing El Salvador's civil war as the subject of his next directorial project, he was handicapping himself. It was a controversial topic that was going to be a hard sell with both viewing audiences and financial backers. But he remained steadfast in his insistence to get the movie made. As he later described it, "I looked at it as my one chance I may get, the only one . . . and I'd take this film, and like a stone, throw it as far and hard as I could."[2]

The idea for *Salvador* came from Stone's encounter in 1984 with an eccentric U.S. journalist, Richard Boyle. Stone first met Boyle in San Francisco in 1977 during an anti–Vietnam War protest. When they reconnected in 1984, Stone discovered that Boyle had a series of unpublished writings about his time as a correspondent in El Salvador. Stone was looking for his next movie project, and between Boyle's eccentricities and his writings on El Salvador, Stone found his inspiration. As Stone later described the film's basic plot:

> It would be about a fuckup journalist whose wife splits in the first scene with their child. He scrounges money to get back to Salvador, where there's a hot war going on and he can make a few bucks through his contacts. Once there, he

hooks back up with a local girlfriend, for whom he develops stronger feelings as he runs into sticky situations and some old enemies—and before long, he's getting squeezed to a pulp, and things get deadly. Would Boyle and his woman and her child make it out of there? Something like that.[3]

He approached Boyle about coauthoring the script and also starring in the lead role. Boyle heartily agreed, and thus the film *Salvador* began.

Stone and Boyle worked furiously to complete an initial draft of the script. When they had done so, they traveled to El Salvador for two weeks in March 1985 to scout possible film locations and to determine if the country, still in the midst of its civil war, could serve as a site for a major motion picture. Boyle insisted that it could, and he assured Stone that his various connections would get Stone the permissions he needed, including the cooperation of the military to provide helicopters and tanks for the battle scenes. The trip was a fiasco, and Stone ended up shooting the film in Mexico. He also replaced Boyle in the lead role with the U.S. actor James Woods. Boyle remained a coauthor of the script, which he and Stone revised after their trip to El Salvador. Stone shot the film during the summer of 1985, and after editing through the fall, it had a limited release in December 1985, then a fuller opening in April 1986.

Salvador was met with mixed reviews and modest ticket sales, and it was soon out of theaters. It seemed to be destined for the same ignominious fate as Stone's first two films, therein, placing Stone's career as a film director further in doubt. But *Salvador*'s fortunes changed at the end of 1986, thanks to three intersecting variables. First, it was released on video, broadening access. Second, the Iran-Contra affair erupted in November 1986, drawing worldwide attention to Central America and increasing popular sympathies for *Salvador*'s ideological perspective. And third, Stone released his next film, *Platoon*, to widespread acclaim. *Platoon* reinvigorated interest in Stone's prior work, and *Salvador* experienced a renaissance. What seemed to be a sure financial loss, *Salvador* ended up roughly doubling the investment that went into making it.[4]

Salvador garnered two Academy Award nominations—best original screenplay by Stone and Boyle and best actor in a lead role by James Woods. Neither won, but having received any nominations after *Salvador*'s inauspicious beginning was a remarkable turnaround. The combination of *Salvador* and *Platoon* launched Stone into the top tier of Hollywood directors. He no longer had to worry about financing or artistic control, and he made ten films in the next ten years. "*Salvador* . . . had given me a foothold," he would later say.[5]

STONE INTERPRETING EL SALVADOR'S CIVIL WAR

The story line of *Salvador* revolves around the character of Richard Boyle, portrayed as a down-on-his-luck reporter/photojournalist looking for a story that will rejuvenate his career. To do so, he needs to be where the action is, which in 1980 is El Salvador. He secures a journalist credential from a small press agency and sets out for El Salvador in a dilapidated red Ford Mustang convertible with his friend, Dr. Rock, a San Francisco DJ.

Once Boyle and Dr. Rock arrive in El Salvador, Stone uses their characters to take viewers on a yearlong odyssey through the country's intensifying civil conflict. Stone places Boyle at the center of some key events that happened that year, including the assassination of Archbishop Romero in March 1980, the exhumation of the four North American churchwomen who were raped and murdered by security forces in December 1980, and the launching of the guerrillas' Final Offensive in January 1981. The latter event allowed Stone to address the accompanying debate inside the U.S. Embassy as to whether the United States should reverse its policy of banning military aid to El Salvador due to the army's heinous record of human rights abuses in order to stave off guerrilla victory. The film portrays the aid as having been released, and the guerrillas were subsequently repulsed, giving the clear implication that the United States' decision turned the tide in favor of the army, narrowly averting a guerrilla victory, akin to Nicaragua in July 1979. Robert White, the U.S. ambassador to El Salvador at the time, says Stone's portrayal of military aid is inaccurate. He says the aid was not released by the Carter administration but rather, by the incoming Reagan administration after January 20, when the Offensive was effectively over.[6]

As Stone navigates Boyle through these events, he introduces us to various characters that become the foil upon which he builds his politicized message. Among them are some Salvadoran military officers and political figures, including Maximiliano Casanova, or Major Max (Tony Plana), a stand-in for the right-wing political leader Roberto D'Aubuisson. He was a former military officer who cofounded the conservative right-wing political party, the National Republican Alliance (ARENA), in 1980. He is widely believed to have headed up one or more paramilitary death squads and to have ordered the assassination of Archbishop Romero in 1980. Other characters include Boyle's friend and traveling companion, Dr. Rock (Jim Belushi), who performs the role of comic sidekick and lightens up the film's darker core; the hardline, anticommunist Pentagon officer, Colonel Bentley Hyde (Will MacMillian); the slick talking, preppily dressed CIA agent Jack Morgan (Colby Chester); the Barbie doll–looking mainstream U.S. reporter Pauline Axelrod (Valerie Wildman); the earnest U.S. ambassador Thomas Kelly

(Michael Murphy), a stand-in for Robert White; the fellow rugged photojournalist John Cassidy (John Savage), a stand-in for the real-life John Hoagland, who indeed died covering the civil war in El Salvador; and finally, Maria (Elpedia Carrillo), Boyle's girlfriend from his previous time in El Salvador, with whom he reconnects in the film.

Stone's overarching message in *Salvador* is expressed by Boyle during one of his many rants, this one directed at Colonel Hyde and Jack Morgan, after they tried to recruit Boyle to spy on the guerrillas for them.

> Oh, come on, you guys have been lying about that [Communist-bloc support for the guerrillas] from the fucking beginning, you never presented one shred of proof to the American public that this is anything other than a legitimate peasant revolution so don't start telling me about the sanctity of military intelligence. Not after Chile and Vietnam. . . .
>
> What are death squads but the CIA's brainchild . . . but you'll run with them, because they're anti-Moscow, you'll let them close the universities, wipe out the Catholic Church, kill whoever they want, wipe out the best minds in the country, but as long as they're no commies, that's okay. That, Colonel, is bullshit. You've created a major Frankenstein, that's what. . . .
>
> So that's why you guys are here, looking for some kind of post-Vietnam experience, like you need a rerun or something? Turn this place into a military zone. Pour in another $120 million so they can get more chopper parades in the sky? . . . All you're doing is bringing misery to these people. For Chrissake, Jack, you gotta take care of the people first, in the name of human decency, something we Americans are supposed to believe in, you've at least gotta try to have something of a just society here![7]

Stone says he got pushback from his producers on the speech as being overly wordy and too blunt, but he insisted that it remain in its entirety because it was, in short, the reason he made the movie. As he put it in his 2020 memoir, "I thought it would probably be my last shot at saying what I believed about our government, Vietnam and Central America. It would be my gravestone speech."[8]

As that speech demonstrates, the primary target for Stone's ire in *Salvador* is the United States and its Cold War foreign policy. As Stone sees it, El Salvador was another Vietnam, a place where the United States was propping up a predatory regime in the name of stopping communism. In the process of doing so, the United States, or at least its military and intelligence wings, was willing to turn a blind eye to the various human rights violations and atrocities committed by its local allies.

The Salvadoran civil war was a series of tremendously complex, sprawling events, but Stone was either unwilling or unable to explore that complexity. Rather, *Salvador* is set in a didactic landscape of good (the opposition) and evil (the government and military). Therein, he provides few clues as to the war's origins. One exception is a brief encounter between Boyle and an elderly woman in a cantina, when she says, ominously, "We're living in a bad time. Like 1932 again, I detect a bad feeling in the air." Her reference to 1932 alludes to a tragic event in El Salvador's history known as *La Matanza* (The Massacre).

In late January 1932, a few hundred, or perhaps as many as a couple thousand peasants, many of them indigenous, rose up in rebellion in the coffee-growing region of El Salvador's western countryside. The rebels attacked approximately one dozen towns, occupied half of them, and killed close to 100 people in the process, including soldiers during the fighting. The military was initially caught off guard, but it regrouped quickly and regained control of the occupied towns within three days. Military reinforcements arrived on that third day and although the rebellion was effectively over, the killing had just begun.

In response to the rebellion, heavily armed and fast-moving military units rampaged through the western countryside killing people indiscriminately; the victims' guilt or innocence for participating in the rebellion was irrelevant. The killing lasted roughly two weeks, and in the end, no one knows for sure how many people died at the military's hands. A commonly cited figure is thirty thousand, which seems a little high. Regardless, the army killed many thousands of their fellow Salvadorans during *La Matanza*, making it one of, if not the single, worst episode of state-sponsored repression in modern Latin American history.[9]

To the extent that the government ever attempted to explain or justify its actions, it identified the rebels as communists and said it was saving the nation from communism. Beyond all else, *La Matanza* was an act of mass terrorism that left an indelible scar on the national psyche. In the succeeding decades, the military and the political right preferred to ignore the events of 1932, but whenever they felt it necessary, they dredged up its memory, as either a justification, or a warning, or both.[10]

La Matanza ushered in five decades of uninterrupted military rule in El Salvador, the longest such span in modern Latin America. The military surrendered formal control over the government in 1979, after a reformist coup installed a military–civilian junta. But the power and influence of the military steadfastly remained throughout the 1980s. Only with the end of the civil war in 1992 and the negotiated settlement between the guerrilla army, the Farabundo Martí Front for National Liberation (FMLN), and the government was the influence of the military curtailed.[11]

For Oliver Stone and people who share his views, the events of 1932 predict the civil conflict of the 1980s. From their perspective, the rebels of 1932 were poor, rural people made desperate by the unjust conditions of Salvadoran society at the time, namely, political authoritarianism, racial hierarchy, and economic exclusion. Projecting this perspective forward, the El Salvador that serves as the setting for *Salvador* had changed little since 1932. The rebels in 1980 are once again viewed as the by-product of a population made desperate by military dictatorship and a lack of economic opportunity. Boyle's reference to the conflict as "a legitimate peasant revolution" encapsulates this perspective, and Stone's portrayal of the military and paramilitary characters in the film as universally violent and repressive reinforces that theme.

Boyle's reference to a "legitimate peasant revolution" carries with it an additional meaning, namely, the rejection of the perspective touted by Cold War hawks that the conflict in El Salvador had foreign origins, ultimately from Moscow, but run through local surrogates in Cuba, Nicaragua, and elsewhere. According to them, the Salvadoran rebels were hardline Marxists whose goal was to overthrow the government, establish a Communist dictatorship and cast El Salvador's lot with international Communism. Even if the hawks acknowledge that most of the rebels were poor people from the countryside, they contend that the guerrilla leaders duped them into fighting for a cause they did not understand.

Without belaboring the point too much here, Stone's interpretation of El Salvador's civil war is basically accurate, albeit simplified and lacking in nuance. The war was, at its core, a homegrown mass insurrection by poor, rural Salvadorans who had been living under an oppressive system of economic deprivation and military rule for decades. As we now know, and as was well known by anyone who cared to look at the situation objectively at the time, the army and its paramilitary allies were responsible for the overwhelming number of deaths and human rights violations that occurred during the war. The guerrillas were not blameless, but to draw any comparison between them and the army and its paramilitary allies is a false equivalency. Only the army perpetrated mass killings of innocent civilians and used widespread torture and terror as purposeful policies.[12]

Indeed, in December 1981, just a few months after the film *Salvador* closes, the Salvadoran military perpetrated one of the worst of its many massacres during the civil war. An elite commando unit, the Atlacatl Battalion, killed approximately one thousand civilians, almost all of them women, children, and elderly men, who had taken refuge in and around the hamlet of El Mozote in northeastern El Salvador. One of the first reporters on the scene was Raymond Bonner for the *New York Times*. His reporting on the massacre and the U.S. government's obfuscation about the Salvadoran military's responsibility brought him into conflict with the then owners of the *Times*, and he eventually resigned and wrote the book *Weakness and Deceit* (1984), an analysis of the U.S. role in the Salvadoran civil war. That book was one of the few references outside of Richard Boyle that Oliver Stone relied on

for information about El Salvador. In fact, many scenes from *Salvador* bear a
striking resemblance to the images contained in Bonner's book.[13]

Stone brings his critique of U.S. foreign policy back home to U.S. immigration policy. He uses the closing scene of *Salvador* to criticize the U.S.
government for refusing to take responsibility for the human cost of its policies in Central America. Stone closes *Salvador* with Maria and her children
being arrested by U.S. border patrol officers after entering the U.S. illegally,
pretending to be Boyle's wife. Boyle's desperate pleas that Maria and her
children will be killed upon being returned to El Salvador does nothing to
dissuade the officers from hauling them away and then arresting Boyle for
his overzealous protest.

The U.S. was not monolithic in its policies toward El Salvador, and Stone
manages to hint at some of this complexity in *Salvador*. Indeed, the U.S.
Defense Department/Pentagon was largely responsible for funding and
training the Salvadoran military, including the eighty-thousand-strong paramilitary organization Democratic Nationalist Organization (ORDEN), which
terrorized the countryside throughout the 1970s. But also, at various times,
the U.S. government, through the State Department, and various aid organizations, such as the United States Agency for International Development
(USAID), pressured the Salvadoran government and military to respect
human rights and moderate their policies. During the Carter administration,
the U.S. withheld military aid starting in 1977 because of human rights violations. The U.S. also backed the reformist coup of 1979, which brought a
moderating civil–military junta to power. The junta not only enacted various
social reforms but also abolished ORDEN and purged the military of some
of its most abusive officers. And throughout its involvement in El Salvador,
the United States, even during the Reagan administration, sought to forestall
the rise of the extreme political right, and especially its figurehead, Roberto
D'Aubuisson. While Stone didn't delve deeply into these complexities, he did
suggest them by showing the tense relationship between the representative of
the State Department, Ambassador Kelly, and the respective representatives
of the Pentagon and the CIA, Colonel Hyde and Jack Morgan.[14]

Stone further explores the dichotomous nature of the United States in El
Salvador through his depiction of the rape and murder of the four North
American churchwomen in December 1980, arguably the most disturbing
scene in the film. There were no eyewitnesses to the horrific events, so
Stone's depiction is fictional. But what was known broadly at the time, and
what we now know in greater detail, the four women were driving to the capital city of San Salvador from the international airport when they were pulled
over by four members of the security forces, operating at that moment as an
extrajudicial death squad. The soldiers raped and murdered the four women

and left them lying in the open air. Peasants found the bodies and buried them. Four days later, on December 4, they were exhumed, inciting an international firestorm. It was an act of terrorism, like the murder of Archbishop Romero earlier that year, meant to deliver the message that no one was safe and any-one who identified with the liberationist wing of the Catholic Church was an enemy of the state.

Stone has Ambassador Kelly and Boyle present at the exhumation, and he portrays Kelly as indignant over the events. Indeed, the real ambassador, Robert White, was at the exhumation, and he was outraged. He knew the women and respected their humanitarian work; in fact, he had dined with two of them the previous evening. But members of the incoming Reagan admin-istration wanted to deflect attention, even for such violent acts perpetrated against U.S. citizens. Jeanne Kirkpatrick, Reagan's nominee for UN ambassa-dor, described the churchwomen on December 25, 1980: "The nuns were not just nuns. . . . They were political activists on the behalf of the Frente" (i.e., the FMLN guerrillas). And then in March 1981, Alexander Haig, Reagan's Secretary of State, said before the House Foreign Affairs Committee that the women, "may have tried to run a roadblock, or may have accidentally been perceived of doing so," and were killed in an exchange of gunfire. This sug-gestion that the women were armed gave rise to the aphorism of "gun-toting" or "pistol-packing" nuns, a criticism of how far the Reagan administration's defenders were willing to go to justify their support for the Salvadoran mili-tary. Stone has Boyle using the gun-toting nuns reference when confronting Colonel Hyde about the events.[15] Ironically, a U.S. diplomatic officer in the U.S. embassy in El Salvador eventually discovered the names of the perpetra-tors, which led to their arrest and conviction in 1984.[16]

The heroes, according to *Salvador*, are the hard-nosed journalists willing to risk it all to get the truth. Boyle, of course, is one of them and so too is John Cassidy (i.e., John Hoagland), who Stone has dying a heroic death while pho-tographing a Salvadoran fighter plane strafing a town during the Offensive of January 1981.[17] By contrast, Stone implicates the mainstream U.S. media as being complicit and aping the party line. Stone expresses this perspective through another one of Boyle's rants, this one directed at Pauline Axelrod, as Boyle reads a draft of one of her reports about Salvadoran elections.

> Pauline, this article is totally 100 percent and unequivocally full of shit. . . . You want to analyze the situation, do it right! You don't have one of those *cedulas* [identity cards] stamped election day, you're dead, what kinda democracy is it when you have to vote and if you don't vote you're a commie subversivo? . . . Fucking yuppies. Do a standup from the roof of the Camino Real [Hotel] for CBS. Think they got the whole story. "My two weeks in El Salvador." Hiding

under a bed in the Camino Real. Course they get their stories published. Cause they kiss the right asses in New York.[18]

Stone's celebration of the work of journalists like Boyle and Hoagland is one of the strengths of *Salvador*. If not for their work, often achieved at great personal risk, we would have known a lot less about the civil war than we did. Upward of twenty international journalists lost their lives covering El Salvador's civil war, and dozens more were targeted for death. In March 1982, one of the death squads, the Maximiliano Hernández Martínez Brigade, published the names of thirty-five journalists, identifying them as being "in the service of international subversion" and "condemned to death by patriots of our organization." Among those on the list were Raymond Bonner and John Hoagland.

Some of journalists' deaths were apparently accidents, like Hoagland's. He died from a bullet wound after being caught in crossfire—although the circumstances of his death remain murky. Others were purposefully targeted. One of the more infamous cases was the killing of four Dutch journalists in March 1982 in an ambush by members of the army's Atonal Battalion. Stone referenced these types of events in *Salvador* when he had the Cassidy character say, "they're shooting at us now," as he and Boyle dodge bullets during the 1981 Offensive.[19]

RICHARD BOYLE

From the perspective of those of us who study El Salvador and seek to better understand its history on its own terms, *Salvador* is a problematic film. Historical inaccuracies and Stone's admitted overdramatizations aside, the main issue is that Richard Boyle is the main subject of the film. El Salvador and its civil war are backdrops to Boyle's character and Oliver Stone's ideological waxing. All the other characters are flat, with Boyle being the only one who in the classical definition of a protagonist, shows the capacity to evolve.[20] Few of the Salvadoran characters have speaking lines, and most of them are limited to the caricature-like military officials. Even Maria, the main sympathetic Salvadoran character, has few lines and is one dimensional.[21]

In a 1986 interview, shortly before the film's theatrical release, Stone said, "I didn't set out to make a message movie about El Salvador, I wanted to do a movie about a correspondent."[22] At that time, Stone was prone to downplaying the political aspects of *Salvador* in interviews, fearing that it would depress ticket sales and bias reviewers. He was justified to be concerned. In the words of one reviewer, David Ansen, in *Newsweek* in September 1985, "such a heavy political film will put the American moviegoer to the test."[23]

Stone's claim about not wanting to make a message movie should be taken with a grain of salt. He may not have particularly cared if the movie was set in El Salvador, but he intended to make a political movie.

When it comes to his claim that the movie is first and foremost about a correspondent, we should take Stone at his word. For all intents and purposes, *Salvador* is a biography, if not an autobiography, of Richard Boyle given that the real Boyle cowrote the script. The film could have been set anywhere in the world where Cold War geopolitics were in play, and the script would hardly have needed changing. In fact, after *Salvador* was completed, Boyle suggested to Stone that they do a sequel, essentially make the same movie, this time set in Lebanon, revolving around Boyle's time there as a correspondent, and that they title it "Beirut" or "Boyle Goes to Beirut."[24]

One positive aspect of Boyle's centrality to the film is the way in which the frenetic energy embodied by his character mimics the breakneck pace of El Salvador's unfolding civil conflict. Throughout 1980, unprecedented events and new horrors seemed to occur daily in El Salvador, as the nation hurtled down the path to civil war. Purposeful campaigns of terror indeed caused many people throughout the country to be terrified. It was one of the deadliest years in the entire conflict, with upward of one thousand people dying each month, most of them civilians, at the hands of paramilitary death squads or security forces. It was difficult to make sense of anything. The pacing of *Salvador* and the way in which Stone shot the images, often with handheld cameras, and James Woods's capacity to capture Boyle's energy, in both speech and physical movement, effectively project a sense of chaos and impending doom.

Any understanding of *Salvador* has to begin with the collaboration between Boyle and Stone and the extent to which Stone relied on Boyle for information about El Salvador. It is readily apparent that Stone knew little about El Salvador before launching into *Salvador*. He mentions having read Raymond Bonner's *Weakness and Deceit* (1984), but beyond that, it appears that most everything Stone knew about El Salvador came from Boyle. As Stone put it, "having heard only the U.S. media's antirevolutionary reportage from Central America, I was confused, and Boyle suggested we take a two-week trip to the region."[25]

The real Richard Boyle was a complicated person. As Stone describes him, "Richard was a bighearted, well-meaning alcoholic/druggie/Irish whatever."[26] It was his big heart, his eccentricities, and his progressive politics that drew Stone to Boyle. Stone was a Vietnam veteran, and his experiences there turned him against that war and into a broad critic of U.S. Cold War foreign policy. Boyle had been a correspondent in Vietnam who got kicked out of the country twice for involvement in an underground South Vietnamese antiwar movement and for covering U.S. soldiers' opposition to the war.[27] He wrote a book about the subject, entitled *Flower of the Dragon: The Breakdown of the U.S. Army in Vietnam: An Eyewitness Account of the Day-to-Day Environment of American Soldiers in Vietnam*.[28] Boyle then went on to serve as a correspondent in Cambodia, Lebanon, Nicaragua, and El Salvador, where his experiences only reinforced his progressive political views coming out of Vietnam.

Boyle was a good journalist who did some fine reporting throughout his career, including from El Salvador in the late 1970s and early 1980s. But places like El Salvador were just another hot spot for him—a place where the action was, where an exposé-type story or a captivating image could be found. Of course, to be an effective journalist in any of those places, he had to come to know them and understand them, but his commitment to any one of them was fleeting. It is safe to say that his knowledge of El Salvador was broad but limited.

As a person, Boyle was erratic and at times, dysfunctional. By the time he and Stone decided to make *Salvador* in 1984–1985, he was leaning toward the latter. He had no steady job and little money, and he was abusing drugs and alcohol. As Stone once summarized it, "I was amazed he still had a liver."[29] His personal life was a wreck, highlighted most recently by his Italian-born wife leaving him and taking their newborn son with her because of Boyle's inability to support them. Stone's wife despised Boyle, and Alex Ho, Stone's prospective producer, called him a "conman" and considered him a liability to the film. Stone remained loyal to Boyle, in part out of personal friendship but also because without Boyle, there was no film.[30]

STONE IN EL SALVADOR, 1985

Evidence of the limited basis of information about El Salvador that Stone had at his disposal is provided by the outsized role that his two-week trip to El Salvador in 1985 played in shaping the content of *Salvador*. It was, by all indications, Stone's only personal encounter of the country, and little was known about the trip until Stone detailed it in his 2020 memoir. The 1985 trip was a failure, to the extent that Stone had to shoot the film in Mexico. In hindsight, Stone admitted that it was lunacy to think they could shoot a film in a country that was in the middle of a civil war. One of their contacts in the military, Colonel Ricardo Cienfuegos, was murdered by the guerrillas at his tennis club while Boyle and Stone were in the country. If nothing else, the trip allowed Stone to observe Boyle in action, to meet some high-ranking political and military officials, and to see a few sites and cities. Stone covers the trip in just four pages of his memoir, and yet almost every description he provides ended up as a scene in *Salvador*. A few examples will illustrate the broader whole.

The basic premise for *Salvador* mimics the 1985 trip. The movie is Stone's directorial eye tracking Boyle as he maneuvers his way through El Salvador upon returning in 1980 in hopes of rejuvenating his career. Their trip to El Salvador in 1985 is Stone following Boyle around as he returns to El Salvador in hopes of rejuvenating his career as a filmmaker. Boyle's dysfunctionality dominates Stone's account of their 1985 trip, just as Boyle's character and erratic behavior define *Salvador*.

One of the places that Boyle took Stone to in 1985 was Puerto del Diablo (The Devil's Door), a cliff on the outskirts of the capital city of San Salvador from which death squads used to dump their victims. Stone depicted a similar site in *Salvador*, having Boyle and Cassidy go there to take photographs of cadavers. Another experience from their 1985 trip that ended up in the film is their encounter with a military officer at an air force base who did not remember Boyle and did not like talking to reporters. Boyle pulled out a yellowed newspaper article that he had written years earlier that profiled favorably the officer's actions in the 1969 war with Honduras. The officer changed his mind and invited them to dinner. *Salvador* contains a similar scene shortly after Boyle and Dr. Rock arrive in El Salvador.

Another place that Boyle took Stone that ended up in the movie was the port town of La Libertad. It was a recreational visit, but Boyle also wanted to go there to reconnect with his former girlfriend, Maria. Boyle's encounter with the real Maria did not go as well as it did in the movie; she had fled to Guatemala out of fear of being targeted by the security forces. But once again, Stone was tapping the 1985 trip for film content. Not only was Maria with Boyle throughout the film, but he also had Boyle and Dr. Rock drive to La Libertad to reconnect with her early in the film. Even some of the dialogue in *Salvador* came directly from their 1985 trip. When Stone arrived in El Salvador, he met Boyle in the airport and quotes him as saying, "I love this fucking country. No yuppies, no computer checks, you don't need a driver's license. I hate efficient countries!"[31] In *Salvador*, the Boyle character says almost the same thing to Dr. Rock soon after they arrive in El Salvador. Obviously, the 1985 trip to El Salvador affected Stone, but more substantively, that lone, superficial encounter with the country was his only firsthand knowledge of the place and he had to make the most of it.

HISTORICAL INACCURACIES

Salvador is, ultimately, a simple film, full of overdramatizations and obvious in its messaging. One reviewer described it as full of "hysterical excesses."[32] In later interviews, Stone acknowledges this but claims that he did as such on purpose, "in the tradition of agit-prop cinema." He says he knows that some scenes were "a bit overdone" or "a little on the simplistic side" but because the purpose of the film was to deliver a message, he didn't want complex characters or subtle plotlines to get in the way.[33] As he put it in his 2020 memoir, "If this was my last film, which I was now expecting it to be, I did not want it to be, once again, misunderstood."[34] That may well be true. It's also possible that Stone was engaging in historical revisionism to explain away some mediocre filmmaking. Either way, a number of historical inaccuracies result from Stone's choices.

The portrayal of the death-squad dumping ground is one such example. Stone depicted the scene as dozens upon dozens of bodies, in close proximity to one another, laid out in the open air, as far as the eye could see. That is not what Stone saw in 1985 at Puerto del Diablo, and neither was it what any of the death-squad dumping grounds looked like. In the director's comments to the 2001 DVD rerelease, Stone admits that he purposefully overdid the scene as part of his agitprop messaging, saying that he made it "more exaggerated than it was."[35] In Stone's defense, the sentiment expressed by his imagery reflected a broader reality of El Salvador in 1980, when paramilitary death squads killed hundreds, if not thousands, of people, often leaving their victims in public spaces to sow the seeds of terror. But the simple fact remains, Stone purposefully exaggerated the image.

Another example is Archbishop Romero's assassination. Stone has him being shot at point-blank range before a large crowd in the national cathedral just as Romero offers communion to his assassin. Stone places Boyle and Maria right next to the killer after having received communion from Romero. Stone also had Romero delivering his most renowned sermon, or homily, just prior to being killed, the one in which he called upon soldiers to refuse to follow immoral orders. In actuality, Romero delivered that speech days before he was shot, and the site of his assassination was his local parish, the *Divina Providencia*, with almost no one present. He was shot at a distance by an assassin with a rifle leaning out of a car. The real Richard Boyle and his girlfriend were nowhere near the site of the murder when it happened.[36]

Here again, in Stone's defense, he managed to package a lot of events relating to Romero's murder into a single scene, including one of the most notorious episodes in El Salvador at the time, when the military opened fire on mourners in front of the cathedral during Romero's funeral procession. Some of them were forced to climb over one another in search of refuge inside the cathedral. That terrible event happened days after Romero was killed. But Stone drew upon the imagery in the movie by having people climb over one another to get out of the cathedral in the immediate aftermath of Romero's murder. Stone actually used archival footage of the attack in the opening credits to the film to exude a sense of chaotic violence.

Yet another example of historical inaccuracy is the battle scene during the Final Offensive in January 1981. Stone depicts it as a cavalry charge in which horse-mounted guerrilla fighters head directly into the army's tanks and heavy artillery only to be repulsed and lead to the guerrillas' general retreat. In actuality, there was no cavalry charge in the Final Offensive. In his director's commentary on the 2001 DVD rerelease, Stone admits that he fabricated the cavalry charge as his "ode to Westerns." He went on to say that he most liked the "gringo-south-of-the-border Western" and that while he got a little carried away with the cavalry charge, he justified it by saying, "Hey, it's a Western, you can do what you want."[37]

That admission reveals a conceit on the part of Stone to knowingly sacrifice historical accuracy for artistic license. But again, in Stone's defense, the imagery of guerrillas charging into tanks referenced a broader truth about El Salvador's civil war, namely, that it was a highly asymmetrical conflict. Backed by the virtually unlimited resources of the United States, the Salvadoran army always had more firepower than the guerrillas, including total control of the skies through the use of helicopters and fixed-wing gunships. Regardless of one's political views, the Salvadoran guerrillas have to be recognized for their remarkable accomplishments: surviving for twelve years against overwhelming odds, fighting the army to a stalemate, and forcing the Salvadoran government to negotiate an end to the war and agree to various reforms.

CONCLUSION

Anyone who has an interest in El Salvador and is sympathetic toward Oliver Stone's political views should be grateful that he made *Salvador*. He did so at great personal cost and professional risk, and despite the film's flaws and limitations, it raised awareness internationally about El Salvador's civil war. However, Stone's ambition was to make a name for himself in Hollywood and to build a career as a film director. Understanding the nuances of a tragedy like El Salvador's civil war and perhaps allowing it to challenge one's preconceived notions were tangential. Ultimately, Salvador is less about El Salvador and more about Richard Boyle and Oliver Stone's views on U.S.

foreign policy. Whatever image or meaning comes out of the film will forever be defined by those constraints.

ADDITIONAL RESOURCES

Almeida, Paul. *Waves of Protest: Popular Struggle in El Salvador, 1925–2005.* Minneapolis: University of Minnesota Press, 2008.

Byrne, Hugh. *El Salvador's Civil War: A Study of Revolution.* Boulder, CO: Lynne Rienner, 1996.

Chávez, Joaquín. *Poets and Prophets of the Resistance: Intellectuals and the Origins of El Salvador's Civil War.* New York: Oxford University Press, 2017.

Ching, Erik. *Stories of Civil War in El Salvador: A Battle over Memory.* Chapel Hill: University of North Carolina Press, 2016.

D'Haeseleer, Brian. *The Salvadoran Crucible: The Failure of U.S. Counterinsurgency in El Salvador, 1979–1992.* Lawrence: University Press of Kansas, 2017.

Danner, Mark. *The Massacre at El Mozote.* New York: Vintage, 1994.

Gorkin, Michael, and Marta Pineda. *From Beneath the Volcano: The Story of a Salvadoran Campesino and His Family.* Tucson: University of Arizona Press, 2011.

Gould, Jeffery L., and Aldo Lauria-Santiago. *To Rise in Darkness: Revolution, Repression and Memory in El Salvador, 1920–1932.* Durham, NC: Duke University Press, 2008.

LaFeber, Walter. "Salvador." In *Oliver Stone's USA: Film, History, and Controversy,* edited by Robert Brent Toplin, 93–109. Lawrence: University Press of Kansas, 2000.

Pyes, Craig. *Salvadoran Rightists: The Deadly Patriots.* Albuquerque: Albuquerque Journal, 1983.

Stone, Oliver. *Chasing the Light: Writing, Directing, and Surviving* Platoon, Midnight Express, Scarface, Salvador, *and the Movie Game.* Boston: Houghton Mifflin Harcourt, 2020.

Viterna, Jocelyn. *Women in War: The Micro-Processes of Mobilization in El Salvador.* New York: Oxford University Press, 2015.

NOTES

1. Tommie Sue Montgomery, *Revolution in El Salvador: From Civil Strife to Civil Peace,* second ed. (Boulder, CO: Westview Press, 1995); Hugh Byrne, *El Salvador's Civil War: A Study of Revolution* (Boulder, CO: Lynne Rienner, 1996); and Erik Ching, *Stories of Civil War in El Salvador: A Battle over Memory* (Chapel Hill: University of North Carolina Press, 2016).

2. Oliver Stone, *Chasing the Light: Writing, Directing, and Surviving* Platoon, Midnight Express, Scarface, Salvador, *and the Movie Game* (Boston: Houghton Miflin, 2020), 237.

3. Stone, *Chasing the Light*, 206.

4. Ian Scott and Henry Thompson, *The Cinema of Oliver Stone: Art, Authorship and Activism* (Manchester University Press, 2016), 80–83; and Stone, *Chasing the Light*, 314–16.

5. Stone, *Chasing the Light*, 330; and Scott and Thompson, *The Cinema of Oliver Stone*, 40–41.

6. Robert White, as quoted in the documentary *Into the Valley of Death*. See also, Raymond Bonner, *Weakness and Deceit: U.S. Policy and El Salvador* (New York: Times Books, 1984), 240. However, some form of economic assistance was released on January 14. See Theresa Keeley, *Reagan's Gun-Toting Nuns: The Catholic Conflict Over Cold War Human Rights Policy in Central America* (Ithaca, NY: Cornell University Press, 2020), chapter 4.

7. Stone, *Chasing the Light*, 254–55.

8. Stone, *Chasing the Light*, 255.

9. On 1932, see Jeffery L. Gould and Aldo Lauria-Santiago, *To Rise in Darkness: Revolution, Repression and Memory in El Salvador, 1920–1932* (Durham, NC: Duke University Press, 2008); and Héctor Lindo Fuentes, Erik Ching, and Rafael Lara Martínez, *Remembering a Massacre in El Salvador: The Insurrection of 1932, Roque Dalton and the Politics of Historical Memory* (Albuquerque: University of New Mexico Press, 2007).

10. On the right's use of 1932, see Ching, *Stories of Civil War*, chapter 2.

11. Philip Williams and Knut Walter, *Militarization and Demilitarization in El Salvador's Transition to Democracy* (Pittsburgh: University of Pittsburgh Press, 1997); and William Stanley, *The Protection Racket State: Elite Politics, Military Extortion and Civil War in El Salvador* (Philadelphia: Temple University Press, 1996).

12. While imperfect, the United Nations Truth Commission remains the foundational standard for documenting the disproportionate responsibility for deaths and human rights violations during the war. See United Nations, Commission on the Truth for El Salvador, *From Madness to Hope: The Twelve-Year War in El Salvador* (New York: United Nations Security Council, 1993). For scholarly analyses that address the historiographical landscape of El Salvador's civil war and demonstrate that Stone's interpretation is consistent with the scholarly consensus, see Joaquín Chávez, *Poets and Prophets of the Resistance: Intellectuals and the Origins of El Salvador's Civil War* (New York: Oxford University Press, 2017); Leigh Binford, "Peasants, Catechists and Revolutionaries: Organic Intellectuals in the Salvadoran Revolution, 1980–1992," in *Landscapes of Struggle: Politics, Society, and Community in El Salvador*, ed. Aldo Lauria-Santiago and Leigh Binford (Pittsburgh: University of Pittsburgh Press, 2004), 105–25; and Ching, *Stories of Civil War in El Salvador*.

13. Bonner, *Weakness and Deceit*. On El Mozote, see Mark Danner, *The Massacre at El Mozote* (New York: Vintage, 1994); and Leigh Binford, *The El Mozote Massacre: Human Rights and Global Implications*, rev. ed. (Tucson: University of Arizona Press, 2016).

14. On the complexity of U.S. involvement in El Salvador, before and during its civil war, see Brian D'Haeseleer, *The Salvadoran Crucible: The Failure of U.S.*

Counterinsurgency in El Salvador, 1979–1992 (Lawrence: University Press of Kansas, 2017).

15. Keeley, *Reagan's Gun-Toting Nuns*, chapter 4.

16. Raymond Bonner, "The Diplomat and the Killer," *The Atlantic*, February 11, 2016, accessed October 4, 2021, https://www.theatlantic.com/international/archive/2016/02/el-salvador-churchwomen-murders/460320/.

17. On this notion of heroic journalists, see Brian McNair, "Journalists at War," *Journalism Practice* 5, no. 4 (2011): 492.

18. Oliver Stone, et al., *Salvador*. Special widescreen ed. Santa Monica, CA: MGM Home Entertainment, 2001. DVD.

19. On the death squad list and the murder of the Dutch journalists, see Warren Hoge, "4 Dutch Newsmen Slain on a Trip to Film Guerrillas in El Salvador," *New York Times*, March 19, 1982, accessed August 20, 2021, https://www.nytimes.com/1982/03/19/world/4-dutch-newsmen-slain-on-a-trip-to-film-guerrillas-in-el-salvador.html.

20. On this issue of Boyle's evolution throughout the film, see William Pace, "Salvador: A Personal Cinema," *Creative Screenwriting* (Fall 1996): 83–109.

21. For a similar interpretation, see Walter LaFeber, "*Salvador*," in *Oliver Stone's USA: Film, History, and Controversy*, ed. Robert Brent Toplin, 93–109 (Lawrence: University Press of Kansas, 2000).

22. *Los Angeles Daily News*, March 26, 1986; see also the liner notes to Stone, *Salvador*.

23. David Ansen, "Oh, What an Ugly War," *Newsweek*, September 9, 1985, 89.

24. Stone, *Chasing the Light*, 250.

25. Stone, *Chasing the Light*, 207.

26. Stone, *Chasing the Light*, 214.

27. Mike Ward, "Escaping the Shadow of the Silver Screen: 'Salvador' Portrayal Dogs Screenwriter in Bid for Assembly Seat," *Los Angeles Times*, September 5, 1988, accessed June 15, 2021, https://www.latimes.com/archives/la-xpm-1988-09-15-ga-2882-story.html.

28. Richard Boyle, *Flower of the Dragon: The Breakdown of the U.S. Army in Vietnam: An Eyewitness Account of the Day-to-Day Environment of American Soldiers in Vietnam* (San Francisco: Ramparts Press, 1972).

29. Stone, *Chasing the Light*, 213.

30. Stone, *Chasing the Light*, 209–12.

31. Stone, *Chasing the Light*, 209.

32. David Kehr, *Movies That Mattered: More Reviews from a Transformative Decade* (Chicago: University of Chicago Press, 2017), 199.

33. Stone, *Salvador*.

34. Stone, *Chasing the Light*, 254.

35. Stone, *Salvador*.

36. Matt Eisenbrandt, *Assassination of a Saint: The Plot to Murder Óscar Romero and the Quest to Bring His Killers to Justice* (Berkeley: University of California Press, 2017); and Carlos Dada, "How We Killed Archbishop Romero," *El Faro*, March 25, 2010, accessed July 8, 2021, https://elfaro.net/es/201003/noticias/1416/

How-we-killed-Archbishop-Romero.htm. For an analysis of how the truncation of these events functions cinematographically, see Robert Rosenstone, *History on Film/Film on History* (New York: Routledge, 2004), 111–12.

37. Stone, *Salvador*; and Stone, *Chasing the Light*, 247.

Chapter 14

The Dancer Upstairs and the Hunt for Sendero Luminoso's Presidente Gonzalo

Susan Elizabeth Ramírez

The Dancer Upstairs *(2002): produced by Andrés Vicente Gómez and John Malkovich; directed by John Malkovich; screenplay by Nicholas Shakespeare, based on his novel; color; 132 minutes; Fox Searchlight Pictures and Lolafilms. Detective Agustín Rejas (Javier Bardem) searches for the elusive leader of a revolutionary organization similar to Peru's Shining Path.*

As a tourist destination, Peru captures a person's imagination with pictures of the quaint red-tile roofs and narrow lanes of highland Cuzco and the sculpted ruins of nearby Machu Picchu; the brightly colored tropical birds of the jungle sanctuary of Manu; the enormous anonymous depictions of a monkey, a bird, and a stylized "alien" outlined in stone on the coastal plains of Nazca; and the Pacific surfing beaches of Máncora. But behind these images is the stark reality that Peru is a country divided, divided by culture between the sophisticated Spanish-speaking populations of the major cities and the Quechua- and Aymará-speaking rural-living, farming, and herding natives. Even geography works against unity—from the Pacific coastal plain that narrows toward the south, the ragged Andean mountain highlands, and the eastern jungles. Peru's populations are also segregated economically, divided by wealth and income inequality. In 1980 the per capita annual income of Peru's 17.5 million people was $1,033, but 28.3% of the population lived in "extreme poverty." Life was especially hard for the third of the country who lived in rural areas, especially in the south-central departments of Ayacucho, Apurimac, and Huancavelica.

These three jurisdictions were listed as Peru's neediest departments. All three in the 1970s were isolated with a population of largely uneducated peasants and farmers. They earned little cash, existed without basic human services, remained constantly malnourished, and died young. In Ayacucho alone, 50.8% of the population lived in absolute destitution.[1]

Such conditions invited resentment, protest, and even insurrection. They provide the backdrop and context for scenes in the movie *The Dancer Upstairs*, produced and directed by John Malkovich. To understand better the unfolding story, this essay will, first, provide a short biographical sketch of Manuel Rubén Abimael Guzmán Reynoso (Esequiel in the movie), the mastermind and founder of the Sendero Luminoso (Shining Path) Movement and the leader of the ensuing conflict, before outlining his violent strategy to remake Peruvian society. Finally, I will flesh out the counterinsurgency efforts of the Peruvian state depicted in the film in its efforts to hunt Guzmán and to end Sendero's strategic use of violence.

MANUEL RUBÉN ABIMAEL GUZMÁN REYNOSO

For a philosophy professor at San Cristóbal de Huamanga University in Ayacucho, such overwhelming conditions seemed ripe for the launch of a movement against a corrupt state that had long systematically discriminated against the rural poor, made up mainly of Quechua-speaking indigenous peoples, in the south-central departments. Guzmán, born in 1934 in the village of Tambo, near Mollendo, a port town in the province of Islay, in the Department of Ayacucho, was the son of Abimael Guzmán and Berenice Reynoso. He studied at the Colegio de La Salle, a private Catholic secondary school and at age nineteen entered the National University of San Agustin in Arequipa, majoring in law and philosophy. His dissertation was titled "The Kantian Theory of Space and the Bourgeois Democratic State." After graduating, he was recruited as a professor at the University of San Cristóbal in 1962. It had reopened in 1959, after being closed for seventy years, as a progressive institution redesigned for rural education.[2] The university offered vocational training to increase employment (in such areas as nursing, education, and rural engineering), but jobs rarely materialized for graduates in the remote area. Blessed with charisma and an appealing message, Guzmán attracted a strong, disciplined, and motivated following among students and some faculty. In those early years, his students called him "shampoo" because he could wash your brain and make everything crystal clear. At the university he met and married (in 1964) the daughter of a local Communist Party leader, Agusta de la Torre. This union lasted until her mysterious death in 1988. In the 1960s, he also made three trips to China during the "cultural revolution," where he claimed to have met Mao and learned how to use explosives.[3]

In 1970, Guzmán founded a left-wing extremist party called the Red Flag, based on the teachings of Peruvian José Carlos Mariategui (1894–1930), who espoused a peasant-based nationalist-Marxism and founded Peru's Socialist Party, and Mao Zedong, who taught that political power must be gained through violence. Guzmán separated from the university in 1975 and went underground to organize and spread his ideas—that, parroting Mao, only through uninterrupted revolutionary violence could change be achieved. His Red Flag adherents—young farmers, university students, artists, and upper middle-class youth—joined him. He indoctrinated and trained them for guerrilla warfare. His goal was to forge a peasant army from people who were marginal and exploited to renew the state and society and establish a "new democracy" through waging a "people's war." Through a Marxist-Maoist insurgency, he would create a dictatorship of the proletariat by introducing a cultural revolution. His teachings came to be called "Gonzalo thought," after his nom de guerre "Presidente [or Comrada] Gonzalo" (Presidente Esequiel in the movie).[4]

SENDERO LUMINOSO'S STRATEGIES

Guzmán deemed 1980 as an auspicious time to begin his movement's activities. He wanted to tap local grievances over corruption and injustices and use the discontent as a basis from which to unseat the Peruvian government and its abuses. By then, the movement had taken the name of the Partido Comunista del Perú en el Sendero Luminoso de José Carlos Mariategui (Communist Party of Peru on the Shining Path of José Carlos Mariategui), or Sendero Luminoso, for short. Its philosophy evolved into a hybrid mix of Stalinism, Maoism, and Guzmán's own ideas. One scholar described it as an "opaque assemblage of revolutionary thought," which was poorly understood by low-ranking party members (Senderistas), academics, and Peru's counterrevolutionary forces. Guzmán was convinced that "to kill gave life, that war brought peace, [and] that the most extreme tyranny brought the greatest freedom." Violence promised a renewal and the cleansing of society. Guzmán talked about a "quota," or the sacrifice in lives and blood, that the insurgency would have to make to achieve its ends.[5]

The premiere Sendero Luminoso action occurred on May 17, 1980, when hooded Senderistas burned ballot boxes for national elections in the Ayacuchan village of Chuschi as a protest against the democratic process. Thereafter, to gain local support, it also engaged in vigilante justice against cattle rustlers, corrupt community officials, delinquents, and unfaithful spouses. By 1981,

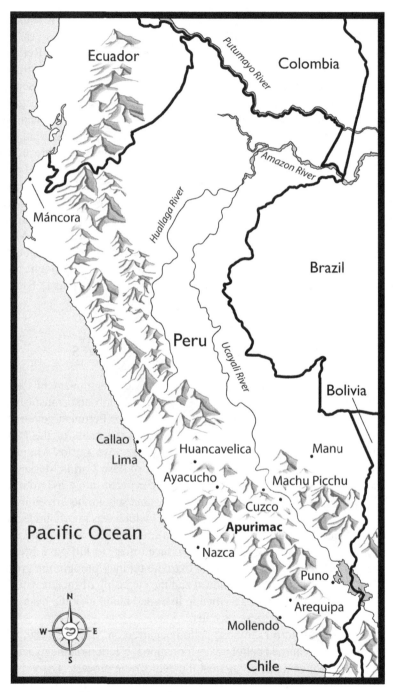

Figure 14.1: Map of Peru. (SEH Mapping)

Sendero Luminoso was attacking banks, mines, government buildings, and police posts. The latter yielded the movement arms and explosives. In early 1982, Sendero Luminoso took over the Ayacucho jail, freeing three hundred prisoners.[6] In April 1983, Senderistas captured the village of Lucanamarca and massacred its seventy residents for not accepting Sendero overtures. They also targeted government functionaries to create a political vacuum and weaken state hold on localities, thus offering respite to the local peasantry. They established something approaching "liberated areas" in Ayacucho and its hinterland between 1980 and 1982. By the mid-1980s, Sendero was targeting foreigners, including professionals, missionaries (represented by the priest in the movie), relief workers, and tourists.[7]

Sendero expanded in rural areas. Children (particularly those between twelve and fifteen years of age) were kidnapped and indoctrinated with "Gonzalo thought." They were compelled to memorize tenets of this "thought" and learn a Maoist hymn in Chinese, syllable by syllable. They were trained in small-unit tactics, the use of explosives, and other aspects of guerrilla warfare. Before being vetted into the insurgent ranks, new members were required to kill a public official, a village leader, or a policeman. But such recruitment fostered resentment and alienated significant sectors of the peasantry throughout the decade of the 1980s.[8]

Sendero Luminoso operated in small (twenty to thirty combatants), disciplined and highly motivated units. Its leaders were mostly in their twenties and thirties. They gathered intelligence and planned operations in the field against government installations, especially electric towers, bridges, and agricultural stations. They used traditional native skills, such as slingshots, which boys used to herd animals in the highlands, to fling dynamite at targets. They also hung dead dogs from light poles, an ancient Inca warning sign, to notify natives of an impending Sendero attack. Since Inca times, dead dogs were buried with the deceased to help lead them across a river to the next life. They slaughtered peasant herds to disrupt the economy. Their goal was to destroy the infrastructure and disrupt agriculture to cut the capital off from the rest of Peru, their "strangle cities" strategy. By mid-1983, they had begun to surround, isolate, and starve Lima. They also destroyed pylons to cut power and blackout the lights.[9]

These activities were carried out by the Presidente Gonzalo–created Ejército Guerrillero Popular (EGP [the Popular Guerrilla Army]), formalized in 1983 as the military arm of the party. Combatants were ruthless, sometimes using peasants as shields in their confrontations with the army or marines. This formalization only increased the killings and reprisals. The movement also tried to decrease agricultural production to a subsistence level, destroy processing plants, and slaughter cattle and alpacas to limit sales. Acreage decreased drastically. In Ayacucho alone, cultivated land dropped from 136,000 hectares in 1980 to 53,000 in 1985.[10]

Until 1986, the military had better weapons than the Senderistas, who relied on seizing and stealing firearms from police outposts. In 1987, however, Sendero forged an alliance with drug traffickers of the Upper Huallaga Valley on the eastern flanks of the Andes Mountains, where coca leaf (and coffee in the movie) was grown on large plantations. Thereafter, Sendero Luminoso generated revenue and received training from the narcotics dealers who operated there in return for providing protection. In this way, Sendero did not have to rely on foreign sources for funding. Sendero Luminoso acquired AK-47 automatic rifles and rocket launchers, which enabled them, subsequently, to step up their hit-and-run tactics. Their highly successful ambushes of state patrols were aided by their arms and knowledge of the mountainous terrain and back roads. They also functioned well in the thin air of the extreme altitudes of the Andes Mountains.[11]

At the same time, Sendero began to expand into the cities. They targeted the "*pueblos jovenes*" (literally, "young towns"; also, *barriadas*, or shantytowns) surrounding Lima, in particular the Villa El Salvador, home to 260,000 inhabitants, adjacent to Lima, on the south. They recruited in Lima's universities and shantytowns before the people were fully aware of Sendero's ideology and intentions. Sendero Luminoso infiltrated local councils and women's clubs and participated in land invasions. As they initially did in the highlands, Sendero gained sympathy by eliminating thieves and other wrongdoers. Such activities were part of Guzmán's plan to bring the "people's war" to the capital. Terror then replaced collaboration.[12]

In 1990, Guzmán ordered assassinations and bombings in Villa El Salvador and later in metropolitan Lima itself. Lima by then was plagued by street crime because of the police assassinations carried out by the insurgents. In the 1990s, Lima was one of the most dangerous cities in the world. A U.S. Embassy confidential cable, dated February 13, 1991, noted that Sendero had bombed the U.S. ambassador's residence and seventeen banks in and around Lima and burned five buses. They also seized trucks and distributed the contents to the poor in places like El Agustino, a pueblo joven.[13]

In 1992, Sendero initiated a series of blasts and sabotage in the capital and its port city of Callao. Police stations, radio broadcasting facilities, and military housing were targets. Simultaneously, Sendero operatives were selectively assassinating people to intimidate residents of poorer neighborhoods. One particularly gruesome murder in February 1992 was that of Maria Elena Moyano, elected deputy mayor in 1989 and former president of the Women's Federation of the Villa of El Salvador, a moderate, very popular leader, who was killed in front of her children. Then, the rebel operatives stuffed her body with explosives and blew it up. Her remains were left in public view.

This type of tactic reflected the traditional Andean belief that an unmutilated victim's spirit could reveal its killers. Months later, on May 22, 1992, a van loaded with three hundred to five hundred kilograms of dynamite exploded at a commercial shopping center in the upper-class neighborhood of San Isidro, killing one and wounding thirteen. About two weeks later, on June 5, a truck bomb carrying six hundred kilograms of explosives demolished a television station, killing five and wounding thirty. Less than a week later, a car bomb with 250 kilograms of explosives destroyed the Bolivian Embassy in San Isidro, injuring fifteen. A car bombing in the Lima seaside suburb of Miraflores killed twenty-five and injured as many as 250 in mid-July. An entire city block was leveled: 183 residences, 400 businesses, and 62 parked cars were destroyed. Evidence of the escalating chaos were the 116 strikes in Lima that left 173 dead in August 1992 alone.[14]

COUNTERINSURGENCY

But the government was not sitting on its hands. Guzmán suffered from psoriasis, which was made worse by the dry highland air, so he moved to the coast, alongside his trusted lieutenants, to a number of safe houses in Lima where he could monitor better the urban terror campaign. This move violated his early Maoist strategy and eventually exposed him and his leadership cadre to capture.[15]

The military gave up power at the national level in July 1980 after a military coup under left-leaning General Juan Velasco Alvarado (1968–1975) had implemented a highly theoretical but less effective agrarian reform, mainly on the coast, which was mostly undone by his successor right-leaning General Francisco Morales Bermúdez (1975–1980). Twelve years of rule exhausted and disheartened the military, as they called elections for a return to civilian rule.[16]

The Servicio de Inteligencia Nacional (SIN, National Intelligence Service) had noted reports of a potential guerrilla campaign planned for Ayacucho as early as 1977. Little was done with the information of seemingly unassociated assassinations here, a blast there, and a robbery elsewhere, as attention was focused on overseeing the transition back to democracy. At the outbreak of Sendero Luminoso activities, President Fernando Belaúnde Terry (1980–1985) could look away no more. He dispatched the Guardia Civil (Civil Guard, police) against them. Counterinsurgency units, called the Sinchis (after the highly visible military operatives who fought for the Incas), battled Sendero but were poorly trained and had little access to intelligence in late 1980 and 1981. Their solution was to use vicious tactics against Sendero or those who they assumed were followers. Army patrols at times looted, lived off the land, stole peasants' possessions, and killed those who protested, including women. These human rights abuses against many innocent peasants resulted in a loss of their potential support. In other words, Sinchi tactics backfired. Instead of gaining the sympathy and support of the rural population, such tactics alienated them and helped Sendero recruit.[17]

On December 27, 1982, Belaúnde began to take Sendero more seriously and escalated his response. He was forced to call in the armed forces to try to defeat the rebels. The military embarked on a "scorched earth" campaign to prove to the peasants that the state was stronger than Presidente Gonzalo's forces. Therefore, the rural population should support the government. The result was a series of well-documented massacres. An ex–Minister of War, General Luis Cisneros, declared that "If to kill 2 or 3 Senderistas it is necessary to kill 80 innocents, then it does not matter. . . . The peasants have to decide where they wish to die: with Sendero or the armed forces." The toll of dead during Belaúnde's term reached six thousand. The overall result of heightened military assaults was to further increase the resentment of the highland population from what they perceived as an invading army from the coast.[18]

Belaúnde's successor, Alan García, president from 1985 to 1990, tried to undercut Guzmán by encouraging the military and police to respect human rights. He initiated an anticorruption campaign and granted some economic aid. These efforts garnered some successes. But he also allowed levels of state-perpetrated violence to increase. In July 1991, a leaked document, cited by Taylor, confirmed that the armed forces were operating under a "shoot to kill" policy. By the end of García's term, more than twenty thousand casualties had been registered, and damages were estimated at $14 billion, while inflation registered 1,000,000% and workers' real wages dropped by two thirds and employees' salaries, by 50%.[19]

Meanwhile, during the Belaúnde and García administrations, economic mismanagement and corruption within the civil service and political class visibly increased, while living standards, foreign investment, and tourism declined. David Scott Palmer provides some telling statistics. From 1976 to the mid-1980s, with the exception 1979–1981, net economic growth was negative, wage settlements fell behind the cost of living, and inflation rates increased from a 20%–30% range to a 75%–125% range. Infant mortality increased, while caloric intake decreased. Such conditions impacted the lower strata of the population especially hard.[20]

The economic crisis, lack of political leadership, and social ills only added to Sendero's ability to recruit. Therefore, from 1983 to 1992, guerrilla activity spread to the departments of Cuzco and Puno to the south, the Upper Huallaga Valley to the east, Junin and surrounding departments in the central highlands, and Cajabamba-Huamachuco and Ancash in the northern mountains. On the coast, rebels moved into the Chancay and Cañete Valleys, north and south, respectively, from Lima. In 1981, under Belaúnde, six provinces were declared in a state of emergency; by December 1989, under García, the figure rose to fifty-six. In 1985, Sendero was entrenched in nineteen of Peru's twenty-four departments. By 1991, Sendero Luminoso was active in all but three.[21]

Whereas Belaúnde had initially responded with the Sinchis, whose unchained violence disaffected the peasantry, and García's "shoot to kill" policies were ineffectual or backfired, Presidente Alberto Fujimori (1990–2000), a former director of the National Agrarian University, moved to grant the military forces a freer hand, which resulted in a new level of street violence, repression, cruelty, and sometimes, indiscriminate counterinsurgency campaigns. Each passing year of Sendero Luminoso's operations deepened the economic crisis and psychological insecurities throughout the country. In the month of February 1992, Sendero bombed the ambassador's residence in Lima, killing three guards. In April 1992, as Lima faced daily water shortages and cuts to electric power and Sendero Luminoso rebels were closing in on Lima, Fujimori, to rule more effectively, he declared, dissolved the Judiciary and Congress in what he called a self-coup (or *auto golpe*) or a *dicta blanda* (a soft dictatorship), replacing them with new institutions and writing a new constitution. Peru suffered "near chaos" as a result of corruption, hyperinflation, mass migration to the cities, and panic emigration of those who could afford it. But these developments also undermined the Peruvian government's legitimacy at home and abroad and allowed Sendero Luminoso to recast its struggles as a fight against dictatorship. The George H. W. Bush administration (1989–1993) cut aid to Peru but allowed a covert CIA operation against Sendero's efforts to continue.[22]

It was in these years, too, that the peasantry who loathed Sendero Luminoso mobilized against it. Although thousands had fled the countryside for the relative safety of the cities, some peasants, reluctant to leave their homes and fields, stayed behind and refashioned an old institution, originally designed to capture rustlers. They formed self-defense committees (*rondas campesinas*) against the insurgents. One of the first was established in the Apurimac Valley, where forty-eight communities united to defend themselves. They were eventually armed and given training. In December 1985, eighty-five participating villages received two hundred hunting rifles, some cash, and tractors from President García himself. News spread. More rondas were established in Huanta, Huancavelica, Puno, and the Mantaro Valley. They became an effective deterrent against Sendero Luminoso's rural operations and provided the state with welcome intelligence. The consequence was another push of Senderistas into the cities.[23]

The Dancer Upstairs

Malkovich's political thriller begins in this phase of the struggle at a rented house at 459 First Street in a quiet middle-class area in the Surquillo neighborhood, where (in the movie) the daughter of a police detective involved in the hunt for Guzmán takes dance lessons from an attractively slender, dark-haired teacher. Two separate investigative units were, at the time, searching for the elusive Presidente Gonzalo and his partisans. One was led by the DINCOTE, the government anti-terrorist police, known for its harsh methods. They used torture, beatings, shock, and dunking people in cold water. One U.S. official who served in Lima admitted that it was not high tech but "nothing real useful either." DINCOTE agents were not always on the up-and-up and trustworthy. Some had posed as terrorists themselves, kidnapping and ransoming victims.[24]

At this juncture in 1991, the Bush administration increasingly worried that Sendero Luminoso would take over in Peru. Bernard Arenson, Bush's assistant secretary of state for Latin America, read reports on Sendero Luminoso's brutality. He urged the clandestine division of the CIA to get involved. As the situation deteriorated and Sendero Luminoso controlled more and more of the population in an ever-tightening noose around Lima, the CIA decided to become more active by aiding the government forces. It sent a CIA agent, nicknamed by his Peruvian collaborators as "Superman" for his tall build, dark hair, and uncanny resemblance to Christopher Reeve (Clark Kent in the Superman movies). He and allied agents traveled to Peru to train, equip, finance, and coach the Peruvian police. In addition, they provided them with vehicles and translated captured documents.[25]

Eventually, the CIA set up an "academy" at DINCOTE headquarters to teach personnel how to analyze, cross-reference, and classify documents. The CIA joined Britain's Scotland Yard to instruct agents on how to conduct surveillance in disguise—as street money changers, fruit vendors, and even a homeless schizophrenic. They stood behind two-way mirrors to watch police interrogate suspects, then advised them on their technique.[26]

The second investigative unit was led by an idealistic policeman, Major Benedicto Jiménez (who is called Agustín Rejas in the movie), who was leading a middle-class life with his trendy wife and daughter (Laura in the movie). He was the son of an Afro-Peruvian father and a Greek immigrant mother. He trained as a detective and army commando. In the late 1980s, he had worked in joint operations with the U.S. Drug Enforcement Administration. In March 1990, he formed a special unit to capture the leaders of Sendero Luminoso. He advocated using old-fashioned means: tailing suspects, stakeouts, cultivating informants, and poring over captured documents. Torture was not mentioned. At the beginning, Jiménez operated out of a tiny office;

his efforts were understaffed, and he had almost no budget. (Note that the detective seemed always short of cash in the movie.) DINCOTE personnel were hostile and derisive.[27]

Jiménez asked the CIA for help, but they demurred until he showed them a captured video of Guzmán, dancing to the music of *Zorba the Greek*. Then, the CIA gave Jiménez gear: telephoto cameras, listening devices, night-vision goggles, and a video camera that could be concealed in a briefcase. The agency also rented cars so that suspects could be followed from a variety of vehicles. The CIA even provided cash to buy meals for the underpaid agents, who earned little for their twelve-to-fifteen-hour shifts. All this cost about $5,000 per month.[28]

Fujimori's government also helped. Jiménez's unit was increased to eighty-two members by mid-1992. The president's advisor and de facto head of intelligence, Vladimiro Montesinos, who favored repressive tactics, began giving Jiménez $500 per month in early 1992, along with two video cameras. He also promised Jiménez two cars if he would hire four military intelligence analysts. They reported, it was soon learned, back to Montesinos, so Jiménez fired them and Montesinos stopped his aid. The four analysts, it turned out, made up an army intelligence death squad, called the Colina Group. Fujimori and Montesinos plotted to keep any arrest secret to be able to execute Guzmán extrajudicially.[29]

Jiménez's measures helped turn the tide against Sendero Luminoso. By the middle of June 1990, the Sendero general headquarters and temporary residence of Guzmán had been discovered. War plans and other documents were captured. In another residence at 459 Calle 2 (Second Street), Urbanización Ramon Castilla, in Monterrico Norte, an exclusive residential neighborhood in Lima, police found electoral documents used to make false identification papers and ten tons of propaganda. Guzmán, it was determined, had been there within the last two weeks. He left behind prescription glasses, medicine for his persistent psoriasis, and a wig. There and in five more safe houses used by Sendero Luminoso, authorities captured over two dozen members, including Elvira Nila Zamabria, a psychologist and Sendero's general secretary of press and propaganda; Carlos Manuel Torres Mendoza, an engineer who was in charge of the Movimiento Revolucionario de Defensa del Pueblo (Revolutionary Movement to Defend the People); Sybila Arredondo, a member of Sendero's Central Committee; and Delia Navidad Taquiri, an important political and military leader of Lima operations.[30]

In mid-1992, Sendero exploded twenty-two car bombs that claimed over a thousand casualties. An armed strike (*paro armado*) of seven thousand public buses paralyzed Lima. Truck bombs destroyed Canal 2, a television station, and a bridge. The central highway linking Lima with the highlands was bombed and closed. During these bloody emergencies, the police raided a Lima college, arresting several members of the Sendero Luminoso Central Committee and finding computers and diskettes full of information on their plans.[31]

Meanwhile, Jiménez identified more hideouts and arrested other members, including a sociologist, a teacher, a medical doctor, a diesel mechanic, and a journalist for the national newspaper, *La República*. Guzmán had not been seen in public for a number of years, fueling rumors among the populace that he was everywhere. Jiménez found proof that Guzmán was alive. He learned that Sendero Luminoso's logistics and financial chief was in the capital. Tailing him led to other conspirators. Peruvian police arrested him on June 22, 1992. He confessed that Guzmán was in Lima, living in a rented house at 459 First Street, Urbanización Los Sauces, Surquillo.[32]

There are several stories about the hideaway on First Street, where Guzmán and his associates would eventually be taken. One story relates that the dancer, Maritza Garrido Lecca Risco, Yolanda in the movie, bought the house. More often, other testimonies claim that either she or her architect boyfriend, Carlos Inchástegui, rented the house. She taught contemporary and classical dance on the first floor and rented the second floor to a certain Rayda Oscate, actually Elena Iparraguirre, member of the Permanent Committee and future wife of Guzmán. Maritza was from a well-off family and twenty-seven years old when arrested. She was born in Lima's seaport of Callao in 1965 and became one of the most recognized dancers in the nation. It is reported that she came in contact with Sendero Luminoso through an aunt, Nelly Marión Evans Risco, a former nun who herself had been recruited by Sendero Luminoso while she was a teacher in the capital. At the time of Evans's arrest in 1991, her apartment was full of Senderistas.[33]

When Surquillo was identified as the possible location of Guzmán, the neighborhood was saturated by undercover agents, some posing as street sweepers, meter readers, itinerant vendors, and adolescent lovers. The young male architect and his girlfriend, the attractive dance instructor, were the home's only visible occupants. But the undercover investigators led by Jiménez noticed that the dancer bought a lot of bread, too much for two people to eat. Sanitation workers (represented by Sargeant Sucre in the film), who combed through the garbage left on the street for pickup, found evidence that told other stories. Five different types of hair had been discarded. The rubbish contained packaging and cigarette butts, which revealed that someone inside was smoking Winston Lights, Guzmán's preferred brand. It also contained wrappers for medicine for psoriasis, which Superman identified as a Swedish ointment for the scaly condition. The investigators got the government to restrict the sale of the medicine used by Guzmán to only two pharmacies, and they recorded who bought it. Superman also identified the discarded labels of Absolut Vodka, known to be Guzmán's drink. Fish bones suggested that someone, like Guzmán, was on a low-fat diet. Chicken bones pointed to Guzmán's favorite dinner. Also, one night, an agent thought he saw Guzmán's profile outlined in shadow behind the curtains of the upstairs apartment.[34]

Finally, on September 12, 1992, some visitors knocked on the door of the house, and Jiménez, trusting his gut feeling, ordered the raid. Agents barged in after them. They found a middle-aged man with a salt and pepper scraggly beard and thick glasses who walked with a limp and suffered from psoriasis, known by then to be the elusive and even legendary figure of *"Puka Inti"* (Red Sun), aka Presidente Gonzalo to his adherents (also notorious as the fourth Sword of Communism and heir to Marx, Lenin, and Mao) or known as the exterminator and monster according to President Fujimori.[35] Other top people arrested that night included Elena Iparraguierre Revoredo (also known as Miriam and future wife of Guzmán), María Pantoja Sánchez (a lawyer, known as Julia), and Laura Zambrano Padilla (code named comarada Meche, a one-time leader of actions in Lima). All the occupants were taken into custody with no resistance, other than some shouting of Sendero Luminoso slogans. Guzmán stayed calm, noting that although he might die, his "thought" would survive. Rejas called a press conference to publicize the interdiction so that clandestine agents of the Fujimori government could not murder the detainees and make them "disappear."[36]

When police radioed headquarters that Guzmán had been nabbed, Superman was there to hear the news and join the celebration. The U.S.

Figure 14.2: "Finally, we captured President Gonzalo." (Photofest)

government found out before the Peruvian president or his intelligence chief Montesinos did. DINCOTE's General Antonio Vidal Herrera, an intelligence officer trained in Russia and the United States who had been appointed by Montesinos to head the unit, rushed to the house with two highly appreciated bottles of whiskey to commemorate the date. They found papers and compact discs with plans for a huge October surprise offensive planned against Lima. In the following days, two hundred more Senderistas were arrested. A 1992 amnesty program and promise of good treatment offered by Fujimori further depleted Sendero's ranks.[37]

But Sendero Luminoso continued to carry out retaliatory, strike-anywhere attacks, killing several police officers. According to a U.S. Embassy cable (dated November 27, 1992), through October 1992, 1,242 random terrorist attacks claimed 1,270 civilian lives. Police detained the leader of "Socorro Popular" (People's Aid), a key Sendero Luminoso organization in Lima. In November, another car bomb filled with 250 kilograms of explosives went off in Miraflores, killing three and wounding almost two dozen.[38]

EPILOGUE

The upshot of this civil war is that Guzmán, a frustrated intellectual, was tried for treason and the use of explosives in a military court in October and sentenced to life without parole as Prisoner 1509.[39] He was imprisoned on the Island of San Lorenzo, off the coast of Lima's port of Callao. He subsequently was known to advocate for a political solution to Peru's many problems. Elena Iparraguirre, Laura Zambrano, and Maria Pantoja likewise, got life. In November, Marta Huatay, leader of "Socorro Popular" (People's Aid), received life and was sent to a jail in Puno, a frigid place high in the south Andes Mountains. Maritza, too, got life, but this sentence was subsequently reduced to twenty-five years. She served in a prison in Ancon, a seaside resort close to Lima, where she would not be subject to the frigid temperatures of the highlands. She was released in 2017, still unrepentant. Her architect boyfriend, Carlos Inchástegui, was released after serving twenty-two years in 2014. Superman disappeared, like the Lone Ranger, who always appeared behind a mask. He never revealed his identity, and those who knew him are mum. Peru suffered $20 to $22 billion in damages and circa 69,280 were killed from 1980 to 2000, according to the Truth and Reconciliation Report. A government-offered million-dollar ($10 million in the movie) reward for the capture of Presidente Gonzalo, dead or alive, was split between Vidal, Jiménez, and their men. Vidal was promoted to other police posts. Jiménez was posted at the Peruvian Embassy in Panama as a police attaché. Another key figure in Jiménez's unit took a job in Bolivia. Jiménez stated that one of his best CIA-trained agents now works as a jail guard. By the end of 1993, the group that captured Guzmán was dissolved.[40]

But the conditions for insurrection remain. And the fact that in the last scene, Rejas perceives an imaginary Maritza and what she represents embodied in his dancing daughter clad in red suggests that the struggle between haves and have-nots is not over.

ADDITIONAL RESOURCES

Camino, Gustavo. "Capture of the Leader of Shining Path: A Dermatologic Disease Changes the Course of History." *American Journal of Dermatopathology* 15, no. 5 (1993): 385–87.

Dillon, Sam. "Guzman Was Hard to Find." *New York Times* (East Coast, late edition), September 25, 1994, A3.

Erulkar, Eliab S. "The Shining Path Paradox." *Harvard International Review* 12, no. 2 (1990): 43–45.

Hammack, Dan W. "Understanding the Path of Terrorism." *Security Management* 37, no. 1 (1993): 26.

Holmes, Jennifer S. "Sendero Luminoso after Fujimori: A Sub-National Analysis." *Latin Americanist* 59, no. 2 (2015): 29–50.

Jacyk, W. K. "Capture of Abimael Guzman." *American Journal of Dermatopathology* 16, no. 3 (1994): 349.

Lane, Charles. "'Superman' Meeting Shining Path: Story of a CIA Success." *Washington Post*, December 7, 2000.

Manwaring, Max G. "Peru's Sendero Luminoso: The Shining Path Beckons." *Annals of the American Academy of Political and Social Science* 541 (1995): 157–66.

Masterson, Daniel M. "The Devolution of Peru's Sendero Luminoso: From Hybrid Maoists to Narco Traffickers?" *History Compass* 8, no. 1 (2010): 51–60.

Palmer, David S. "Rebellion in Rural Peru: The Origins and Evolution of Sendero Luminoso." *Comparative Politics* 18, no. 2 (1986): 127–46.

Robinson, Linda. "No Holds Barred." *U.S. News and World Report* 113, no. 12 (September 28, 1992): 49.

Taylor, Lewis. "Counter-Insurgency Strategy, The PCP-SL and the Civil War in Peru, 1980–1996." *Bulletin of Latin American Research* 17, no. 1 (1998): 35–58.

U.S. Embassy, Peru. Confidential Cable. February 13, 1991.

U.S. Embassy, Peru. "Peru: 1992 Annual Terrorist Report." November 27, 1992.

Vargas Llosa, Mario. "Prisoner 1509." *Index on Censorship* 5–6 (1993): 37–39.

Venon, Lieutenant-Colonel Gerald N. Jr. "Sendero Luminoso: A Failed Revolution in Peru?" Strategy Research Project, Carlisle Barracks, PA: U.S. Army War College, 1998.

Watson, Russell, and Brook Larmar. "It's Your Turn to Lose." *Newsweek* 120, no. 13 (September 28, 1992): 28.

NOTES

1. Peru, World Bank Documents, Socio-Economic Database, 1980s; DataBank, World Development Indicators; Mario Vargas Llosa, "Prisoner 1509," *Index on Censorship* 5–6 (1993): 38; and David S. Palmer, "Rebellion in Rural Peru: The Origins and Evolution of Sendero Luminoso," *Comparative Politics* 18, no. 2 (1986): 130 for 1981 figures. Palmer also reminds readers that the city of Ayacucho was not tied to the capital until a road was built in 1924 ("Rebellion in Rural Peru," 132). As late as the 1960s, fewer than 100 cars and trucks circulated in the city. Two buses provided transportation. Quechua was the native language of most adults. In 1961, per capita income for farmers was less than $100 per year (Palmer, "Rebellion in Rural Peru," 133). In 1981, illiteracy stood at 54% of the total population. Ayacucho's 500,000 inhabitants could count on only thirty doctors and 366 hospital beds and 827 telephones. Life expectancy was forty-four years. Seven percent of the residents had running water and 14% had electricity (Palmer, "Rebellion in Rural Peru," 138–39).

2. A thumbnail sketch of the history of the university is provided by Palmer, "Rebellion in Rural Peru," 127.

3. Daniel M. Masterson, "The Devolution of Peru's Sendero Luminoso: From Hybrid Maoists to Narco Traffickers?" *History Compass* 8, no. 1 (2010): 51; Palmer, "Rebellion in Rural Peru," 135–36; Dan W. Hammack, "Understanding the Path of Terrorism," *Security Management* 37, no. 1 (1993): 26.

4. Gustavo Camino, "Capture of the Leader of Shining Path: A Dermatologic Disease Changes the Course of History," *American Journal of Dermatopathology* 15, no. 5 (1993): 385–87; Russell Watson and Brook Larmar, "It's Your Turn to Lose," *Newsweek* 120, no. 13 (September 28, 1992): 28; and Masterson, "Devolution of Peru's Sendero Luminoso," 51. On the Red Flag party, see Palmer, "Rebellion in Rural Peru," 128, 138.

5. Masterson, "Devolution of Peru's Sendero Luminoso," 50–60; Palmer, "Rebellion in Rural Peru," 128.

6. Deaths attributed to Sendero Luminoso stood at 2 in 1980, 8 in 1981, 171 in 1982, and 3,028 in 1983 (Palmer, "Rebellion in Rural Peru," 139). In 1989, Sendero attributed deaths were 1,016 civilians and 289 soldiers; Eliab S. Erulkar, "The Shining Path Paradox," *Harvard International Review* 12, no. 2 (1990): 43. On the attack on the jail, see Hammack, "Path of Terrorism," 26; Max G. Manwaring, "Peru's Sendero Luminoso: The Shining Path Beckons," *Annals of the American Academy of Political and Social Science* 541 (1995): 162.

7. Lewis Taylor, "Counter-Insurgency Strategy, The PCP-SL and the Civil War in Peru, 1980–1996," *Bulletin of Latin American Research* 17, no. 1 (1998): 35, 37, 41–42; Palmer, "Rebellion in Rural Peru," 129, 139; Hammack, "Path of Terrorism," 26.

8. Watson and Larmar, "It's Your Turn," 28; U.S. Defense Intelligence Agency Secret Defense Intelligence Terrorism Summary, June 15, 1987; Masterson, "Devolution of Peru's Sendero Luminoso," 51–60.

9. Taylor, "Counter-Insurgency Strategy," 49; Masterson, "Devolution of Peru's Sendero Luminoso," 51–60; Manwaring, "Peru's Sendero Luminoso," 161.

10. Refworld.org, US Department of State, Annual Reports, Country Reports on Terrorism, 2013. Foreign Terrorist Organizations: Shining Path; Taylor, "Counter-Insurgency Strategy," 46.

11. Masterson, "Devolution of Peru's Sendero Luminoso," 51–60; Palmer, "Rebellion in Rural Peru," 140; Hammack, "Path of Terrorism," 26.

12. Masterson, "Devolution of Peru's Sendero Luminoso," 51–60.

13. U.S. Embassy, Peru, Confidential Cable, February 13, 1991, "Sendero Bombs Banks, As the Search for 'Presidente Gonzalo' Continues," 1–6; U.S. Embassy, Peru, Unclassified Cable, November 27, 1992, 3–6.

14. Linda Robinson, "No Holds Barred," *U.S. News and World Report* 113, no. 12 (September 28, 1992): 49; U.S. Defense Intelligence Agency Secret Defense Intelligence Terrorism Summary, June 15, 1987; U.S. Embassy Peru, Unclassified Cable, 2–4; Masterson, "Devolution of Peru's Sendero Luminoso," 51–60.

15. W. K. Jacyk, "Capture of Abimael Guzman," *American Journal of Dermatopathology* 16, no. 3 (1994): 349.

16. Masterson, "Devolution of Peru's Sendero Luminoso," 51–60; Palmer, "Rebellion in Rural Peru," 137, for a discussion of the effects of agrarian reform in Ayacucho.

17. Taylor, "Counter-Insurgency Strategy," 37, 42, 46; Masterson, "Devolution of Peru's Sendero Luminoso," 51–60.

18. Taylor, "Counter-Insurgency Strategy," 42–43; Palmer, "Rebellion in Rural Peru," 139.

19. Taylor, "Counter-Insurgency Strategy," 44; Vargas Llosa, "Prisoner 1509," 39; Erulkar, "The Shining Path Paradox," 44.

20. Palmer, "Rebellion in Rural Peru," 130.

21. Taylor, "Counter-Insurgency Strategy," 45; Palmer, "Rebellion in Rural Peru," 129, 139. See also Hammack, "Path of Terrorism," 26; and Erulkar, "The Shining Path Paradox," 44.

22. Taylor, "Counter-Insurgency Strategy," 49; Watson and Larmar, "It's Your Turn," 28; Charles Lane, "'Superman' Meeting Shining Path: Story of a CIA Success," *Washington Post*, December 7, 2000; Hammack, "Path of Terrorism," 26.

23. Taylor, "Counter-Insurgency Strategy," 48–49; Manwaring, "Peru's Sendero Luminoso," 163.

24. On DINCOTE abuses, see Taylor, "Counter-Insurgency Strategy," 51; Lane, "'Superman' Meeting."

25. Lane, "'Superman' Meeting."

26. Lane, "'Superman' Meeting."

27. Taylor, "Counter-Insurgency Strategy," 46; Lane, "'Superman' Meeting."

28. Taylor, "Counter-Insurgency Strategy," 51; Lane, "'Superman' Meeting."

29. Sam Dillon, "Guzman Was Hard to Find," *New York Times* (East Coast, late edition), September 25, 1994, A3; Lane, "'Superman' Meeting."

30. U.S. Defense Intelligence Agency, Secret Intelligence Information Report.

31. U.S. Embassy Peru, Unclassified Cable, 2.

32. U.S. Embassy, Peru, Confidential Cable, 2; Lane, "'Superman' Meeting."

33. Robinson, "No Holds Barred," 49.

34. Camino, "Capture of the Leader of Shining Path," 385–87; Watson and Larmar, "It's Your Turn," 28; Lane, "'Superman' Meeting."

35. Bob Edwards, *Morning Edition*, National Public Radio Broadcast, September 14, 1992; Watson and Larmar, "It's Your Turn," 28.

36. Manwaring, "Peru's Sendero Luminoso," 158.

37. Watson and Larmar, "It's Your Turn," 28; Lane, "'Superman' Meeting."

38. Robinson, "No Holds Barred," 49; Watson and Larmar, "It's Your Turn," 28; U.S. Embassy Peru, Unclassified Cable, 2–3.

39. Vargas Llosa, "Prisoner 1509," 37–39.

40. Watson and Larmar, "It's Your Turn," 28; U.S. Embassy Peru, Unclassified Cable, 6–8; Jennifer S. Holmes, "Sendero Luminoso after Fujimori: A Sub-National Analysis," *Latin Americanist* 59, no. 2 (2015): 29–50; Lane, "'Superman' Meeting."

Chapter 15

También la Lluvia

Screening Resistance to Columbus and Bolivia's Anti-Neoliberal Water War

Leo J. Garofalo

También la Lluvia (2010); produced by Juan Gordon; directed by Icíar Bollaín; written by Paul Laverly; color; 103 minutes; Morena Films. In early twenty-first century Bolivia, a movie crew attempts to make a film about the arrival of the Spanish in the Caribbean five hundred years earlier.

Rarely can one feature film allow us to think about two distinct historical moments simultaneously. *También la lluvia* (Even the Rain), directed by Spanish filmmaker Icíar Bollaín, creates this dual perspective by placing a story within a story, or in this case, makes a film about making a historical film (the film-in-production). Bollaín's film revisits two transformative moments in Latin American and world history: the arrival of the Spanish in the Caribbean and the opening of national economies to multinational corporations (1990s–2000s). Both Christopher Columbus's disastrous attempts to get rich quick and the privatization of basic services during economic liberalization constitute historical watersheds in the Americas. Powerful coalitions of outsiders invade and exploit labor and resources, both efforts met fierce resistance, and both used violence and local allies to try to quell opposition. The film's dramatization of these parallel stories offers ample opportunities for teachers and students to explore the complex histories and multiple historical actors involved in both turning points. We can deepen our understanding of the film and these periods of transformation by drawing upon an array of easily accessible and highly relevant primary and secondary sources, including other films and documentaries.

POLITICAL FILMS AND MAKING FILMS ABOUT FILMS

Film critics, such as Manuel Quinto, place director Icíar Bollaín's *También la lluvia* squarely in the tradition of powerful political films, such as those of Costa-Gavras (*State of Siege*), Francisco Rosi (*The Mattei Affair*), Volker Schlöndorf (*The Circle of Deceit*), and Ken Loach (*Carla's Song*).[1] Paul Laverty, the screenwriter for *También la lluvia*, wrote the script for many of Ken Loach's films, and he spent years in Nicaragua, Guatemala, and El Salvador in the 1980s, during their civil wars. From Madrid and usually writing her own films, Icíar Bollaín examined contemporary social issues, such as immigration and domestic violence, in her earlier full-length films *Flores del otro mundo* (1999) and *Te doy mis ojos* (2003). Challenging with her work the inequalities between women and men in cinema both in on-screen representations and behind the camera, Bollaín also famously and playfully critiqued both the patriarchal film industry and the label of feminist filmmaking.[2] This is her first Americas-themed work. With *También la lluvia*, Bollaín shows herself to be a capable political filmmaker. The central actors—Mexican actor Gael García Bernal, Spanish actor Luis Tosar, and Bolivian actor Juan Carlos Aduviri—deliver strong performances. They interpret three characters who almost function as archetypes of the figures in any modern political drama or social struggle: the well-meaning and idealistic outsider who wants to flee when disaster strikes (Sebastián), the hard-nosed realist who discovers he has a heart (Costa), and the fearless plebeian leader who propels this transformation and is at the center of a wider struggle (Daniel). This is also a film to draw in film enthusiasts with a narrative tone and visual style similar to those of Terrence Malick in *The New World* and Werner Herzog's *Fitzcarraldo*.[3] And like these iconic films, *También la lluvia* grapples with the foundational traumas of the Americas through its critiques of power and its abuse, especially economic exploitation and violence, against indigenous and marginalized peoples.

También la lluvia presents the making of a present-day film, the film-in-production, in Bolivia about the history of brutal exploitation of the people of Española (modern Haiti/Dominican Republic) and Cuba in the Caribbean when they were forced—in the days of Columbus—to produce gold, suffering dismemberment if failing to fill quotas and slaughter if openly resisting. The fictional filmmaking by a Spanish and Mexican film crew and actors in the twenty-first century is given a historically accurate setting: Cochabamba, Bolivia, in 1999–2000 just as a powerful, cross-class alliance—the Coordinadora in Defense of Water and Life—is holding town-hall meetings and taking to the streets to stop municipal and national elites from selling the country's resources and rights to overcharge water consumers to the highest bidder, international conglomerate Bechtel.[4] Some of the local protest leaders in the Cochabamba Water War are among the Bolivians hired by the day as low-paid extras for the filming; one comes to portray a main character in the resistance to the first Spanish invaders—the historical Taíno leader Hatuey. This parallel exploration in film of two time periods allows for a rigorous double critique in classes on Latin America and Spain: first, of the role of Columbus and the Church in the devastation of the West Indies, which can be paired with primary source readings by Columbus and his younger contemporaries such as Hieronymite friar Ramón Pané, and later, Dominican Bartolomé de Las Casas (1484–1566), and second, of the innovative and democratic social movements that arose in resistance in Bolivia and across the hemisphere during the post-authoritarian era to challenge a neoliberal hegemony promoted by the United States and central governments throughout the hemisphere. This portrayal of Bolivia's Water War against an unfair economic system and stubborn national elites helps classes explore historical and social inequalities through the perspective of people like Coordinadora leader and shoemaker Oscar Olivera and other Bolivians mobilizing to defend their national resources and further open their political system to popular participation.

The film-in-production uses historical records that are read on-screen and incorporated into its script, and it is set on two Caribbean islands during the first two decades of the Spanish invasion, from 1492 to 1512. Shooting the film in the highlands of landlocked Bolivia among largely Spanish-and Quechua-speaking populations raises one of the ironies that infuses the plot and animates debates by the characters and film critics alike: indigenous people throughout the Americas are treated as interchangeable and largely without voice, and production costs are kept low in a foreign film denouncing colonial exploitation of Amerindians by Europeans precisely by exploiting cheap labor and Bolivia's relative impoverishment. The film-in-production also compresses time and events and collapses distances in order to bring historical figures onto the set at the same time and into dialogue with each other in ways that did not occur in the historical era represented.

COLUMBUS AND SOURCES AND OTHER FILMS
ON THE INVASION OF THE CARIBBEAN

Columbus (1451–1506) made four voyages to the Americas: 1492–1493; 1493–1496, when he attempted colonization; 1498–1500; and 1502–1504.

The actor portraying Columbus in the film-in-production complains of the script's simplistic characterization of Columbus as a man motivated solely by greed and a love for gold. He perhaps has a point. Although Columbus is rightly held up by his contemporaries and ours as a despised symbol of the atrocities committed in that era, the historical sources on Columbus, flawed as they are, hint at a man with more than one motive: a desire to prove himself an unmatched navigator and explorer and hopes for a hereditary title of nobility, wealth through trade (including of enslaved people), and ways to support his royal patrons' championing of Christianity and battles against Muslims. Failing to find the promised trade routes to China or rich trade goods to export from the Americas, he tried his hand at governing settler colonization and placer gold mining, all powered by indigenous laborers with disastrous results. The film-in-production highlights some of the worst and most chilling consequences of this merciless, squeezing exploitation: chopping off hands, setting dogs upon people, and mothers killing their own babies.[5]

Three sets of primary sources facilitate an approximation to Columbus and are as close as we can get to his own words: a handful of his published letters and navigational records; Las Casas's selective quoting and paraphrasing of a now-lost logbook made by Columbus on the first voyage; and Hernando Colón's history of his father's endeavors, also based on the original logbooks from the four voyages and other lost manuscripts also made by Columbus.[6] Even for scholars, approximating Columbus is notoriously difficult: his handwriting was hard to decipher, often surviving only in copies or copies of copies; his Spanish was that of a foreigner, full of idiosyncrasies, inaccuracies, allusions, and borrowings from Portuguese, Italian, and his native Genoese; and Las Casas and Hernando Colón each pursued his own agenda in selecting what to reproduce.[7] Las Casas sought to revindicate the Indians by collecting materials that reflected well on their rationality, goodness, legitimate governments and rulers, and natural rights to freedom and self-rule. Las Casas also believed that the discovery of the New World by Columbus was divinely preordained for a time propitious for saving the souls of the inhabitants of the Americas; therefore, he admired Columbus for his role as a divine tool to spread Christianity. Consequently, Las Casas sought out the passages and words in Columbus's accounts that confirmed this belief. This was a belief that Columbus also apparently found convenient to occasionally highlight or to reassure himself by mentioning. With his history, Hernando Colón sought to revindicate his family's good name and restore its privileges.[8] Finding the "real" Columbus to teach or put in a film is no easy task.

Around the Columbus quincentennial in 1992 marking the first voyage, a number of films came out; some lionized him, others pointed out "tragic flaws." The 2012–2014 Televisión Española (TVE) historical fiction series *Isabel* dedicated some episodes to Columbus and the dilemmas he faced at court and with his misgovernment and interests in profiting from a slave trade in Amerindian people. Neither the earlier films nor the highly entertaining Spanish television series provide much material useful for a history class or a serious scholar attempting to reveal a historical Columbus. The texts described above—especially when curated by experts, such as Professor Felipe Fernández-Armesto in the collection cited above—provide a much better grounding for learning about the more complex Columbus than the fictional actor called for.[9]

For those seeking to pair *También la lluvia* with other feature-length films on the early—often unsuccessful—years of the Spanish invasion and efforts at evangelization in the circum-Caribbean, *Cabeza de Vaca* and *Jericó* might fit the bill nicely. Based on the published account of the consequences of a real misadventure that occurred in 1528, the 1990 Mexican film *Cabeza de Vaca* begins with Alvar Núñez Cabeza de Vaca's account of the 1527 Pánfilo de Narváez expedition's shipwreck off Florida in North America. He went on to gain fame in Europe with the publication of this account (and he later returned to the Americas authorized to carry out his own mission of conquest). The 1528 shipwreck set off an eight-year trek by boat and land for the dwindling number of survivors along the Gulf coasts, inland through Texas, all the way to Mexico City.[10] The author, two other Spaniards, and Esteban (Estevanico or Estevan de Dorantes or Mustafa Azemmouri, d. 1539, is the first-known African to traverse this part of North America) become immersed in a string of diverse Native American societies along the way, and these remnants of an Iberian and African world must come to understand Native American societies on their own terms in order to survive and continue on.[11] Directed by Mexican ethnologist Nicolás Echevarría, it presents an indigenous history usually ignored in films about conquest and colonization, and it dramatizes the director's interest in the shamanism and mysticism that draws in the main character and wins him over if the sixteenth-century account and the film can be believed.

In a similar fashion, Venezuelan director Luis Alberto Lamata's *Jericó* (1991) further decenters the story of invading warriors and missionaries and examines the activities and values of a Carib village and family in the coastal Venezuela region that adopt, incorporate, and "convert" to their ways a Spanish Dominican friar who alone survived a disastrous *entrada* (royally sanctioned private expedition to conquer and claim territory and its residents for the Crown and Christianization). In this region, Germans carried out the expeditions licensed by the Spanish Crown. Much of the filming occurred in Kariña villages. These films give voice and space to indigenous people and their resistance and to the moral and spiritual dilemmas of individuals from the invading forces.[12] These treatments of resistant discourses in the Americas and the discordance among the invading Europeans and Africans plumb deeper into the depths of the traumas that made these Americas and continue to reproduce them today. These treatments offer glimpses of unique local histories and invite audiences to identify with the disempowered, not just pity them. An approach like these, which disrupt established narratives, is hampered in *También la lluvia* by the ways that it silences Bolivians and Taínos and constantly foregrounds outsiders who never really view Bolivians and Taínos as more complex than subjects or victims—whether piteous or admirably heroic.[13] Even the term Taíno conceals an ethnic plurality that included Aïtïj, Bohio, Boriqua, Caribe, Canima, Ciboney, Ciguayo, and Lucayas. In this sense, *También la lluvia* re-creates "official discourses" of conquest and colonization—whether celebratory or critical. These discourses effectively silence a diversity of autonomous indigenous histories and also oversimplify the complexity and variability of European and African experiences in the Americas.[14] Pairing *También la lluvia* with these and other films from a critical postcolonial tradition can expand the discussion.

Digging more deeply into the writings and histories of Columbus's near contemporaries and critics can also deepen the discussion. Some are named characters in the film-within-the-film, and others are not. But their presence can almost be felt. Inspired by the news of Columbus's voyage and a fervent missionary, the young Catalan friar Pané joined the second expedition in 1493, and Columbus sent him to live for several years among the people of Española and record their customs. The friar paid particular attention to their religious beliefs and practices because his goal was their conversion to Christianity. Historians do not know when he was born or died. His account, completed in 1498, informed many of Las Casas's later writings, and Las Casas corrected some of Pané's misunderstandings. Therefore, although not a character in the film-in-production, Pané's descriptions survive today for us to analyze as an example of early Spanish attempts to learn the Taíno language, concepts, origin stories, medicine, and reverence for deities and ancestral spirits and the carved objects housing them, as well as expressing some of the first criticisms of his countrymen for taking land by force.[15] As with Columbus's own accounts, it shows how early European desires to spread Christianity clashed with those to acquire land, wealth, and power, usually at the expense of local populations and their rights to live unmolested.

As a boy, Las Casas saw Columbus parade through the streets of Seville on Palm Sunday, March 31, 1493, and was inspired to join the conquest. In 1502, he crossed the Atlantic to assist as a chaplain. He spent much of 1502–1506 traveling around the island of Española. From there, he passed to Cuba with an expedition. As a reward, he was allowed to join other members of the Spanish population in holding indigenous people as tributaries in *encomienda* (royal license to exploit the labor of indigenous people in exchange for Christianizing them, collecting Crown tribute, and suppressing rebellion).

Those subject to the encomienda were technically not enslaved, but in practice their experience in those early days in the Caribbean was very close to
enslavement and an almost total denial of their personhood. Moving to Cuba
with Spanish forces, Las Casas was involved in the 1511–1512 campaign,
which would capture and execute Hatuey.[16] The flight of the *cacique* (an
honorific title meaning king or chieftain) Hatuey and many of his followers
from his homeland on Española to Cuba helps bring these different chapters
and theaters of the early conquest and evangelization together into the same
frame for the film-in-production in *También la lluvia*. The film anachronistically puts all these figures together in the same place at the same time.

The populations of the Caribbean were the first to deal with the Europeans
and negotiate new realities; they endured disease-driven demographic collapse, societal crises, and ecological change in the key 1492–1580 period.[17]
In 1495, heavily armed Spanish troops defeated the combined forces of
Española's principal *caciques*, torturing to death the leaders captured. Out
of this destruction, Guarionex emerged as a mediator with the Spanish,
until 1497 when famine, epidemic disease, and divisions among the Spanish
provoked a conspiracy to rebel. More *caciques* were killed, and Guarionex
was turned into a puppet for the Columbus family.[18] By 1500, native polities
no longer operated autonomous on the island. A similar story of conquest
then unfolded in Jamaica, Puerto Rico, the Lucayas (Bahamas), and Cuba,
with native societies destroyed and dispersed. Some were subjugated, others
enslaved and sold, and still others escaped to the Lesser Antilles, where resistance lasted longer and was joined by escaping Africans as well.

Fleeing the invaders' avarice and savagery in Española, Hatuey brought
a warning to Cuba. He counseled other *caciques* against compromise or
alliance with the Spanish, and he organized stiff resistance among those
he influenced. In 1511, a license to occupy Cuba was granted, and troops
assembled in Jamaica and Española, including Las Casas, for whom this
experience proved critical to forming his condemnation of conquest and
defense of Indians. Thus it was that Las Casas came to Cuba with an army
to face this foe of colonial occupation in 1511. As these two forces overran
Cuba by March 1512, Las Casas witnessed an incident so horrific it became
a foundational story and image of the Black Legend derived in part from his
published writings that would emerge among the empire's opponents about
Spanish cruelty and tyranny. This incident was the burning alive of resistance
leaders, including an uncowed and defiant Hatuey, depicted in *También la
lluvia* and re-created in the famous engravings by Flemish-born, German
engraver and editor Theodor de Bry.[19] These adorn most modern editions
of Las Casas, as well as those printed outside Spanish-controlled areas,
during the Empire's heyday in the 1500s and 1600s. Although he heard the
Dominican Montesinos preach against these abuses in church in 1511, and

he saw Montesinos refuse to give communion to anyone holding Indians in encomienda or as slaves, Las Casas did not fully commit to castigating the Spanish occupation until 1514. Las Casas came to believe that the cross could not follow the sword, and he argued that no true conversion could be made through war or in its aftermath. Nevertheless, Las Casas never abandoned his belief that Europeans had a right and a providential opportunity to be in the Americas to convert this branch of humanity.

Las Casas remained an active reader, writer, and campaigner throughout fifty years of his life from 1516 to 1566, and his views and arguments changed over that time, even though historians and other modern writers present a static or one-sided version of what he represented or advocated. One of the best introductions in English to his labors and an excellent teaching anthology in an accessible format is provided in a brief history with documents edited by Lawrence A. Clayton and David M. Lantigua.[20] There is much in Las Casas's corpus today's teachers and students find problematic (e.g., his views on those who practiced Islam). His most widely noted position that troubles the vision of him as a hero in the face of the brutality and immorality of invasion and colonization was his early support for some petitions to the Spanish Crown by individual sugar mill owners to import enslaved Africans. Las Casas hoped these would prevent the enslavement and mistreatment of indigenous people on those Caribbean islands. However, once he studied the chronicles and accounts of the conquests of the Canary Islands and other parts of Africa, he concluded in his published works that those acts and the enslavement of African peoples were just as egregious and reprehensible as the mistreatment of indigenous people in the Americas. But this reversal is rarely acknowledged or examined. In the rush to celebrate Las Casas or to condemn him, we can overlook who he really was and the significance of his actions and writings for the stories told in this film and laid open to our teaching and learning. Even though the Spanish actor portraying Las Casas in the film-within-a-film might at times seem overshadowed on-screen by the awakening consciousness of the fictional Spanish producer (Costa), the topics Las Casas raised remained painful thorns in the side of Spanish imperialism and Catholic evangelization. In fact, they still trouble powerholders' belief in resource extractivism and neoliberal economic models throughout the hemisphere today, from northern Canada to the Mapuche lands in Argentina and Chile.

COCHABAMBA "WATER WAR" AGAINST
NEOLIBERALISM IN BOLIVIA

Just as the Caribbean featured in *También la lluvia* constituted the epicenter of the world-changing conquest of America in one era, the Bolivia of our present era appearing in *También la lluvia* constituted the world's front line against neoliberalism in the early 2000s.[21] Over the 1980s and 1990s, Latin American governments of the right or those assuming democratic power as military dictatorships receded worked with the IMF and the World Bank to implement neoliberal reforms of economic liberalization, decentralization, structural readjustment, welfare state retrenchment, and privatization. Limiting government spending and opening the economy plunged many millions into poverty. To survive the effects of this harsh economic crisis, the poor, working classes, and women joined community organizations to address collective problems. In Bolivia, citizens' frustration with neoliberal policies boiled over in 2000; the national government had gained international financial support by trading to a U.S.-based consortium control of Cochabamba's municipal water supply and the water of its surrounding countryside, including the rain falling on it ("also the rain," hence the name of the film). Citizens from within the city and outside it, and representing all sectors and most social classes, marched; they blocked streets and clashed with national police, who shot and killed a teenager, in what became known as the "Water War." And that was only the beginning of what was to come.[22] This was a reinvention of democracy fueled initially by economic conditions and the callous response of elected officials and security forces. In this repudiation and reinvention, Bolivia for a time led the way. That is what inspired this film. Before there was Podemos in Spain and other European anti-austerity movements, before the Arab Spring, and before there was Occupy in the United States, there was Cochabamba in Bolivia and its victory in the "Water War."

También la lluvia shows us glimpses of the new forms of organizing and grassroots empowerment in this rapidly expanding local movement, which would be replicated across the nation. Prior to this, the economic world order had been targeted by protestors for decades at World Trade Organization protests, and the Zapatistas in Mexico had risen and secured autonomy in their communities. But those movements had not succeeded in stopping governments or overturning the system. Part of what made Cochabamba's movement so strong and resilient in the face of official defiance of such a clear manifestation of the public will were its organizing strategies, its awareness and connection to past movements and history, and its involvement of indigenous and women leaders and their modes of mobilization. Organized indigenous women have long been a force in Bolivia's labor movement and politics. They actively undermined the military dictatorships in the 1960s and 1970s, and they opposed the neoliberal presidents in the 1980s and 1990s.[23] Thus, indigenous women were already active in several groups, and they spearheaded the blocking of key roads and launched pivotal protests in the "Water War" (and in a later national struggle over nationalizing the exploitation of gas reserves known as the "Gas War"). Their prominence in these efforts solidified their place within the broader indigenous rights movement. And after later electoral victories, they gained positions in government and placed their issues on the national agenda. In addition, water activist Oscar Olivera pointed out key strategies learned over the years that functioned to protect the movement; these included having many leaders, not just one (to prevent opponents taking out an essential figure); taking all decisions in public townhall meetings (to avoid corrupt deal making or cooptation); seeking consensus rather than majority rule (to preserve a wide coalition); and studying history and economics in order to understand their present moment and how the economic system was stacked against their interests.[24] In some ways, Olivera perhaps presented director Bollaín and screenwriter Laverty with an attractive model for the fictive Daniel as a well-informed and politically astute plebeian protest leader. And the Aymara-speaking actor (and film-school teacher) Juan Carlos Aduviri, from the great proletarian city of El Alto, breathes further life and passion into the part.[25] Unfortunately, the film does not allow for a fuller profile of this or the other kinds of leaders that made the struggle so successful, much less give its audience an inside view of the movement's modus operandi. However, the clarity of purpose in defending a basic necessity essential to all human life—water—does come across forcefully in the film. The imperative to defend access to water of all things, lent powerful momentum to this struggle. Several instructive documentaries featured the clash over the rain in Cochabamba.[26] Today, water defenders are continually in the news, fighting everywhere to preserve this resource for all. Most often they are indigenous, frequently women, and always operating in coalitions.[27] Once again, the treatment in *También la lluvia* of the "Water War" serves as a jumping-off point for a deeper dive into Bolivian history, racialized and class exclusion, indigenous politics, and the underpinnings of what was once termed the Latin American Pink Tide of left-of-center elected governments that came into power in the twenty-first century.

Two years after the citizenry won the "Water War," Bolivia's president pushed through and refused to reverse a wildly unpopular plan to export the nation's natural gas through neighboring Chile. Protests calling for the nationalization of the gas, originally organized in El Alto and the neighboring political capital La Paz, quickly gained momentum. They grew even stronger as the government deployed army troops and military convoys to break through blocked streets. In the "Gas War," protestors used many of the

organizational techniques seen in Cochabamba, built on existing organizations, and kept the focus on defending a national resource belonging to all
Bolivians and condemning an elected government that showed itself unfit
to rule through its reactions. Targeted and indiscriminate shooting with tear
gas canisters, rubber bullets, and live ammunition killed sixty-seven civilians
and one soldier shot by his own commanding officer for refusing to fire on
protestors (the bloodiest day was Columbus Day, October 12, 2003, when
the army killed twenty-nine civilians). The protests toppled the president,
who fled to Miami and then Washington, DC. *Crisis Is Our Brand* documents how a president more popular in Washington than in Bolivia could
win a national election with a plurality of the vote but not a majority and then
misunderstand his own people so profoundly as to be driven from office,
even when employing the most expensive polling firm in the United States.[28]
Further insight into this groundswell, so surprising to outsiders, can be gained
by looking back to a few years prior at more overt meddling by the U.S.
Ambassador to undermine the candidacies and platform of Evo Morales, then
a congressman from the coca-growing region and representing the coca leaf
growers' unions. This interference seemed to have the opposite effect to the
one Washington intended; many Bolivians from other regions and the cities
asserted their national autonomy and rallied to his cause and the defense of
the much-maligned coca leaf and its small-scale, rural growers and workers.
Coca leaf growers and workers were most often indigenous migrants to low-
land areas from the highlands. Two additional documentaries on Morales help
us see and hear these marginalized social sectors and recognize the power
of their local organizations and discourses of revindication of rights often
dismissed by national, political elites and Washington and presented on the
streets in *También la lluvia*.[29] Over the months following the "Gas War," these
rapidly associating social movements continued to gain momentum, pushing
out of office a vice president and other interim leaders until a national election
was scheduled for December 2005.

Evo Morales won that election with a 54% majority in the first round, and
his party—the MAS (the Movement toward Socialism)—dominated congress
and scheduled a Constitutional Assembly. They swept aside the customary
power of the elite parties. After beginning his first five-year presidency in
2006, this popular mandate allowed him to regain state control of privatized hydrocarbon resources, increase taxes, and raise royalties. Left-wing
presidents in Brazil and Argentina—which bought Bolivia's gas exports
(and soybeans)—worked with the new government rather than blocking it.
With this election, the left and popular nationalism had returned in Bolivia.
But much more was gained with this election: Bolivia elected its first
self-identified indigenous president. Historian José Antonio Lucero explains
that "it is important to situate this victory within the centuries-long history

of indigenous resistance in Bolivia. In every century, Bolivia has seen major indigenous uprisings. These conflicts have left deep imprints on Bolivian politics. . . . [And they are] present across a wide spectrum of contemporary Bolivian political discourses."[30] Lucero contextualizes this historic victory that challenged "the nation's long history of exclusion and racism" and makes available Morales's two inaugural speeches from 2006 along with two telling photos of Morales as president.[31] Political scientist Shawnna Mullenax further explains the forces behind this win and that sustained its political power for more than a decade:

> Morales was the candidate of the poor and middle class, the traditionally mar-
> ginalized, and the ideologically Left. Morales and the MAS owed their success
> to a wide range of active social movements, including the indigenous women's
> movement. . . . Living at the intersection of two systematically disadvantaged
> groups, indigenous women were disproportionately affected by the late-twenti-
> eth-century neoliberal policies. . . . Their support for Morales was, and remains,
> crucial to his success.[32]

Even after a coup forced Morales from office and the country in 2019, these popular movements returned MAS to the presidency with 55% of the vote and control of both chambers of the legislature in 2020.

Political victories of anti-neoliberal movements and indigenous President Morales's long stretch in office (2006–2019) opened a new chapter in Latin America's history. However, Bolivia and all the other countries in the Americas remain dependent on a model of extraction and expropriation of resource wealth in order to sustain or expand redistributive policies that address inequalities in social welfare, health, housing, education, and jobs.[33] Left-leaning and even indigenous governments like that of President Morales could no more fully shake dependence on the extraction of natural resources than could more conservative governments. These contradictions came to the fore as President Morales and MAS militants trampled on indigenous rights to territory and decision-making in order to build highways, pipelines, and gas fields. The entanglements of colonialism and neocolonialism cannot be easily escaped. Just as the protagonists in *Cabeza de Vaca* and *Jericó* are awoken to another way of thinking and another way of living only to be forced back into the brutal logics of invading armies, are we inspired by *También la lluvia* and shown a way of valuing life and each other and *Pachamama* (Mother Earth) by brave water defenders only to be dragged unwillingly back to the depressing reality that we and our societies are the products and the perpetuators of conquest, settler colonialism, and extractivism? The film provokes many more questions than it answers.

My students in history and colleagues in Hispanic Studies always react enthusiastically to this film. When I co-teach with those colleagues, we invariably screen *También la lluvia* and debate its approach to art and history. As a historian of the colonial era and a teacher of the modern era, I find it less a faithful mirror of any historical events than a compelling and passionate call to look honestly at those events and to see our modern selves and our present societies both as a product of them and still ensnared in their ugly realities and unresolved struggles over resources, autonomy, agency, and survival. What could be a more relevant historical lesson to teach or learn?

ADDITIONAL RESOURCES

Primary Sources

John Carter Brown Library and Research Center (Providence, Rhode Island), online access to digitized books, maps, and images for conquest and colonial period. https://jcblibrary.org/collection/digital-images.

Library of Congress (Washington, DC), online images from the Jay I. Kislak Collection. https://www.loc.gov/collections/jay-i-kislak-collection/?fa=original-format:web+page.

Museo de América (Madrid), website with catalogue of images and artefacts. https://www.culturaydeporte.gob.es/museodeamerica/coleccion.html.

Print

Arce, Moisés. *Resource Extraction and Protest in Peru.* Pittsburgh: University of Pittsburgh Press, 2014.

Fernández-Armesto, Felipe. *Columbus on Himself.* Cambridge: Hackett Publishing, 2010.

Garofalo, Leo J. "Christopher Columbus Evaluates Indigenous Societies" and "European Priests Discuss Ruling Indigenous and African Peoples." In *Documenting Latin America: Gender and Race, Empire and Nation,* edited by Erin O'Connor and Leo J. Garofalo, Vol. 1, 6–15, 57–68. New York: Pearson/Prentice Hall, 2010.

Kohl, Benjamin H., and Linda C. Farthing. *Impasse in Bolivia.* New York: Zed Books, 2006.

Las Casas, Bartolomé de. *An Account, Much Abbreviated, of the Destruction of the Indies,* edited by Franklin W. Knight. Translated by Andrew Hurley. Indianapolis: Hackett Publishing, 2003.

Lucero, José Antonio. "'We Are All Presidents': Evo Morales and the Challenges of an Indigenous-Popular Government in Bolivia (2006)." In *Documenting Latin America: Gender, Race, and Nation,* edited by Erin O'Connor and Leo J. Garofalo, Vol. 2, 270–78. New York: Pearson/Prentice Hall, 2011.

Meyer, Lois, and Benjamín Maldonado Alvarado. *New World of Indigenous Resistance*. San Francisco: City Lights, 2010.

Olivera, Oscar with Tom Lewis, *¡Cochabamba! Water War in Bolivia*. Cambridge: South End Press, 2004.

Pané, Ramón. *An Account of the Antiquities of the Indians: Chronicles of the New World Encounter*, edited and translated by José Juan Arrom. Durham, NC: Duke University Press, 1999.

Prashad, Vijay, and Teo Ballvé. *Dispatches from Latin America: On the Frontlines against Neoliberalism*. Cambridge: South End Press, 2006.

Whitehead, Neil L. "The Crises and Transformations of Invaded Societies: The Caribbean (1492–1580)." In *Cambridge History of Native Peoples*, edited by Frank Salomon and Stuart B. Schwartz, Vol. 3, Part 1, 864–903. Cambridge: Cambridge University Press, 1999.

Zamora, Margarita. *Reading Columbus*. Berkeley: University of California Press, 1993.

Video

Berta Caseres Vive, Vimeo video online.

Cabeza de Vaca, dir. Nicolaìs Echevarrìia (Mexico: Producciones Iguana, Instituto Mexicano de Cinematografiìa, 1991).

Coca and the Congressman, dir. Jon Alpert (New York: Films for the Humanities and Sciences, 2006).

Cocalero, dir. Alejandro Landes and Julia Solomonoff (First Run Features, 2006).

Crisis Is Our Brand, dir. Rachel Boyton (Port Washington: Koch Lober Films, 2005).

Jericó, dir. Luis Alberto Lamata (Venezuela: Bolívar Films, 1991).

"Leasing the Rain," *Frontline* (Alexandria: PBS, 2002).

"Thirst," PBS, *Point of View*, season 17, dir. Alan Snitow and Deborah Kaufman (Bullfrog Films, 2004).

NOTES

1. Manuel Quinto, "'También la lluvia,'" *El Ciervo* 60, no. 719 (February 1, 2011): 37.

2. Icíar Bollaín, "Cine con Tetas," in *La mitad del cielo. Directoras españolas de los años 90*, ed. Carlos F. Heredero (Málaga: Primer Festival de Cine Español de Malaga, 1998), 51–53. Republished in English in *Film Manifestos and Global Cinema Cultures: A Critical Anthology*, ed. Scott MacKenzie (Oakland: University of California Press, 2014) 566–569.

3. Joshua Lund, *Werner Herzog* (Urbana: University of Illinois Press, 2020).

4. Oscar Olivera with Tom Lewis, *¡Cochabamba! Water War in Bolivia* (Cambridge: South End Press, 2004).

5. Here, there are resonances with *King Leopold's Ghost* (1998) on the atrocities committed in the Congo between 1885 and 1908 to enrich the King of Belgium and documentary filmmaker Raoul Peck's more recent and wide-ranging exploration of colonialism and the origins of white supremacy in *Exterminate All the Brutes* (2021).

6. Fernando Colombo, *The Life of the Admiral Christopher Columbus by His Son Ferdinand*, trans. Benjamin Keen (New Brunswick, NJ: Rutgers University Press, 1992).

7. Hernando Colón later sought to build a great Renaissance library. José María Pérez Fernández and Edward Wilson-Lee, *Hernando Colón's New World of Books: Toward a Cartography of Knowledge* (New Haven, CT: Yale University Press, 2021).

8. Felipe Fernández-Armesto, *Columbus on Himself* (Cambridge, MA: Hackett Publishing, 2010).

9. Fernández-Armesto, *Columbus on Himself*.

10. Alvar Núñez Cabeza de Vaca, *The Narrative of Cabeza de Vaca*, ed. and tran. Patrick Charles Pautz and Rolena Adorno (Lincoln: University of Nebraska Press, 2003).

11. Dennis Herrick, *Esteban: The African Slave Who Explored America* (Albuquerque: University of New Mexico Press, 2018); Robert Goodwin, *Crossing the Continent, 1527–1540: The Story of the First African-American Explorer of the American South* (New York: Harper, 2008).

12. Luisela Alvaray, "Imagi(ni)ng Indigenous Spaces: Self and Other Converge in Latin America," *Film & History* 34, no. 2 (2004): 58–64.

13. Michel-Rolp Trouillot, *Silencing the Past: Power and the Production of History* (Boston: Beacon Press, 2015).

14. The New Conquest History for Mesoamerica is a good place to start unpacking these complexities. See, for example, Matthew Restall, *Seven Myths of the Spanish Conquest* (New York: Oxford University Press, 2003).

15. Ramón Pané, *An Account of the Antiquities of the Indians: Chronicles of the New World Encounter*, ed. and trans. José Juan Arrom (Durham, NC: Duke University Press, 1999).

16. Bartolomé de Las Casas, *An Account, Much Abbreviated, of the Destruction of the Indies*, ed. Franklin W. Knight, trans. Andrew Hurley (Cambridge, MA: Hackett Publishing, 2003).

17. In Española, the population declined from perhaps 1 million in 1492 to 30,000 in 1514, and only a handful in the mid-1500s. Neil L. Whitehead, "The Crises and Transformations of Invaded Societies: The Caribbean (1492–1580)," in *Cambridge History of Native Peoples*, vol. 3, part 1, ed. Frank Salomon and Stuart B. Schwartz (Cambridge: Cambridge University Press, 1999), 864–903.

18. Columbus employed practices of negotiation and deceit with *caciques* throughout the Antilles and across his four voyages, sometimes finding allies to turn upon others, other times kidnapping and holding hostage or for ransom these local leaders. Columbus and the conquistadores and governors who came after him were always trying to find ways to use the established social order to their benefit. In some ways, missionary orders in the Americas and at home in Europe would pursue similar strategies of courting and converting leaders to serve as examples to their people and tools

for indirect rule and control over labor and other resources. Missionaries depended on indigenous labor and resources, too. Instead of building family fortunes and seeking hereditary feudal privileges, they used this influence to build churches and monasteries and root upon the land and among the populace their order's missions and jurisdictional claims, often bestowed by the Spanish Crown through the right of royal patronage (*patronato real*) over Church appointments in Spain's territories.

19. Many of these images and multiple editions in several languages of Las Casas's books can been seen in their entirety in the online collections of digitized illustrations, maps, and books at the John Carter Brown Library, https://jcblibrary.org/collection/digital-images.

20. *Bartolomé de Las Casas and the Defense of Amerindian Rights: A Brief History with Documents*, ed. Lawrence A. Clayton and David M. Lantigua (Tuscaloosa: University of Alabama Press, Atlantic Crossings Series, 2020).

21. Vijay Prashad and Teo Ballvé, *Dispatches from Latin America: On the Frontlines Against Neoliberalism* (Cambridge: South End Press, 2006).

22. Benjamin H. Kohl and Linda C. Farthing, *Impasse in Bolivia: Neoliberal Hegemony and Popular Resistance* (New York: Zed Books, 2006).

23. A classic in the testimonial genre of personal accounts of struggle that treats these periods is Domitila Barrios de Chungara and Moema Viezzer, *Let Me Speak! Testimony of Domitila, A Woman of the Bolivian Mines*, trans. Victoria Ortiz (New York: Monthly Review Press, 1978).

24. Oscar Olivera, "They Cannot Privatize Our Dreams," in Oscar Olivera with Tom Lewis, *¡Cochabamba! Water War in Bolivia* (Cambridge: South End Press, 2004), 175–89.

25. https://www.gosua.com/juan-carlos-aduviri/.

26. "Leasing the Rain," *Frontline* (Alexandria: PBS, 2002); "Thirst," PBS, *Point of View*, season 17, dir. Alan Snitow and Deborah Kaufman (Bullfrog Films, 2004); and *The Corporation*, dir. Mark Achbar, Jennifer Abbott, and Joel Bakan (New York: Zeitgeist, 2004).

27. Documentaries on Peruvian and other Latin American cases provide helpful comparisons and further insight into community-level organizing, awareness building, and cross-class potential as well as divisions and failure. *Choropampa: The Price of Gold*, dir. Ernesto Cabellos and Stephanie Boyd (Brooklyn: First Run/Icarus Films, 2002); *Tambogrande: Mangos, Murder, Mining*, dir. Ernesto Cabellos and Stephanie Boyd (Brooklyn: First Run/Icarus Films, 2007); and *Berta Caceres Vive*, Vimeo video online.

28. *Crisis Is Our Brand*, dir. Rachel Boyton (Port Washington: Koch Lober Films, 2005).

29. *Cocalero*, dir. Alejandro Landes and Julia Solomonoff (First Run Features, 2006); and *Coca and the Congressman*, dir. Jon Alpert (New York: Films for the Humanities and Sciences, 2006).

30. José Antonio Lucero, "'We Are All Presidents': Evo Morales and the Challenges of an Indigenous-Popular Government in Bolivia (2006)," in *Documenting Latin America: Gender, Race, and Nation*, vol. 2, ed. Erin O'Connor and Leo J. Garofalo (New York: Pearson/Prentice Hall, 2011) 271.

31. Lucero, "'We Are All Presidents,'" 270–78.

32. Shawnna Mullenax, "De Jure Transformation, De Facto Stagnation: The Status of Women's and LGBT Rights in Bolivia," in *Seeking Rights from the Left: Gender, Sexuality, and the Latin American Pink Tide*, ed. Elisabeth Jay Friedman (Durham, NC: Duke University Press, 2018), 176–77.

33. Bret Gustafson, "Amid Gas, Where Is the Revolution?" *Real World Latin America*, second ed., ed. Fred Rosen and Alejandro Reuss, *The North American Congress on Latin America, and the Dollars and Sense Collective* (Boston: Economic Affairs Bureau, 2013), 55–61.

Index

About the Contributors

Jürgen Buchenau is professor of history and Latin American studies at UNC-Charlotte, where he is also chair of the Department of History. He received his PhD from UNC-Chapel Hill in 1993 and has authored and edited ten books, including *Plutarco Elías Calles and the Mexican Revolution* (2007), winner of the Alfred B. Thomas Book Award of the Southeastern Council of Latin American Studies, and *Mexico's Once and Future Revolution: Social Upheaval and the Challenge of Rule since the Late Nineteenth Century* (2013, with Gilbert M. Joseph). His research has been funded by the National Endowment of the Humanities and the American Philosophical Society.

Erik Ching is the Walter Kenneth Mattison Professor of History at Furman University. He received his PhD from the University of California, Santa Barbara in 1997. His field is modern Latin America with a research specialization in twentieth-century El Salvador. Ching has authored or co-authored numerous books and articles on Salvadoran history, including *Modernizing Minds in El Salvador* (2012), *Authoritarian El Salvador* (2014), and *Stories of Civil War in El Salvador* (2016).

Kevin Coleman is associate professor of history at the University of Toronto. He is the author of *A Camera in the Garden of Eden: The Self-Forging of a Banana Republic* and co-editor (with Daniel James) of *Capitalism and the Camera: Essays on Photography and Extraction*. His research has been funded by the Andrew W. Mellon Foundation and the American Council of Learned Societies, the Social Sciences and Humanities Research Council of Canada, and the Fulbright-Hays Program. He is currently writing a book on Saint Oscar Romero.

Thomas C. Field Jr. received his PhD from the London School of Economics and is professor of social sciences at Embry-Riddle Aeronautical University. He is author of *From Development to Dictatorship: Bolivia and the Alliance* *for Progress in the Kennedy Era* (2014), which won the 2015 Thomas McGann Book Award from the Rocky Mountain Council for Latin American Studies. His research articles on international development and foreign policy have received the 2012 Bernath Article Prize from the Society for Historians for American Foreign Relations and the 2020 Cherny Article Prize from the Pacific Coast Branch of the American Historical Association.

Leo J. Garofalo is associate professor of history and former director of the Center for the Comparative Study of Race and Ethnicity at Connecticut College. He researches market and ritual activities in Andean cities and seafaring by black Europeans from Iberia. He co-edited *Documenting Latin America: Gender, Race, and Empire*; *Afro-Latino Voices: Narratives from the Early Modern Ibero-Atlantic World, 1550–1812*; and *Más allá de la dominación y la resistencia*. Currently, he is researching and writing about freed and enslaved Asians in the sixteenth-and seventeenth-century Andes and Africans and Afro-Andeans in Cuzco.

James N. Green is the Carlos Manuel de Céspedes Professor of Latin American History at Brown University and professor of Portuguese and Brazilian studies. He is the author of *Beyond Carnival: Male Homosexuality in Twentieth-Century Brazil* (1999); *We Cannot Remain Silent: Opposition to the Brazilian Military Dictatorship in the United States* (2010); and *Exile within Exiles: Herbert Daniel, Gay Brazilian Revolutionary* (2018), all three also published in Portuguese. Green is the co-author or co-editor of nine additional works that include *The Brazil Reader: History, Culture and Politics* (2019) and *Brazil: Five Centuries of Change*, third ed. (2020). He is the national co-coordinator of the U.S. Network for Democracy in Brazil and the president of the board of directors of the Washington Brazil Office.

Madison Green is a graduate student at the University of North Carolina at Charlotte graduating in May 2022 with a Master of Arts in Spanish and Latin American Studies. She received her Bachelor of Arts from Western Carolina University, studying Spanish and international studies. As a graduate assistant for the Conference of Latin American History, she studies Mexican literature and film and has a particular interest in Colonial Mexico and gender studies. She has presented her research at the Southeastern Council of Latin American Studies, the Midwest Political Science Association Conference, and the National Conference of Undergraduate Research.

Thomas H. Holloway is professor emeritus of history at the University of California, Davis. He previously taught at Cornell University and earned a PhD in Latin American history from the University of Wisconsin in

1974. He is the author of *Immigrants on the Land: Coffee and Society in São Paulo* (1980) and *Policing Rio de Janeiro: Repression and Resistance in a Nineteenth Century City* (1993) and is the editor of *A Companion to Latin American History* (2008). He was the 2020 recipient of the Lifetime Distinguished Service Award from the Conference on Latin American History.

Mohamed Kamara, professor of French at Washington and Lee University in Virginia, has a BA and a diploma in secondary education from Fourah Bay College (Sierra Leone), an MA from Purdue University, and a PhD from Tulane University. His teaching and research interests include French and Francophone literatures and cultures, with specific focuses on African and eighteenth-century French women writers, French colonialism, and human rights. He has published short stories; a play; and articles on human rights, the African child soldier, French colonial education, and other areas of African literature. He is completing a monograph on the French colonial school.

Daniel O. Mosquera is professor of Spanish and Latin American and Caribbean studies, former director of the Latin American and Caribbean studies program, and chair of the Department of Modern Languages and Literatures (2020–2023) at Union College. He has published on Latin American colonial historiography and transatlantic studies, blackness and popular culture and politics, Latin American cinema, and cultural studies and cultural theory. He has directed and co-produced two documentaries on Afro-Colombian, or *chocoano*, religious practices and popular culture and is also a published translator. A former member of the editorial board in the *Journal of Latin American Cultural Studies*, he currently serves on the journal's advisory board.

Susie S. Porter, professor of history and gender studies at the University of Utah, is the author of two award-winning books: *Workingwomen in Mexico City: Public Discourses and Material Conditions, 1879–1931* (2003) and *From Angel to Office Worker: Middle-Class Identity and Female Consciousness in Mexico, 1890–1950* (2018). Both were also published in Spanish by El Colegio de Michoacán (2008 and 2020, respectively). Porter is co-editor of *Orden social e identidad de género*, with María Teresa Fernández Aceves and Carmen Ramos Escandón (2006); *Género en la encrucijada de la historia social y cultural*, with María Teresa Fernández Aceves (2015); and *Mexican History: A Primary Source Reader*, with Nora Jaffray and Ed Osowski (2009).

Susan Elizabeth Ramírez is the Neville G. Penrose chair of history and Latin American studies at Texas Christian University. Her publications include *Provincial Patriarchs: Land Tenure and the Economics of Power in Colonial Peru*; *The World Upside Down: Cross Cultural Contact and Conflict in Colonial Peru*; *To Feed and Be Fed: The Cosmological Bases of Authority and Identity in the Andes*; *Al servicio de Dios y Su Magestad: Los orígenes de las escuelas públicas para niños indígenas en el norte del Perú en el siglo XVIII*; and *Colonial Latin American History from First Encounters to Independence.* Her next book, to be published in 2022, is *In Praise of the Ancestors: Names, Memory, and Identity in Africa and the Americas.*

Donald F. Stevens is professor emeritus of history at Drexel University. He edited *Based on a True Story: Latin American History at the Movies* (1997) and was the editor of *The Americas*, where he served on the editorial board for twenty-four years. His research has been supported by the National Endowment for the Humanities, the Social Science Research Council, and the American Council of Learned Societies, Joint Committee on Latin American Studies. He is the author of two award-winning books: *Mexico in the Time of Cholera* (2019) and *Origins of Instability in Early Republican Mexico* (1991).

Camilla Townsend is Board of Governors Distinguished Professor of History at Rutgers University, New Brunswick. She has extensive publications on Indigenous history, focusing primarily on the surviving Nahuatl-language sources that illuminate the world we refer to as "Aztec." Her latest book is *Fifth Sun: A New History of the Aztecs* (2019), which won the 2020 Cundill History Prize. Townsend's research has been supported by such entities as the American Philosophical Society, the National Endowment for the Humanities, and the John Simon Guggenheim Memorial Foundation.

Made in the USA
Monee, IL
18 January 2023

25566000R00193